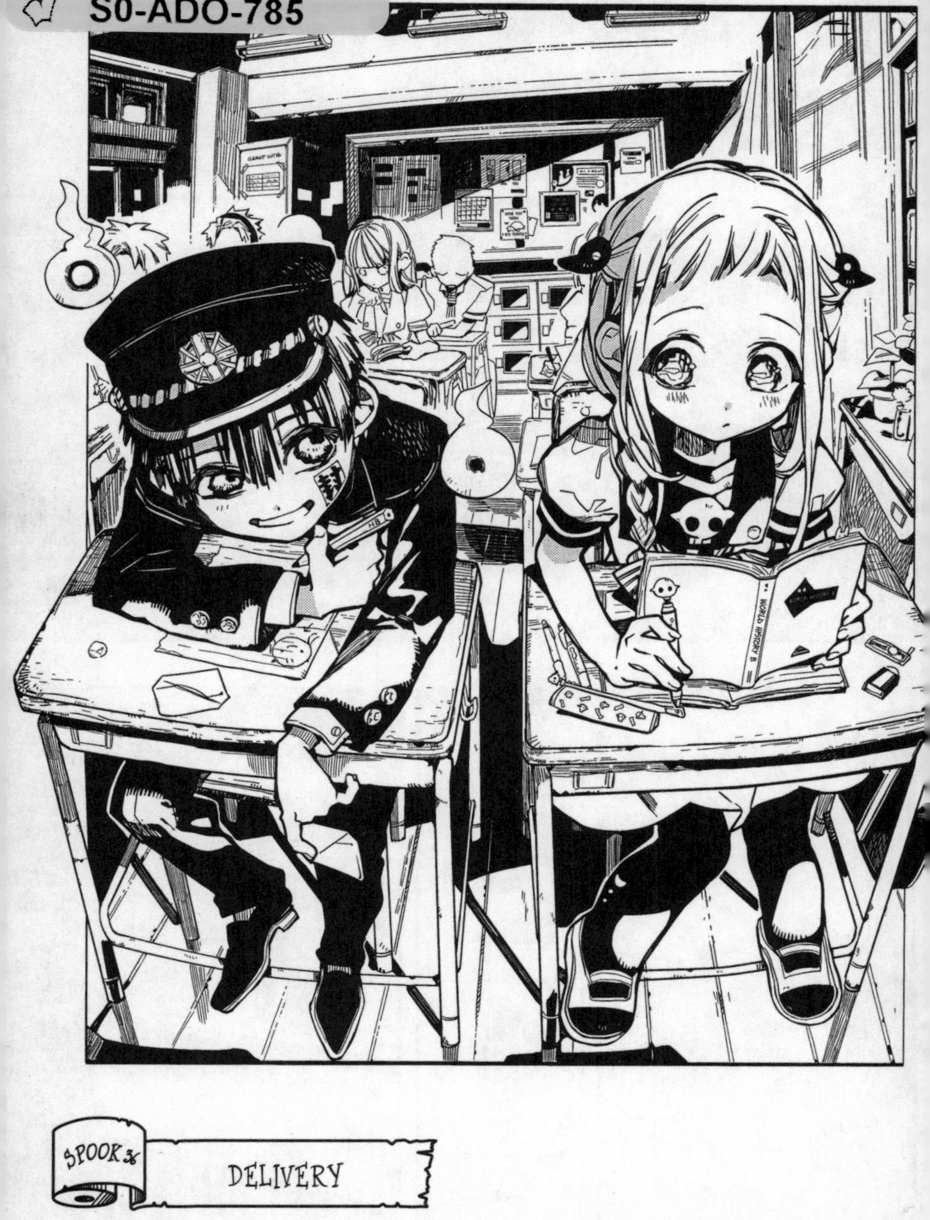
HB
WORLD HISTORY B

SPOOK 36

DELIVERY

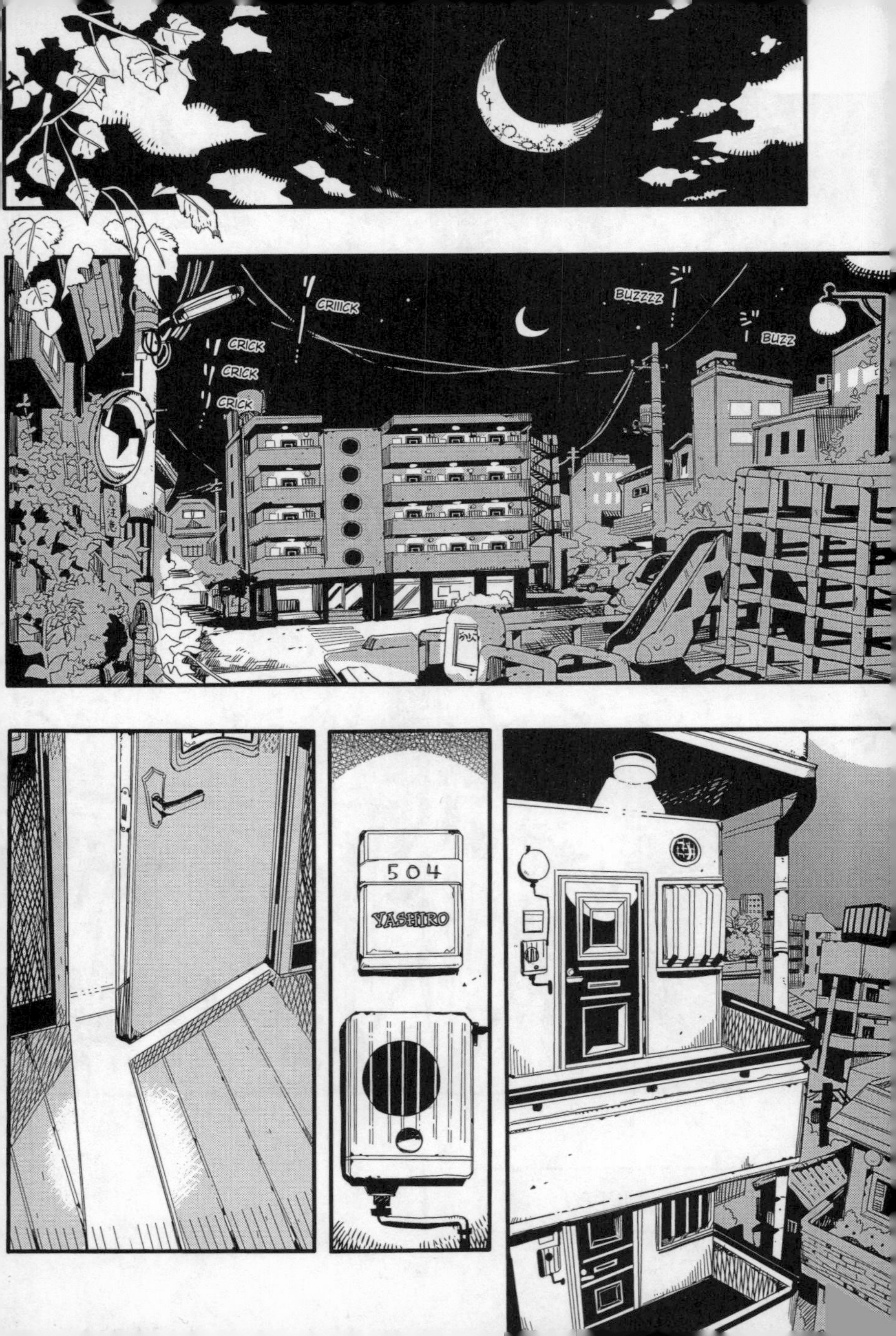
BUZZ
BUZZZZ
CRIIICK
CRICK
CRICK
CRICK
504
YASHIRO

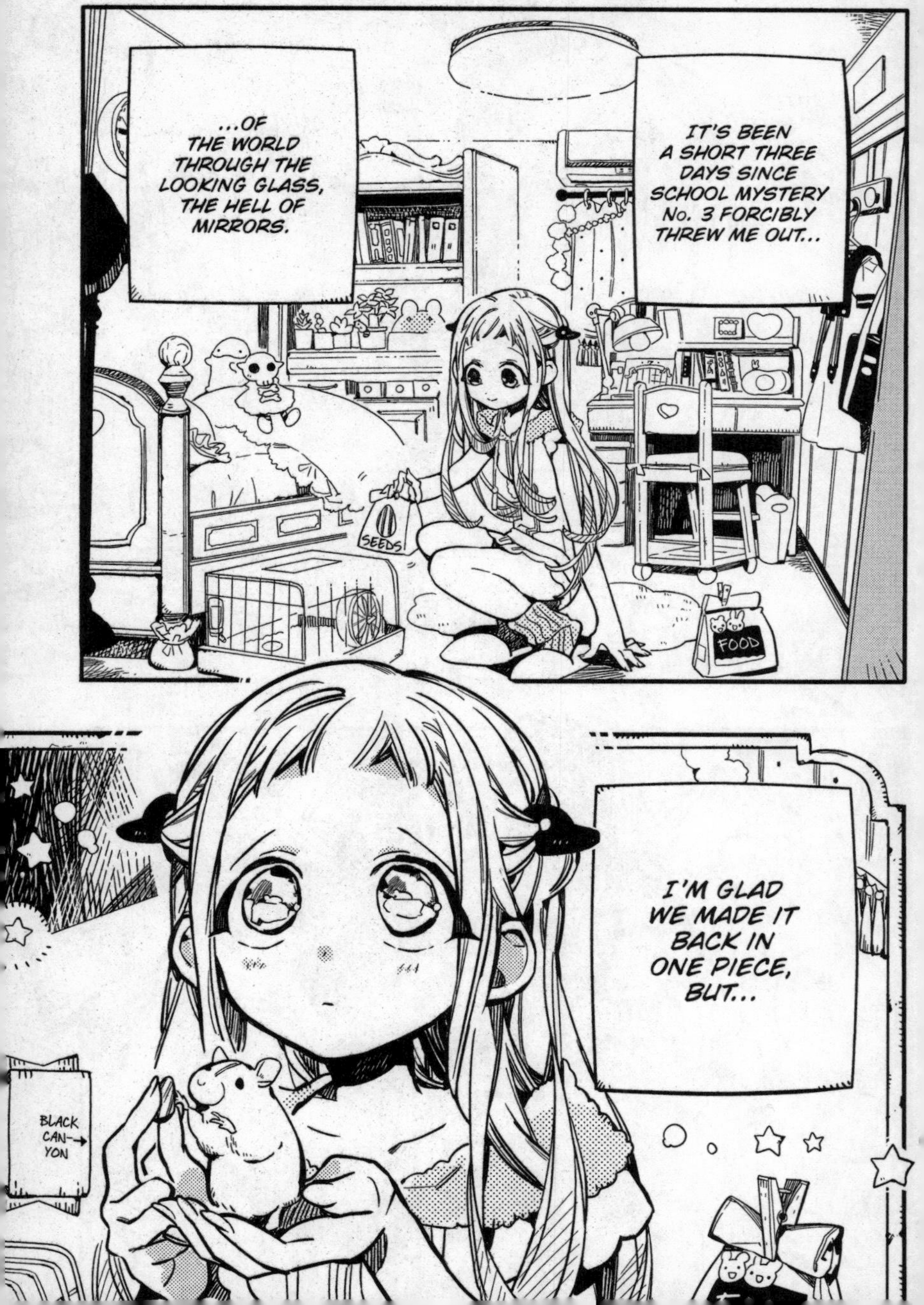
IT'S BEEN A SHORT THREE DAYS SINCE SCHOOL MYSTERY No. 3 FORCIBLY THREW ME OUT...
...OF THE WORLD THROUGH THE LOOKING GLASS, THE HELL OF MIRRORS.
SEEDS
FOOD
I'M GLAD WE MADE IT BACK IN ONE PIECE, BUT...
BLACK CAN-YON

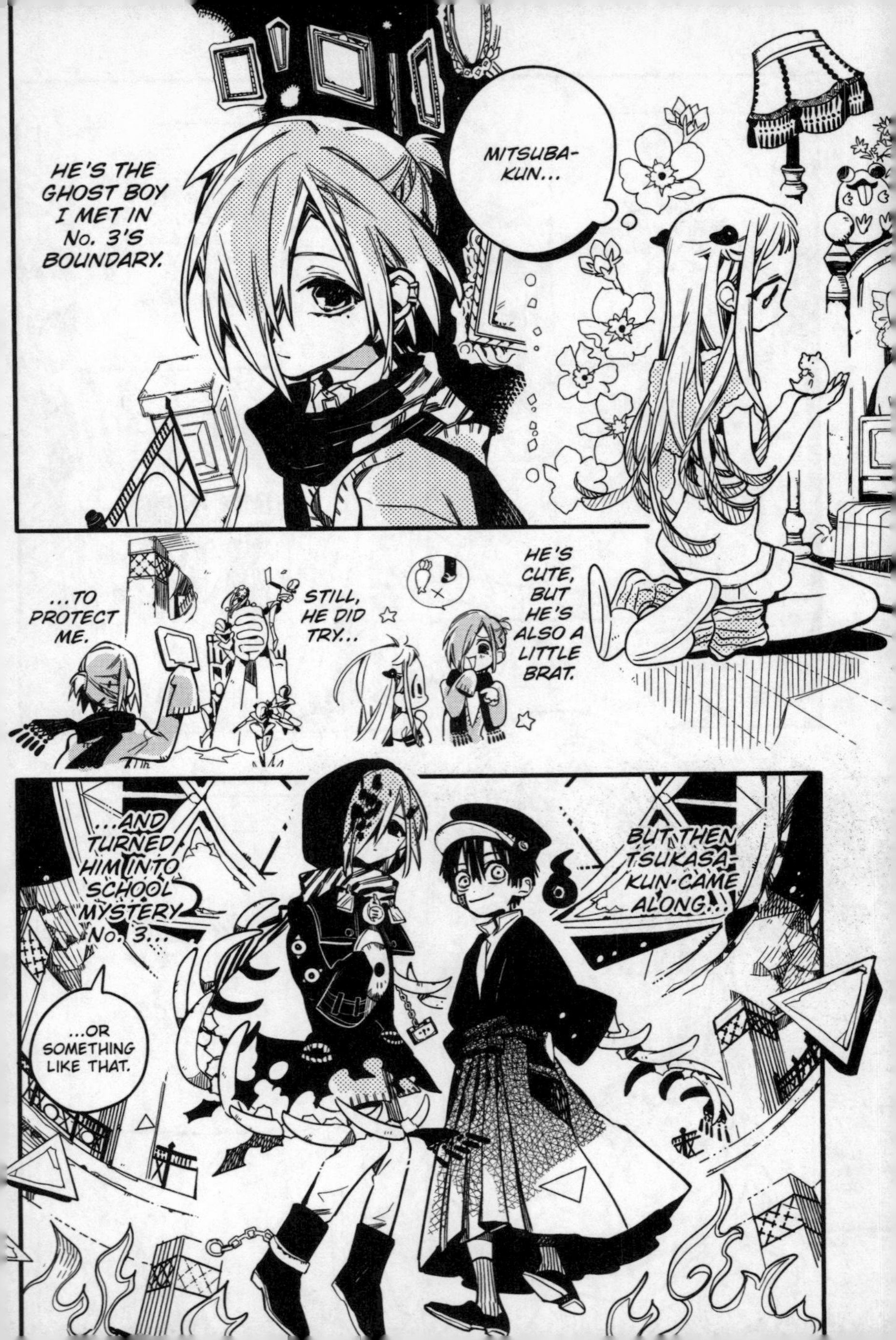
MITSUBA-KUN...
HE'S THE GHOST BOY I MET IN No. 3'S BOUNDARY.
HE'S CUTE, BUT HE'S ALSO A LITTLE BRAT.
STILL, HE DID TRY...
...TO PROTECT ME.
BUT THEN TSUKASA-KUN CAME ALONG...
...AND TURNED HIM INTO SCHOOL MYSTERY No. 3...
...OR SOMETHING LIKE THAT.

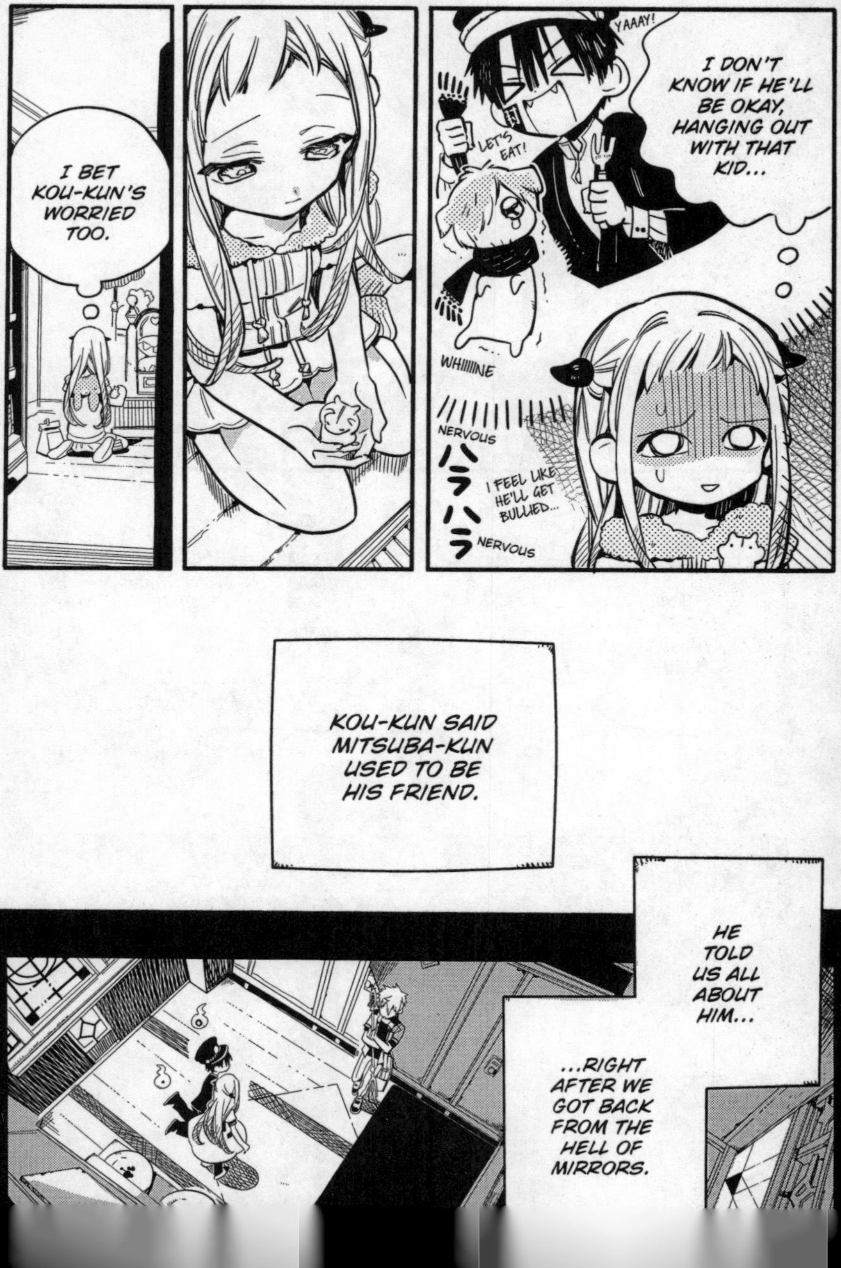
I DON'T KNOW IF HE'LL BE OKAY, HANGING OUT WITH THAT KID...
YAAAY!
LET'S EAT!
WHIIIINE
NERVOUS
ハラハラ
NERVOUS
I FEEL LIKE HE'LL GET BULLIED...
I BET KOU-KUN'S WORRIED TOO.
KOU-KUN SAID MITSUBA-KUN USED TO BE HIS FRIEND.
HE TOLD US ALL ABOUT HIM...
...RIGHT AFTER WE GOT BACK FROM THE HELL OF MIRRORS.

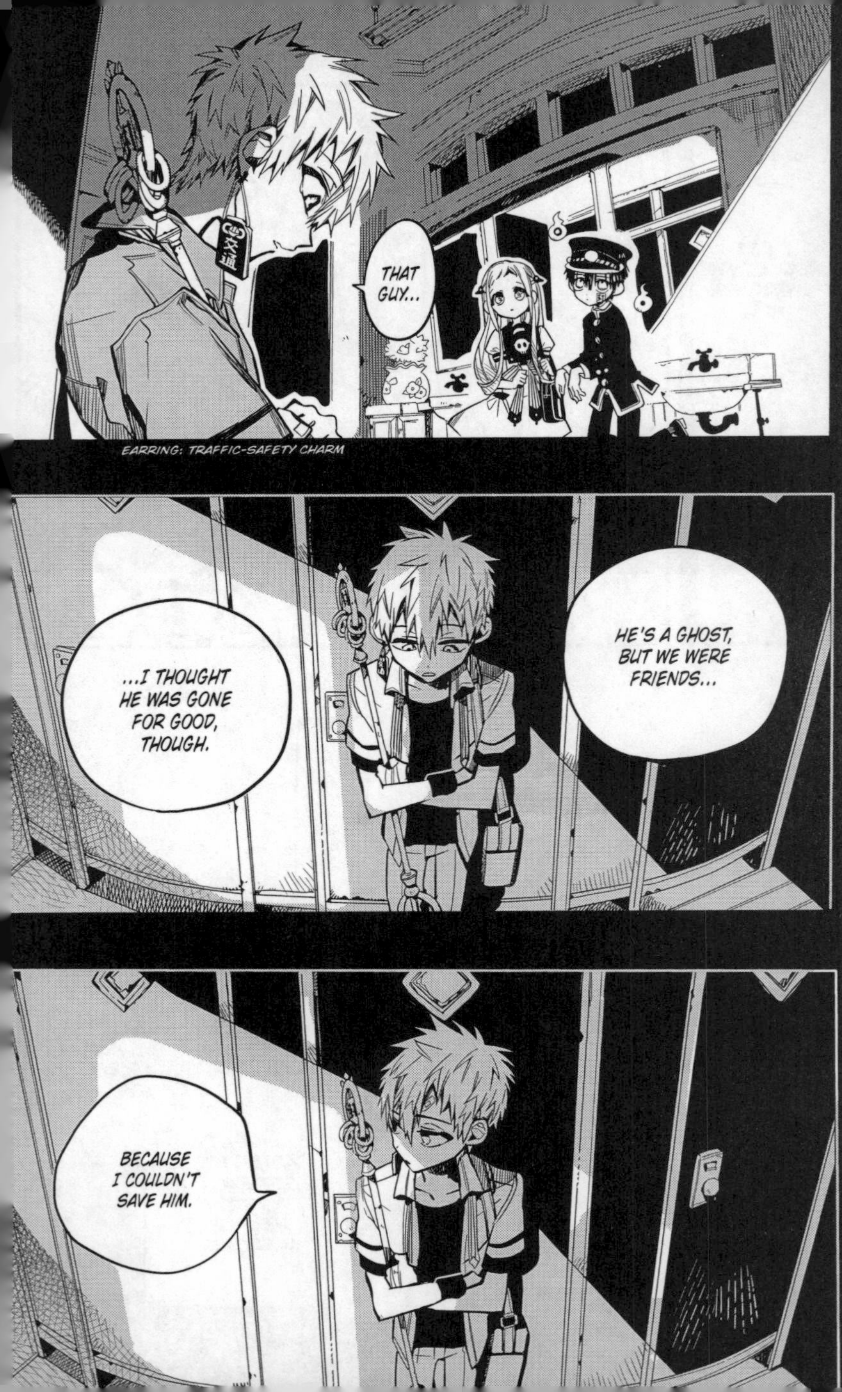
THAT GUY...
交通
EARRING: TRAFFIC-SAFETY CHARM
HE'S A GHOST, BUT WE WERE FRIENDS...
...I THOUGHT HE WAS GONE FOR GOOD, THOUGH.
BECAUSE I COULDN'T SAVE HIM.

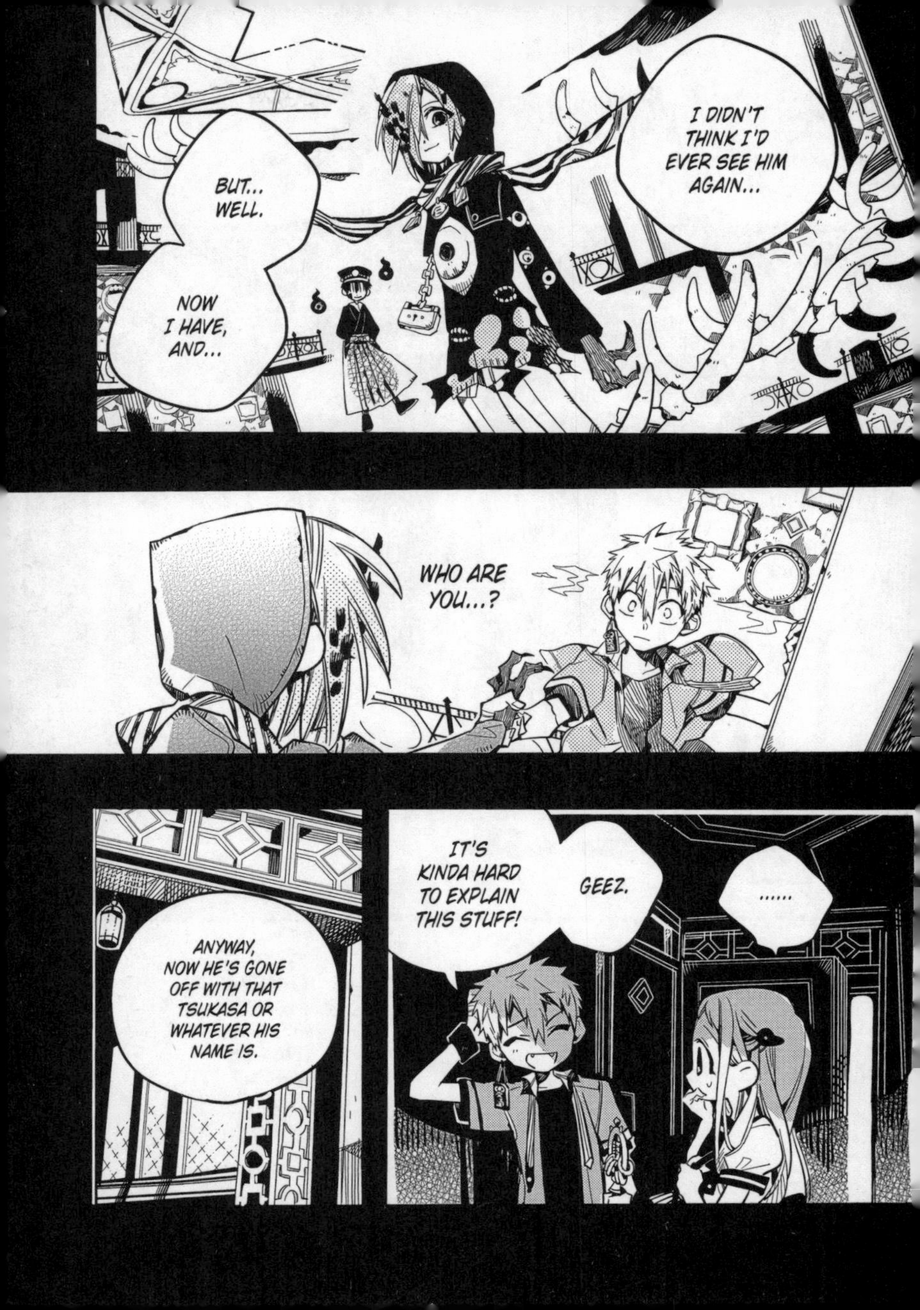
I DIDN'T THINK I'D EVER SEE HIM AGAIN...
BUT... WELL.
NOW I HAVE, AND...
WHO ARE YOU...?
......
GEEZ.
IT'S KINDA HARD TO EXPLAIN THIS STUFF!
ANYWAY, NOW HE'S GONE OFF WITH THAT TSUKASA OR WHATEVER HIS NAME IS.

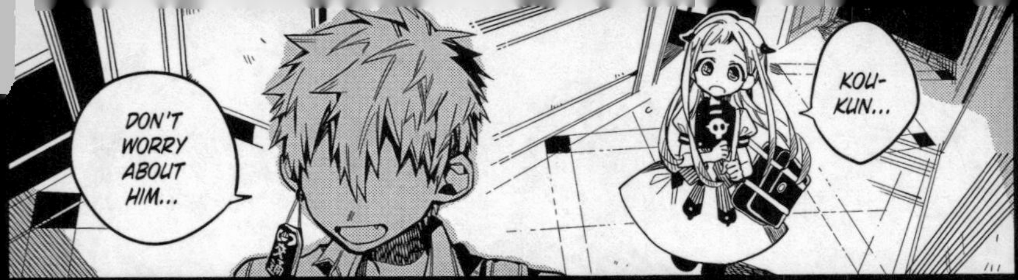
KOU-KUN...
DON'T WORRY ABOUT HIM...

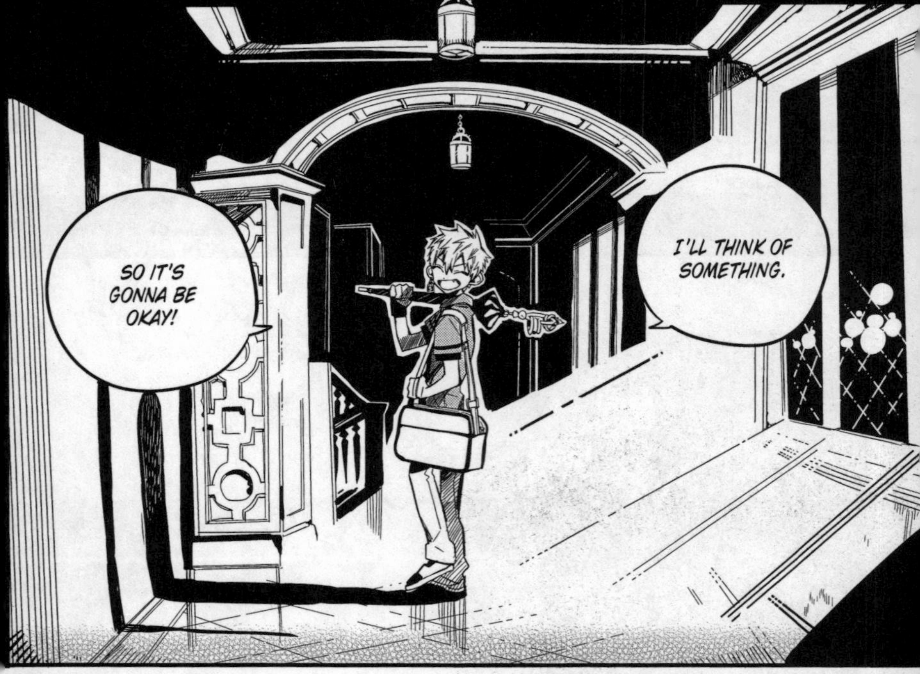
I'LL THINK OF SOMETHING.
SO IT'S GONNA BE OKAY!

THAT'S WHAT HE SAID AFTER HE TOLD US ABOUT MITSUBA-KUN.

HE WAS EVEN SMILING.

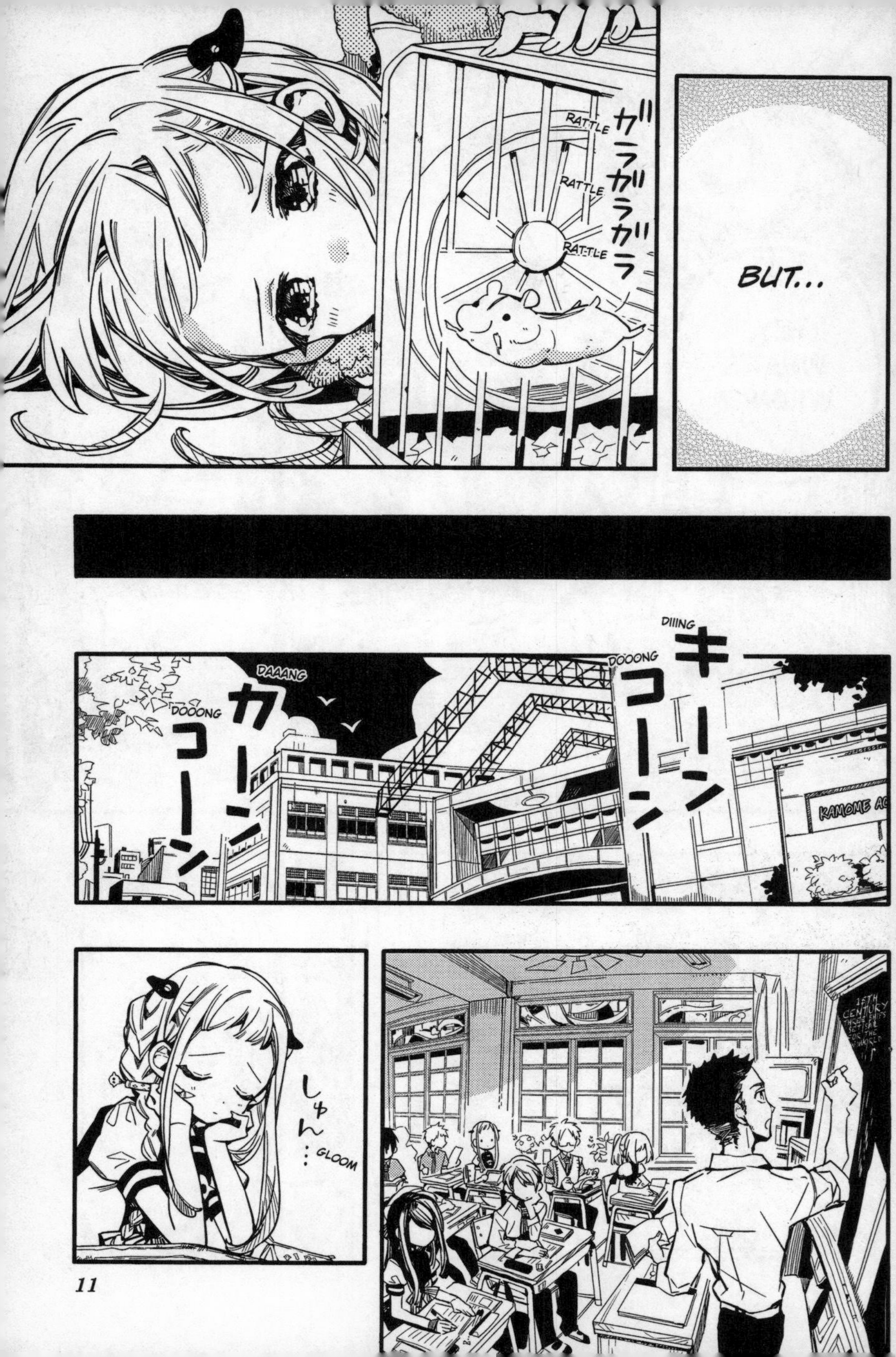
BUT...
ガラガラガラ
RATTLE
RATTLE
RATTLE
キーンコーン
DIIING
DOOONG
カーンコーン
DAAANG
DOOONG
KAMOME AC
しゅん…
GLOOM

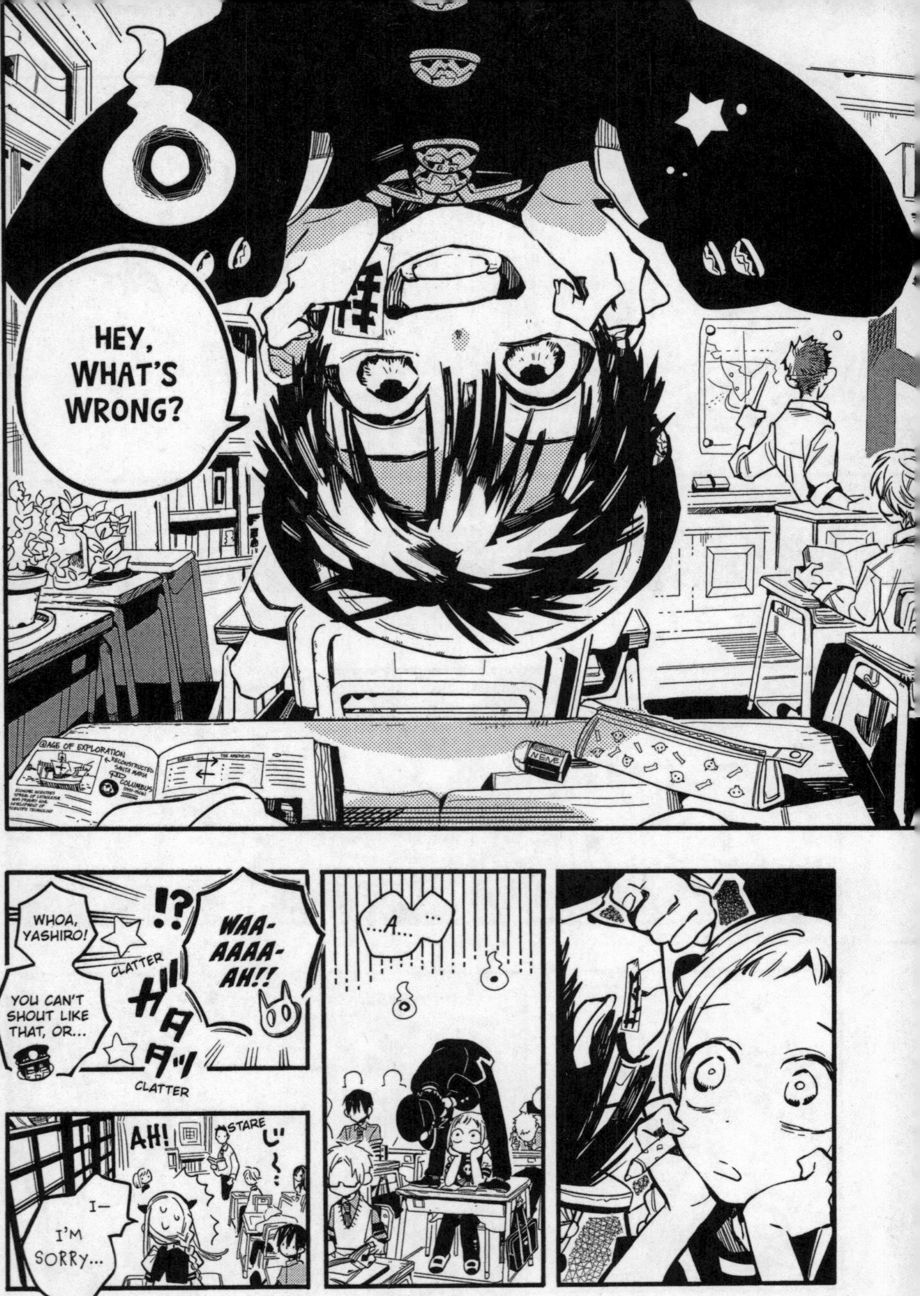
HEY, WHAT'S WRONG?
AGE OF EXPLORATION
RECONSTRUCTED SANTA MARIA
COLUMBUS
NENE
...A...
...
WAA-AAAA-AH!!
!?
CLATTER
ガタタッ
CLATTER
WHOA, YASHIRO!
YOU CAN'T SHOUT LIKE THAT, OR...
STARE
じ~
AH!
I—
I'M SORRY...

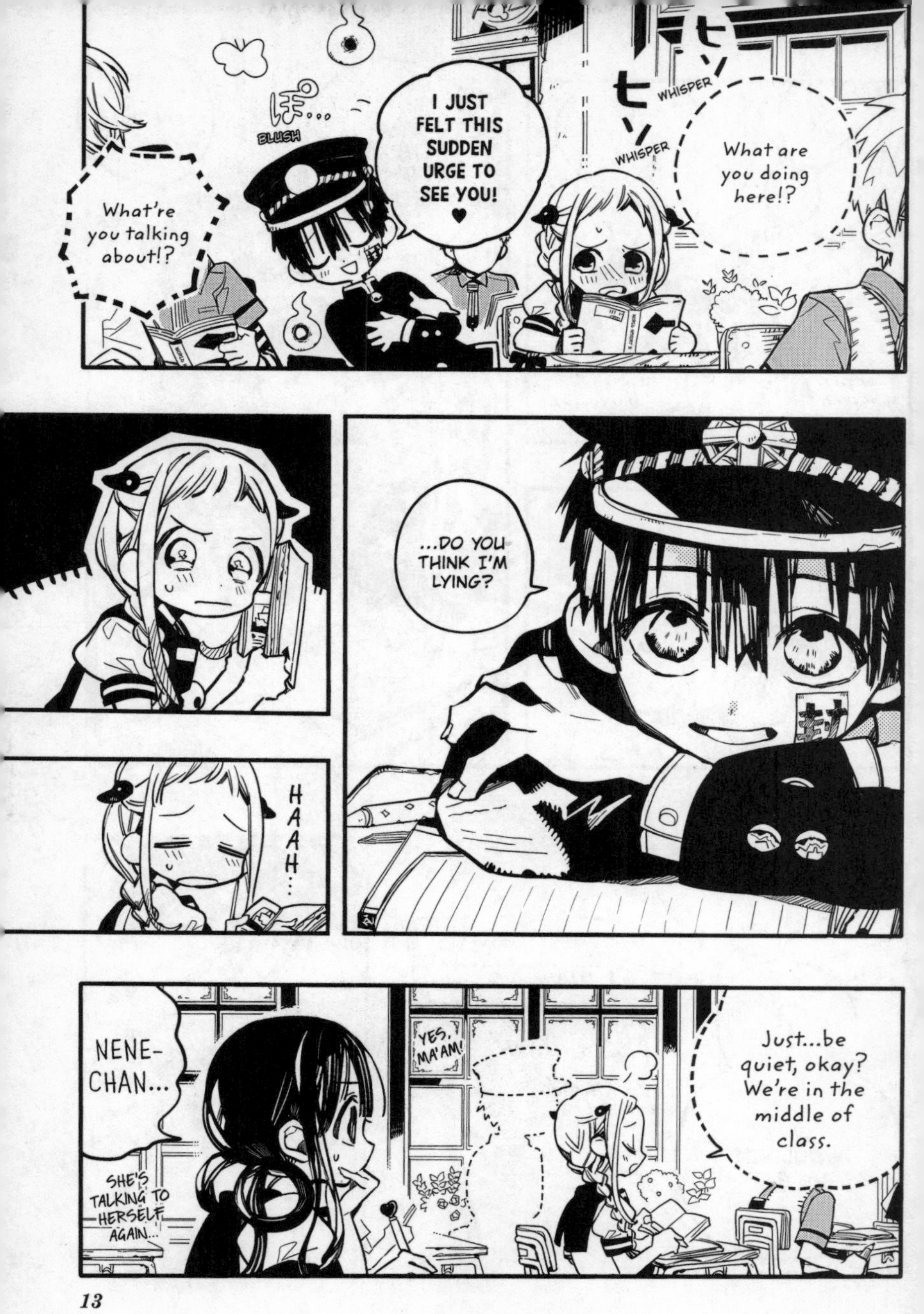
What are you doing here!?
ヒソ WHISPER
ヒソ WHISPER
I JUST FELT THIS SUDDEN URGE TO SEE YOU! ♥
ぽ... BLUSH
What're you talking about!?
...DO YOU THINK I'M LYING?
HAAAH...
Just...be quiet, okay? We're in the middle of class.
YES, MA'AM!
NENE-CHAN...
SHE'S TALKING TO HERSELF AGAIN...

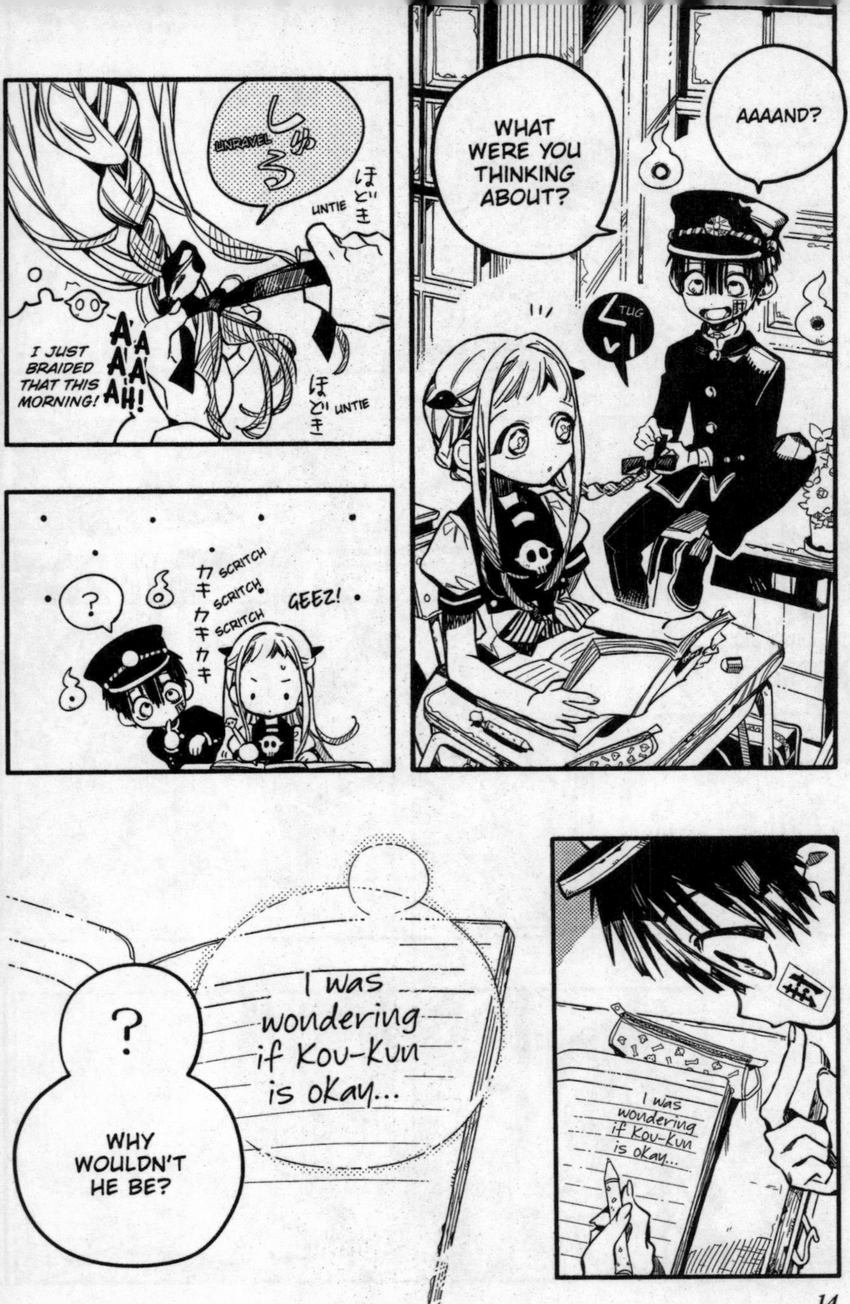

AAAAND?
WHAT WERE YOU THINKING ABOUT?
TUG
しゅる
UNRAVEL
ほどき
UNTIE
ほどき
UNTIE
AAAAH!
I JUST BRAIDED THAT THIS MORNING!
GEEZ!
カキカキカキ
SCRITCH SCRITCH SCRITCH
?
I was wondering if Kou-kun is okay...
I was wondering if Kou-kun is okay...
?
WHY WOULDN'T HE BE?

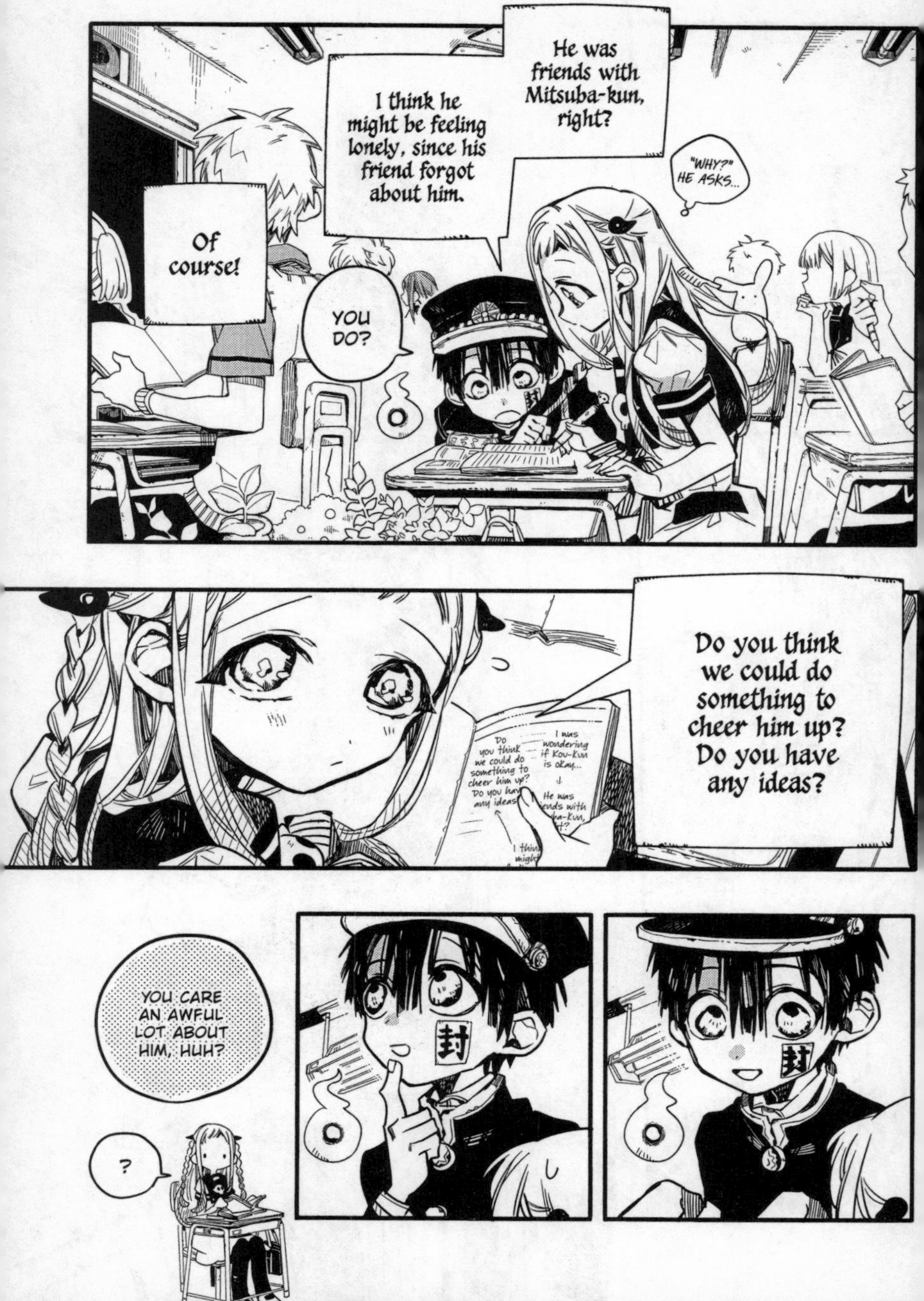
He was friends with Mitsuba-kun, right?
"WHY?" HE ASKS...
I think he might be feeling lonely, since his friend forgot about him.
YOU DO?
Of course!
Do you think we could do something to cheer him up? Do you have any ideas?
I was wondering if Kou-Kun is okay...
Do you think we could do something to cheer him up? Do you have any ideas?
YOU CARE AN AWFUL LOT ABOUT HIM, HUH?
?

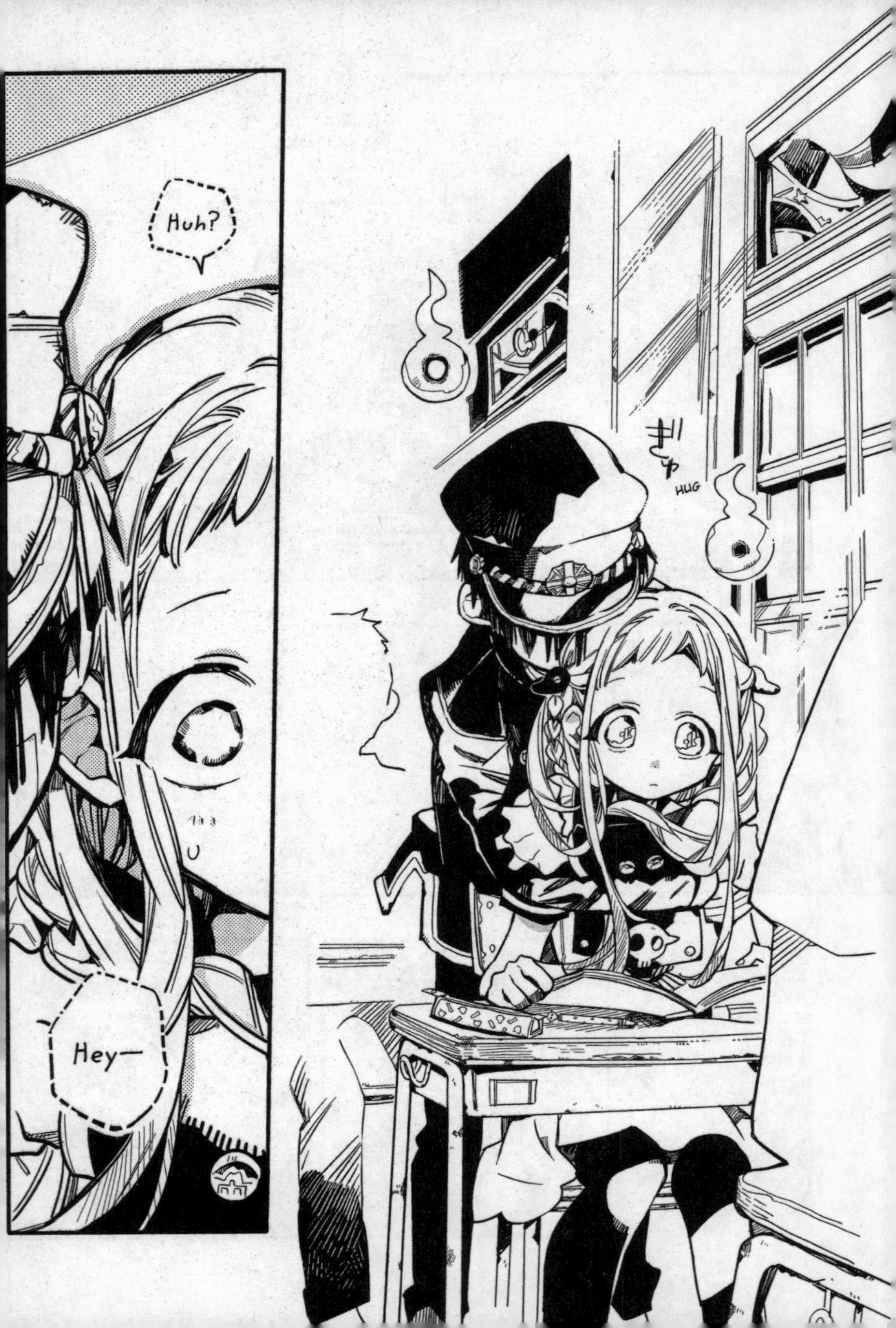
ぎゅ
HUG
Huh?
Hey—

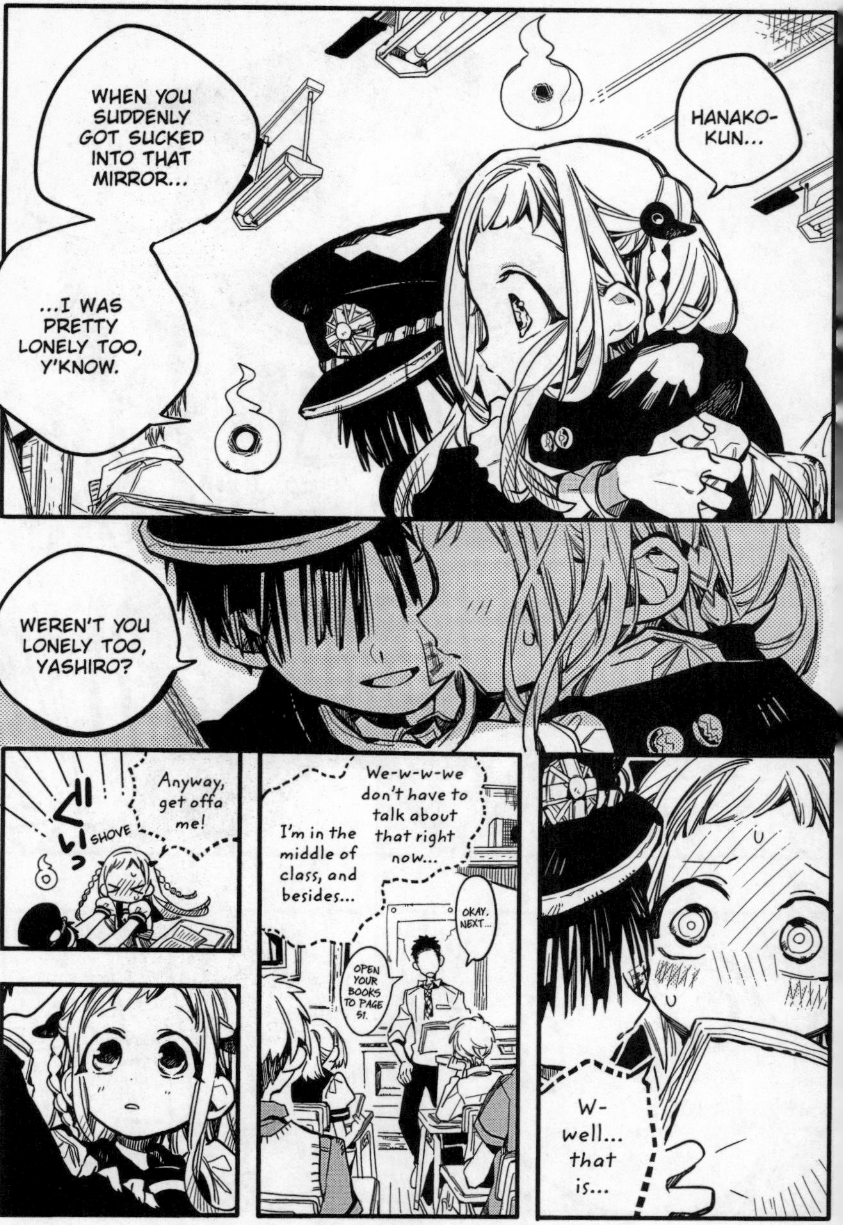
HANAKO-KUN...
WHEN YOU SUDDENLY GOT SUCKED INTO THAT MIRROR...
...I WAS PRETTY LONELY TOO, Y'KNOW.
WEREN'T YOU LONELY TOO, YASHIRO?
W-well... that is...
We-w-w-we don't have to talk about that right now...
I'm in the middle of class, and besides...
OKAY, NEXT...
OPEN YOUR BOOKS TO PAGE 51.
Anyway, get offa me!
ぐいっ
SHOVE

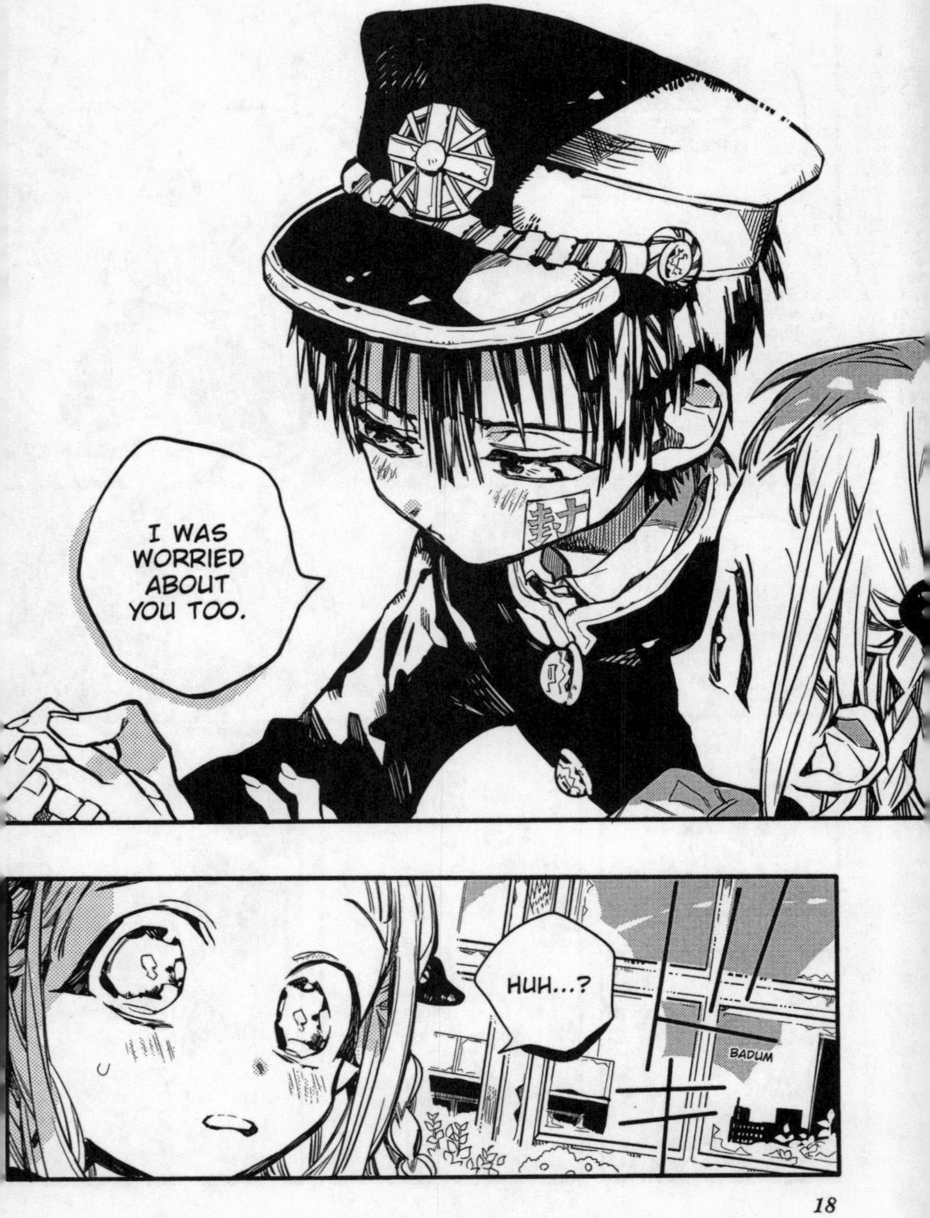
I WAS WORRIED ABOUT YOU TOO.
HUH...?
BADUM

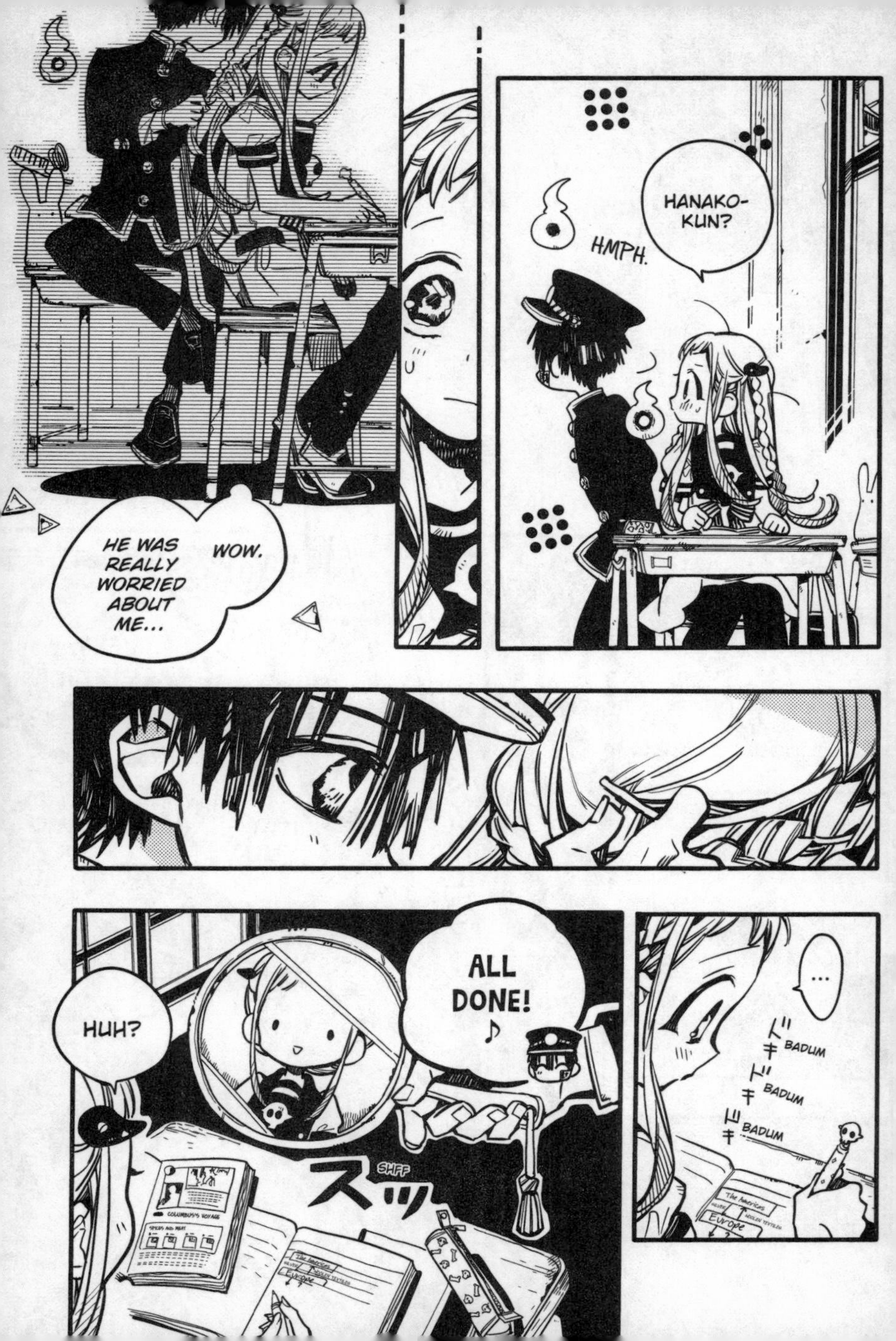
HANAKO-KUN?
HMPH.
WOW.
HE WAS REALLY WORRIED ABOUT ME...
...
ドキ BADUM
ドキ BADUM
ドキ BADUM
ALL DONE! ♪
HUH?
スッ SHFF
COLUMBUS'S VOYAGE
SPICES AND MEAT
The Americas
Europe

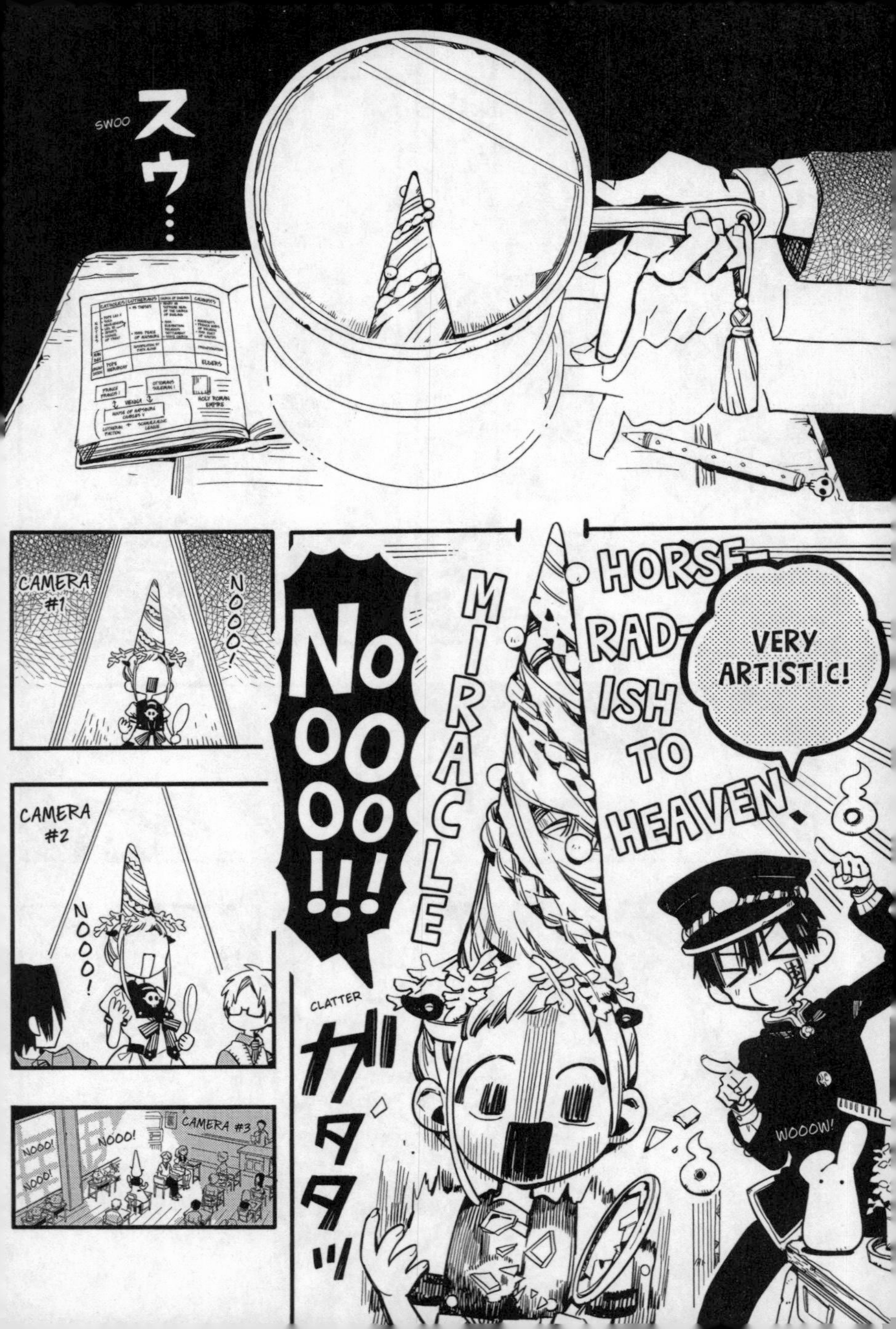
SWOO
スウ…
VERY ARTISTIC!
HORSE-RADISH TO HEAVEN.
MIRACLE
NOOOOOO!!!
WOOOW!
CLATTER
ガタタッ
CAMERA #1
NOOO!
CAMERA #2
NOOO!
CAMERA #3
NOOO!
NOOO!
NOOO!

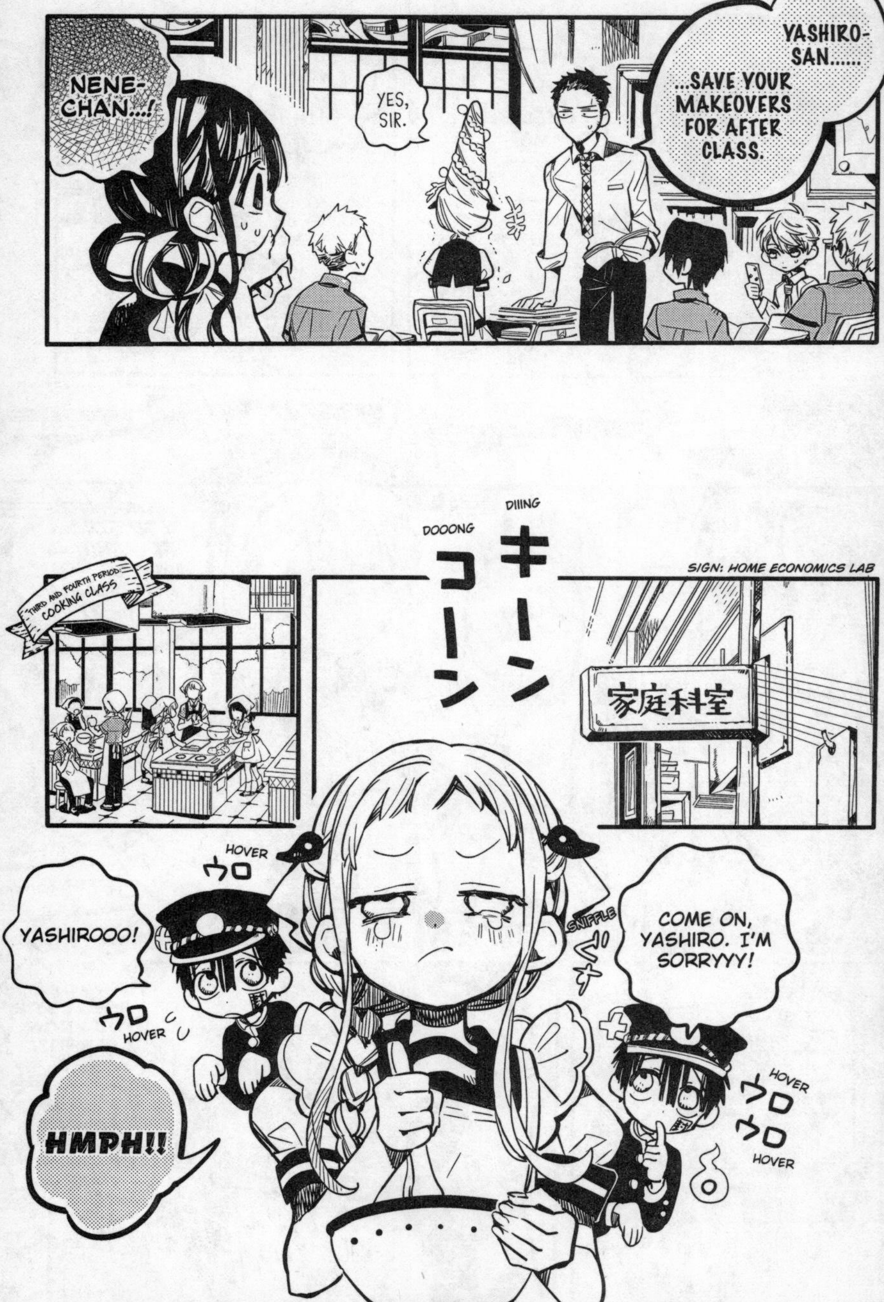
YASHIRO-SAN......
...SAVE YOUR MAKEOVERS FOR AFTER CLASS.
YES, SIR.
NENE-CHAN...!
DIING
キーン
DOOONG
コーン
SIGN: HOME ECONOMICS LAB
家庭科室
THIRD AND FOURTH PERIOD: COOKING CLASS
HOVER
ウロ
ウロ
HOVER
COME ON, YASHIRO. I'M SORRYYY!
SNIFFLE
HOVER
ウロ
YASHIROOO!
ウロ
HOVER
HMPH!!

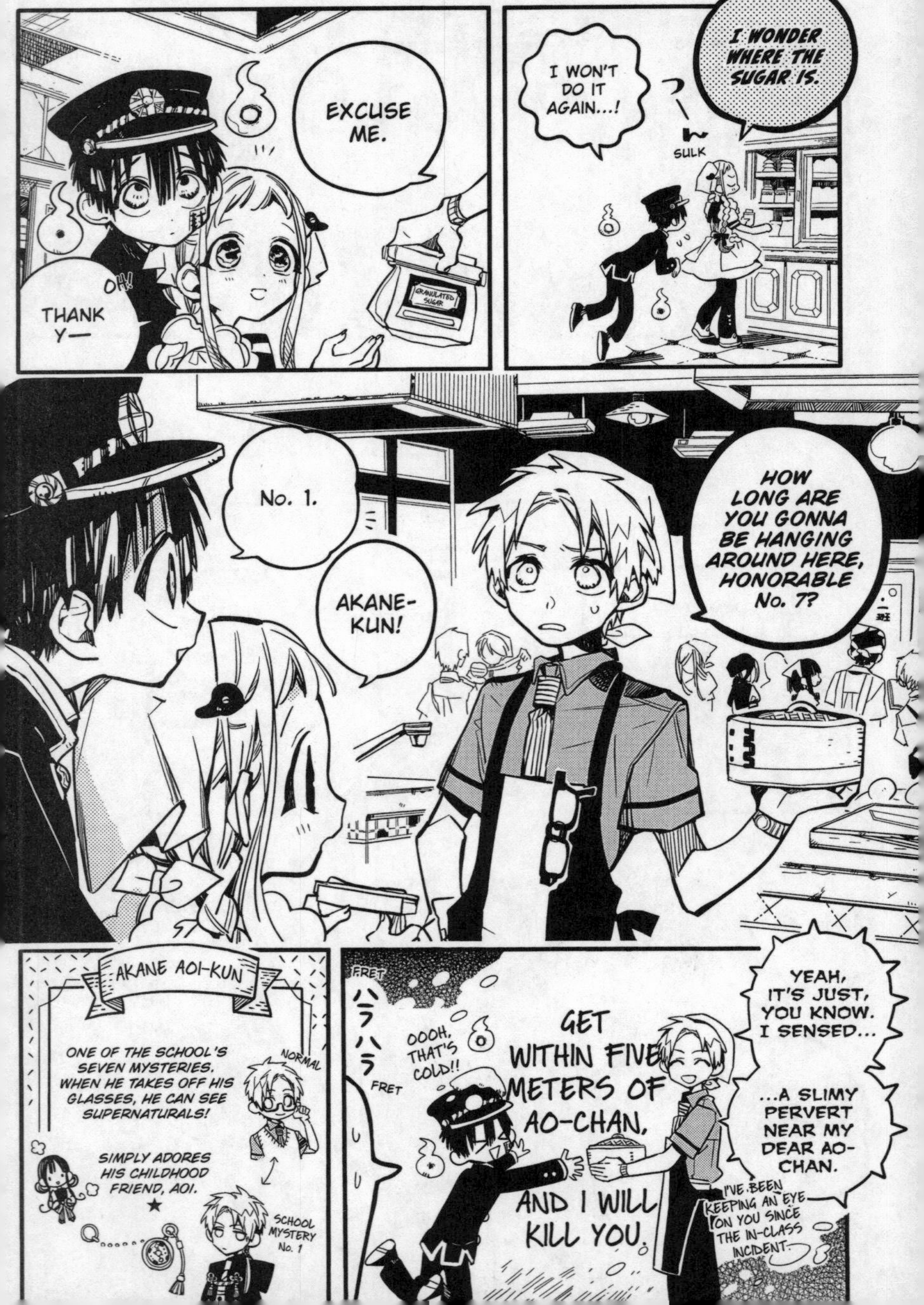
I WONDER WHERE THE SUGAR IS.
I WON'T DO IT AGAIN...!
SULK
EXCUSE ME.
GRANULATED SUGAR
OH!
THANK Y—
HOW LONG ARE YOU GONNA BE HANGING AROUND HERE, HONORABLE No. 7?
AKANE-KUN!
No. 1.
YEAH, IT'S JUST, YOU KNOW. I SENSED...
...A SLIMY PERVERT NEAR MY DEAR AO-CHAN.
I'VE BEEN KEEPING AN EYE ON YOU SINCE THE IN-CLASS INCIDENT.
GET WITHIN FIVE METERS OF AO-CHAN, AND I WILL KILL YOU.
OOOH, THAT'S COLD!!
FRET
ハラハラ
FRET
AKANE AOI-KUN
ONE OF THE SCHOOL'S SEVEN MYSTERIES. WHEN HE TAKES OFF HIS GLASSES, HE CAN SEE SUPERNATURALS!
NORMAL
SIMPLY ADORES HIS CHILDHOOD FRIEND, AOI. ★
SCHOOL MYSTERY No. 1

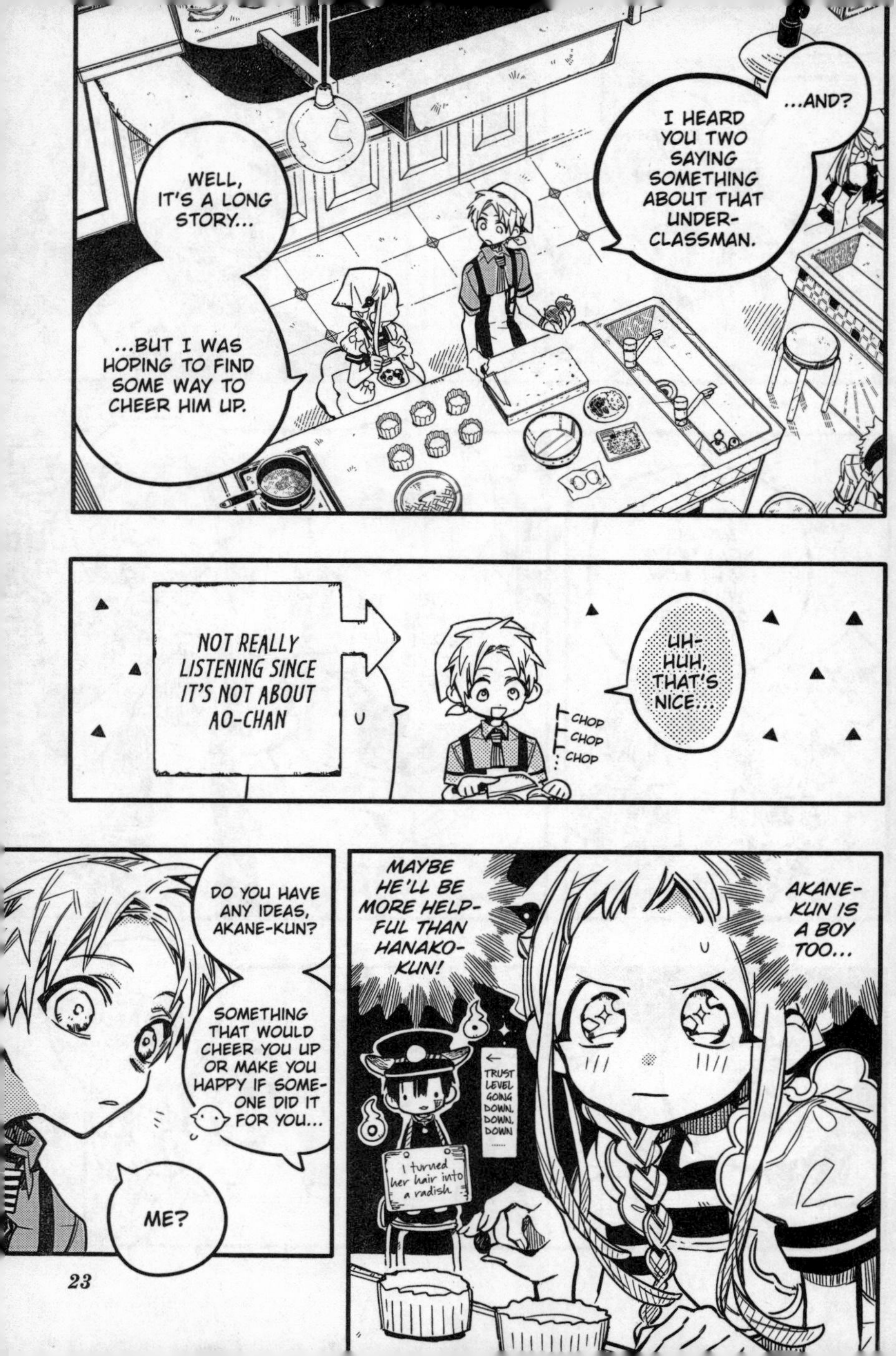
...AND?
I HEARD YOU TWO SAYING SOMETHING ABOUT THAT UNDER-CLASSMAN.
WELL, IT'S A LONG STORY...
...BUT I WAS HOPING TO FIND SOME WAY TO CHEER HIM UP.
UH-HUH, THAT'S NICE...
CHOP CHOP CHOP
NOT REALLY LISTENING SINCE IT'S NOT ABOUT AO-CHAN
AKANE-KUN IS A BOY TOO...
MAYBE HE'LL BE MORE HELP-FUL THAN HANAKO-KUN!
← TRUST LEVEL GOING DOWN, DOWN, DOWN ......
I turned her hair into a radish
DO YOU HAVE ANY IDEAS, AKANE-KUN?
SOMETHING THAT WOULD CHEER YOU UP OR MAKE YOU HAPPY IF SOME-ONE DID IT FOR YOU...
ME?

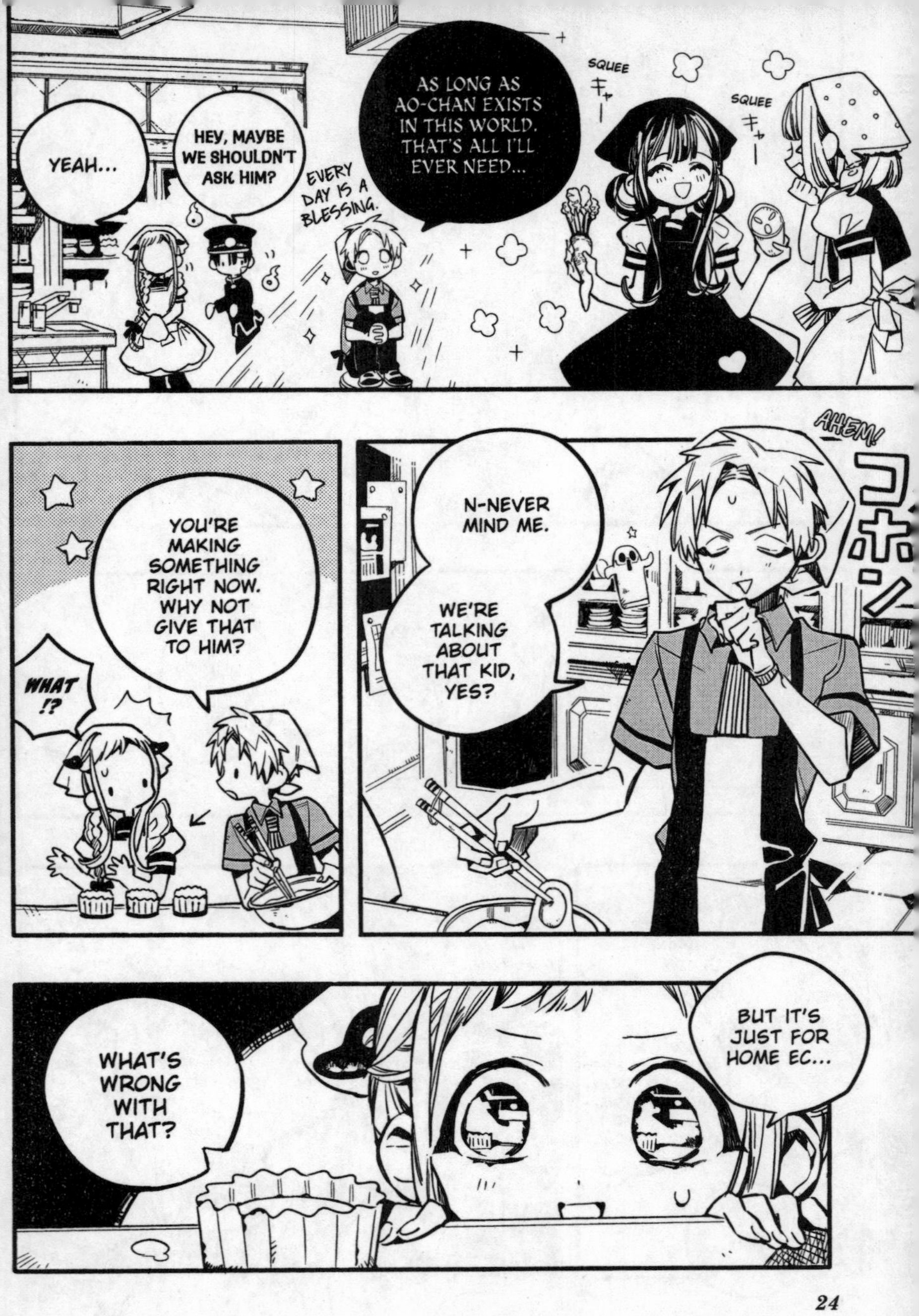
SQUEE
キャー
SQUEE
キャー
AS LONG AS AO-CHAN EXISTS IN THIS WORLD. THAT'S ALL I'LL EVER NEED...
EVERY DAY IS A BLESSING.
HEY, MAYBE WE SHOULDN'T ASK HIM?
YEAH...
AHEM!
コホン
N-NEVER MIND ME.
WE'RE TALKING ABOUT THAT KID, YES?
YOU'RE MAKING SOMETHING RIGHT NOW. WHY NOT GIVE THAT TO HIM?
WHAT!?
BUT IT'S JUST FOR HOME EC...
WHAT'S WRONG WITH THAT?

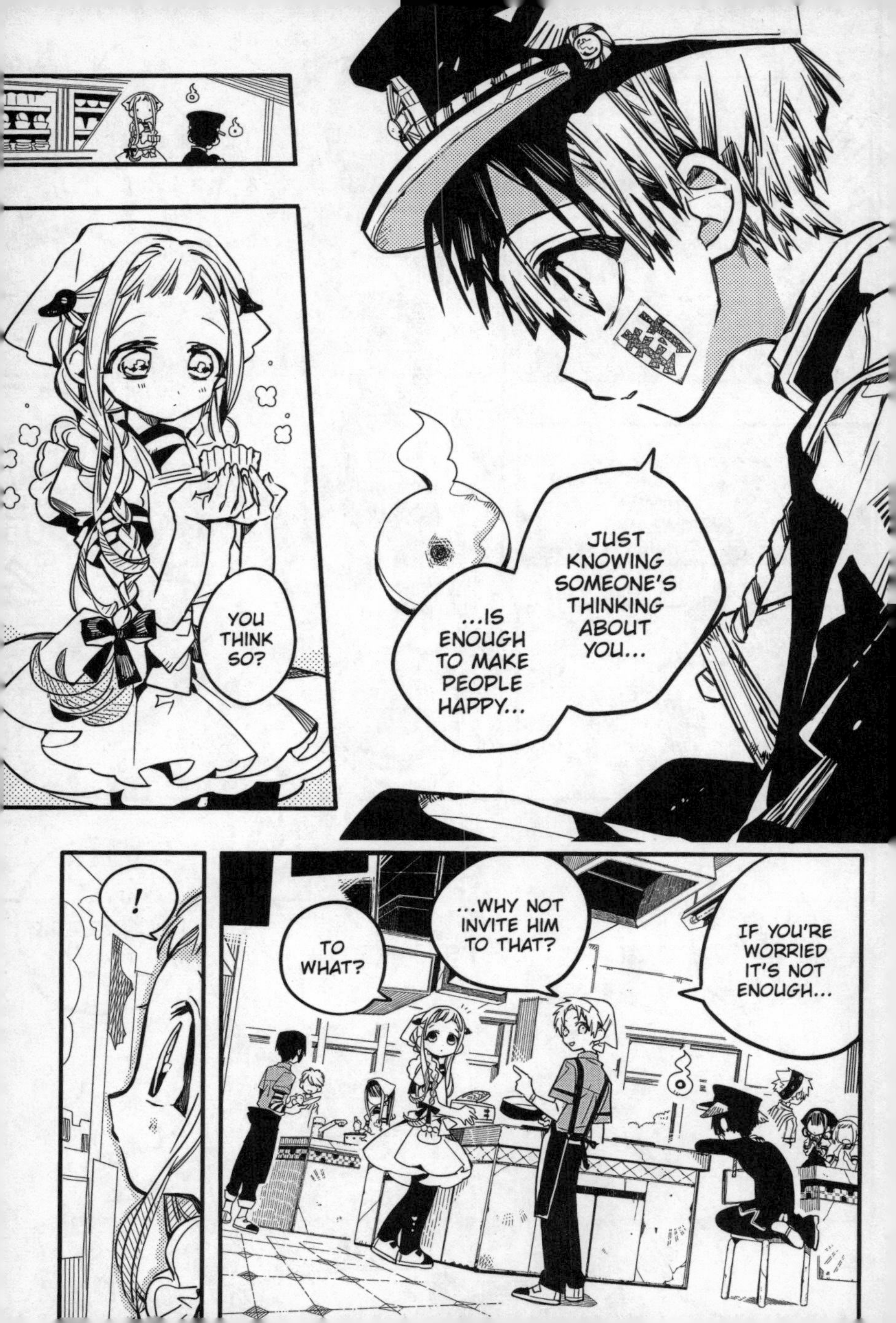
JUST KNOWING SOMEONE'S THINKING ABOUT YOU...
...IS ENOUGH TO MAKE PEOPLE HAPPY...
YOU THINK SO?
IF YOU'RE WORRIED IT'S NOT ENOUGH...
...WHY NOT INVITE HIM TO THAT?
TO WHAT?
!

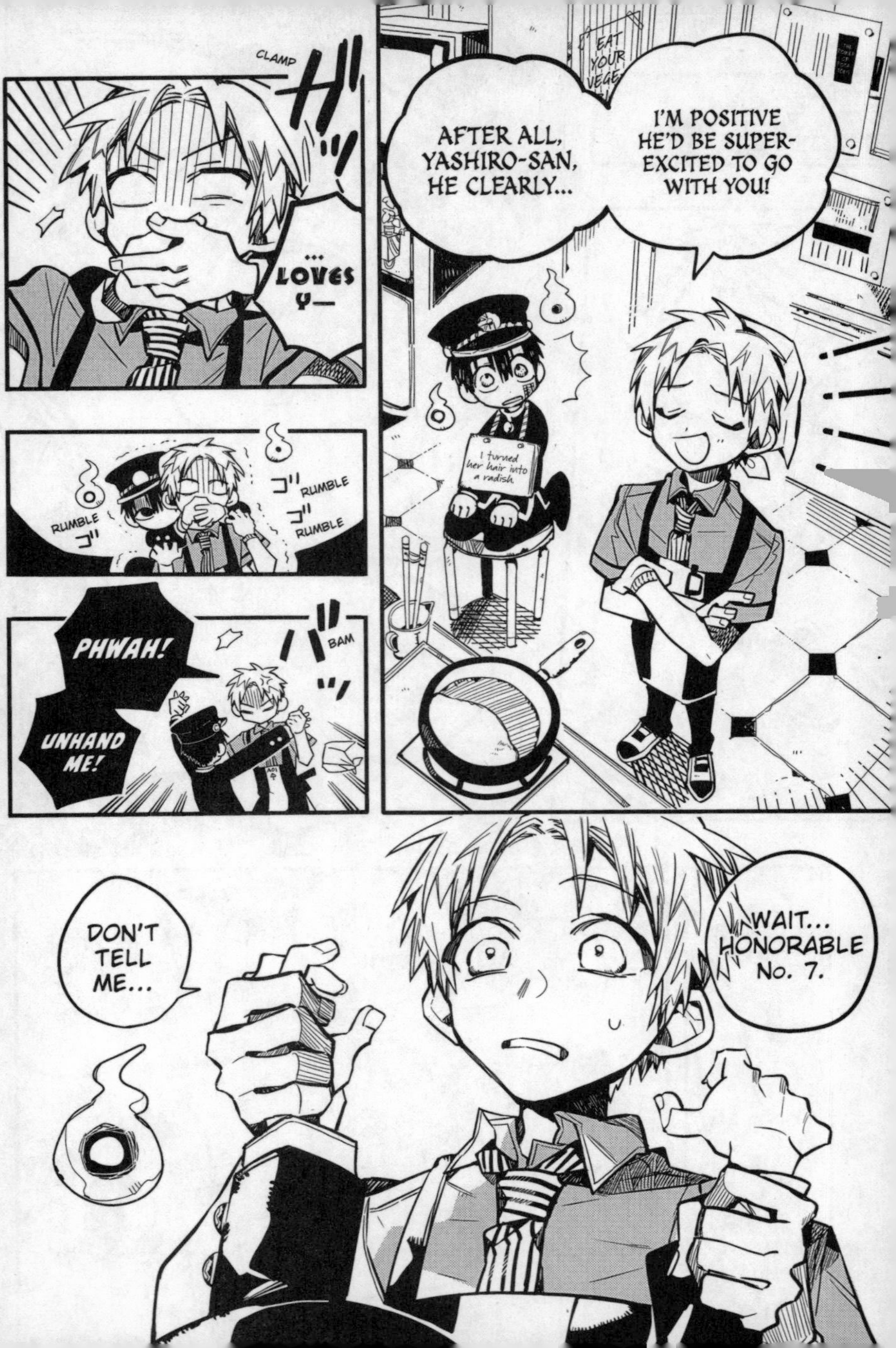
EAT YOUR VEGE
I'M POSITIVE HE'D BE SUPER-EXCITED TO GO WITH YOU!
AFTER ALL, YASHIRO-SAN, HE CLEARLY...
I turned her hair into a radish
CLAMP
...LOVES Y—
RUMBLE
RUMBLE
RUMBLE
BAM
PHWAH!
UNHAND ME!
WAIT... HONORABLE No. 7.
DON'T TELL ME...

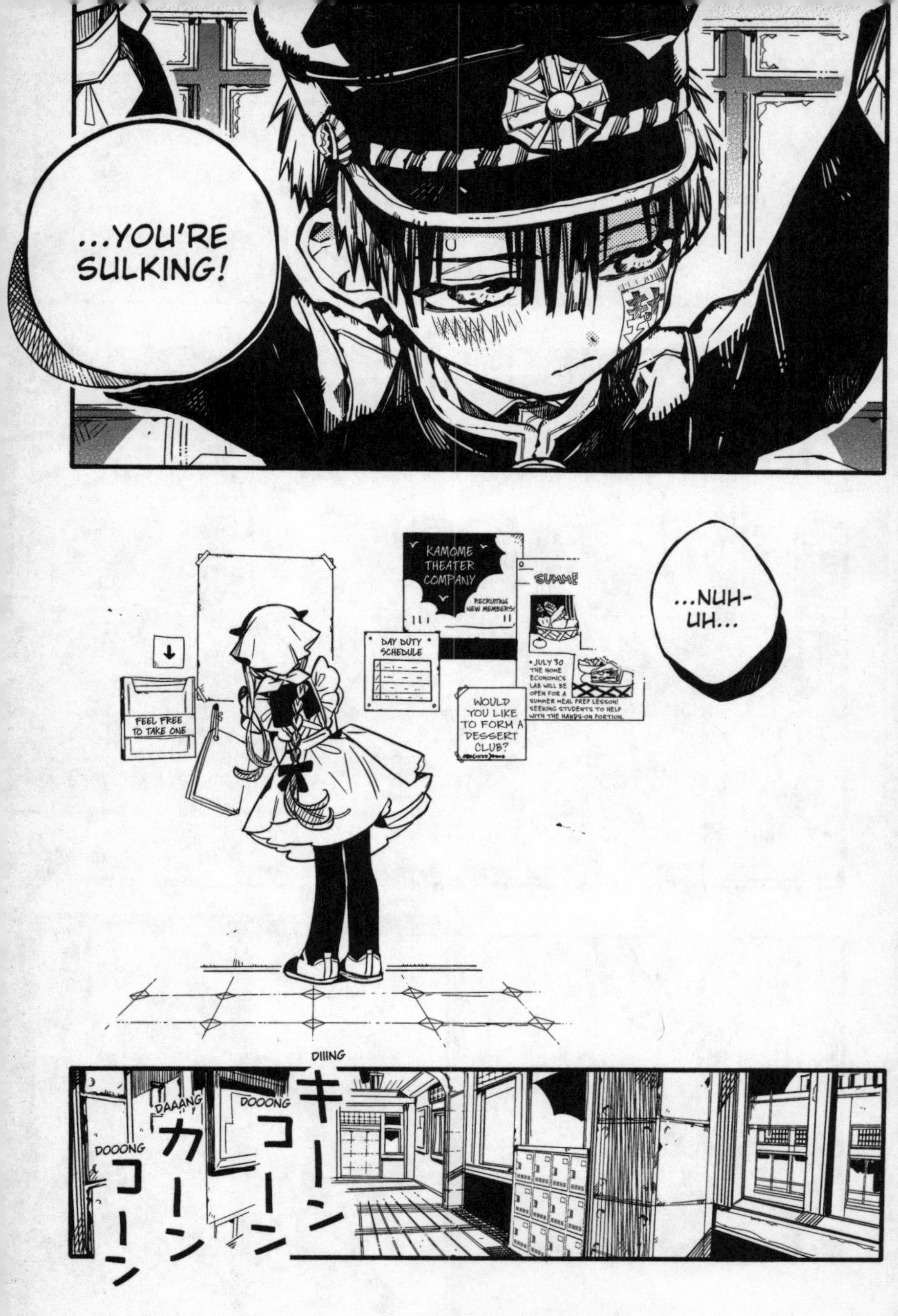
...YOU'RE SULKING!
...NUH-UH...
SUMME
KAMOME THEATER COMPANY
RECRUITING NEW MEMBERS!
• JULY 30 THE HOME ECONOMICS LAB WILL BE OPEN FOR A SUMMER MEAL PREP LESSON! SEEKING STUDENTS TO HELP WITH THE HANDS-ON PORTION.
WOULD YOU LIKE TO FORM A DESSERT CLUB?
DAY DUTY SCHEDULE
FEEL FREE TO TAKE ONE
DIIING
キーン
DOOONG
コーン
DAAANG
カーン
DOOONG
コーン

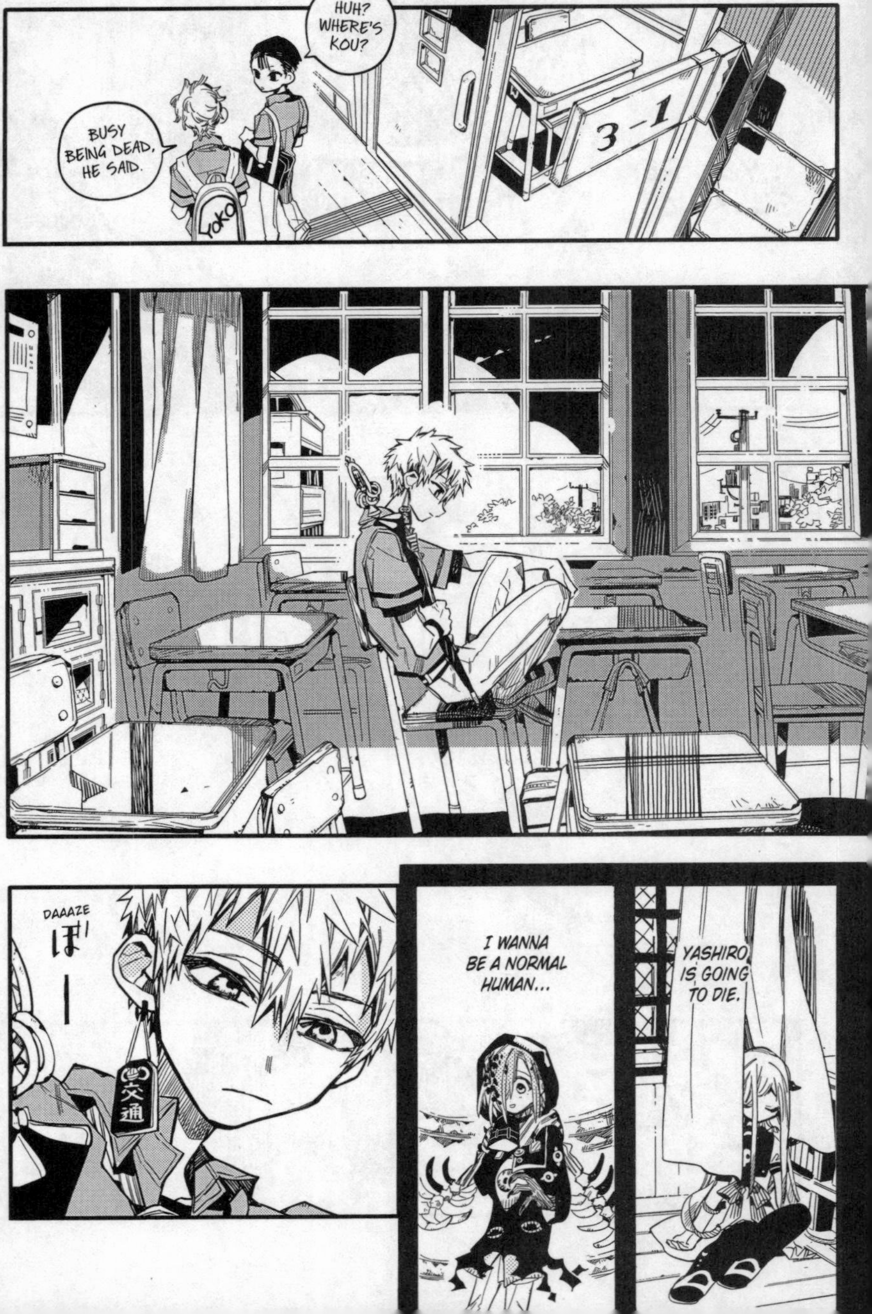
3-1
HUH? WHERE'S KOU?
BUSY BEING DEAD, HE SAID.
YOKO
YASHIRO IS GOING TO DIE.
I WANNA BE A NORMAL HUMAN...
DAAAZE
ぼー
交通

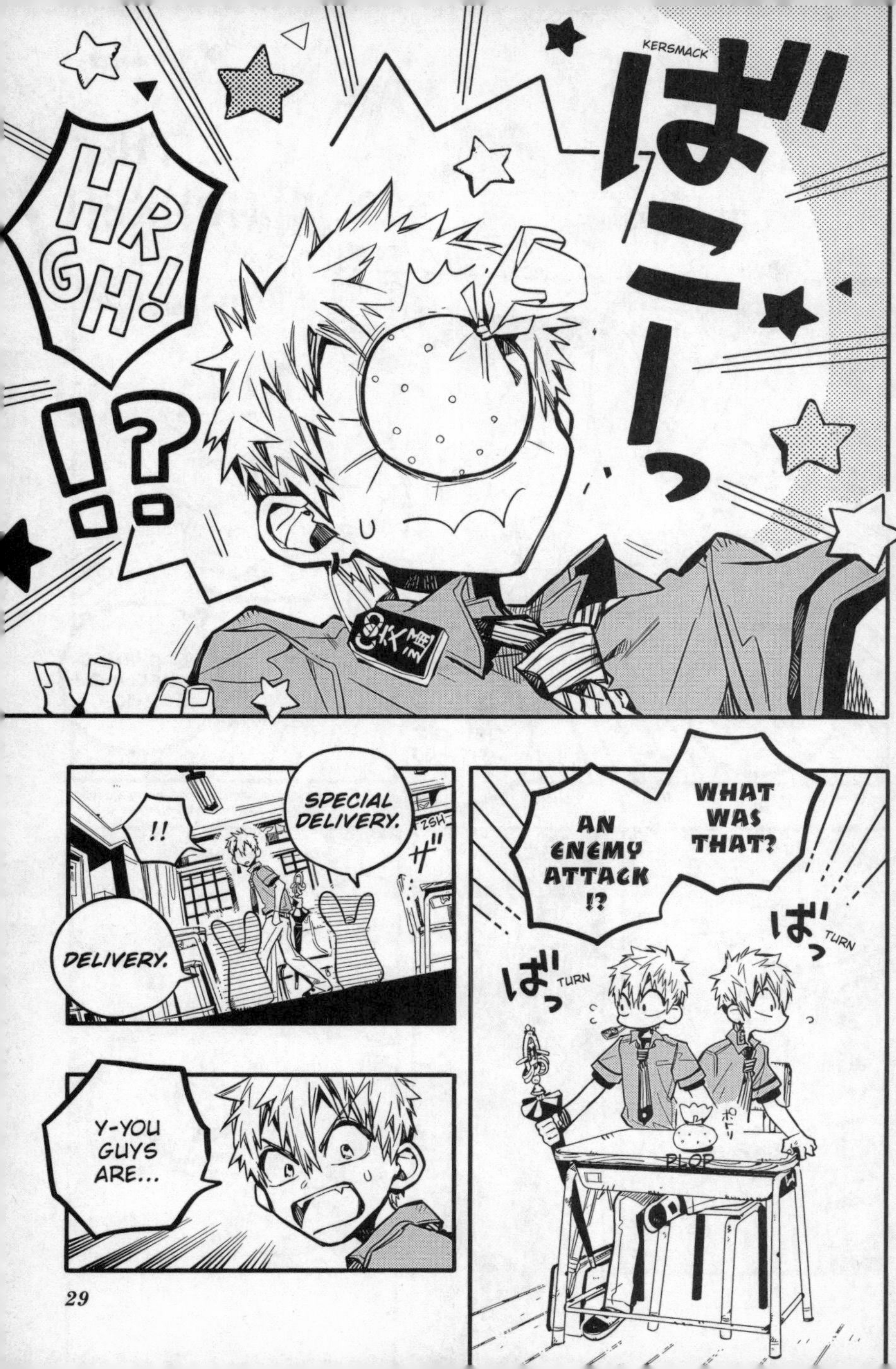
KERSMACK
ばこーっ
HRGH!
!?
WHAT WAS THAT?
AN ENEMY ATTACK!?
ばっ TURN
ばっ TURN
ポトリ
PLOP
SPECIAL DELIVERY.
ZSH
ザ
!!
DELIVERY.
Y-YOU GUYS ARE...

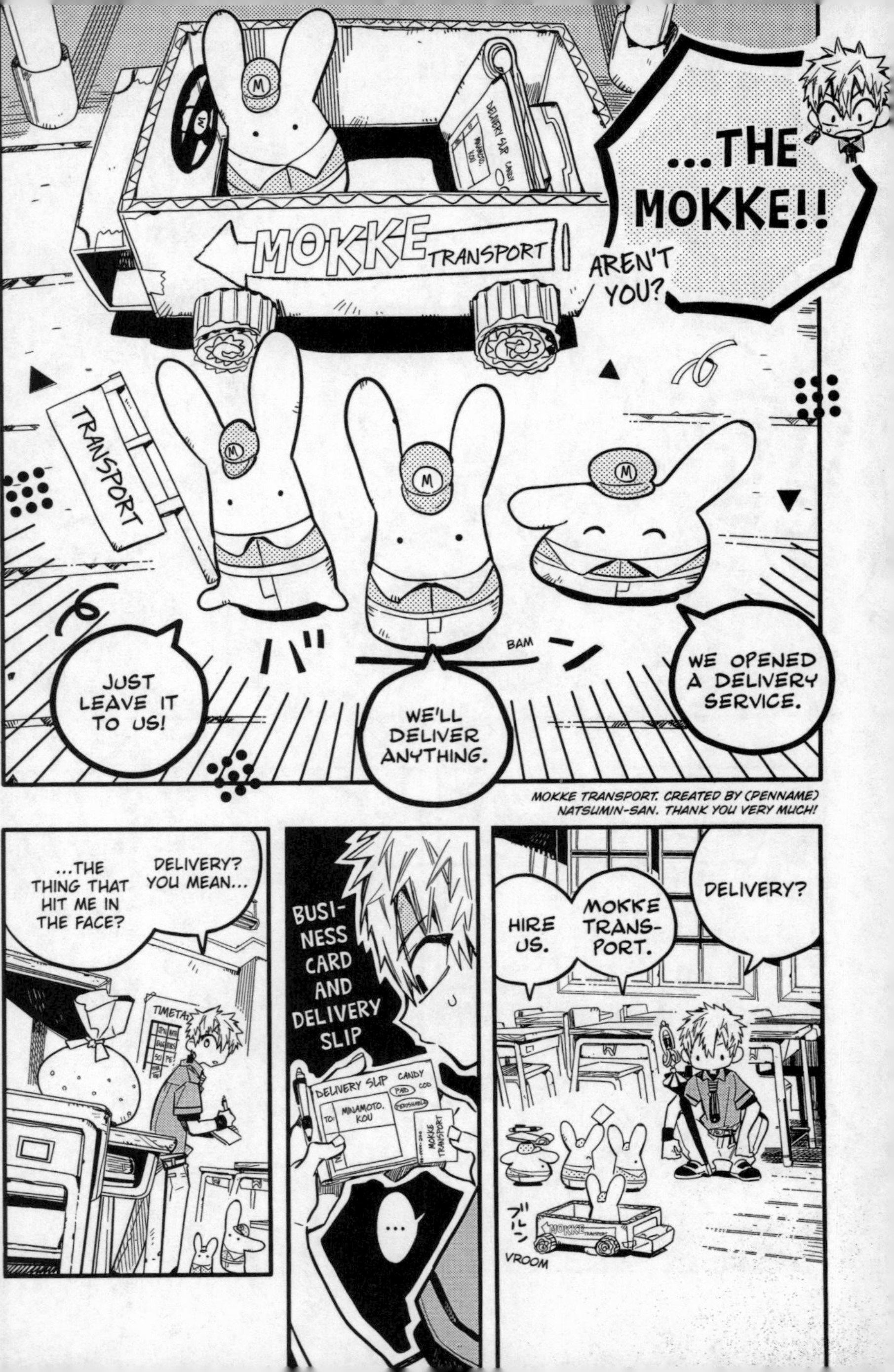
...THE MOKKE!!
AREN'T YOU?
MOKKE TRANSPORT
TRANSPORT
WE OPENED A DELIVERY SERVICE.
BAM
WE'LL DELIVER ANYTHING.
JUST LEAVE IT TO US!
MOKKE TRANSPORT. CREATED BY (PENNAME) NATSUMIN-SAN. THANK YOU VERY MUCH!
DELIVERY?
MOKKE TRANS-PORT.
HIRE US.
VROOM
BUSI-NESS CARD AND DELIVERY SLIP
DELIVERY SLIP CANDY
PAID COD
PERISHABLE
TO: MINAMOTO, KOU
MOKKE TRANSPORT
...
DELIVERY? YOU MEAN...
...THE THING THAT HIT ME IN THE FACE?
TIMETA

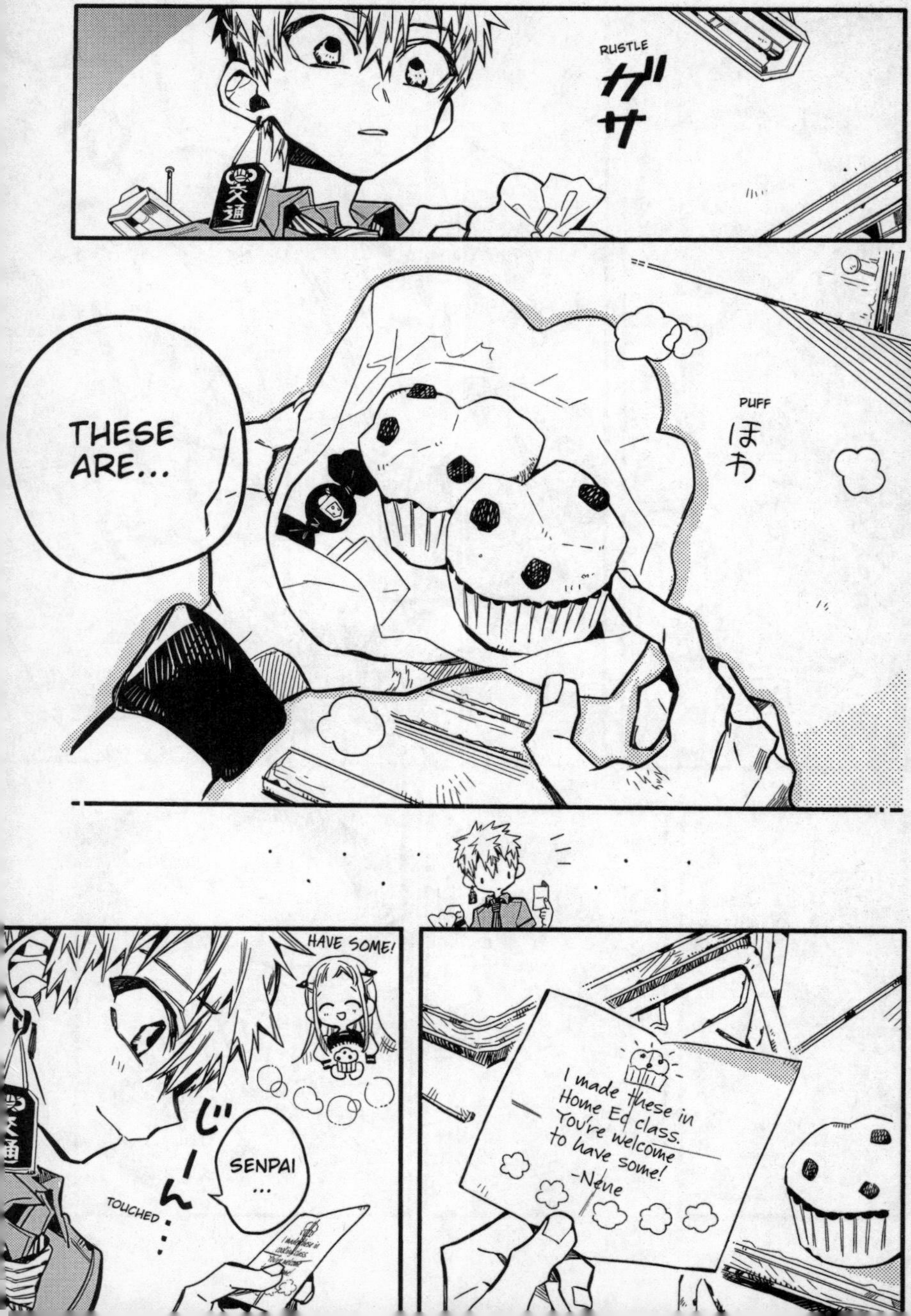
RUSTLE
ガサ
PUFF
ほわ
THESE ARE...
I made these in Home Ec class. You're welcome to have some! -Nene
HAVE SOME!
じーん…
TOUCHED
SENPAI ...

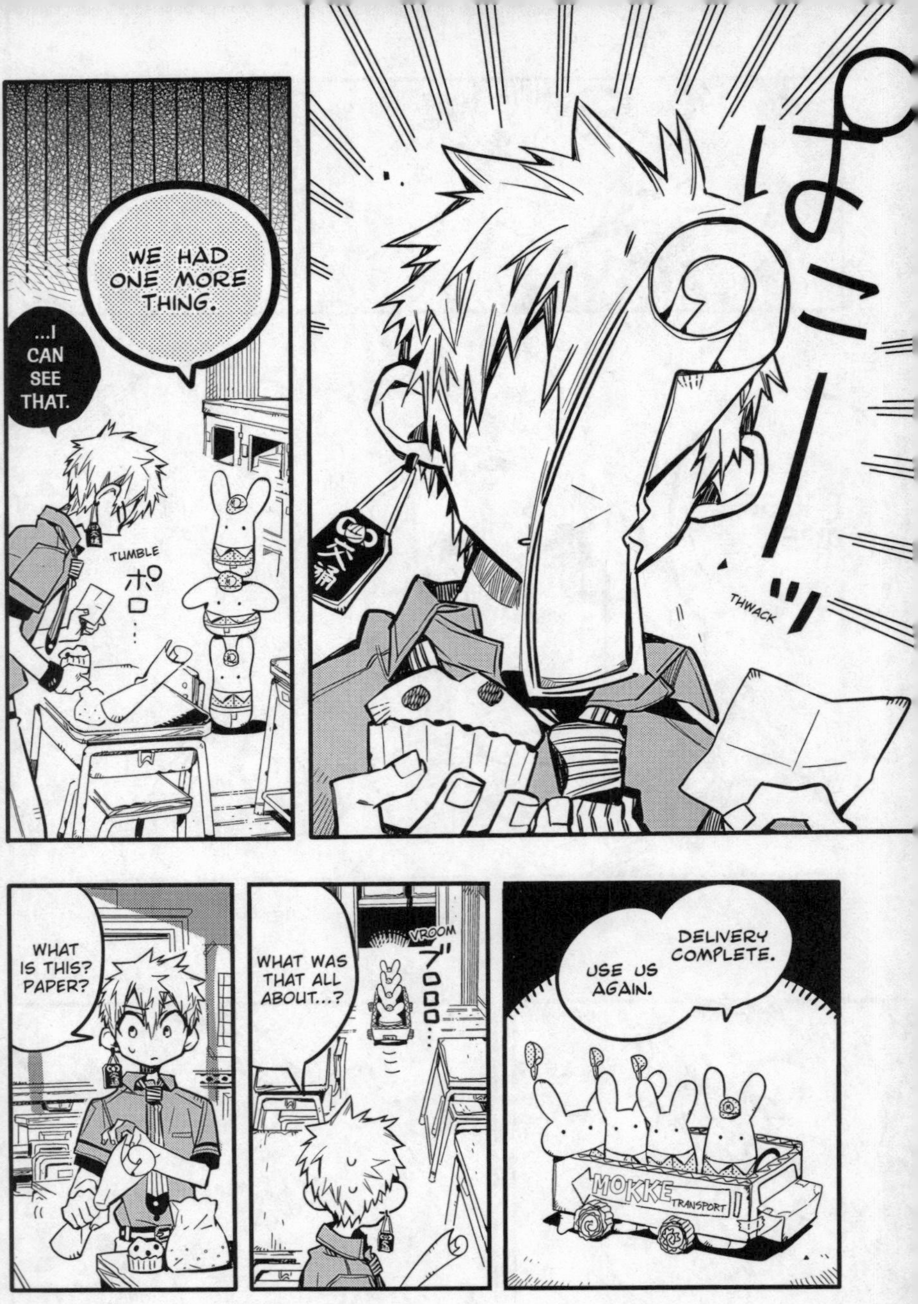

THWACK
WE HAD ONE MORE THING.
...I CAN SEE THAT.
TUMBLE
ポロ...
DELIVERY COMPLETE.
USE US AGAIN.
MOKKE TRANSPORT
VROOM
ブロロロ...
WHAT WAS THAT ALL ABOUT...?
WHAT IS THIS? PAPER?

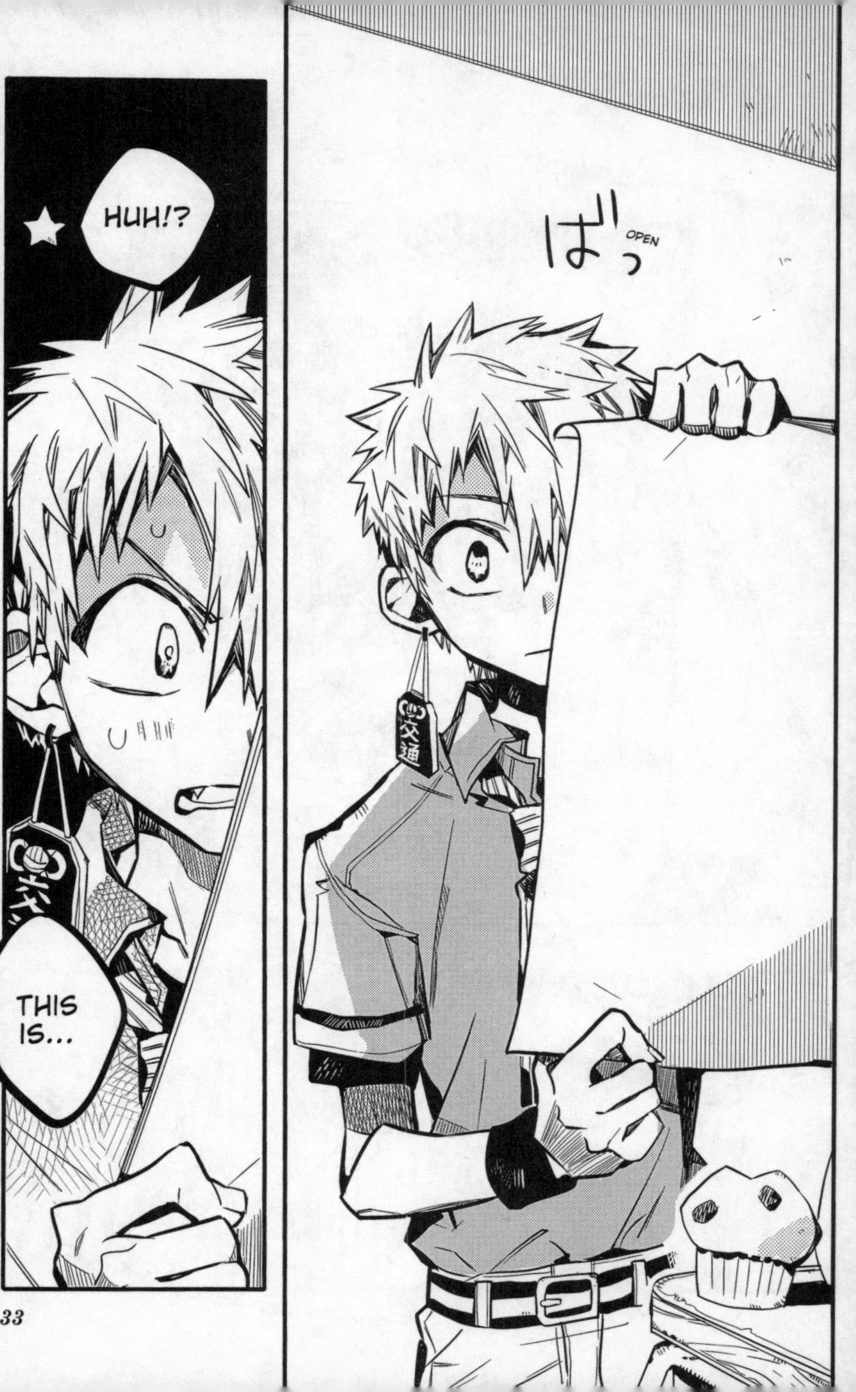
ばっ
OPEN
交通
HUH!?
THIS IS...

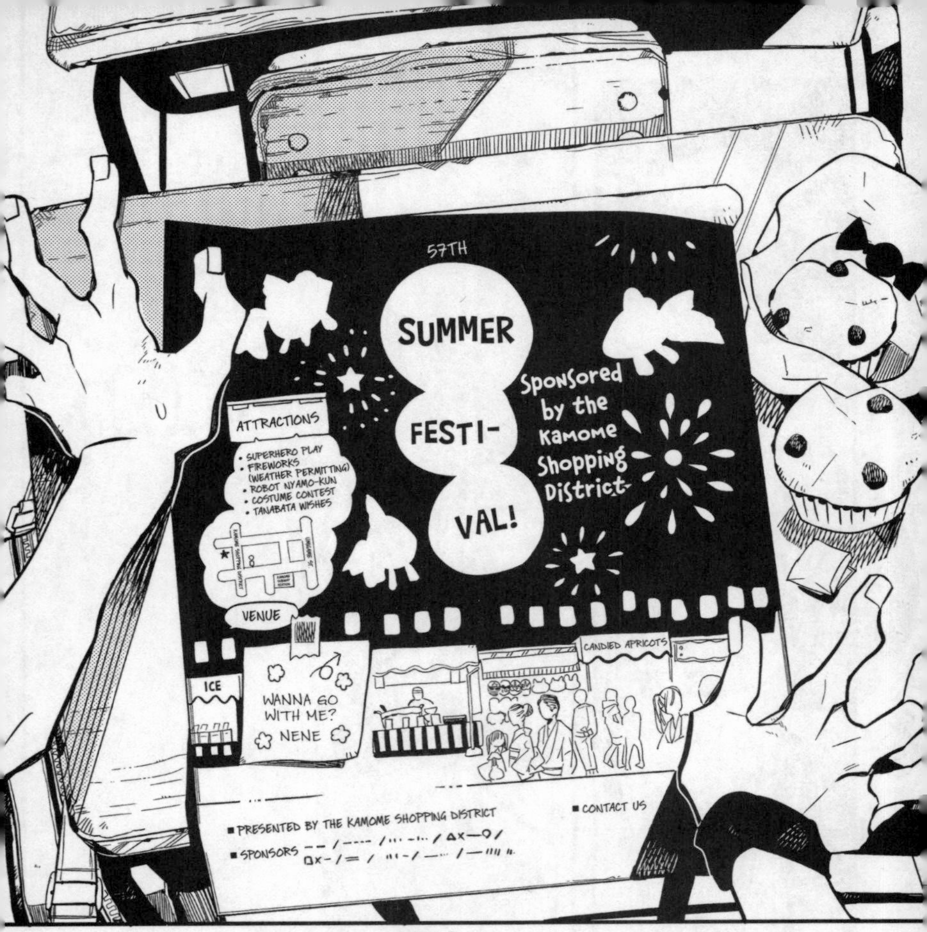
57TH
SUMMER
FESTI-
VAL!
Sponsored by the Kamome Shopping District
ATTRACTIONS
• SUPERHERO PLAY
• FIREWORKS (WEATHER PERMITTING)
• ROBOT NYAMO-KUN
• COSTUME CONTEST
• TANABATA WISHES
VENUE
ICE
WANNA GO WITH ME?
NENE
CANDIED APRICOTS
■ PRESENTED BY THE KAMOME SHOPPING DISTRICT
■ SPONSORS
■ CONTACT US

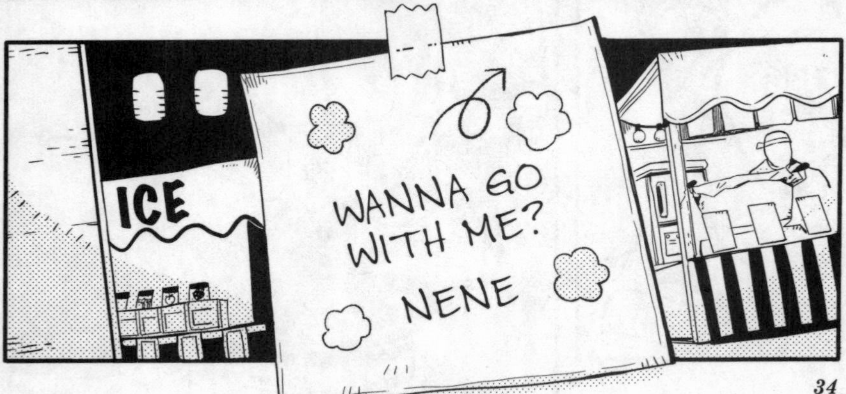
ICE
WANNA GO WITH ME?
NENE

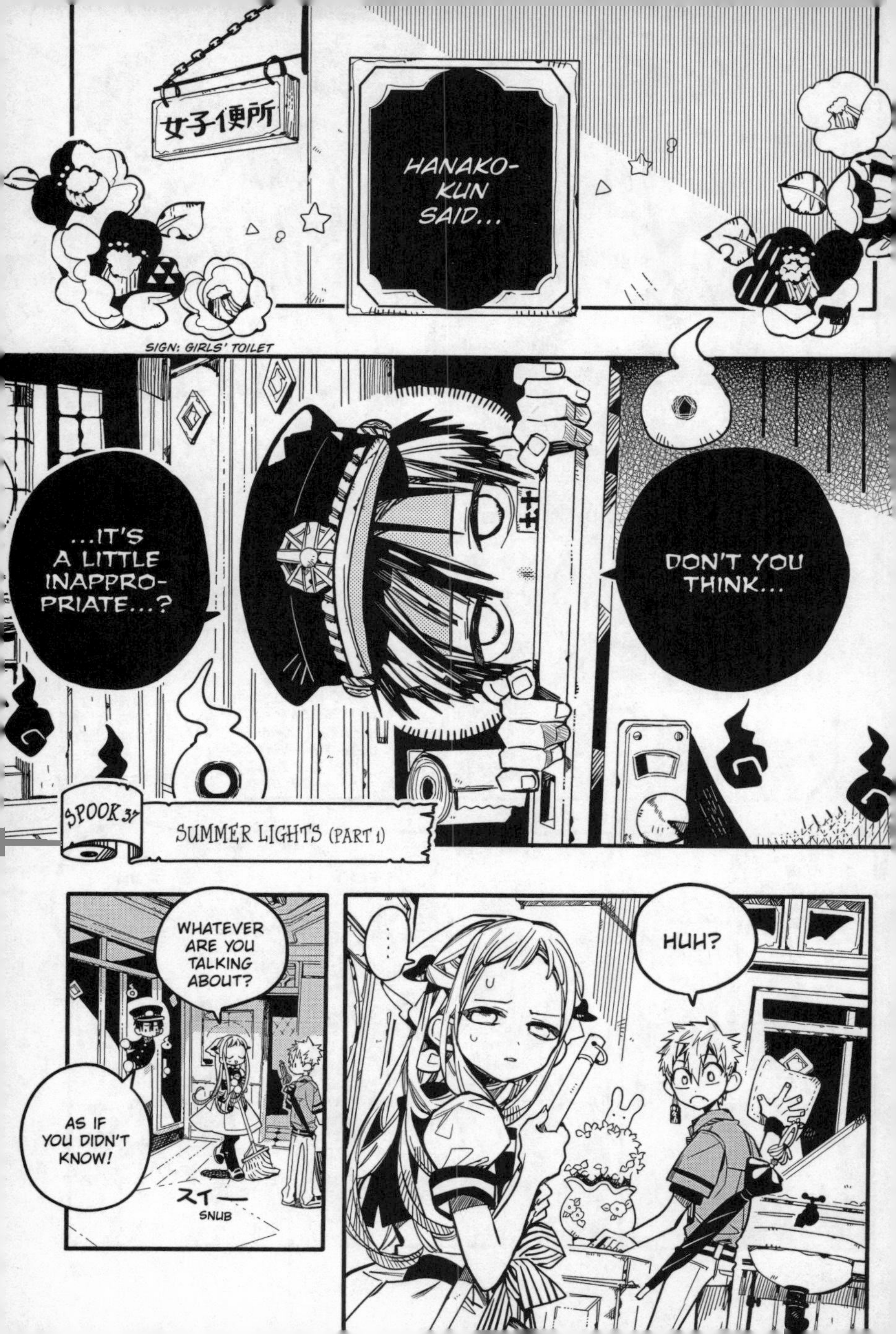
女子便所
HANAKO-KUN SAID...
SIGN: GIRLS' TOILET
DON'T YOU THINK...
...IT'S A LITTLE INAPPROPRIATE...?
SPOOK 37
SUMMER LIGHTS (PART 1)
HUH?
...
WHATEVER ARE YOU TALKING ABOUT?
AS IF YOU DIDN'T KNOW!
スイー
SNUB

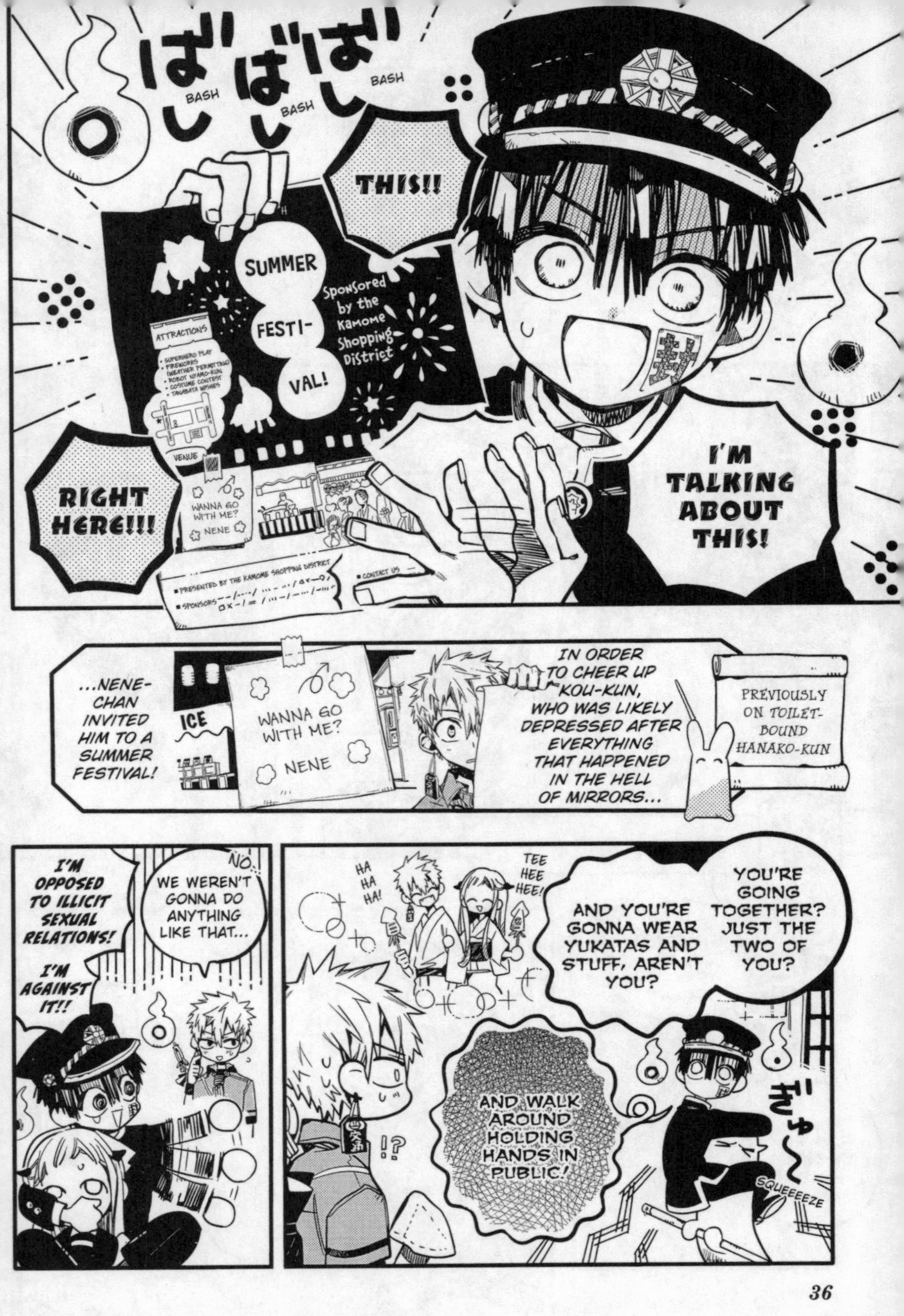
THIS!!
I'M TALKING ABOUT THIS!
SUMMER FESTI-VAL!
Sponsored by the Kamome Shopping District
ATTRACTIONS
• SUPERHERO PLAY
• FIREWORKS (WEATHER PERMITTING)
• ROBOT NYAMO-KUN
• COSTUME CONTEST
• TANABATA WISHES
VENUE
WANNA GO WITH ME? NENE
PRESENTED BY THE KAMOME SHOPPING DISTRICT
CONTACT US
SPONSORS
RIGHT HERE!!!
ばしばしばし
BASH BASH BASH
PREVIOUSLY ON TOILET-BOUND HANAKO-KUN
IN ORDER TO CHEER UP KOU-KUN, WHO WAS LIKELY DEPRESSED AFTER EVERYTHING THAT HAPPENED IN THE HELL OF MIRRORS...
WANNA GO WITH ME? NENE
ICE
...NENE-CHAN INVITED HIM TO A SUMMER FESTIVAL!
YOU'RE GOING TOGETHER? JUST THE TWO OF YOU?
AND YOU'RE GONNA WEAR YUKATAS AND STUFF, AREN'T YOU?
TEE HEE HEE!
HA HA HA!
AND WALK AROUND HOLDING HANDS IN PUBLIC!
ぎゅ〜
SQUEEEEZE
!?
NO...
WE WEREN'T GONNA DO ANYTHING LIKE THAT...
I'M OPPOSED TO ILLICIT SEXUAL RELATIONS!
I'M AGAINST IT!!

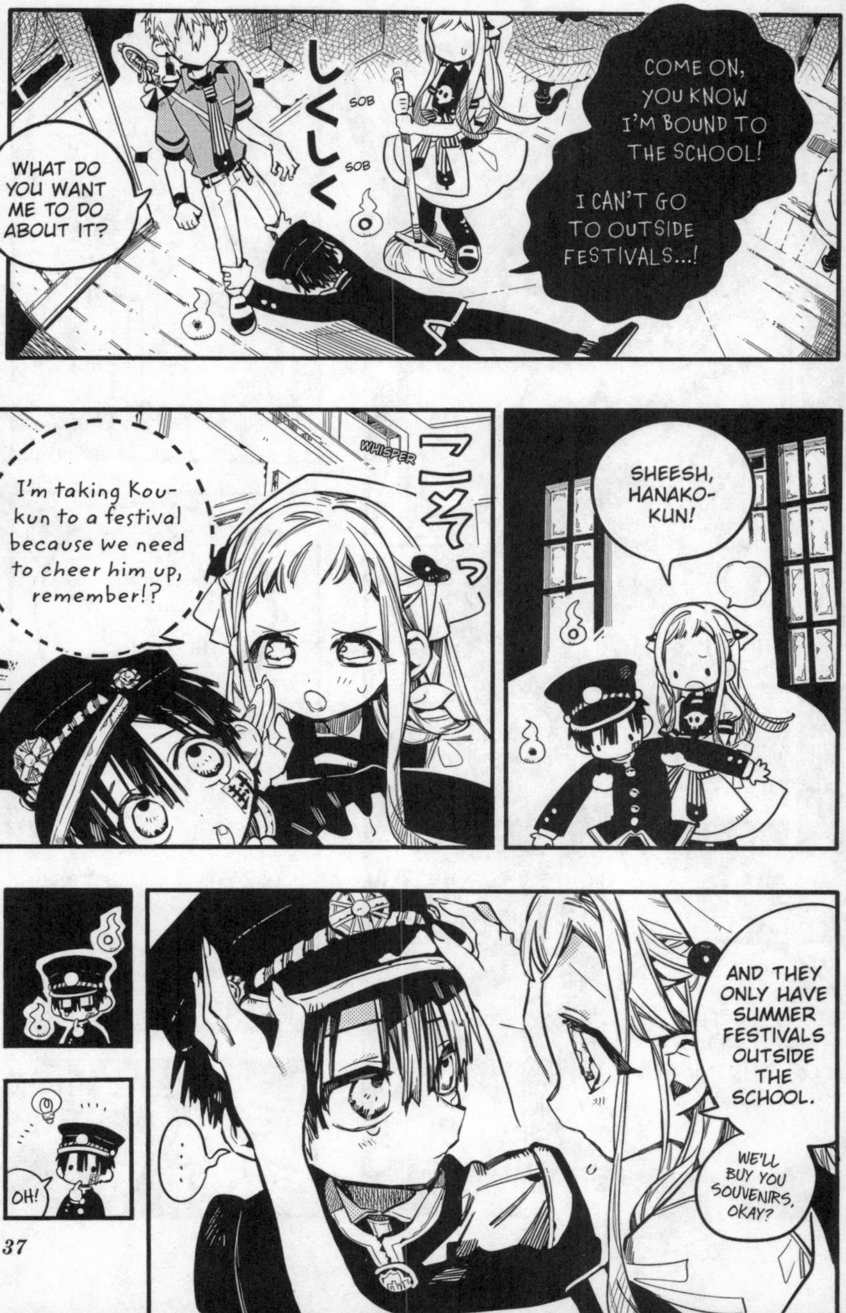
COME ON, YOU KNOW I'M BOUND TO THE SCHOOL!
I CAN'T GO TO OUTSIDE FESTIVALS...!
しくしく
SOB
SOB
WHAT DO YOU WANT ME TO DO ABOUT IT?
SHEESH, HANAKO-KUN!
こそっ
WHISPER
I'm taking Kou-kun to a festival because we need to cheer him up, remember!?
AND THEY ONLY HAVE SUMMER FESTIVALS OUTSIDE THE SCHOOL.
WE'LL BUY YOU SOUVENIRS, OKAY?
....
OH!

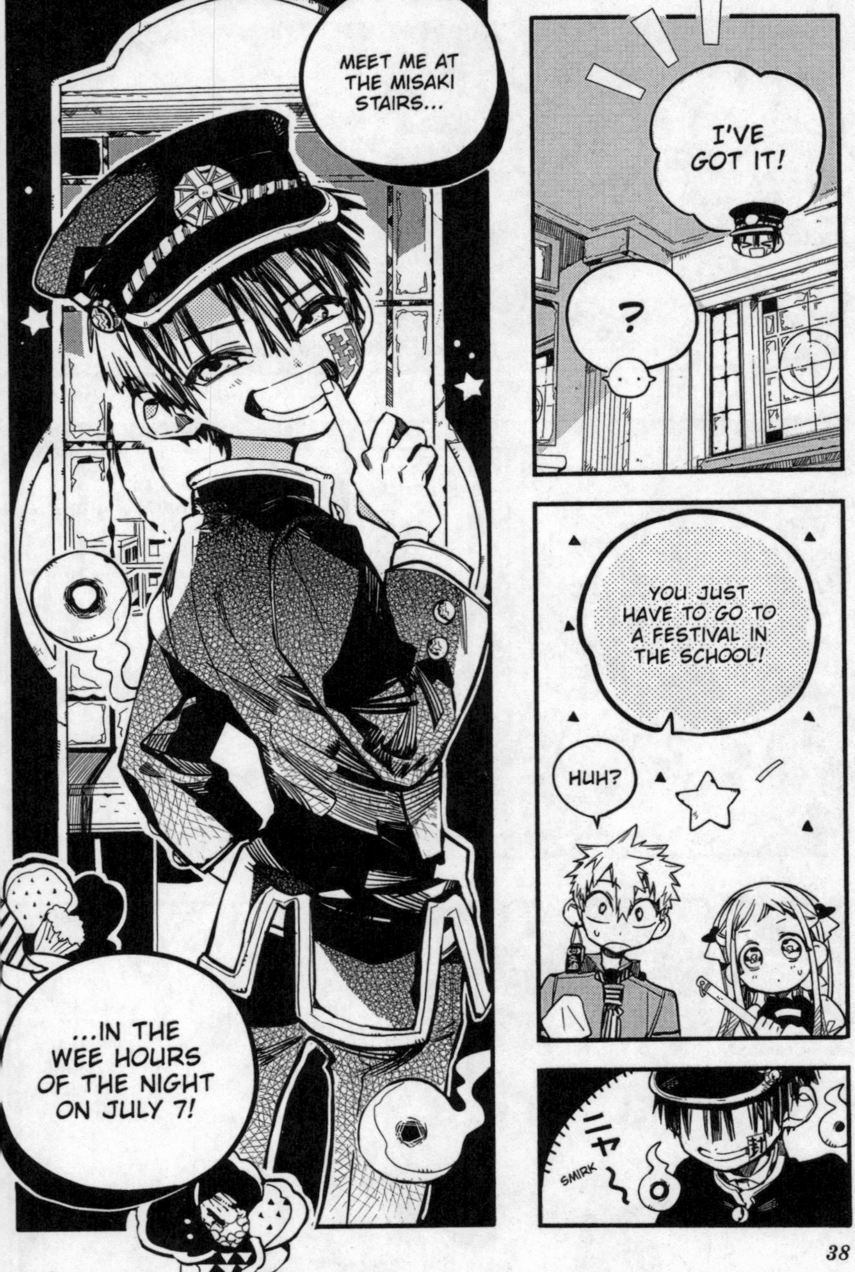
I'VE GOT IT!
?
YOU JUST HAVE TO GO TO A FESTIVAL IN THE SCHOOL!
HUH?
ニヤ～
SMIRK
MEET ME AT THE MISAKI STAIRS...
...IN THE WEE HOURS OF THE NIGHT ON JULY 7!

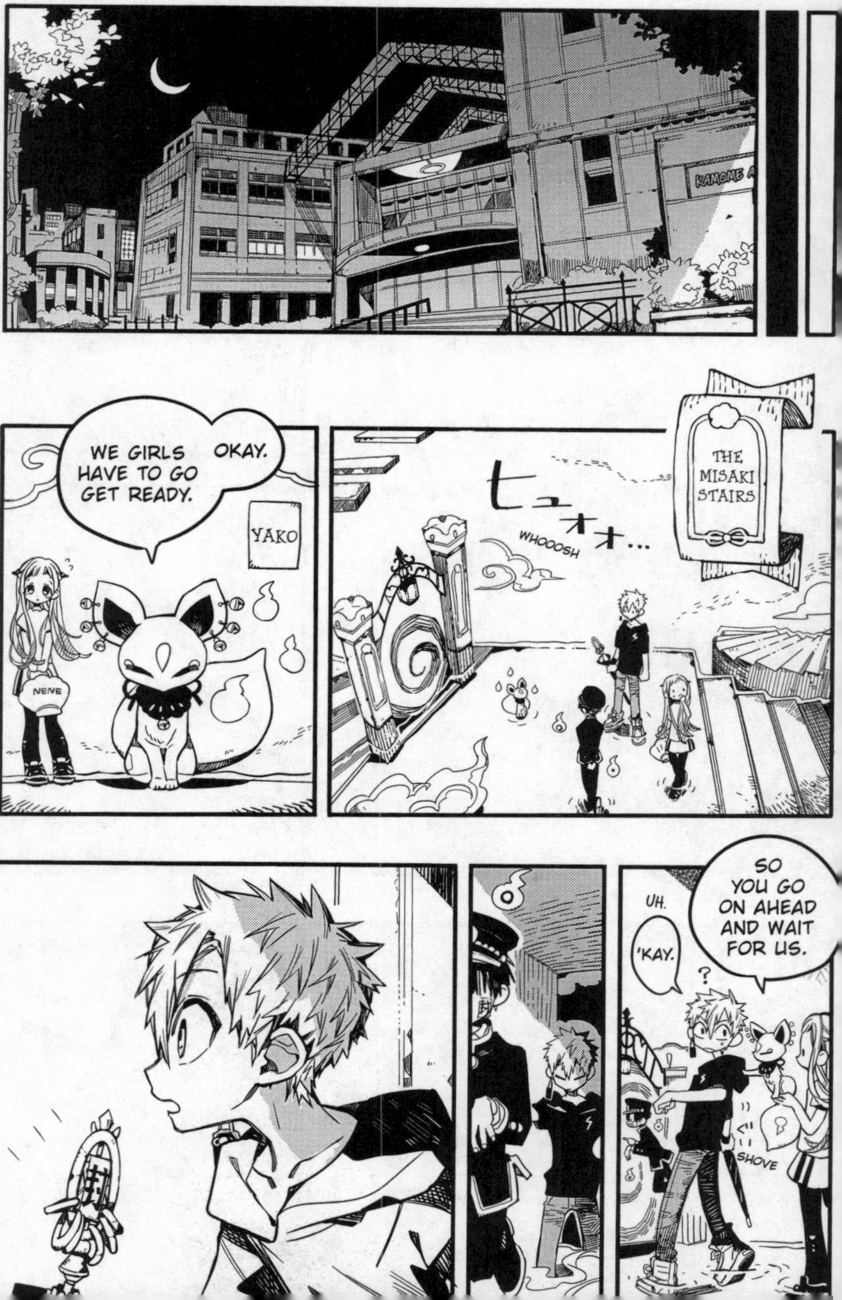
KAMOME A
THE MISAKI STAIRS
ヒュオオ…
WHOOOSH
WE GIRLS HAVE TO GO GET READY.
OKAY.
YAKO
NENE
SO YOU GO ON AHEAD AND WAIT FOR US.
UH.
'KAY.
?
SHOVE

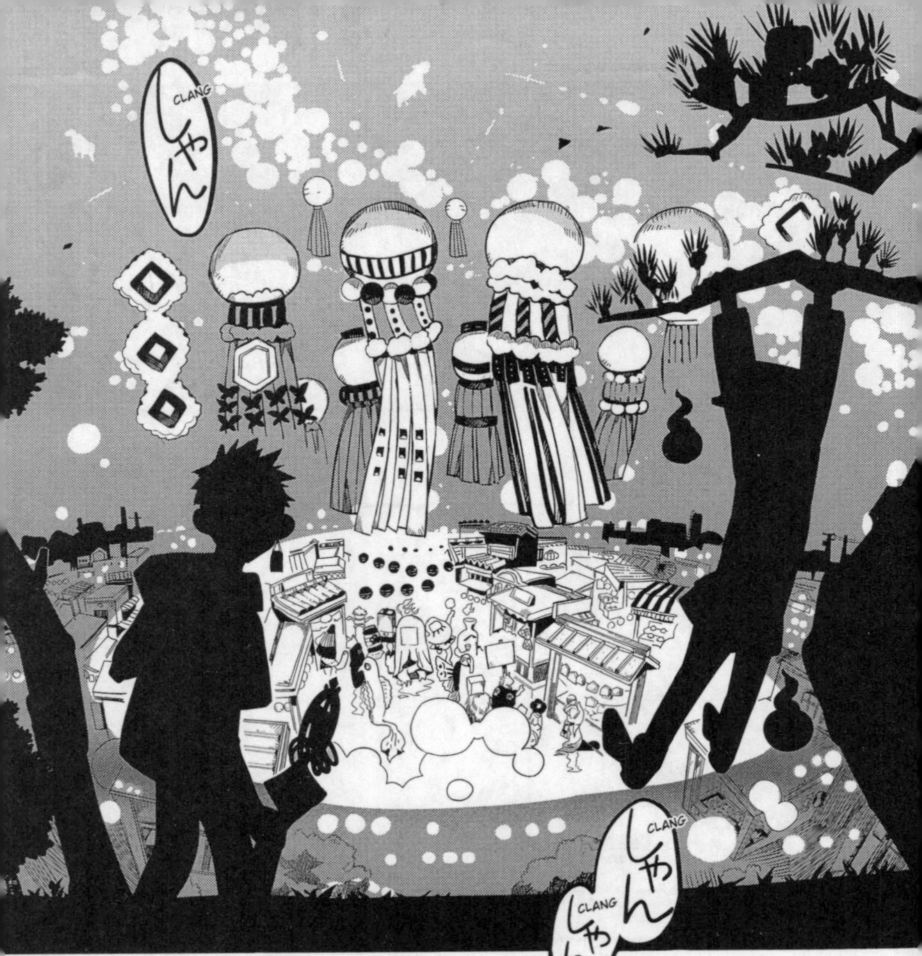

しゃん
CLANG
しゃん
CLANG
しゃん
CLANG

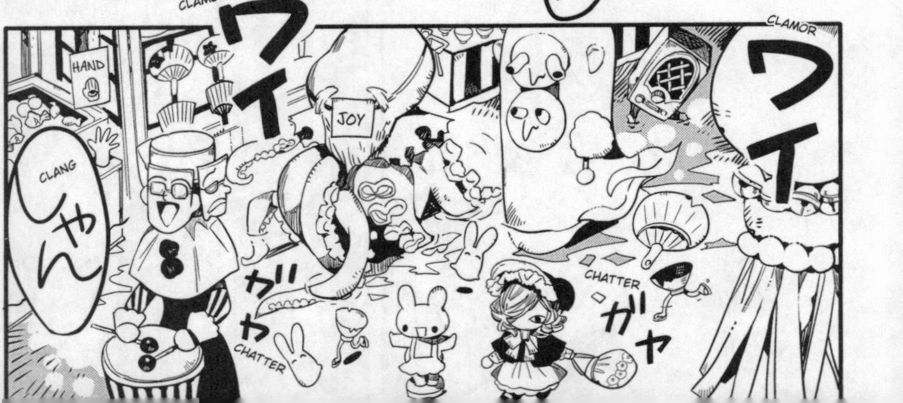

ワイ
CLAMOR
ワイ
CLAMOR
JOY
HAND
ガヤ
CHATTER
しゃん
CLANG
ガヤ
CHATTER

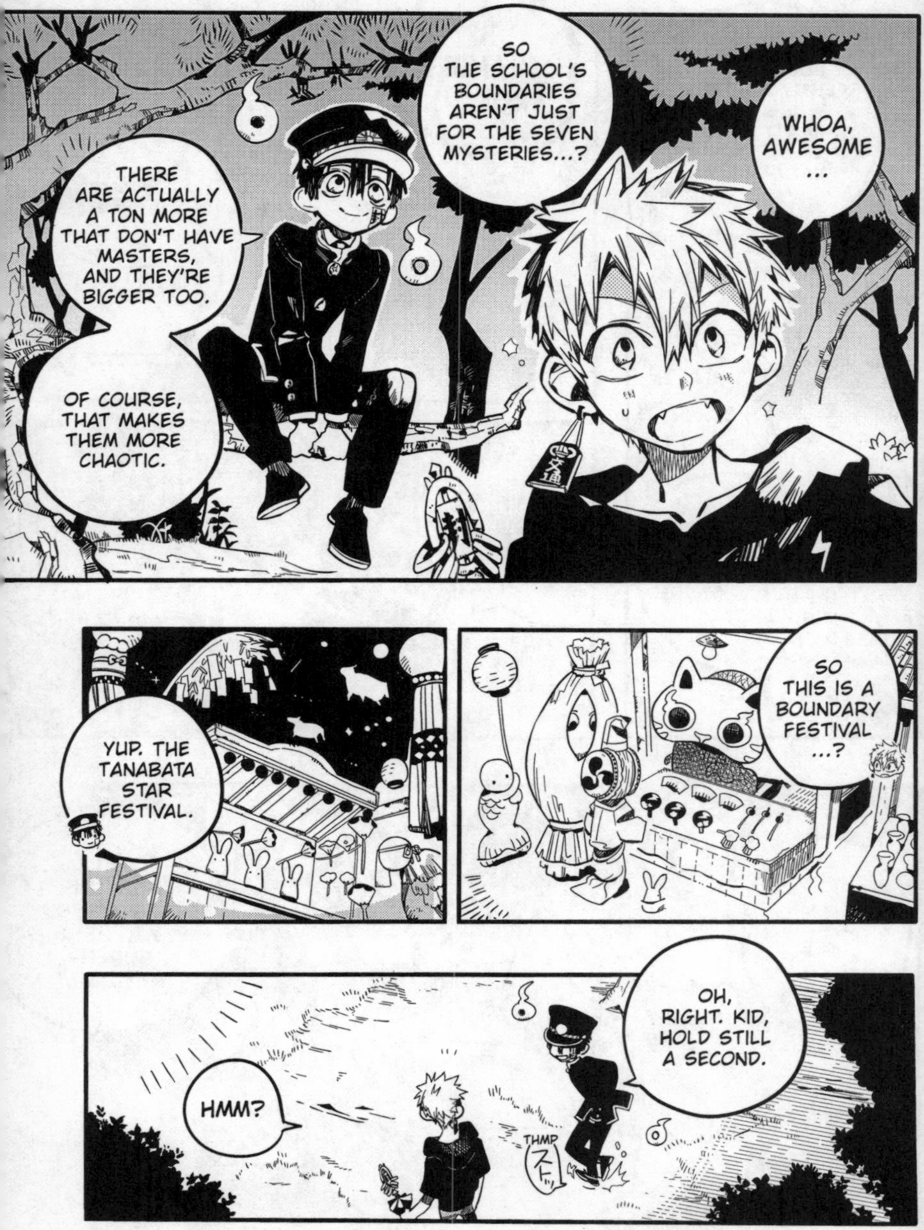
WHOA, AWESOME ...
SO THE SCHOOL'S BOUNDARIES AREN'T JUST FOR THE SEVEN MYSTERIES...?
THERE ARE ACTUALLY A TON MORE THAT DON'T HAVE MASTERS, AND THEY'RE BIGGER TOO.
OF COURSE, THAT MAKES THEM MORE CHAOTIC.
SO THIS IS A BOUNDARY FESTIVAL ...?
YUP. THE TANABATA STAR FESTIVAL.
OH, RIGHT. KID, HOLD STILL A SECOND.
THMP
HMM?

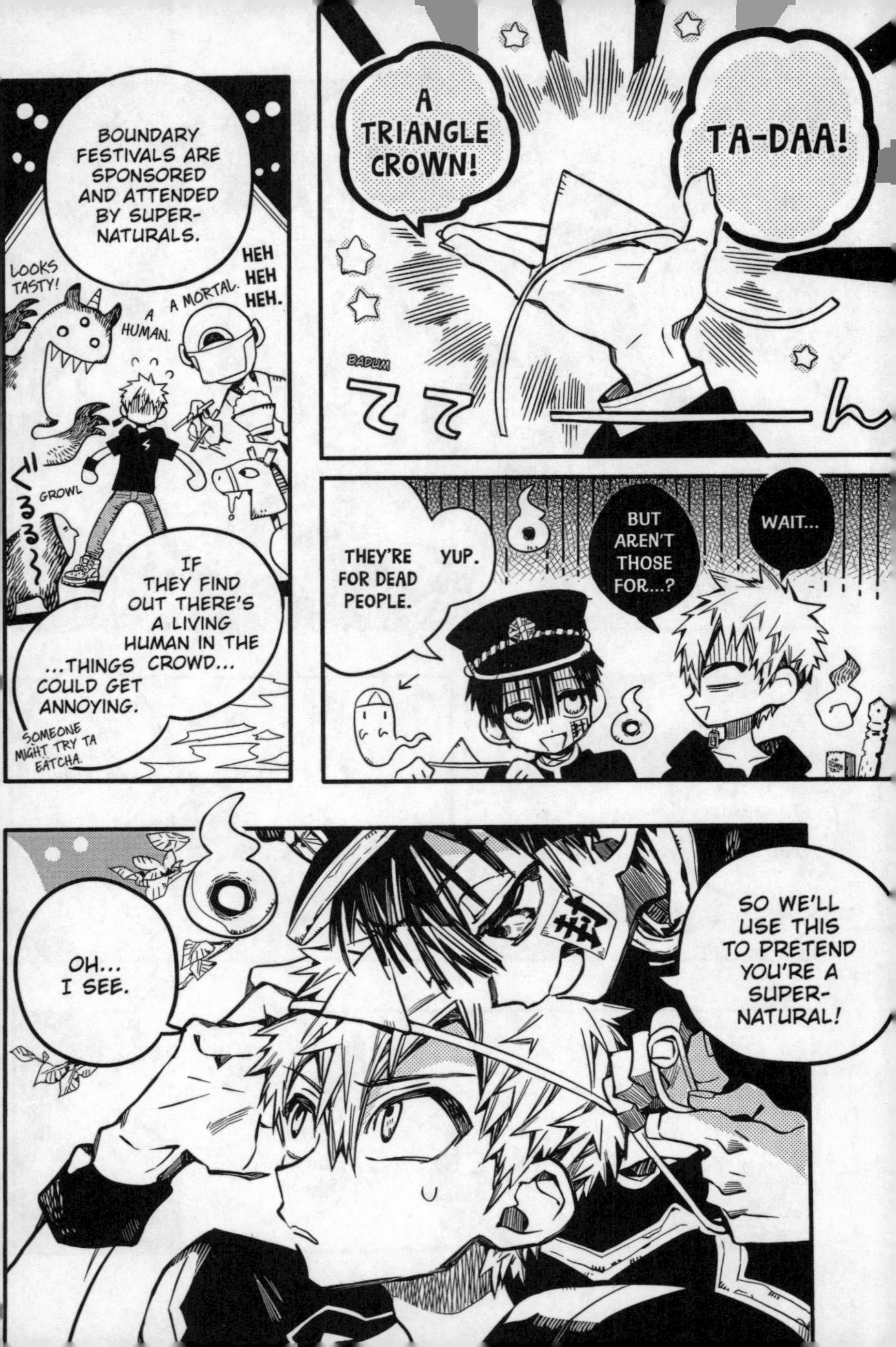
TA-DAA!
A TRIANGLE CROWN!
BADUM
ててーん
WAIT...
BUT AREN'T THOSE FOR...?
YUP.
THEY'RE FOR DEAD PEOPLE.
BOUNDARY FESTIVALS ARE SPONSORED AND ATTENDED BY SUPER-NATURALS.
HEH HEH HEH.
A MORTAL.
A HUMAN.
LOOKS TASTY!
ぐるる～
GROWL
IF THEY FIND OUT THERE'S A LIVING HUMAN IN THE CROWD... ...THINGS COULD GET ANNOYING.
SOMEONE MIGHT TRY TA EATCHA.
SO WE'LL USE THIS TO PRETEND YOU'RE A SUPER-NATURAL!
OH... I SEE.

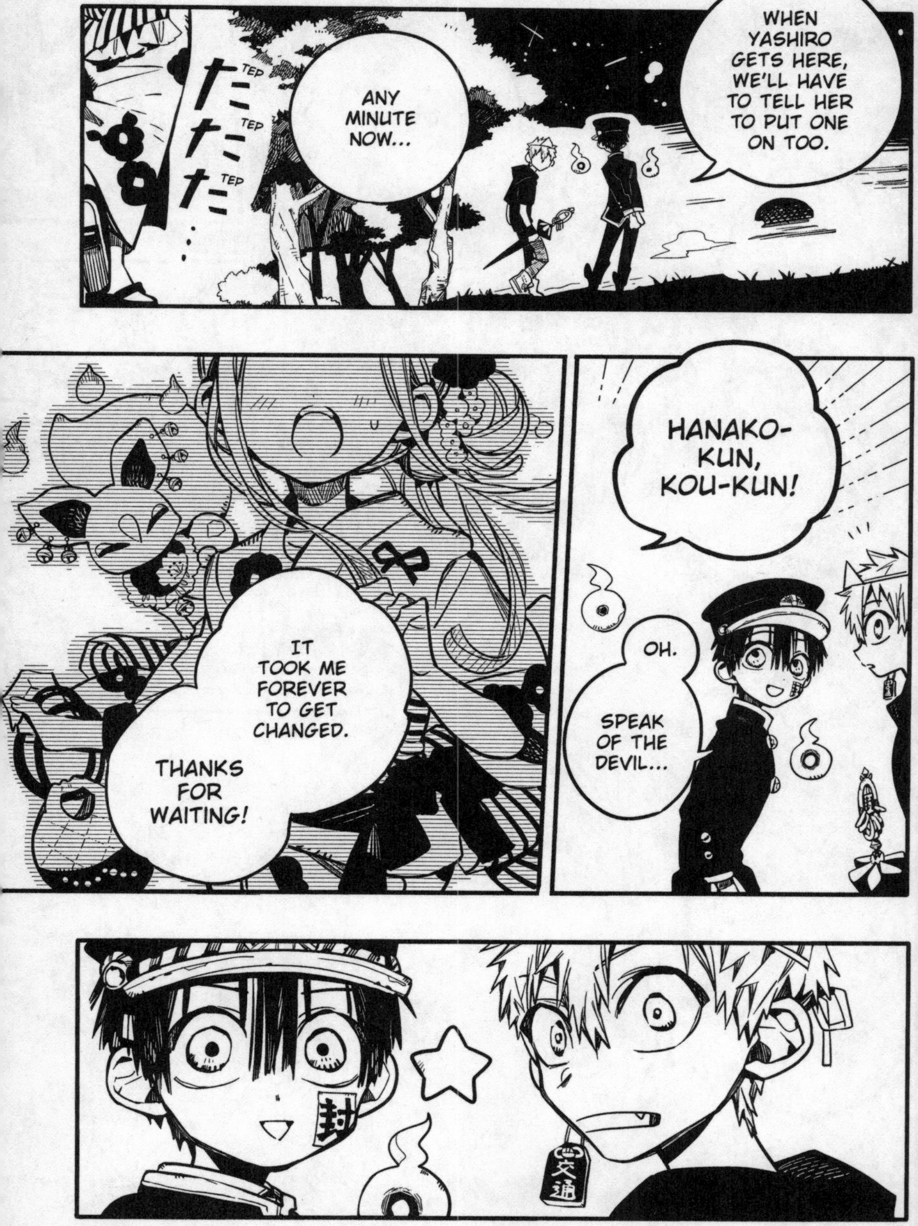
WHEN YASHIRO GETS HERE, WE'LL HAVE TO TELL HER TO PUT ONE ON TOO.
ANY MINUTE NOW...
たたた
TEP TEP TEP
HANAKO-KUN, KOU-KUN!
OH.
SPEAK OF THE DEVIL...
IT TOOK ME FOREVER TO GET CHANGED.
THANKS FOR WAITING!

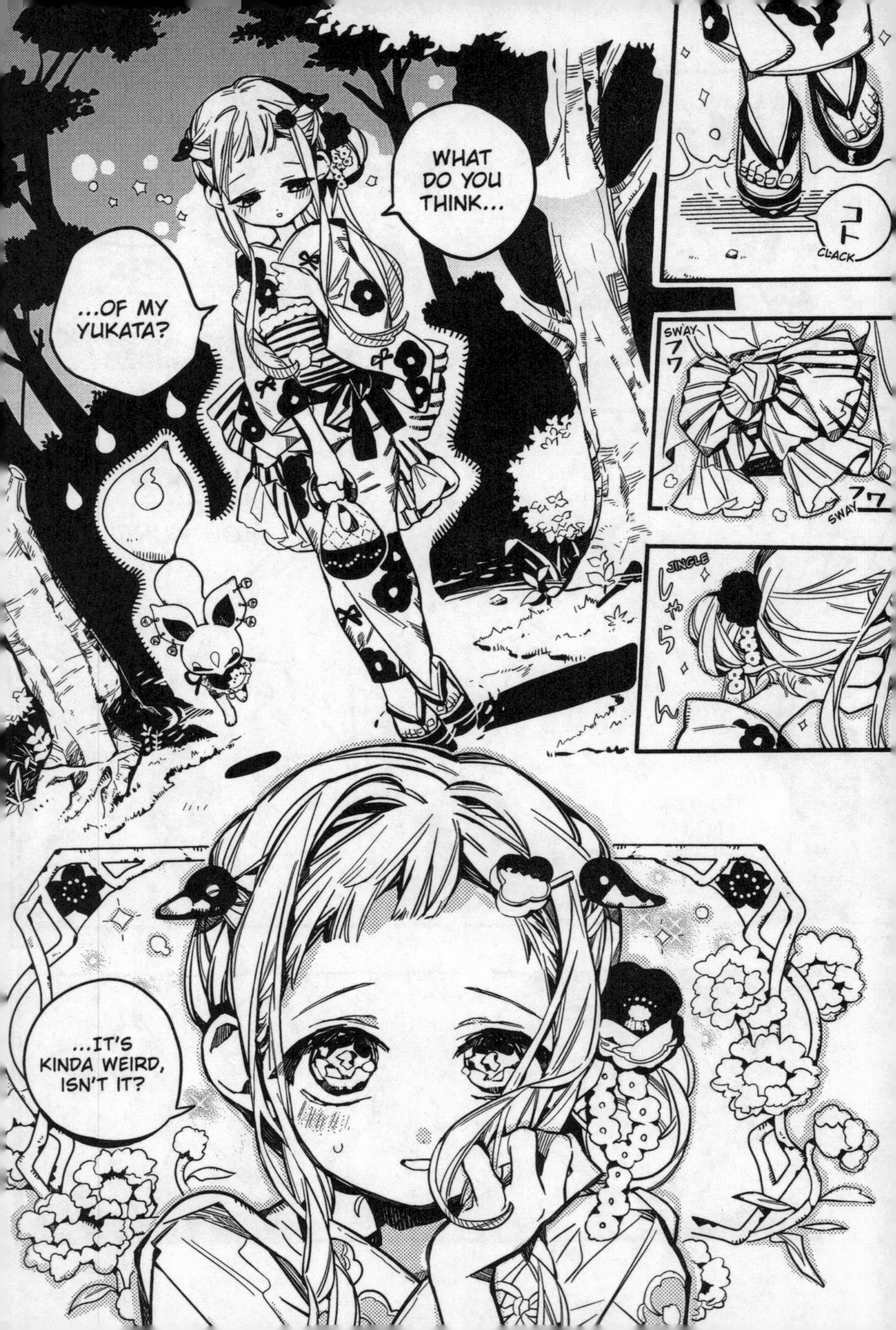
コト
CLACK
SWAY フワ
フワ SWAY
JINGLE しゃらーん
WHAT DO YOU THINK...
...OF MY YUKATA?
...IT'S KINDA WEIRD, ISN'T IT?

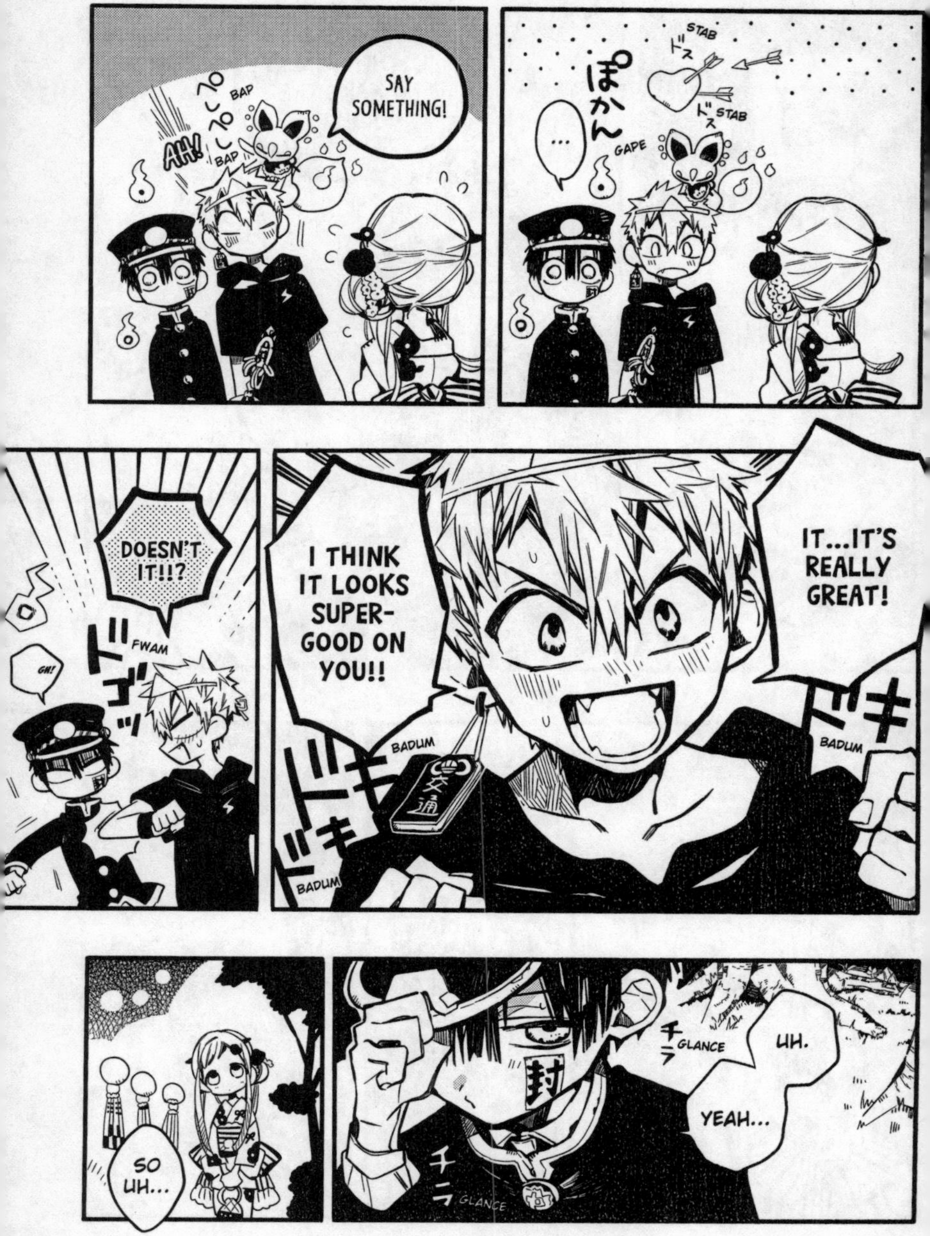
ドス
STAB
ぽかん
GAPE
...
ドス
STAB
SAY SOMETHING!
ぺしぺし
BAP
BAP
AH!
IT...IT'S REALLY GREAT!
I THINK IT LOOKS SUPER-GOOD ON YOU!!
ドキ
BADUM
ドキ
BADUM
ドキ
BADUM
DOESN'T IT!!?
ドゴッ
FWAM
GH!
チラ
GLANCE
UH.
YEAH...
チラ
GLANCE
SO UH...

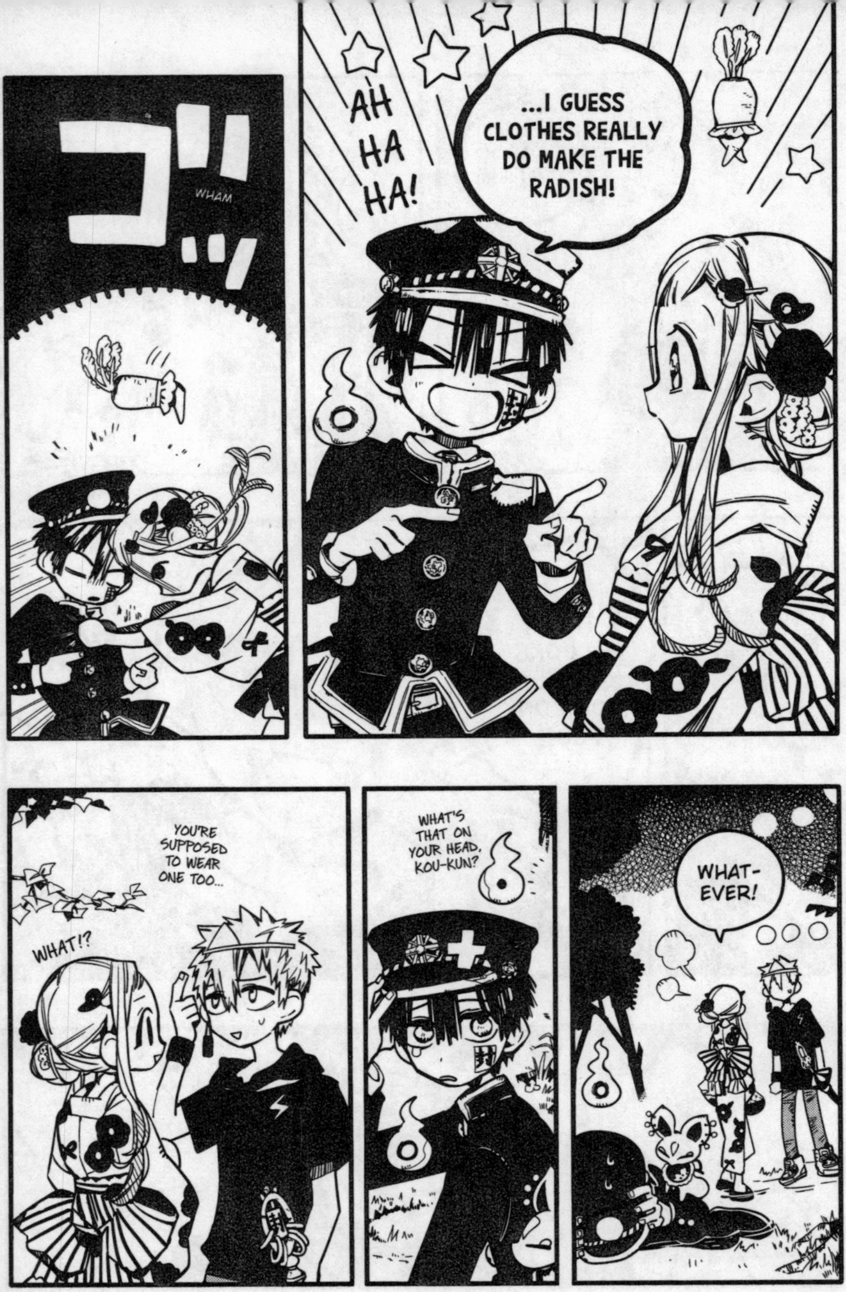
...I GUESS CLOTHES REALLY DO MAKE THE RADISH!
AH HA HA!
WHAM
WHAT-EVER!
WHAT'S THAT ON YOUR HEAD, KOU-KUN?
YOU'RE SUPPOSED TO WEAR ONE TOO...
WHAT!?

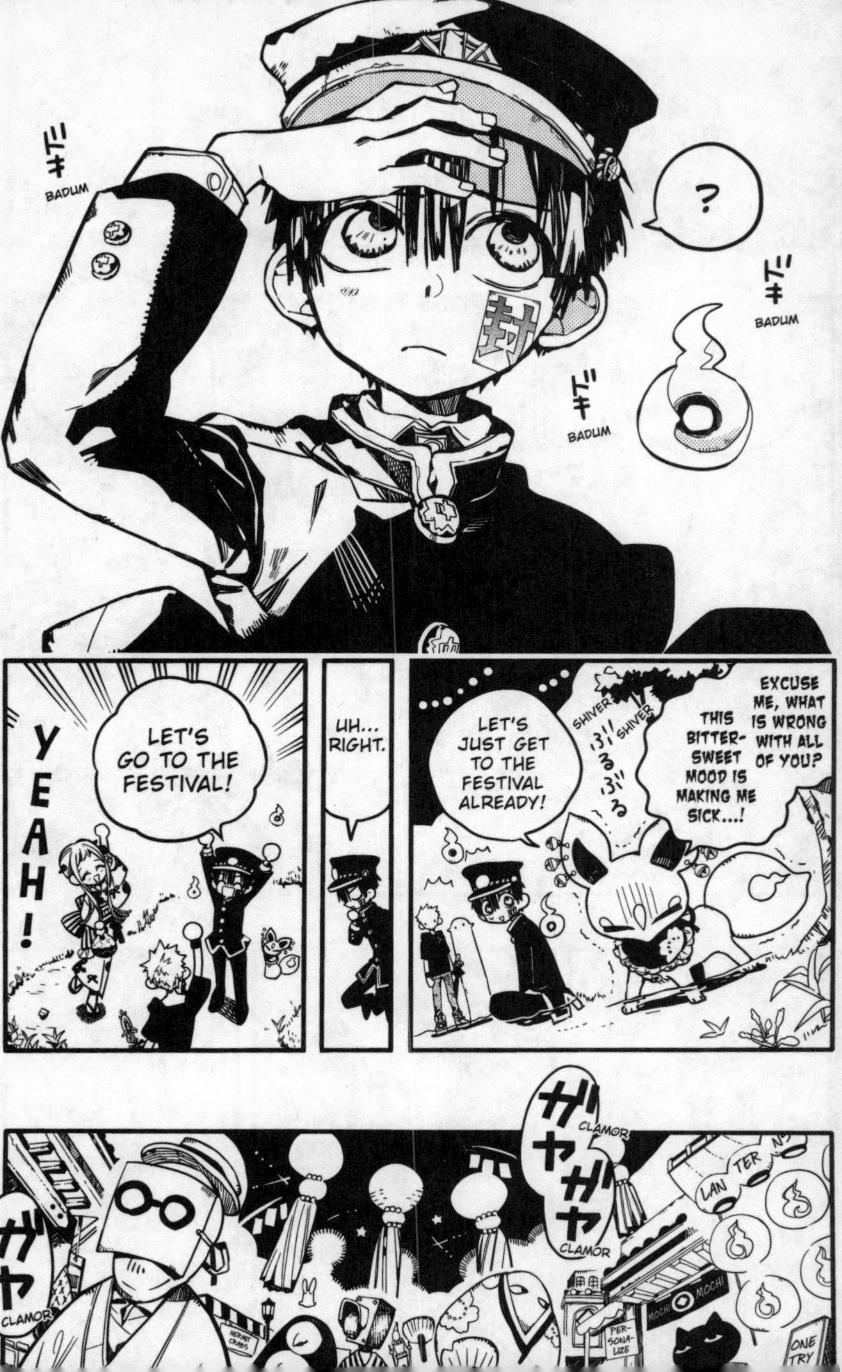
?
ドキ
BADUM
ドキ
BADUM
ドキ
BADUM
EXCUSE ME, WHAT IS WRONG WITH ALL OF YOU?
THIS BITTER-SWEET MOOD IS MAKING ME SICK...!
SHIVER SHIVER
ぷるぷる
LET'S JUST GET TO THE FESTIVAL ALREADY!
UH... RIGHT.
LET'S GO TO THE FESTIVAL!
YEAH!
ガヤガヤ
CLAMOR
CLAMOR
LANTERN
MOCHI MOCHI
ONE TRY
PERSONALIZE
HERMIT CRABS
ガヤ
CLAMOR

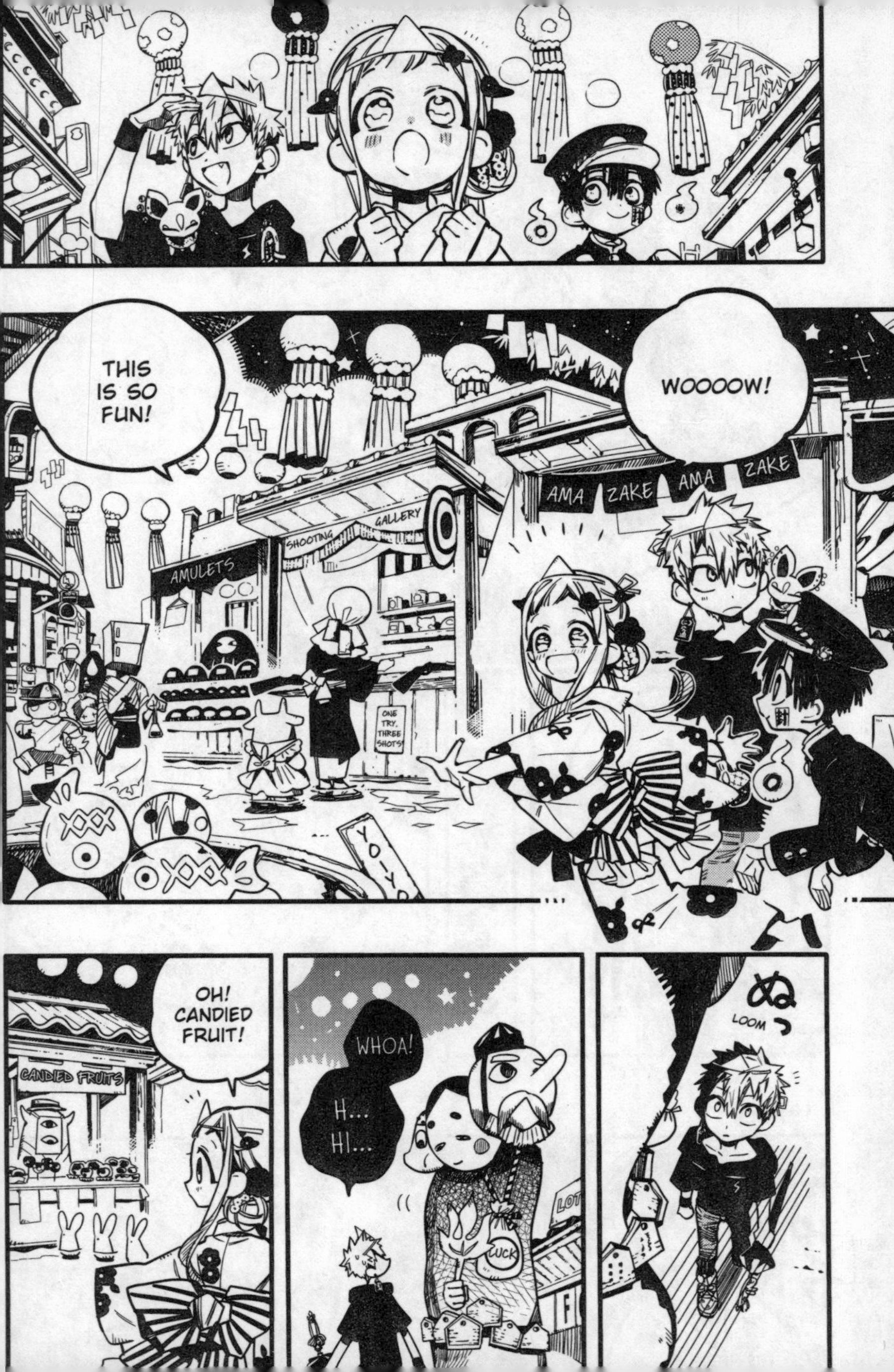
WOOOOW!
AMA ZAKE AMA ZAKE
THIS IS SO FUN!
SHOOTING GALLERY
AMULETS
ONE TRY, THREE SHOTS!
ぬ
LOOM
WHOA!
H... HI...
LUCK
OH! CANDIED FRUIT!
CANDIED FRUITS

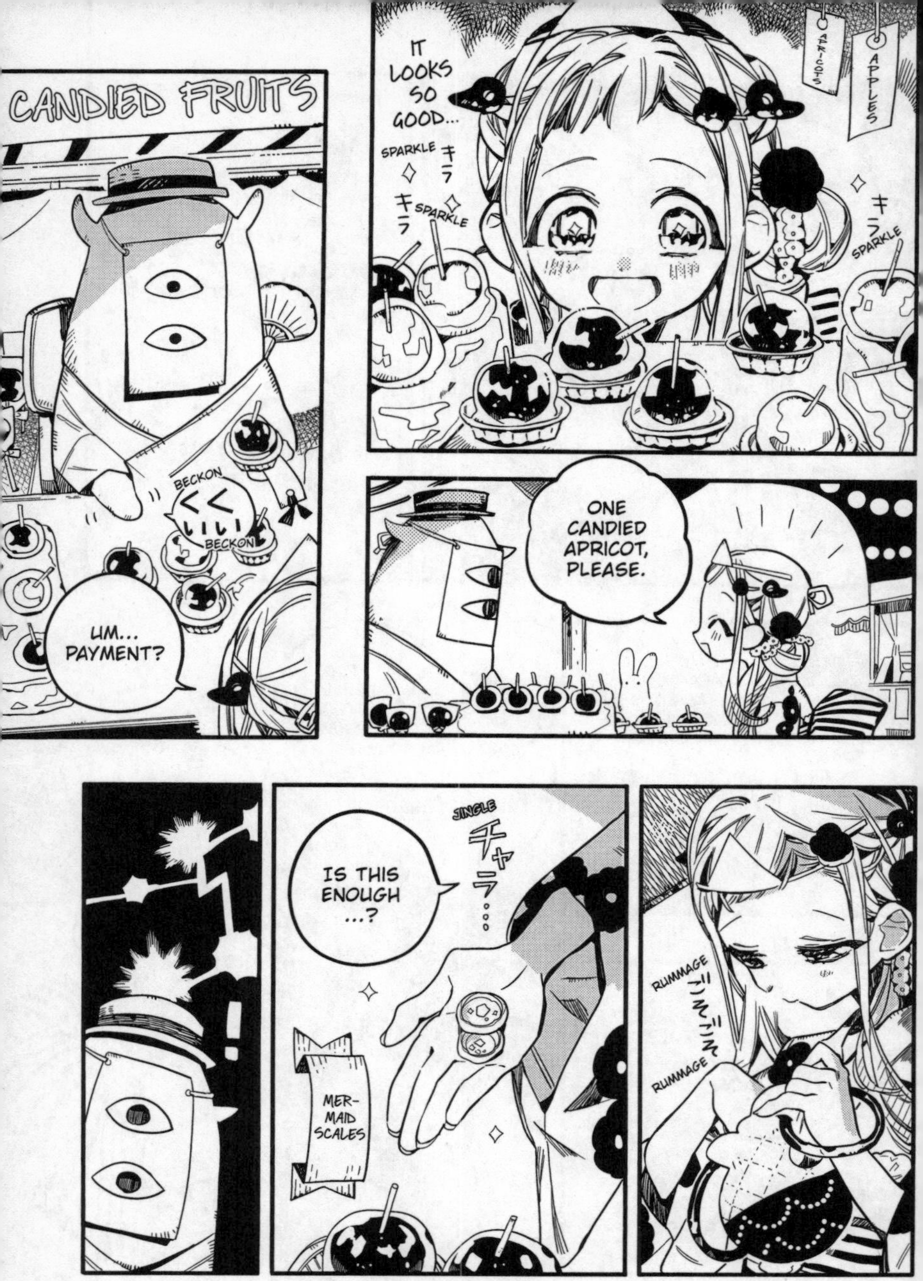
APRICOTS
APPLES
IT LOOKS SO GOOD...
SPARKLE キラ
キラ SPARKLE
キラ SPARKLE
ONE CANDIED APRICOT, PLEASE.
CANDIED FRUITS
BECKON
BECKON
UM... PAYMENT?
RUMMAGE
RUMMAGE
JINGLE
チャラ…
IS THIS ENOUGH ...?
MER-MAID SCALES

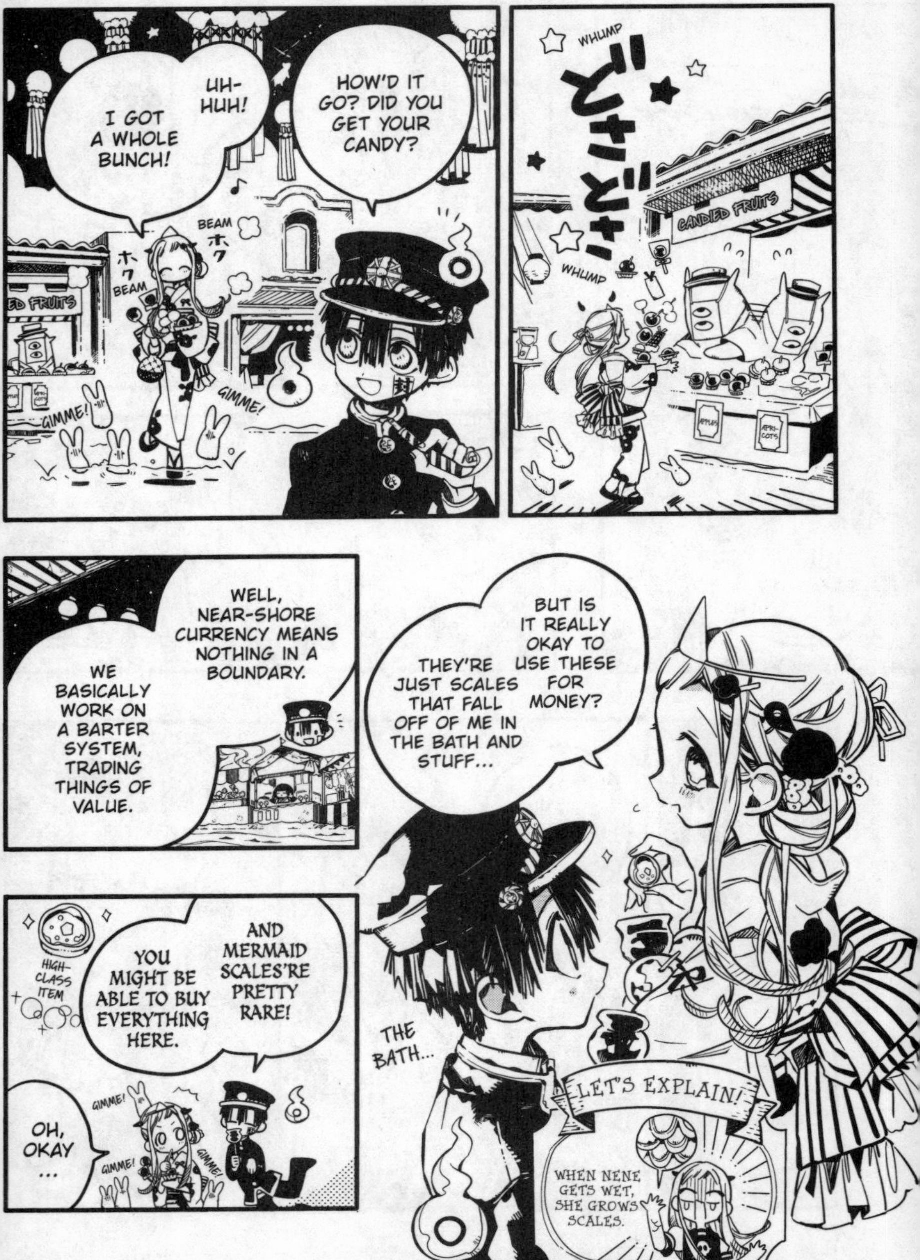
WHUMP
どさどさ
WHUMP
CANDIED FRUITS
APPLES
APRI-COTS
HOW'D IT GO? DID YOU GET YOUR CANDY?
UH-HUH!
I GOT A WHOLE BUNCH!
BEAM ホクホク BEAM
GIMME!
GIMME!
BUT IS IT REALLY OKAY TO USE THESE FOR MONEY?
THEY'RE JUST SCALES THAT FALL OFF OF ME IN THE BATH AND STUFF...
THE BATH...
LET'S EXPLAIN!
WHEN NENE GETS WET, SHE GROWS SCALES.
WELL, NEAR-SHORE CURRENCY MEANS NOTHING IN A BOUNDARY.
WE BASICALLY WORK ON A BARTER SYSTEM, TRADING THINGS OF VALUE.
HIGH-CLASS ITEM
AND MERMAID SCALES'RE PRETTY RARE!
YOU MIGHT BE ABLE TO BUY EVERYTHING HERE.
GIMME!
GIMME!
GIMME!
OH, OKAY...

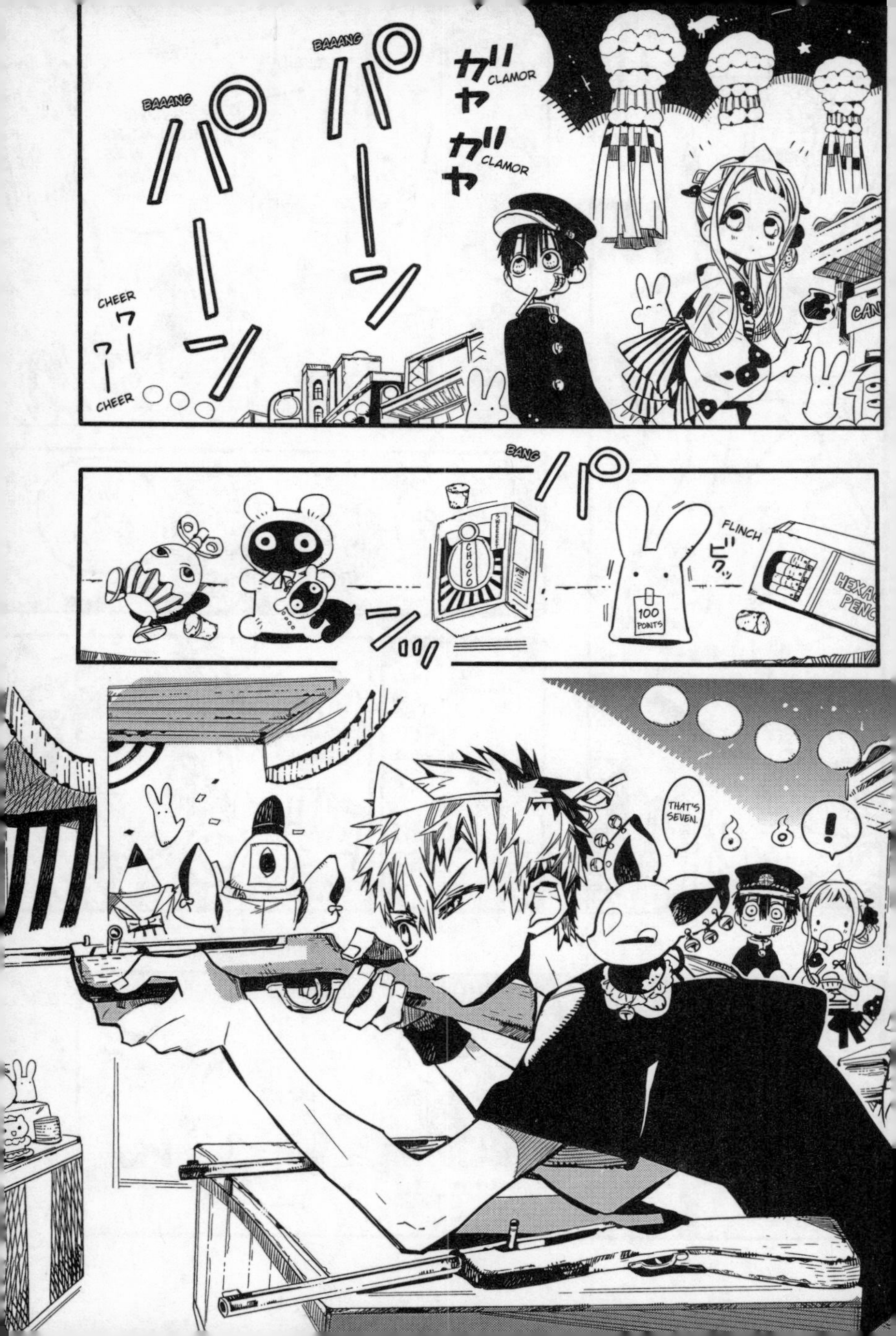
ガヤガヤ
CLAMOR
CLAMOR
パーン
BAAANG
パーン
BAAANG
ワーワー
CHEER
CHEER
パ
BANG
ビクッ
FLINCH
100 POINTS
CHOCO
THAT'S SEVEN.
!

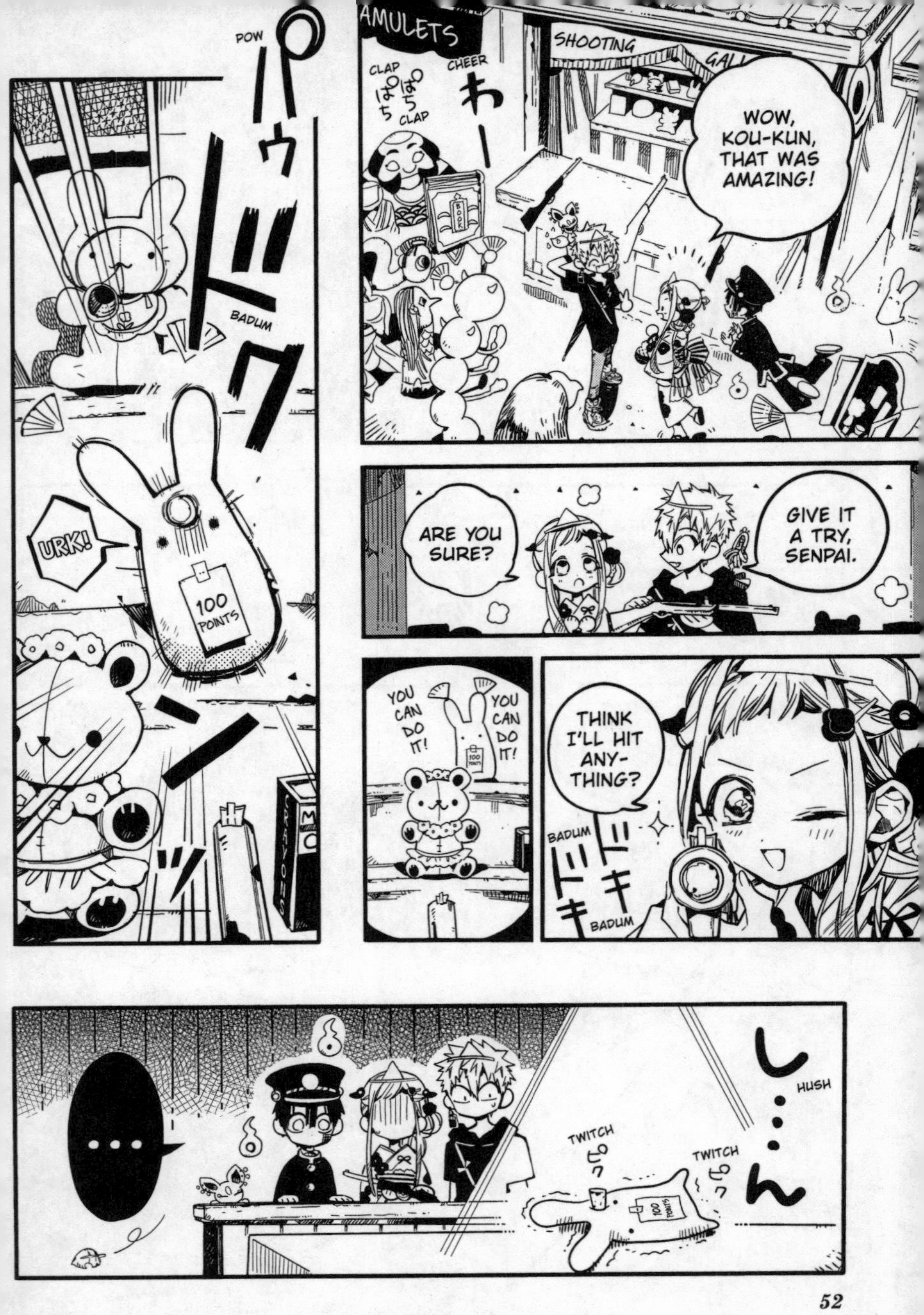
SHOOTING GALL
WOW, KOU-KUN, THAT WAS AMAZING!
AMULETS
CHEER
わー
CLAP
ぱち ぱち
CLAP
BOOK
GIVE IT A TRY, SENPAI.
ARE YOU SURE?
THINK I'LL HIT ANYTHING?
BADUM
ドキドキ
BADUM
YOU CAN DO IT!
YOU CAN DO IT!
100 POINTS
POW
パウ
ドッ
BADUM
ク
URK!
100 POINTS
CRAYONS
HUSH
し…ん
TWITCH
ピク
TWITCH
ピク
100 POINTS
...

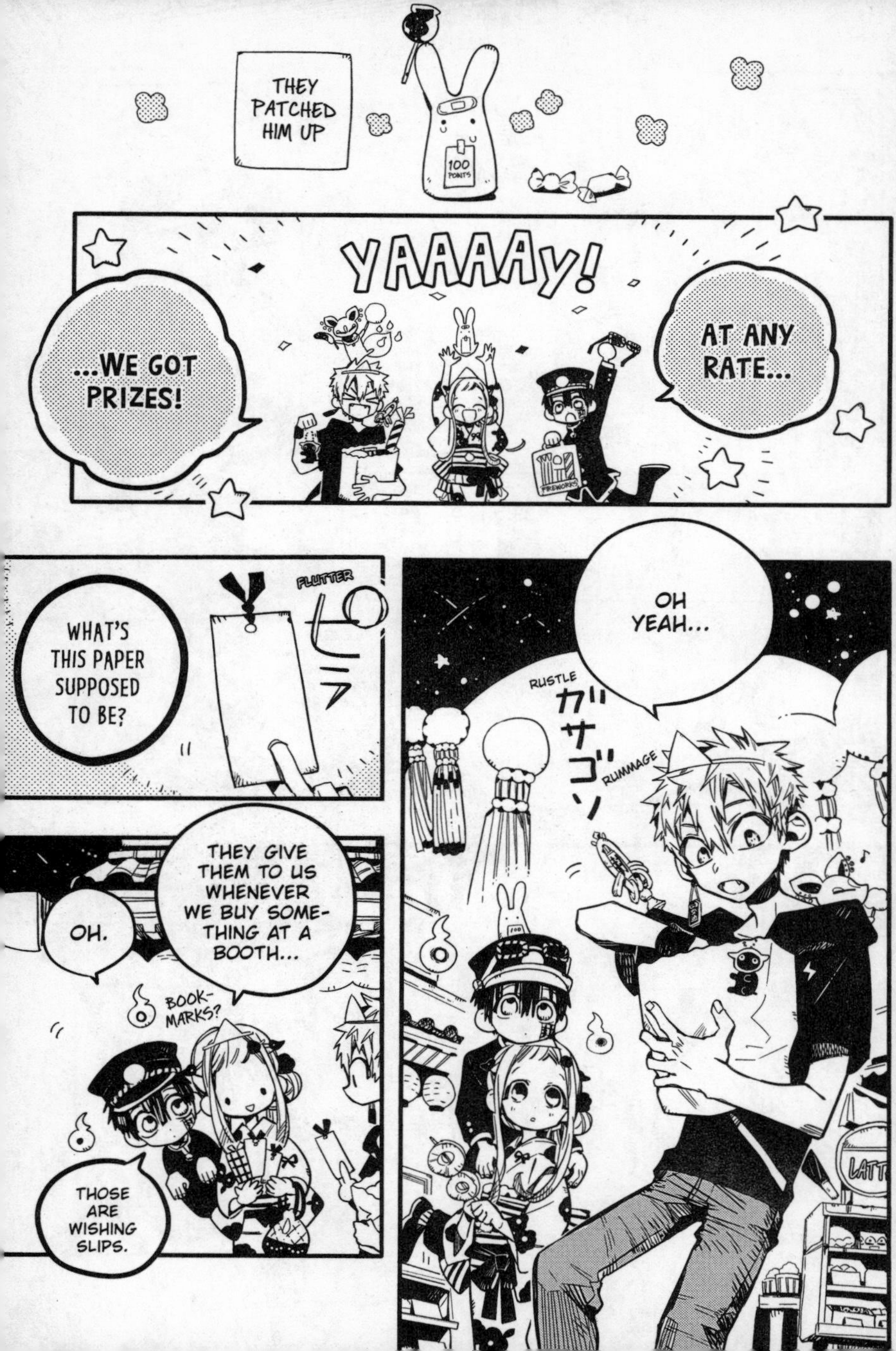
THEY PATCHED HIM UP
100 POINTS
AT ANY RATE...
YAAAAY!
...WE GOT PRIZES!
FIREWORKS
OH YEAH...
RUSTLE
ガサ
RUMMAGE
ゴソ
FLUTTER
ピラ
WHAT'S THIS PAPER SUPPOSED TO BE?
THEY GIVE THEM TO US WHENEVER WE BUY SOME-THING AT A BOOTH...
OH.
BOOK-MARKS?
THOSE ARE WISHING SLIPS.

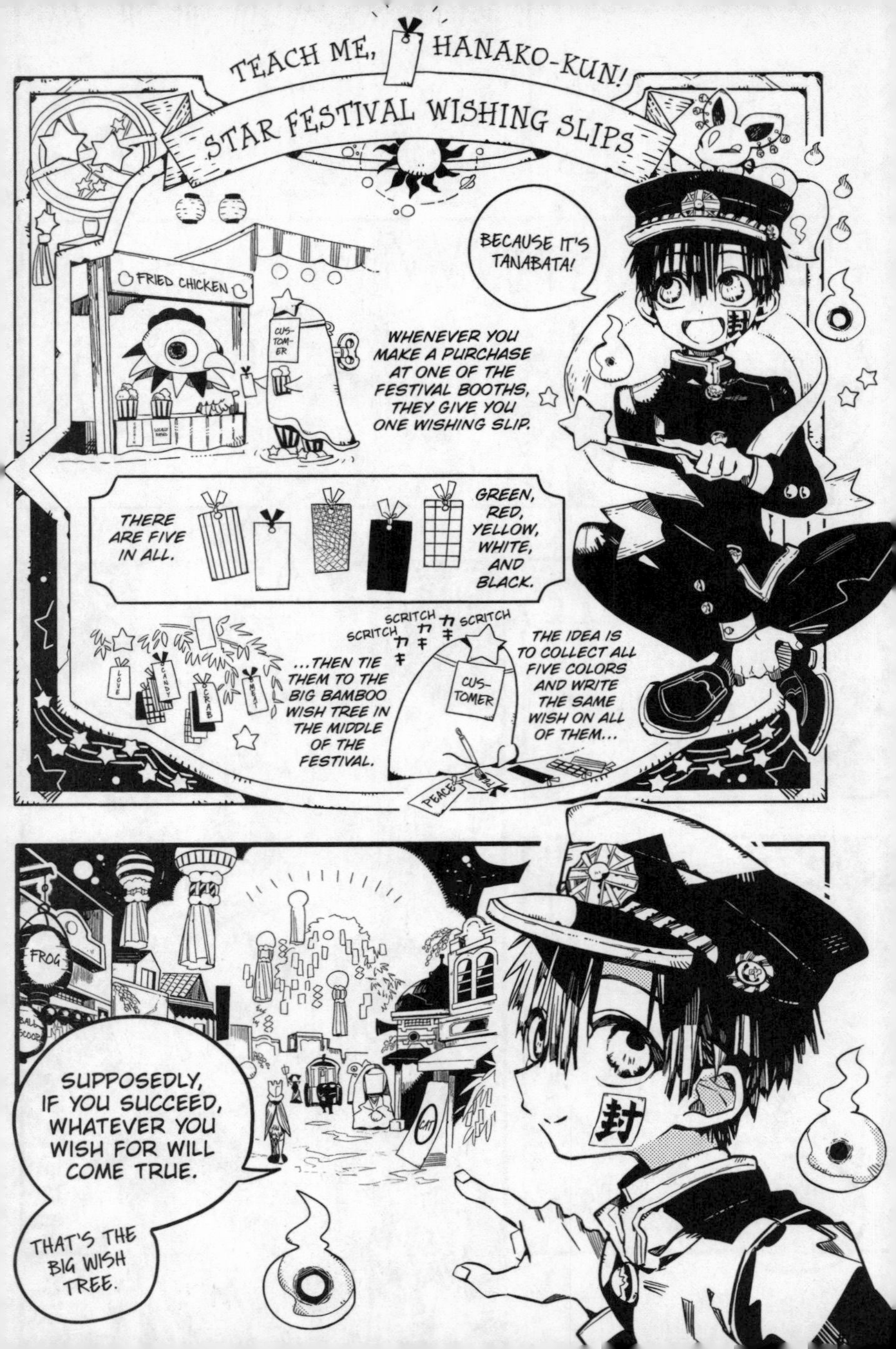
TEACH ME, HANAKO-KUN!
STAR FESTIVAL WISHING SLIPS
BECAUSE IT'S TANABATA!
WHENEVER YOU MAKE A PURCHASE AT ONE OF THE FESTIVAL BOOTHS, THEY GIVE YOU ONE WISHING SLIP.
FRIED CHICKEN
CUS-TOM-ER
THERE ARE FIVE IN ALL.
GREEN, RED, YELLOW, WHITE, AND BLACK.
THE IDEA IS TO COLLECT ALL FIVE COLORS AND WRITE THE SAME WISH ON ALL OF THEM...
SCRITCH SCRITCH
カキ カキ
CUS-TOMER
PEACE
...THEN TIE THEM TO THE BIG BAMBOO WISH TREE IN THE MIDDLE OF THE FESTIVAL.
LOVE
CANDY
CRAB
MEAT
FROG
CAT
SUPPOSEDLY, IF YOU SUCCEED, WHATEVER YOU WISH FOR WILL COME TRUE.
THAT'S THE BIG WISH TREE.

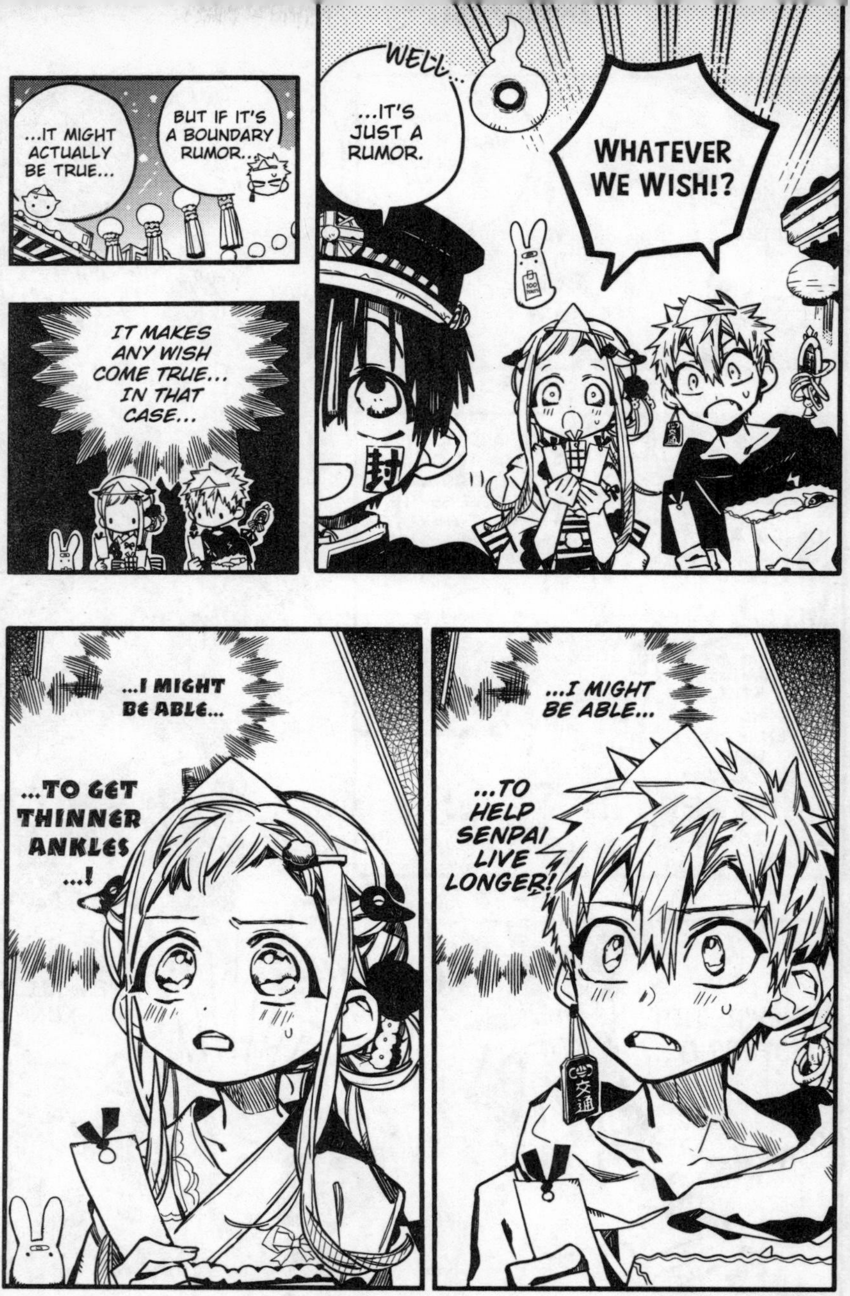
WHATEVER WE WISH!?
WELL...
...IT'S JUST A RUMOR.
BUT IF IT'S A BOUNDARY RUMOR...
...IT MIGHT ACTUALLY BE TRUE...
IT MAKES ANY WISH COME TRUE... IN THAT CASE...
...I MIGHT BE ABLE...
...TO HELP SENPAI LIVE LONGER!
...I MIGHT BE ABLE...
...TO GET THINNER ANKLES ...!

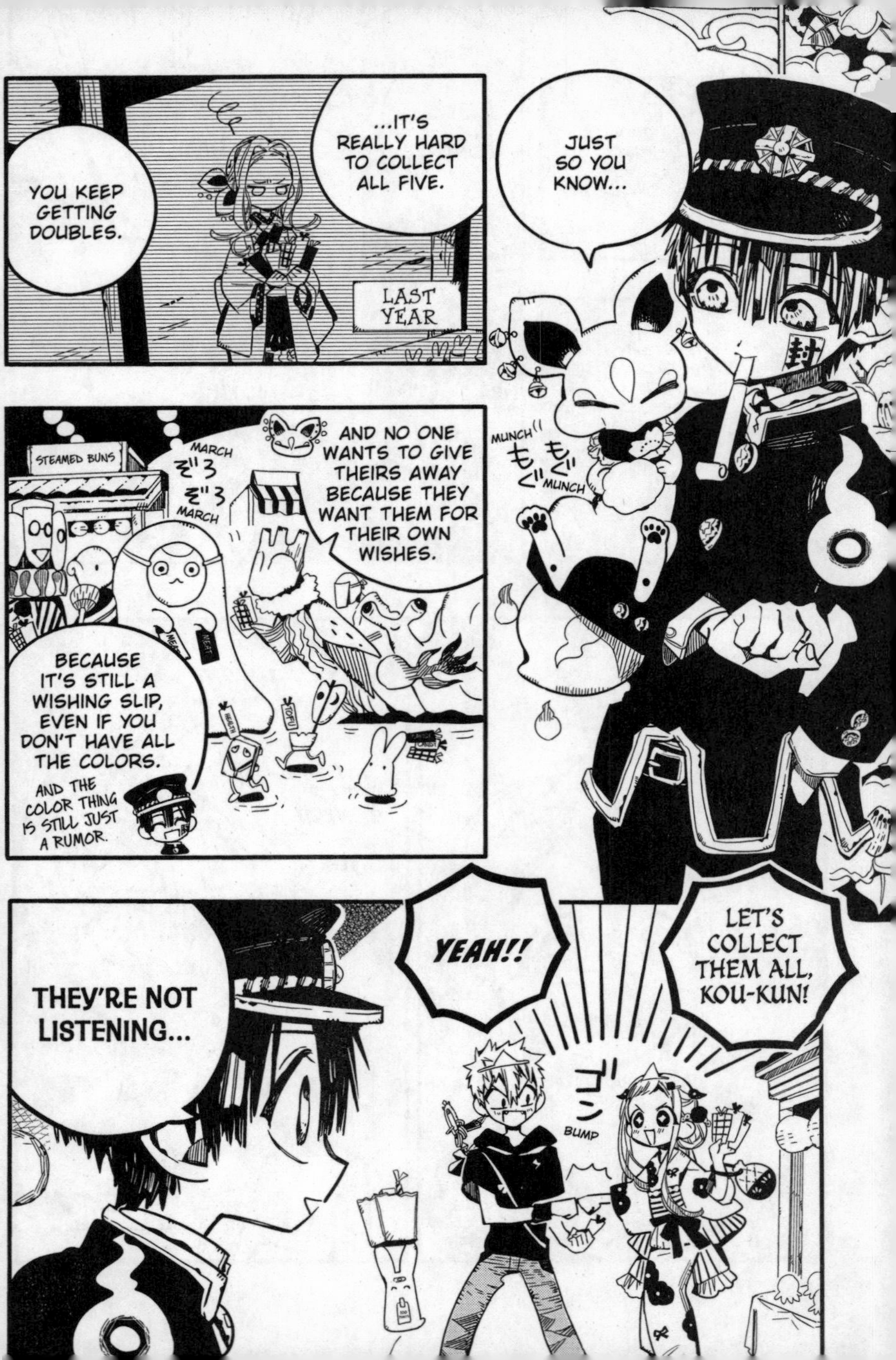
JUST SO YOU KNOW...
MUNCH MUNCH
...IT'S REALLY HARD TO COLLECT ALL FIVE.
YOU KEEP GETTING DOUBLES.
LAST YEAR
AND NO ONE WANTS TO GIVE THEIRS AWAY BECAUSE THEY WANT THEM FOR THEIR OWN WISHES.
MARCH MARCH
STEAMED BUNS
BECAUSE IT'S STILL A WISHING SLIP, EVEN IF YOU DON'T HAVE ALL THE COLORS.
AND THE COLOR THING IS STILL JUST A RUMOR.
LET'S COLLECT THEM ALL, KOU-KUN!
YEAH!!
BUMP
THEY'RE NOT LISTENING...

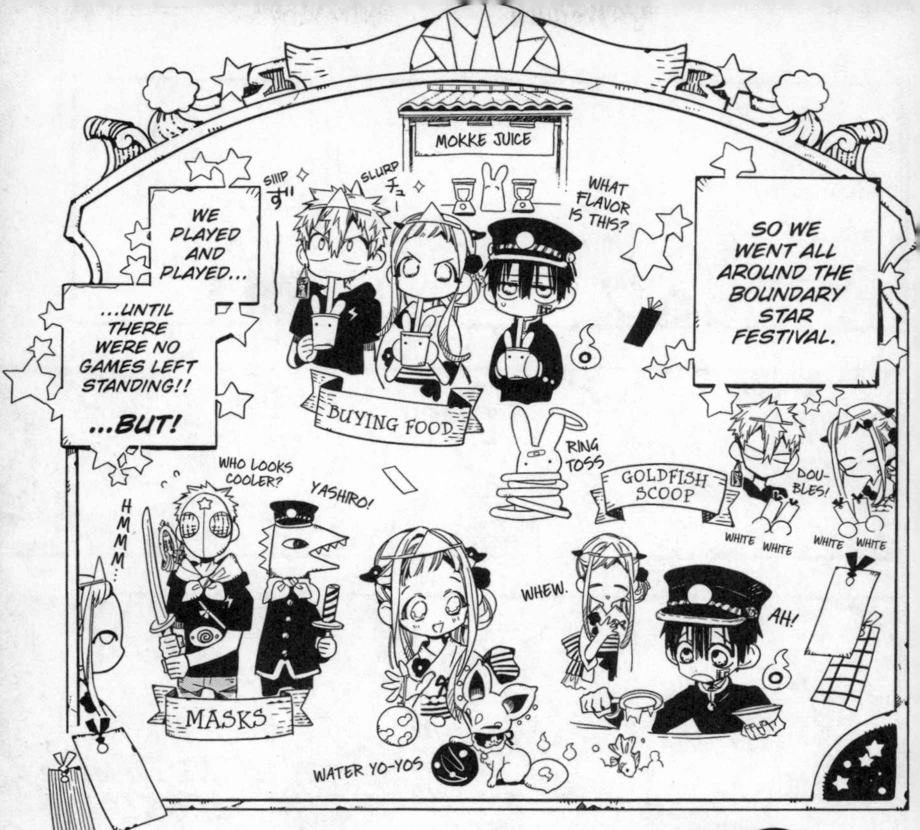
SO WE WENT ALL AROUND THE BOUNDARY STAR FESTIVAL.
MOKKE JUICE
WHAT FLAVOR IS THIS?
SLURP チュー
SIIIP ず
WE PLAYED AND PLAYED...
...UNTIL THERE WERE NO GAMES LEFT STANDING!!
...BUT!
BUYING FOOD
DOU-BLES!
WHITE WHITE
WHITE WHITE
GOLDFISH SCOOP
RING TOSS
AH!
WHEW.
YASHIRO!
WHO LOOKS COOLER?
HMMM...
MASKS
WATER YO-YOS

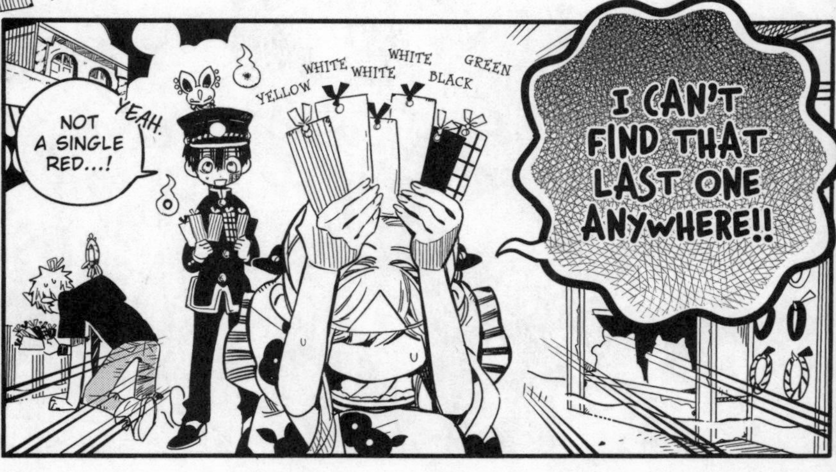
I CAN'T FIND THAT LAST ONE ANYWHERE!!
GREEN
BLACK
WHITE
WHITE
WHITE
YELLOW
YEAH.
NOT A SINGLE RED...!

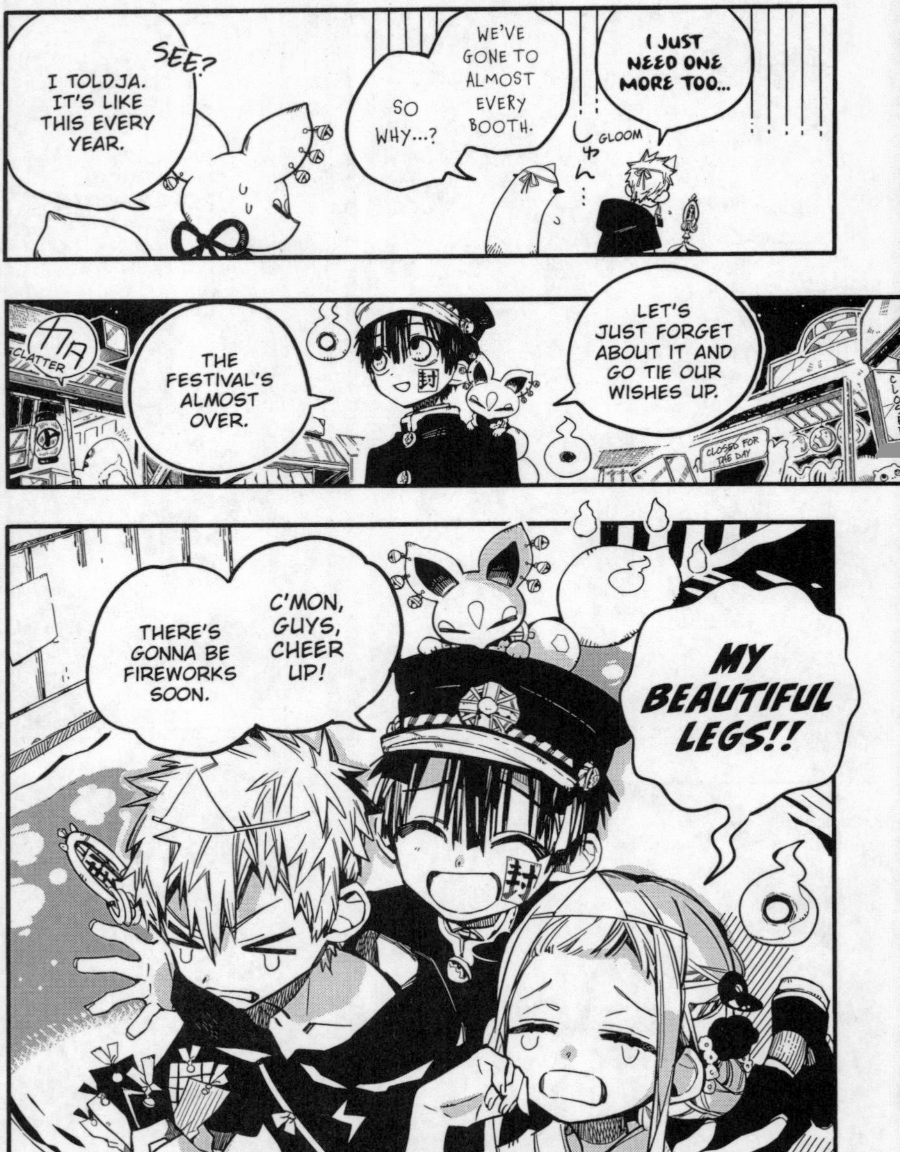
I JUST NEED ONE MORE TOO...
しゅん...
GLOOM
WE'VE GONE TO ALMOST EVERY BOOTH.
SO WHY...?
SEE?
I TOLDJA. IT'S LIKE THIS EVERY YEAR.
LET'S JUST FORGET ABOUT IT AND GO TIE OUR WISHES UP.
CLOSED
CLOSED FOR THE DAY
THE FESTIVAL'S ALMOST OVER.
カタ
CLATTER
MY BEAUTIFUL LEGS!!
C'MON, GUYS, CHEER UP!
THERE'S GONNA BE FIREWORKS SOON.

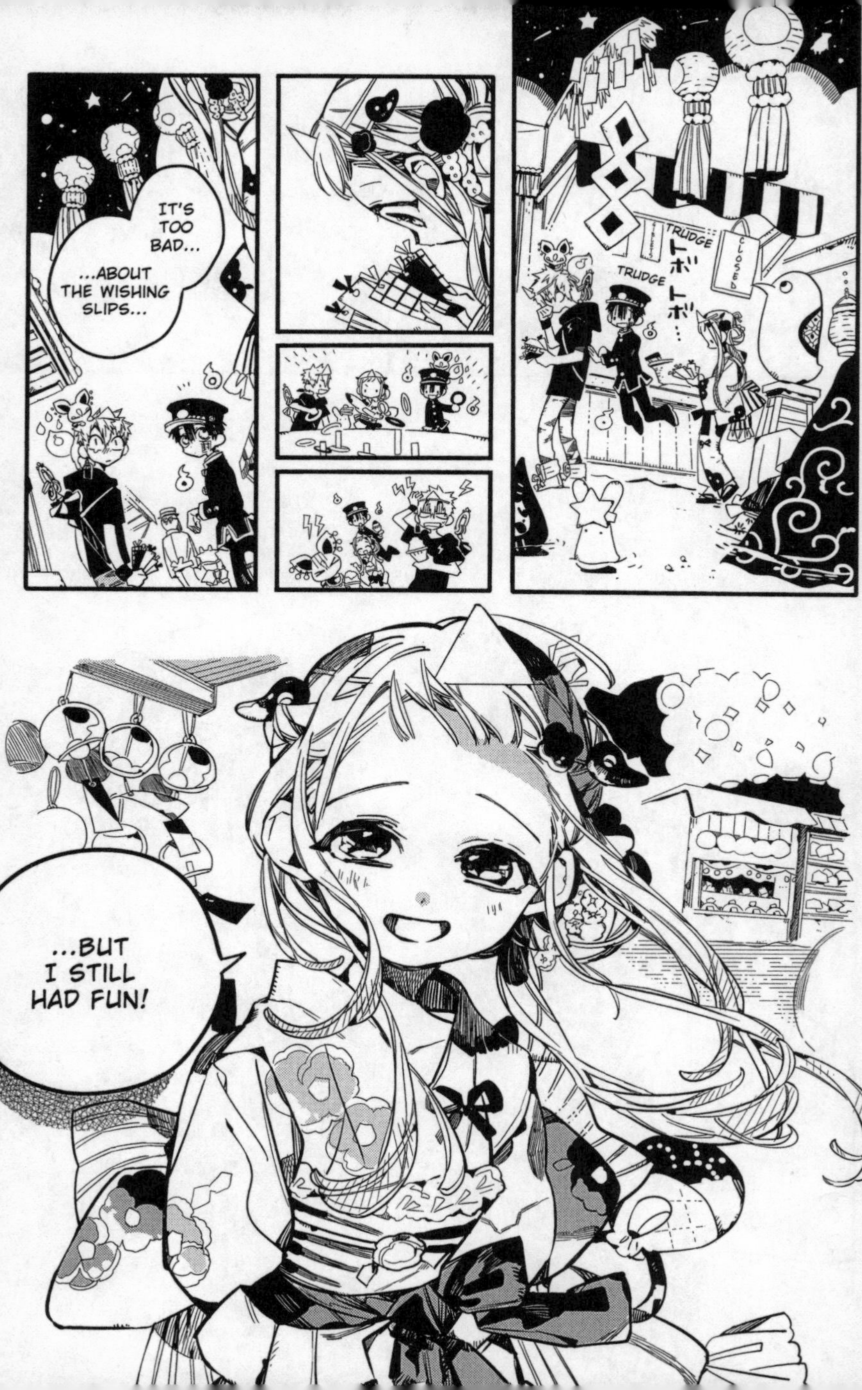
TRUDGE
トボ
TRUDGE
トボ…
CLOSED
IT'S TOO BAD…
…ABOUT THE WISHING SLIPS…
…BUT I STILL HAD FUN!

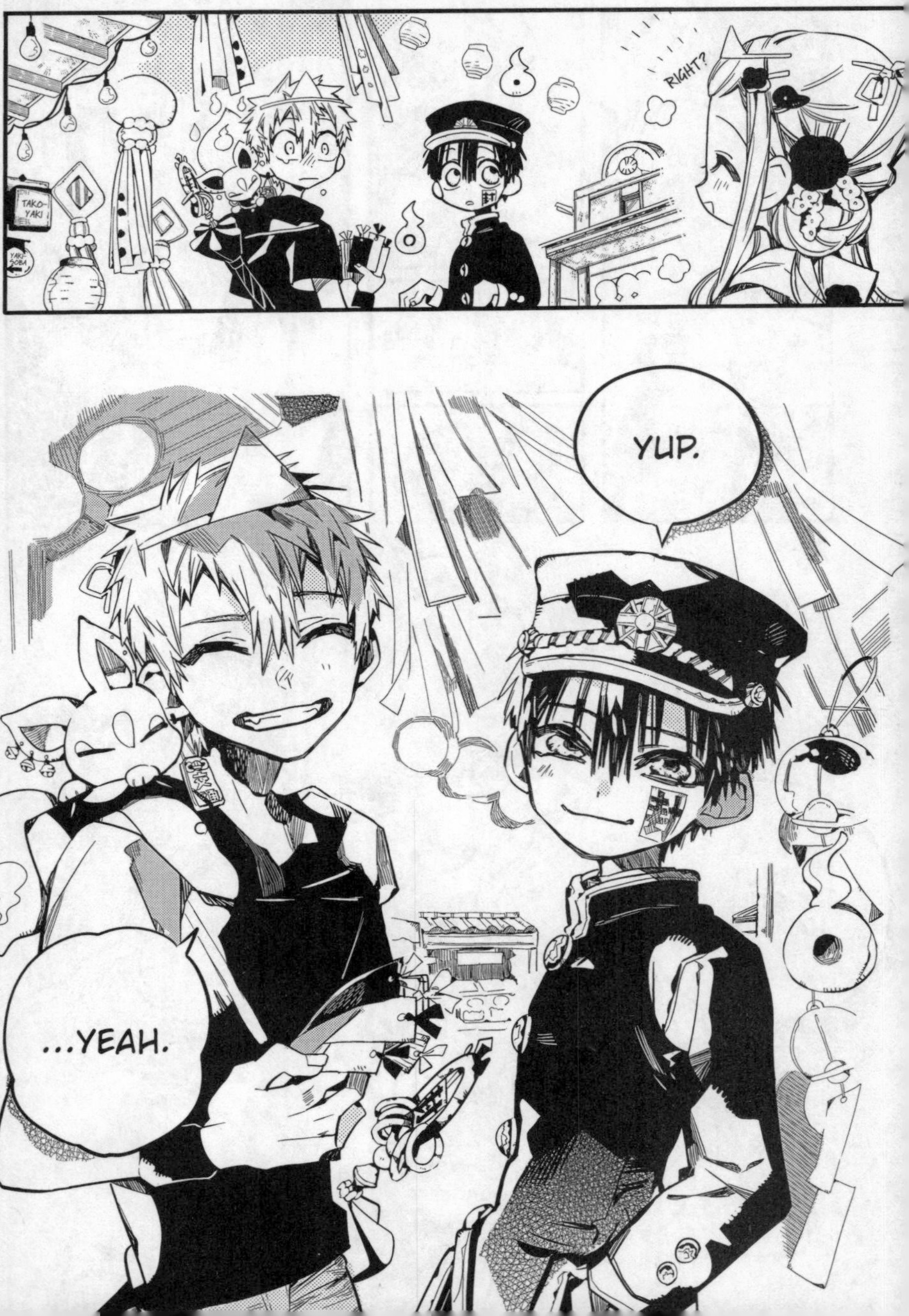
RIGHT?
TAKO-YAKI
YAKI-SOBA
YUP.
...YEAH.

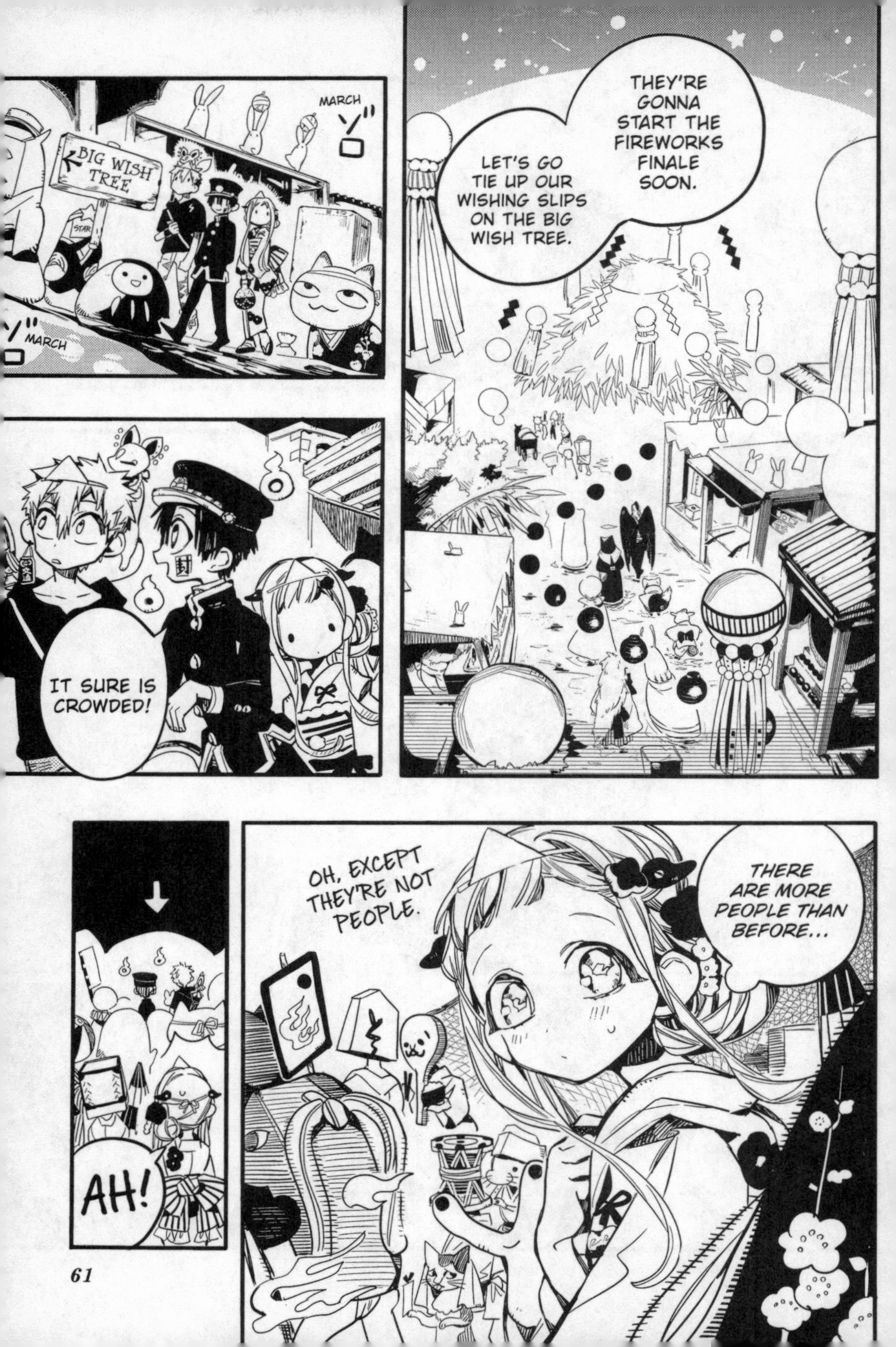
THEY'RE GONNA START THE FIREWORKS FINALE SOON.
LET'S GO TIE UP OUR WISHING SLIPS ON THE BIG WISH TREE.
MARCH
BIG WISH TREE
STAR
MARCH
IT SURE IS CROWDED!
THERE ARE MORE PEOPLE THAN BEFORE...
OH, EXCEPT THEY'RE NOT PEOPLE.
AH!

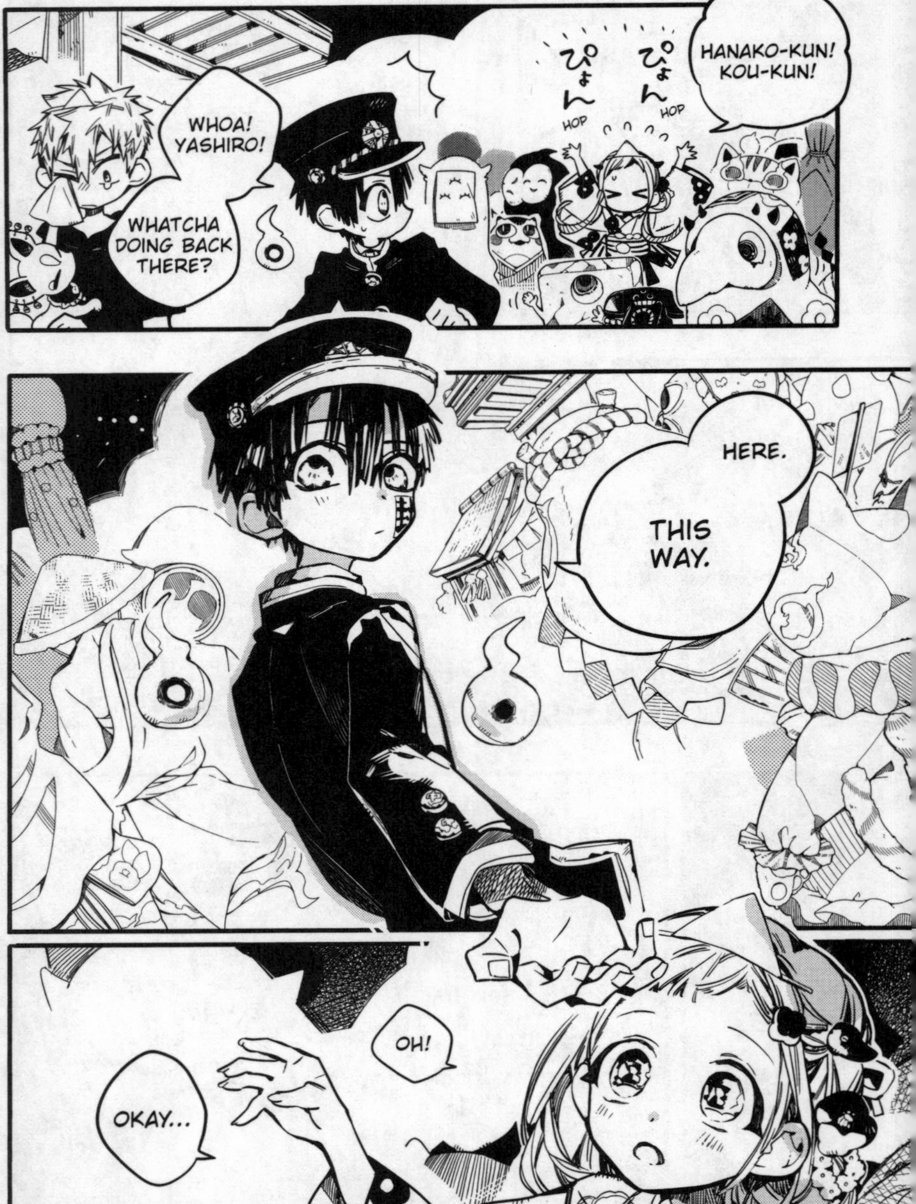
HANAKO-KUN! KOU-KUN!
ぴょん HOP
ぴょん HOP
WHOA! YASHIRO!
WHATCHA DOING BACK THERE?
HERE.
THIS WAY.
OH!
OKAY...

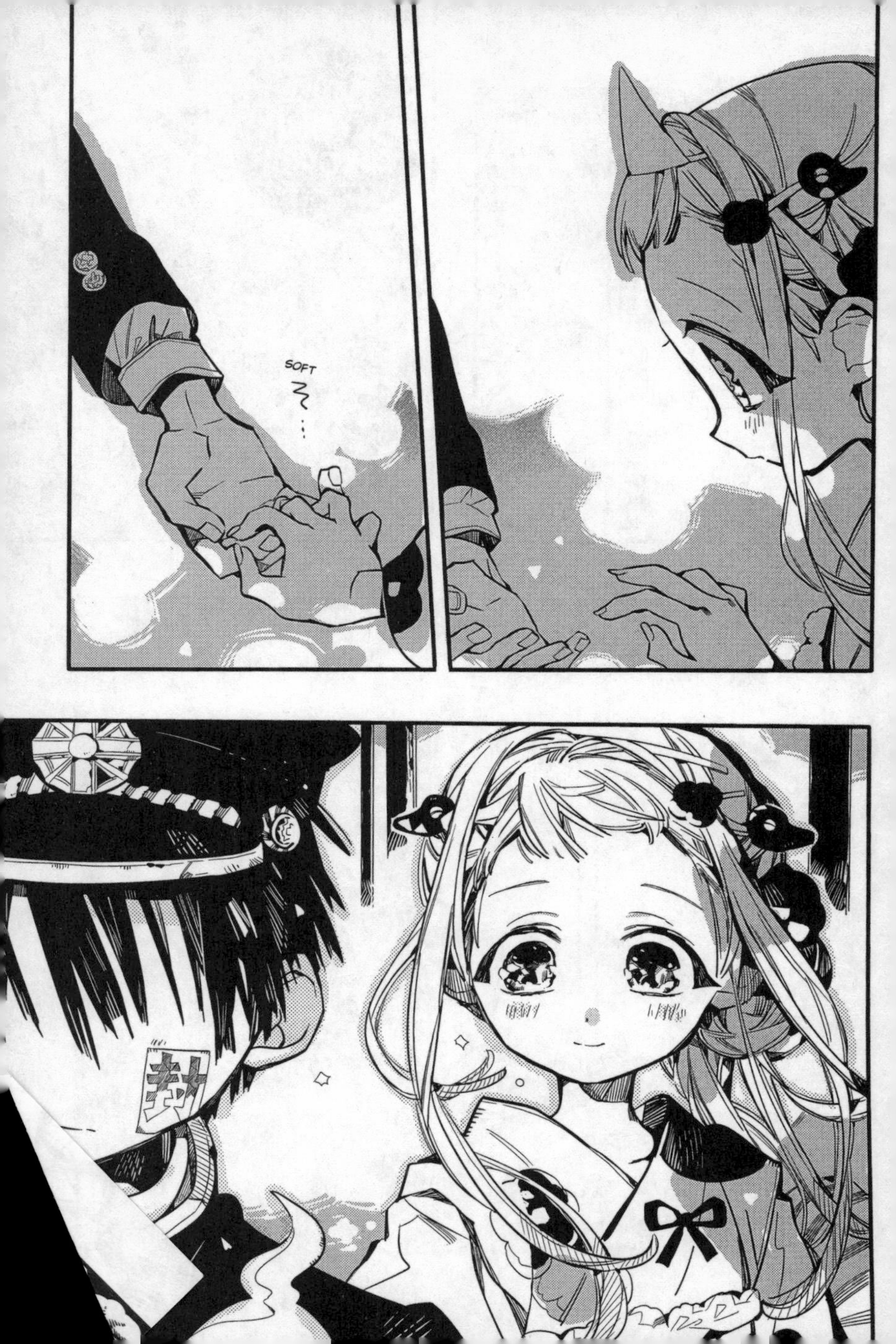
SOFT

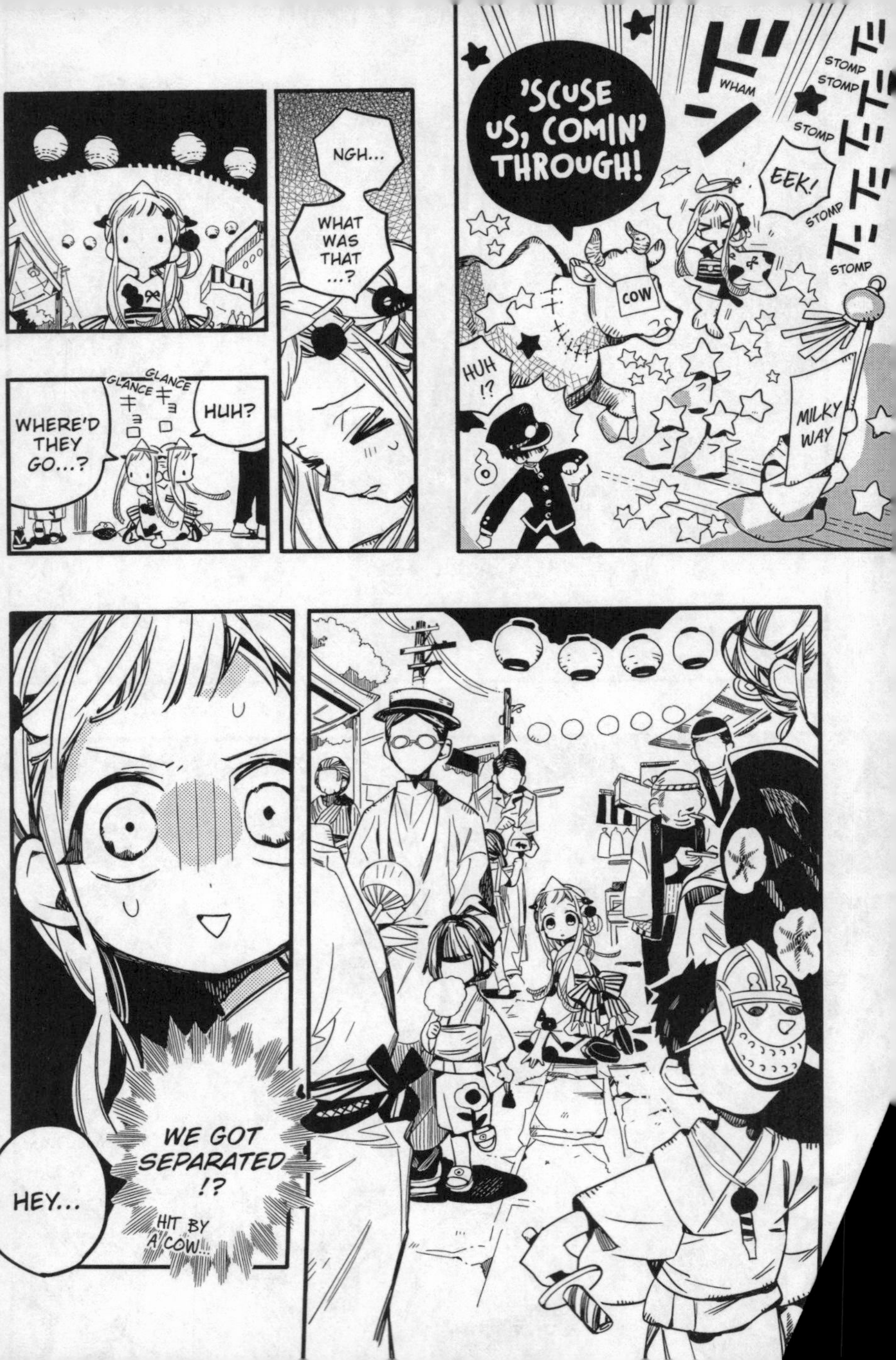

ドン
WHAM
STOMP
STOMP
STOMP
STOMP
STOMP
'SCUSE US, COMIN' THROUGH!
EEK!
COW
HUH!?
MILKY WAY
NGH...
WHAT WAS THAT ...?
GLANCE キョロ
GLANCE キョロ
HUH?
WHERE'D THEY GO...?
HEY...
WE GOT SEPARATED !?
HIT BY A COW...

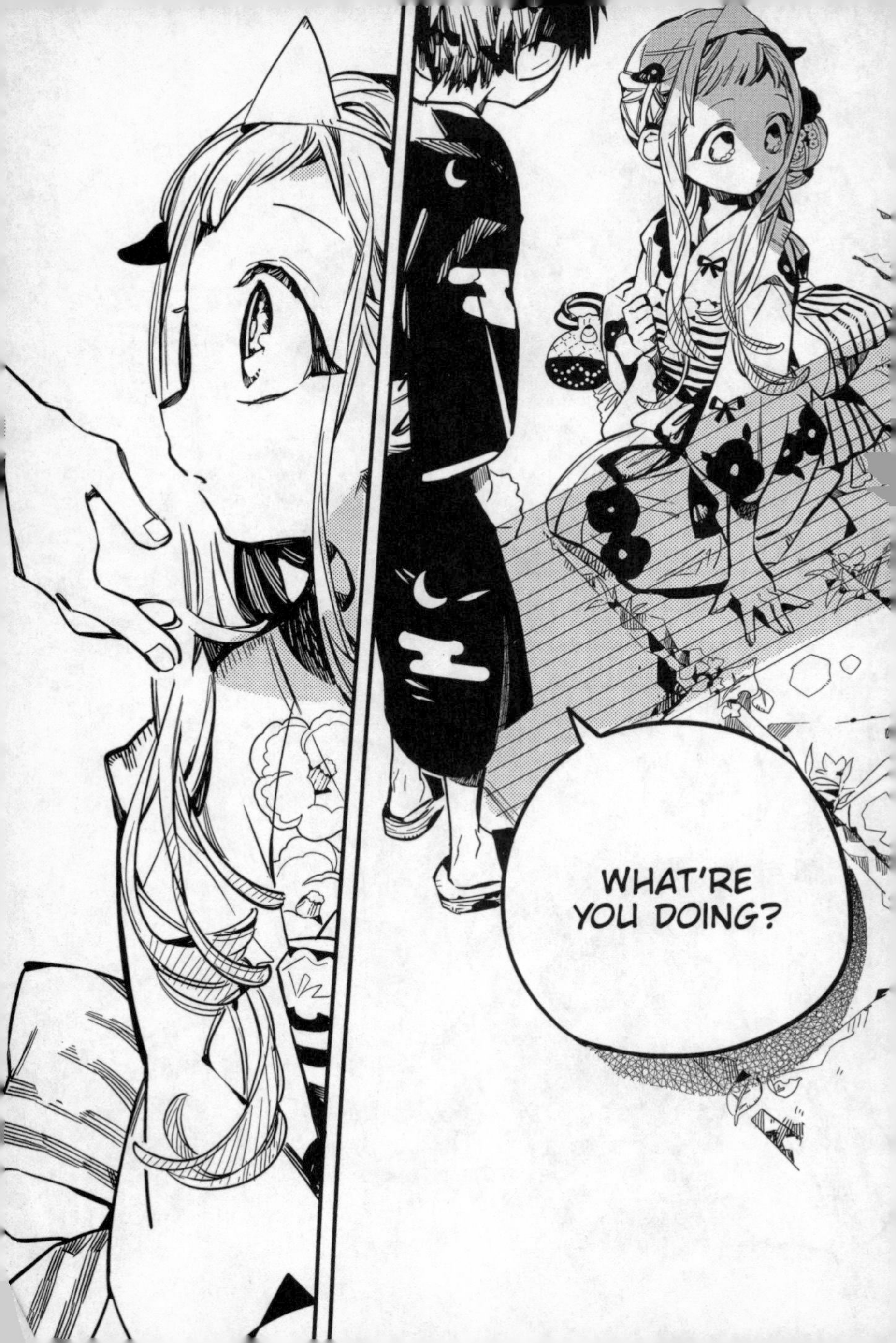
WHAT'RE YOU DOING?

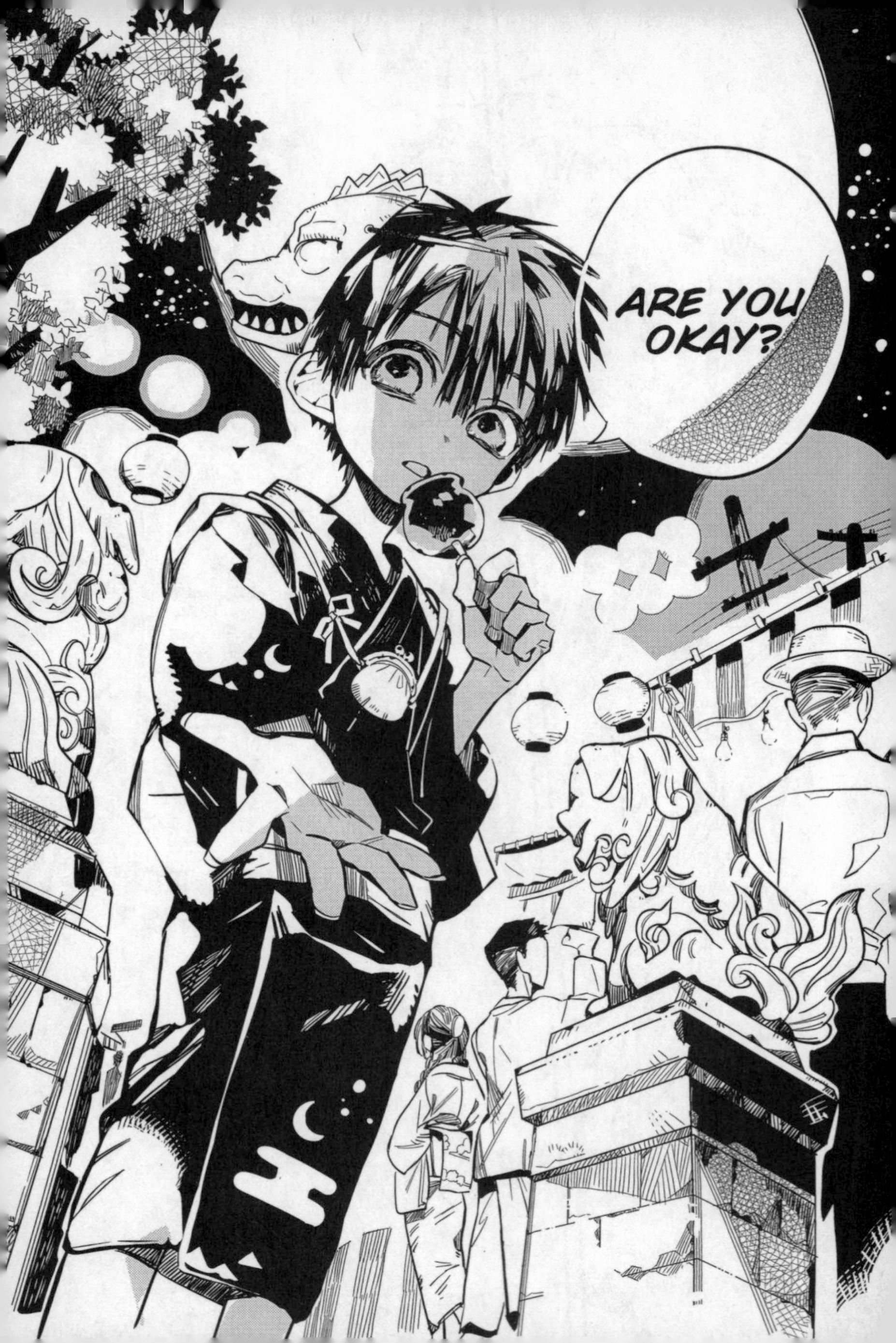
ARE YOU OKAY?

 SPOOK 38   SUMMER LIGHTS (PART 2)

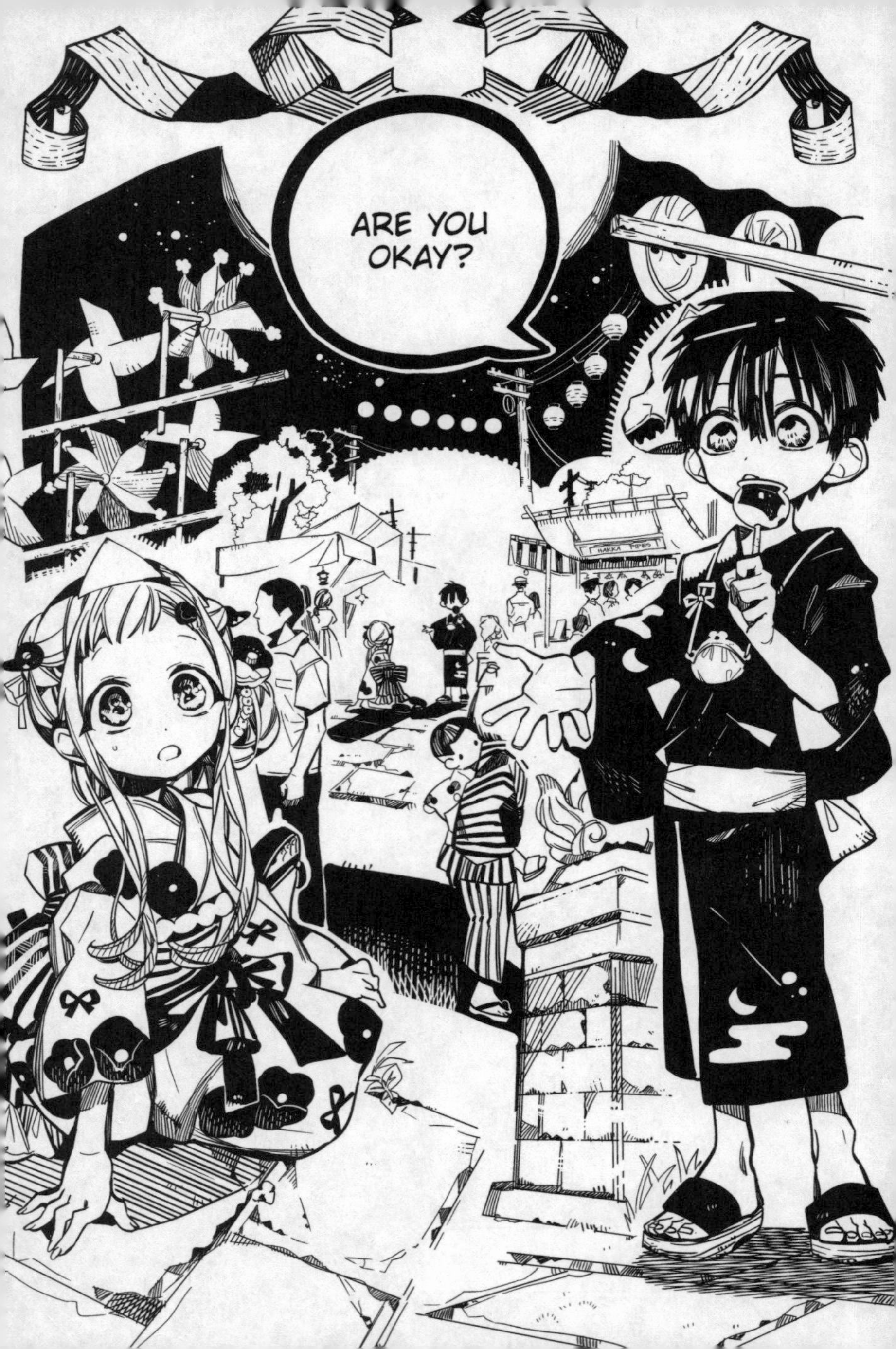
ARE YOU OKAY?
HAKKA PIPES

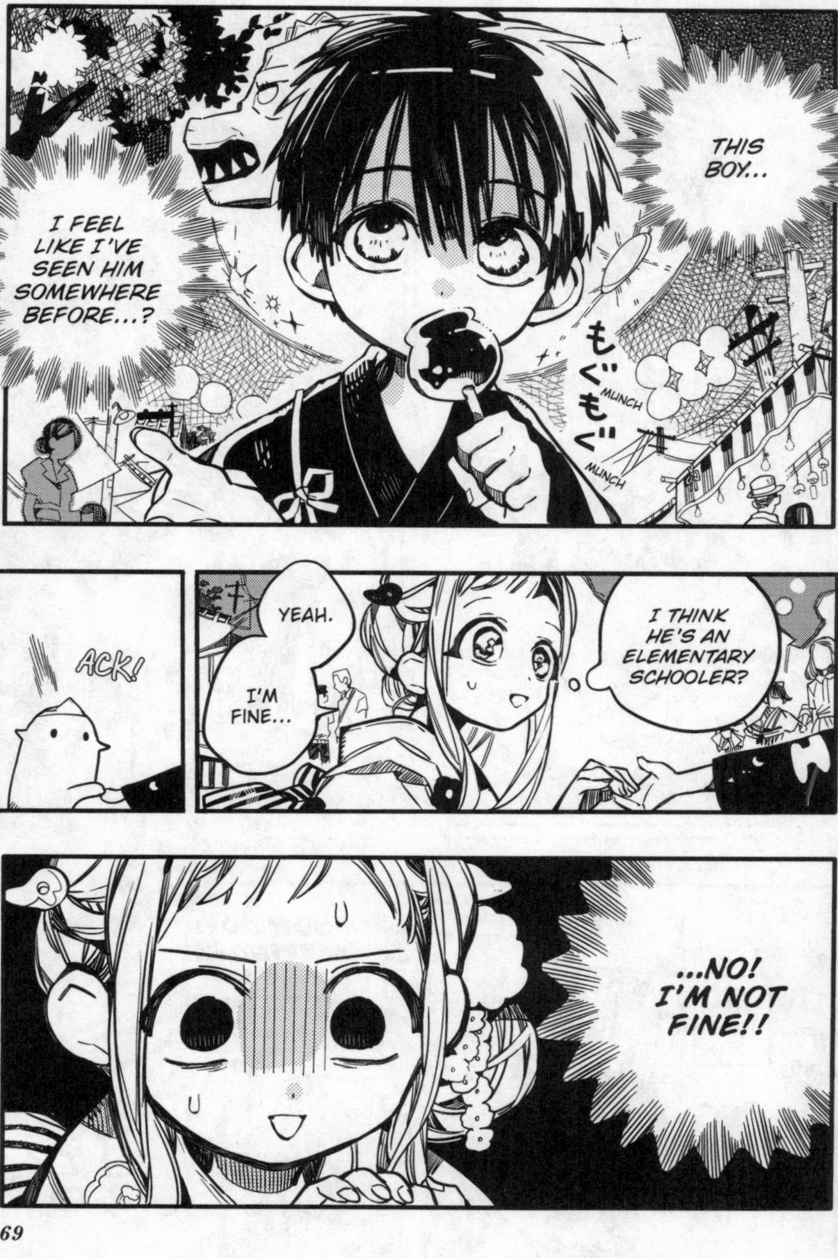
THIS BOY...
I FEEL LIKE I'VE SEEN HIM SOMEWHERE BEFORE...?
もぐもぐ
MUNCH
MUNCH
I THINK HE'S AN ELEMENTARY SCHOOLER?
YEAH.
I'M FINE...
ACK!
...NO! I'M NOT FINE!!

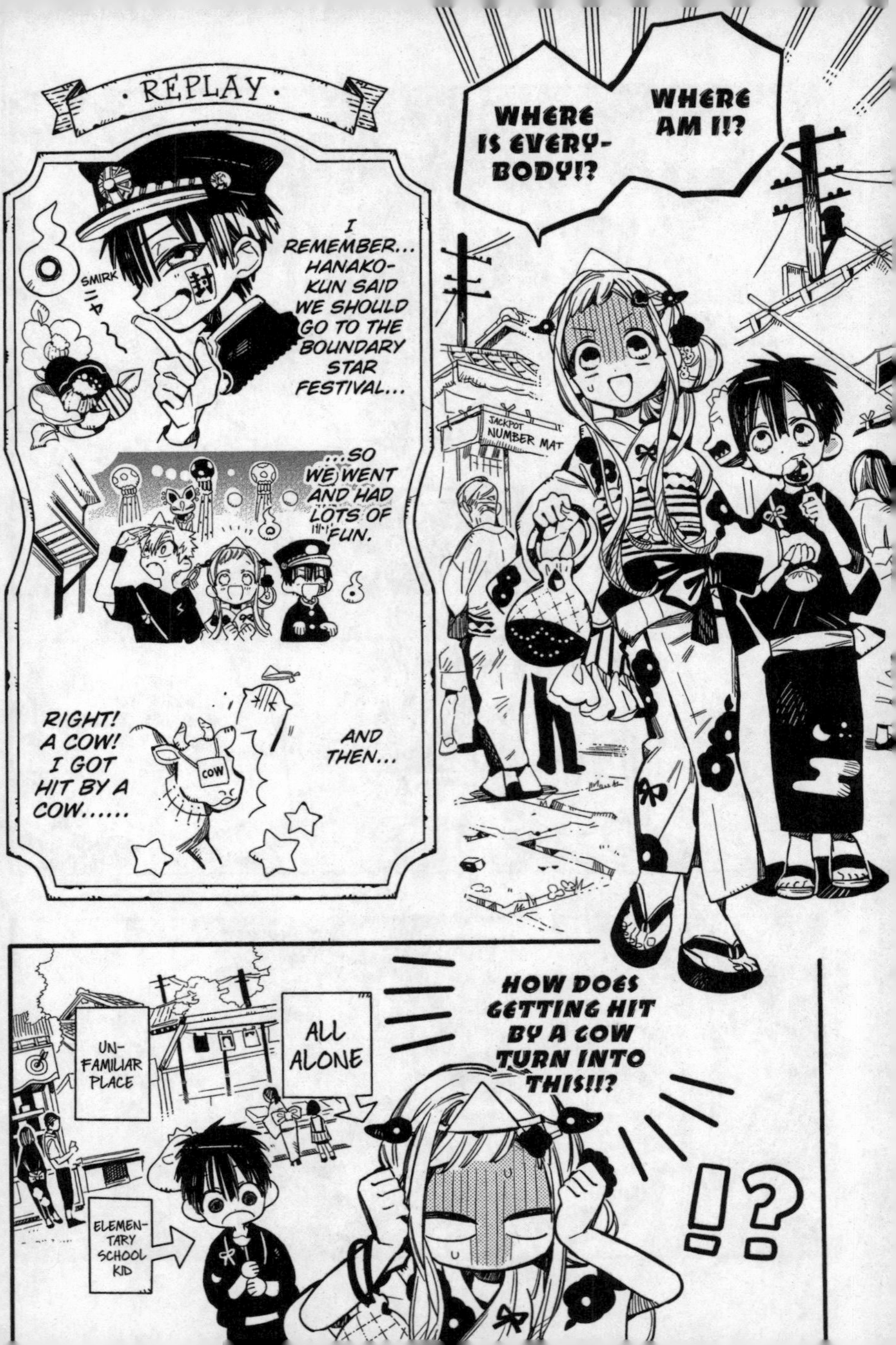

WHERE AM I!?
WHERE IS EVERY-BODY!?
JACKPOT NUMBER MAT
REPLAY
I REMEMBER... HANAKO-KUN SAID WE SHOULD GO TO THE BOUNDARY STAR FESTIVAL...
SMIRK
ニヤ〜
...SO WE WENT AND HAD LOTS OF FUN.
AND THEN...
COW
RIGHT! A COW! I GOT HIT BY A COW......
HOW DOES GETTING HIT BY A COW TURN INTO THIS!!?
!?
ALL ALONE
UN-FAMILIAR PLACE
ELEMENTARY SCHOOL KID

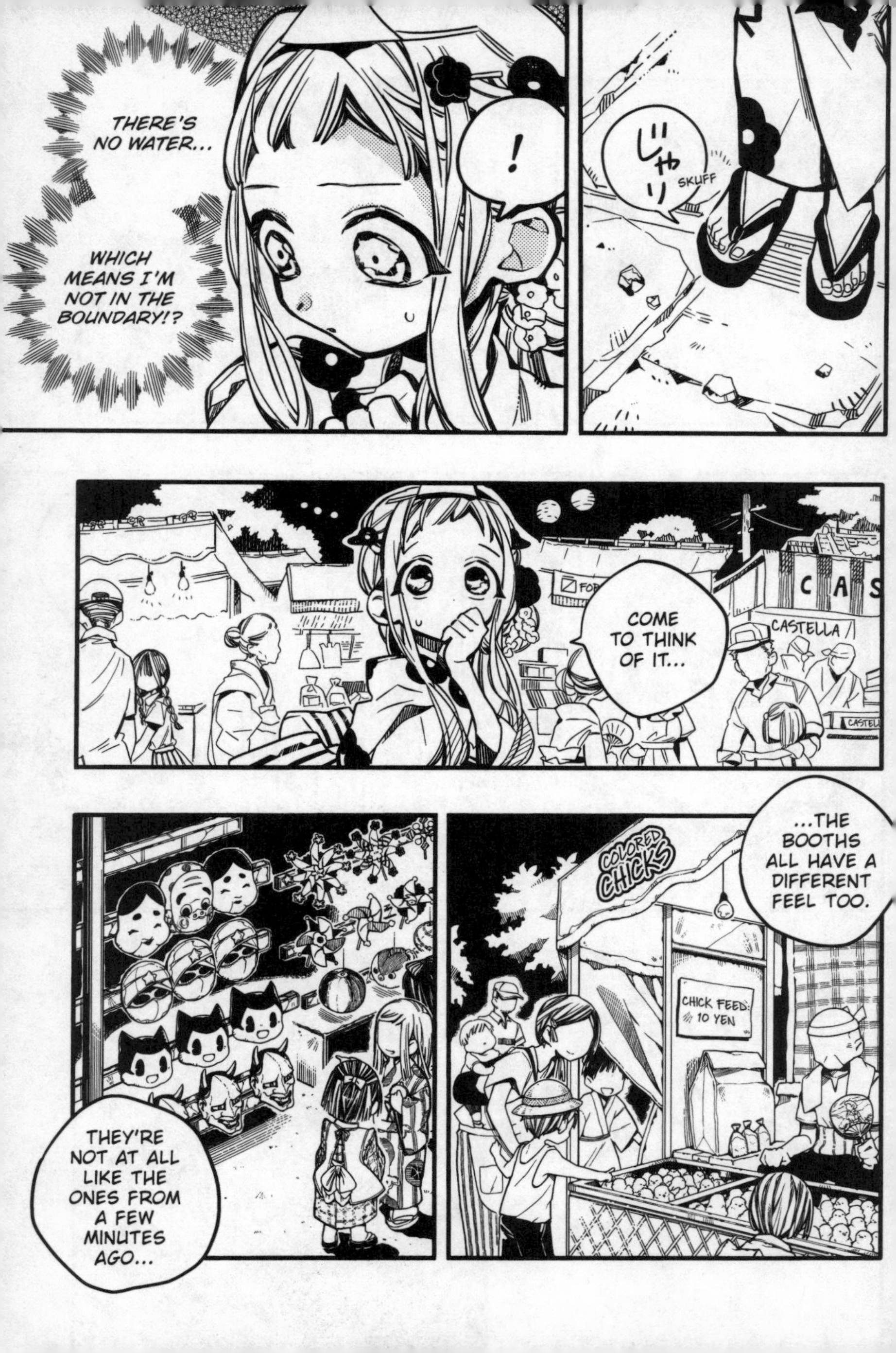
じゃり
SKUFF
!
THERE'S NO WATER...
WHICH MEANS I'M NOT IN THE BOUNDARY!?
CASTELLA
COME TO THINK OF IT...
...THE BOOTHS ALL HAVE A DIFFERENT FEEL TOO.
COLORED CHICKS
CHICK FEED: 10 YEN
THEY'RE NOT AT ALL LIKE THE ONES FROM A FEW MINUTES AGO...

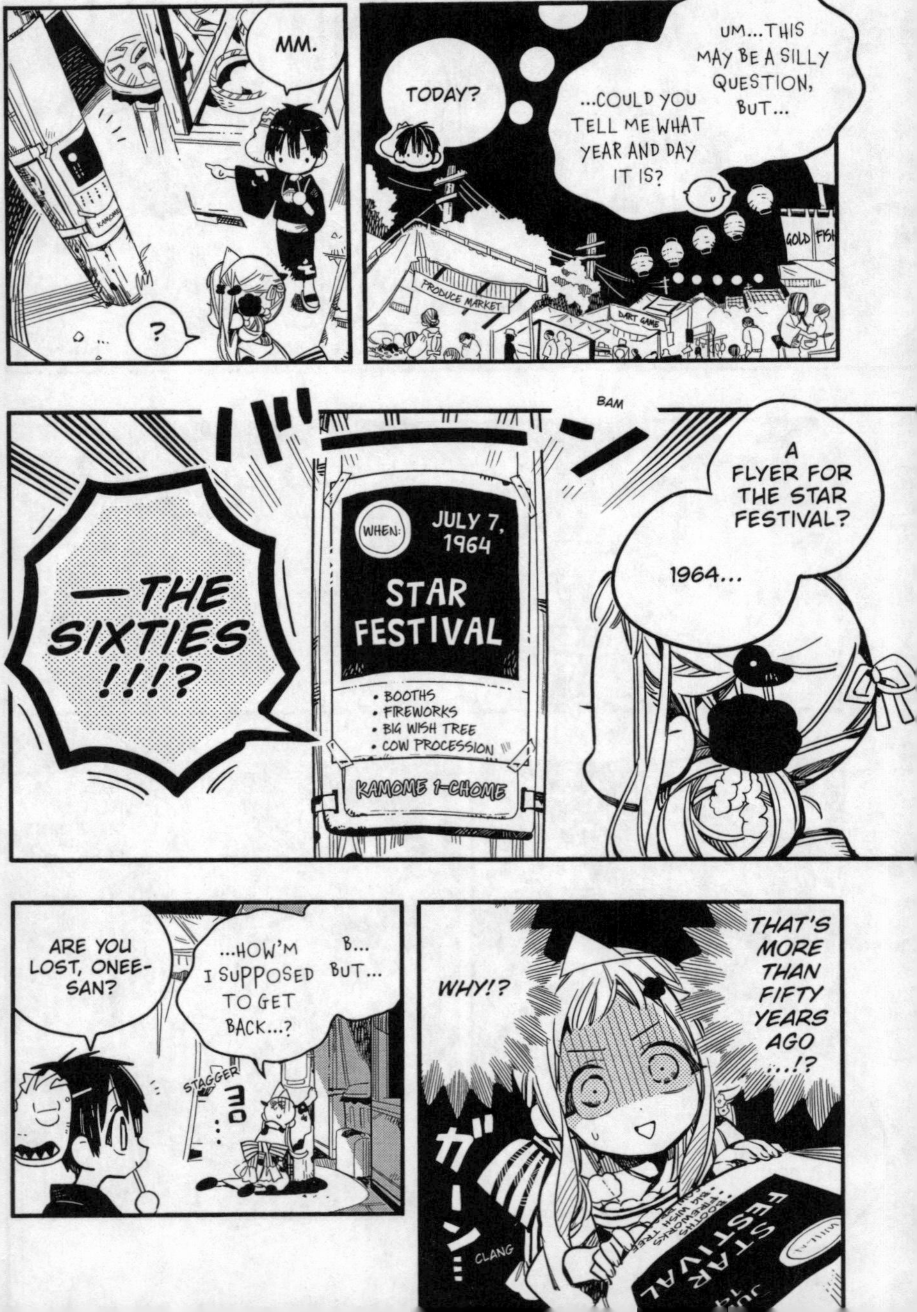
UM...THIS MAY BE A SILLY QUESTION, BUT...
...COULD YOU TELL ME WHAT YEAR AND DAY IT IS?
TODAY?
GOLD FISH
PRODUCE MARKET
DART GAME
MM.
?
BAM
A FLYER FOR THE STAR FESTIVAL?
1964...
WHEN: JULY 7, 1964
STAR FESTIVAL
• BOOTHS
• FIREWORKS
• BIG WISH TREE
• COW PROCESSION
KAMOME 1-CHOME
—THE SIXTIES!!!?
THAT'S MORE THAN FIFTY YEARS AGO...!?
WHY!?
CLANG
B... BUT...
...HOW'M I SUPPOSED TO GET BACK...?
STAGGER
ARE YOU LOST, ONEE-SAN?

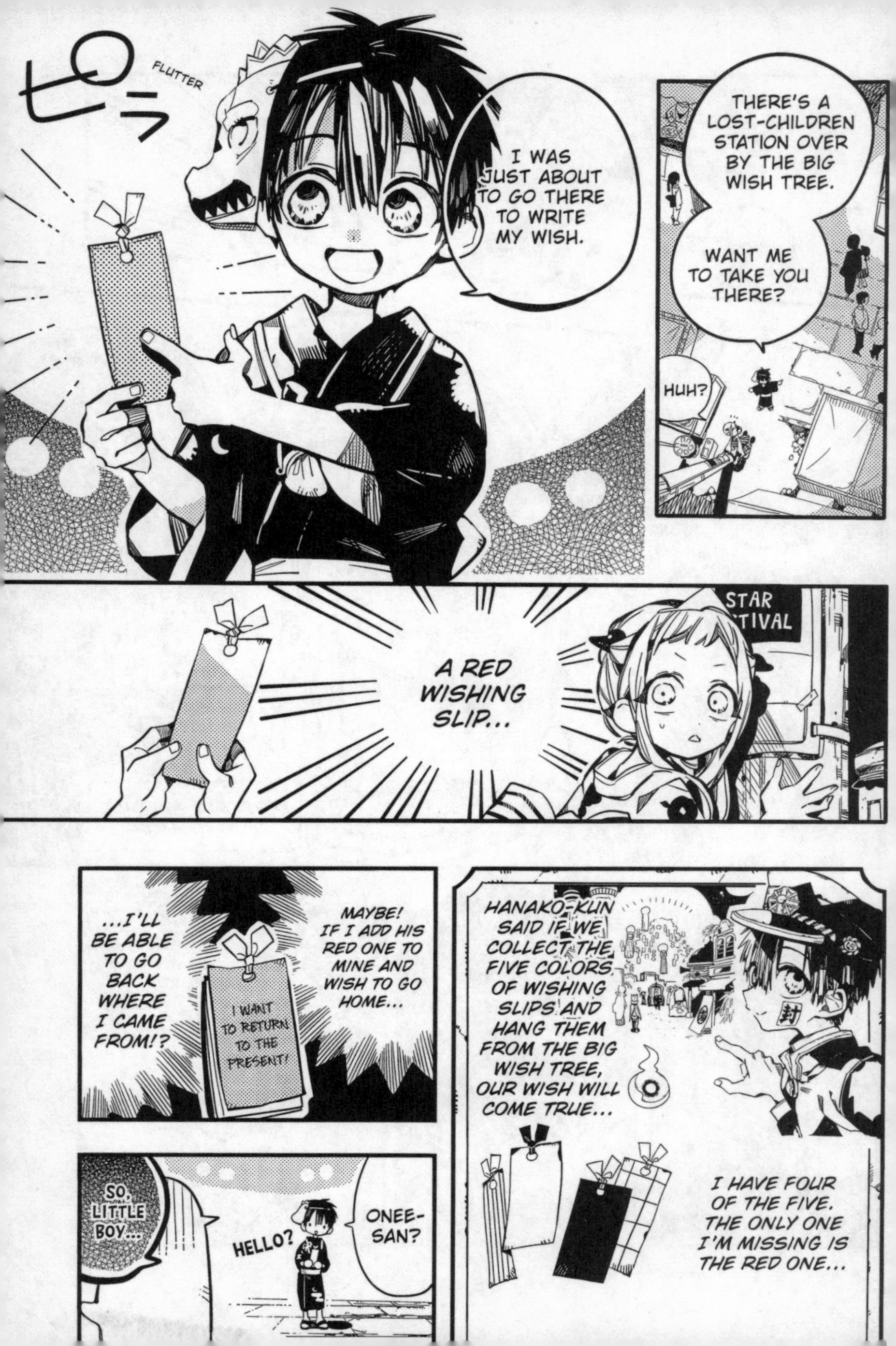
THERE'S A LOST-CHILDREN STATION OVER BY THE BIG WISH TREE.
WANT ME TO TAKE YOU THERE?
HUH?
I WAS JUST ABOUT TO GO THERE TO WRITE MY WISH.
ピラ
FLUTTER
STAR
TIVAL
A RED WISHING SLIP...
HANAKO-KUN SAID IF WE COLLECT THE FIVE COLORS OF WISHING SLIPS AND HANG THEM FROM THE BIG WISH TREE, OUR WISH WILL COME TRUE...
I HAVE FOUR OF THE FIVE. THE ONLY ONE I'M MISSING IS THE RED ONE...
MAYBE! IF I ADD HIS RED ONE TO MINE AND WISH TO GO HOME...
...I'LL BE ABLE TO GO BACK WHERE I CAME FROM!?
I WANT TO RETURN TO THE PRESENT!
ONEE-SAN?
HELLO?
SO, LITTLE BOY...

GRAB
WHOA!
YOUR WISHING SLIP... I DON'T SUPPOSE YOU'D BE WILLING TO GIVE IT TO ME...?
NOTE: THE HEROINE OF THIS STORY
HUH!?
THAT THERE...
...RED WISHING SLIP...
I SIMPLY MUST HAVE IT...
HFF...
HFF...
PLEASE? PRETTY PLEASE ...?
I'LL DO ANY-THING...
BADUM
BADUM
E-EEK...
BADUM

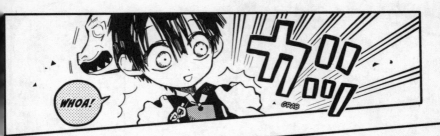

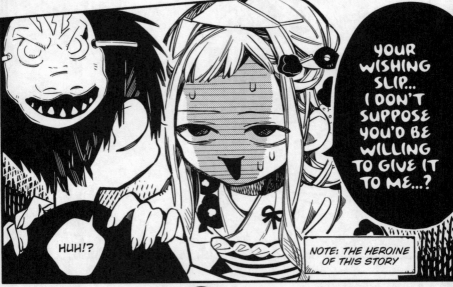

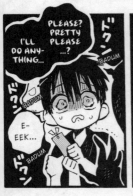

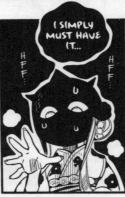

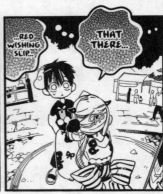

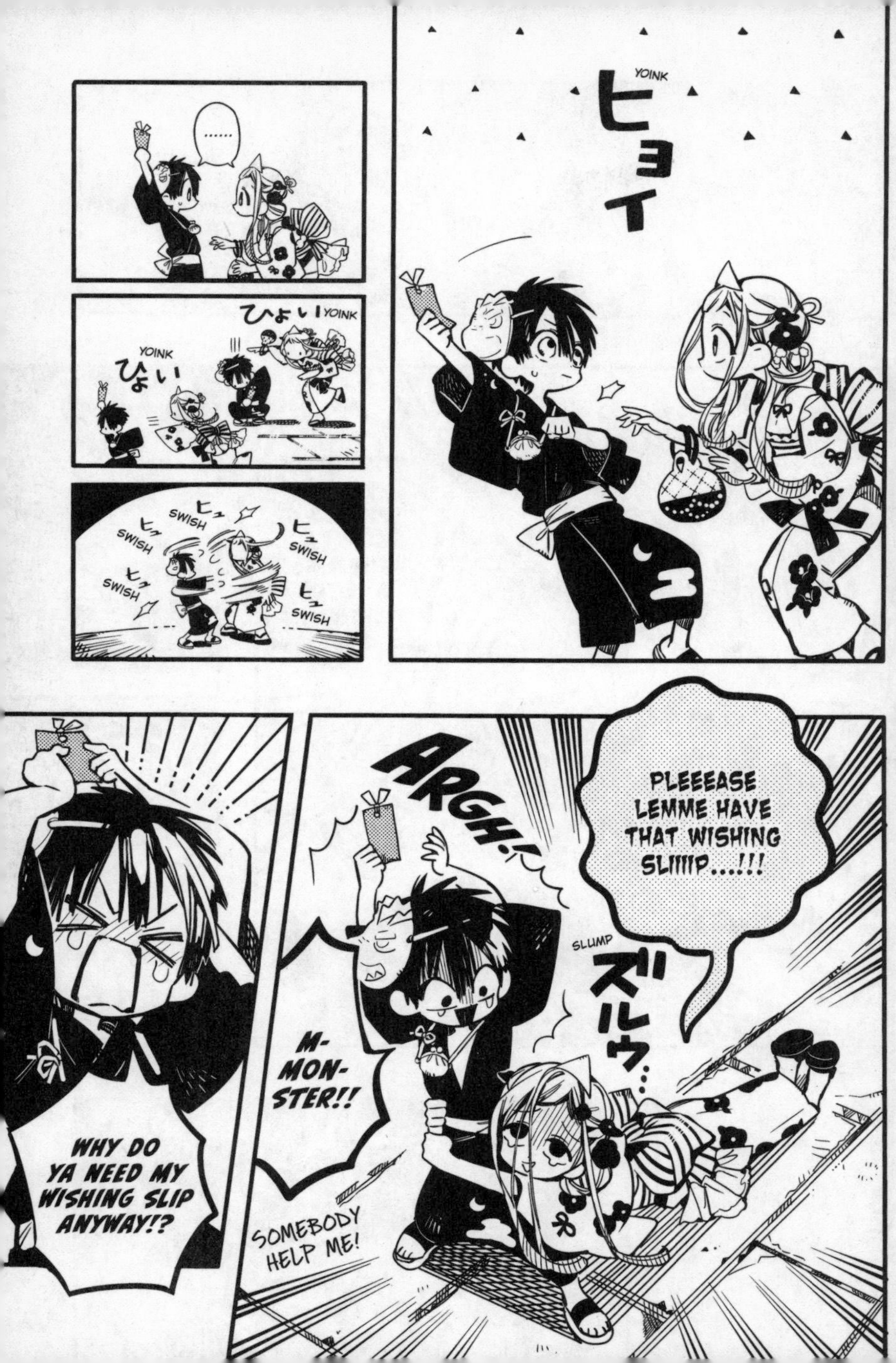
YOINK
ヒョイ
......
ひょい! YOINK
YOINK
ひょい
ヒュ SWISH
ヒュ SWISH
ヒュ SWISH
ヒュ SWISH
ヒュ SWISH
ARGH!!
PLEEEASE LEMME HAVE THAT WISHING SLIIIIP...!!!
SLUMP
ズルゥ...
M-MON-STER!!
SOMEBODY HELP ME!
WHY DO YA NEED MY WISHING SLIP ANYWAY!?

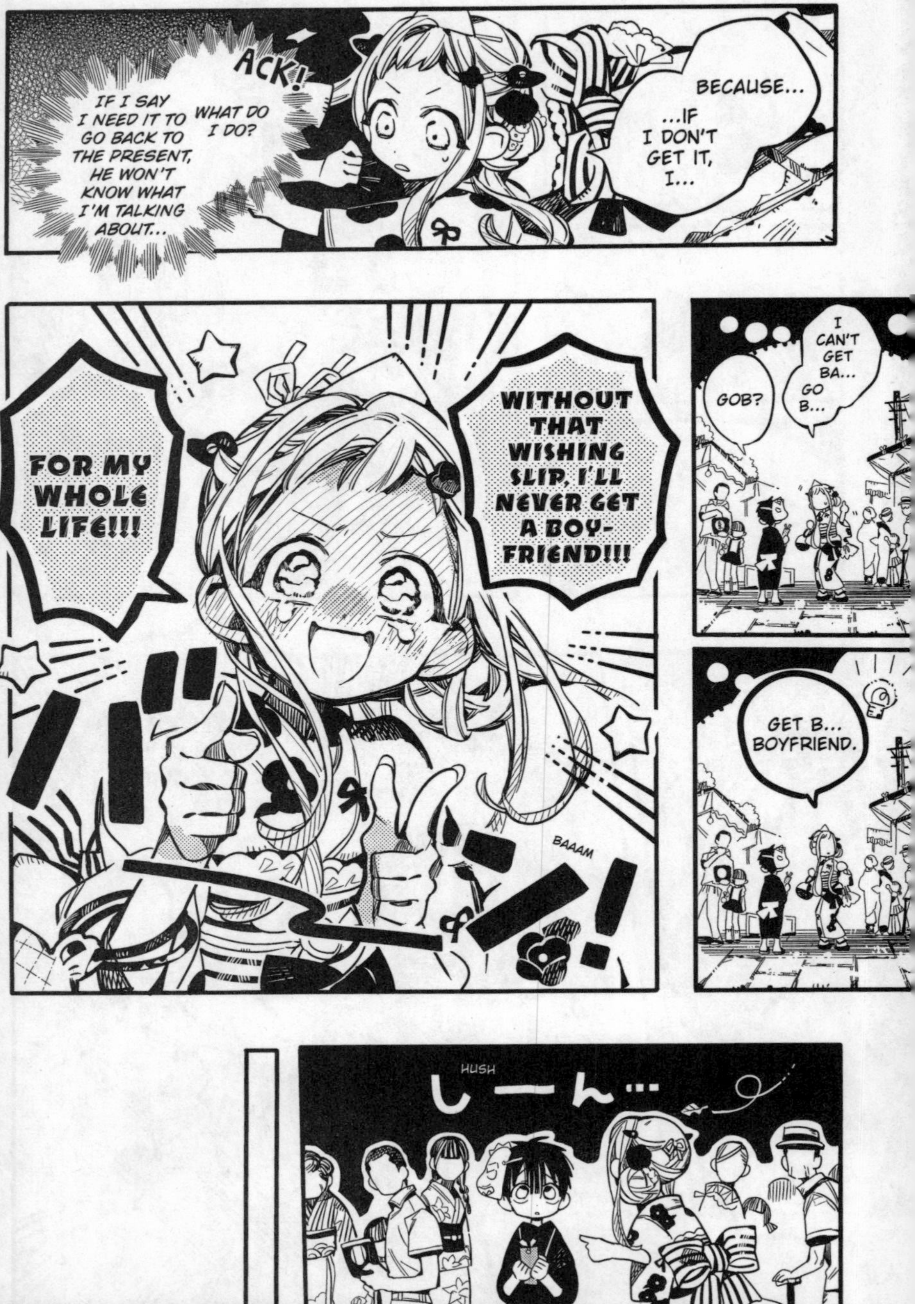
BECAUSE...
...IF I DON'T GET IT, I...
ACK!
WHAT DO I DO?
IF I SAY I NEED IT TO GO BACK TO THE PRESENT, HE WON'T KNOW WHAT I'M TALKING ABOUT...
I CAN'T GET BA... GO B...
GOB?
GET B... BOYFRIEND.
WITHOUT THAT WISHING SLIP, I'LL NEVER GET A BOY-FRIEND!!!
FOR MY WHOLE LIFE!!!
BAAAM
HUSH
しーん…

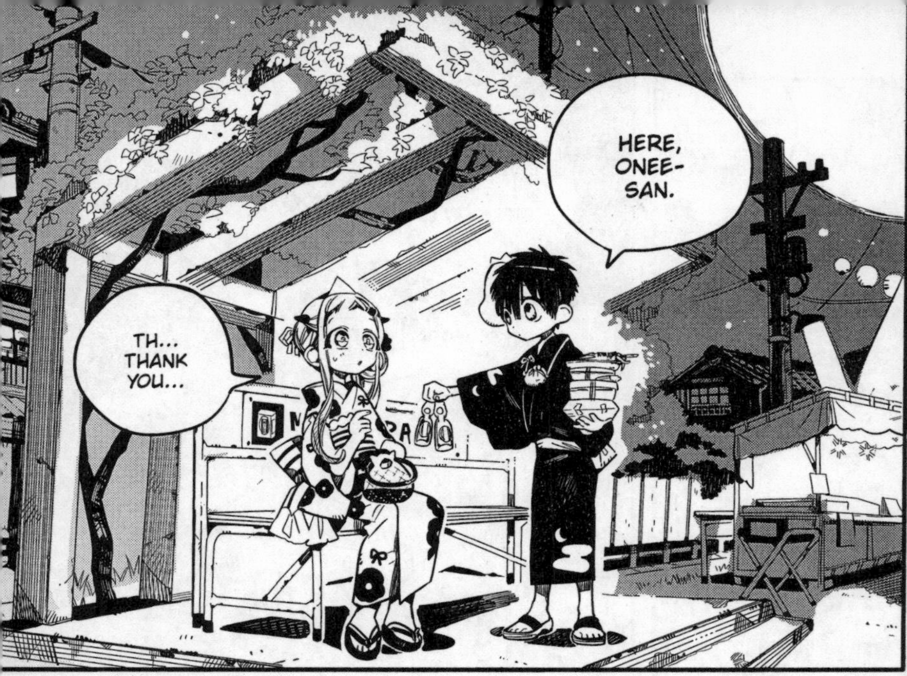
HERE, ONEE-SAN.
TH... THANK YOU...

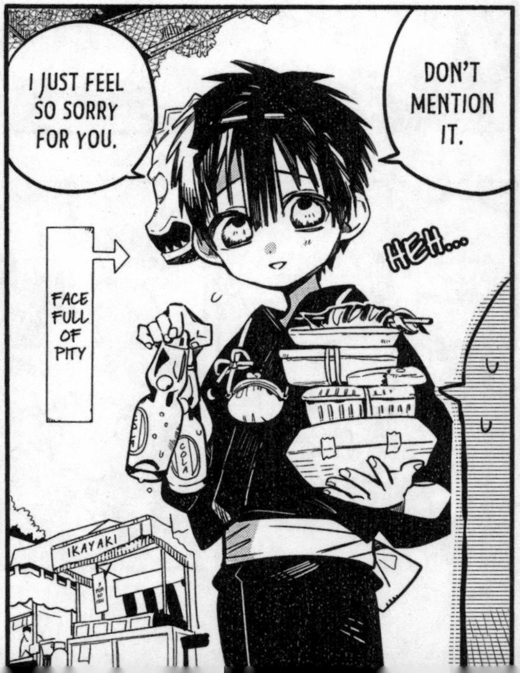
DON'T MENTION IT.
I JUST FEEL SO SORRY FOR YOU.
HEH...
FACE FULL OF PITY
COLA
IKAYAKI

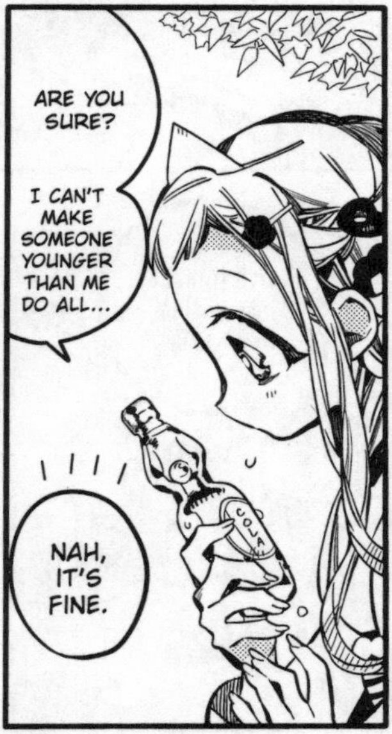
ARE YOU SURE?
I CAN'T MAKE SOMEONE YOUNGER THAN ME DO ALL...
NAH, IT'S FINE.
COLA

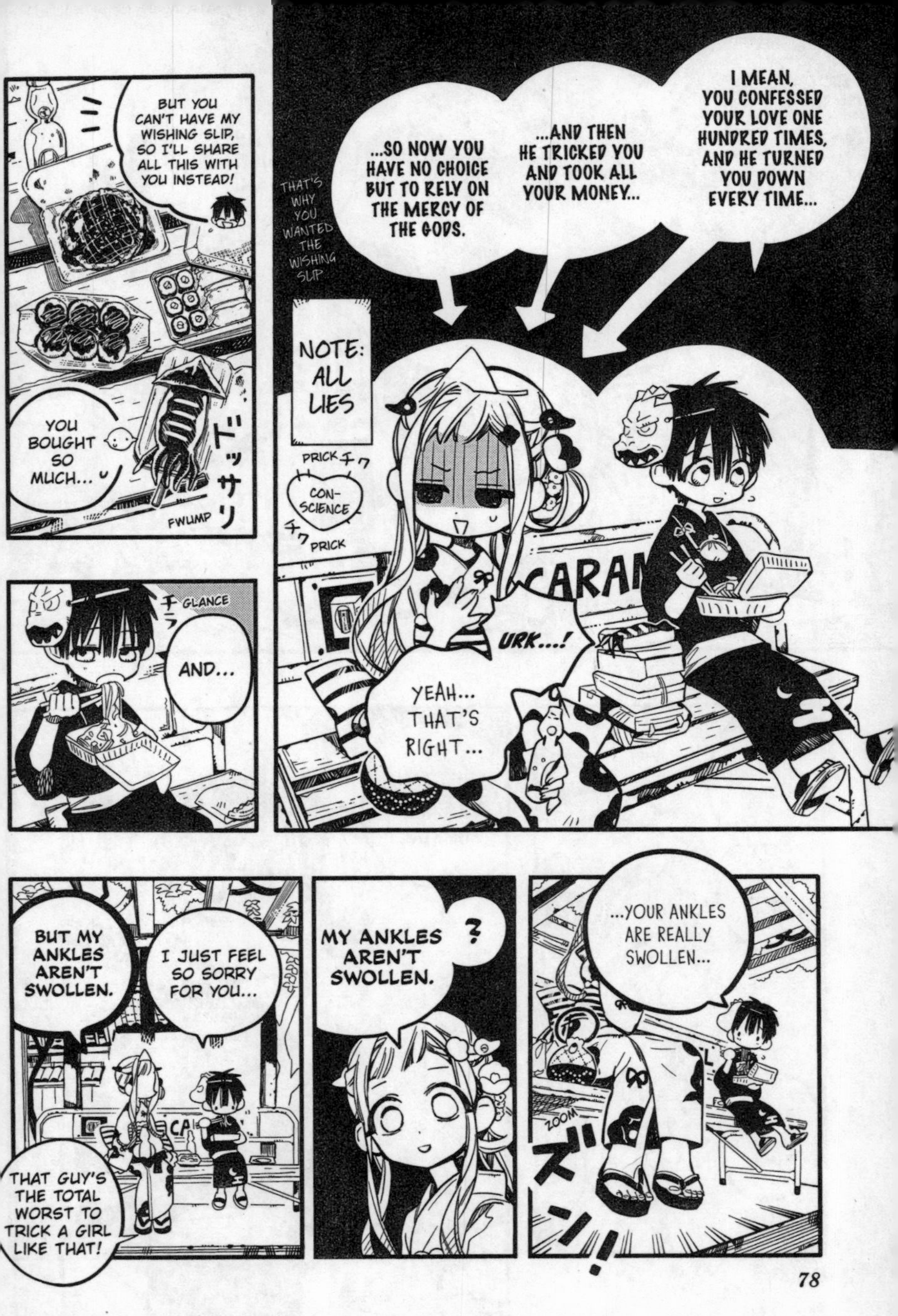
I MEAN, YOU CONFESSED YOUR LOVE ONE HUNDRED TIMES, AND HE TURNED YOU DOWN EVERY TIME...
...AND THEN HE TRICKED YOU AND TOOK ALL YOUR MONEY...
...SO NOW YOU HAVE NO CHOICE BUT TO RELY ON THE MERCY OF THE GODS.
THAT'S WHY YOU WANTED THE WISHING SLIP
NOTE: ALL LIES
PRICK チク
CON-SCIENCE
チク PRICK
CARAM
URK...!
YEAH... THAT'S RIGHT...
BUT YOU CAN'T HAVE MY WISHING SLIP, SO I'LL SHARE ALL THIS WITH YOU INSTEAD!
ドッサリ
FWUMP
YOU BOUGHT SO MUCH...
チラ GLANCE
AND...
...YOUR ANKLES ARE REALLY SWOLLEN...
ZOOM
ズーン!!
?
MY ANKLES AREN'T SWOLLEN.
I JUST FEEL SO SORRY FOR YOU...
BUT MY ANKLES AREN'T SWOLLEN.
CA
THAT GUY'S THE TOTAL WORST TO TRICK A GIRL LIKE THAT!

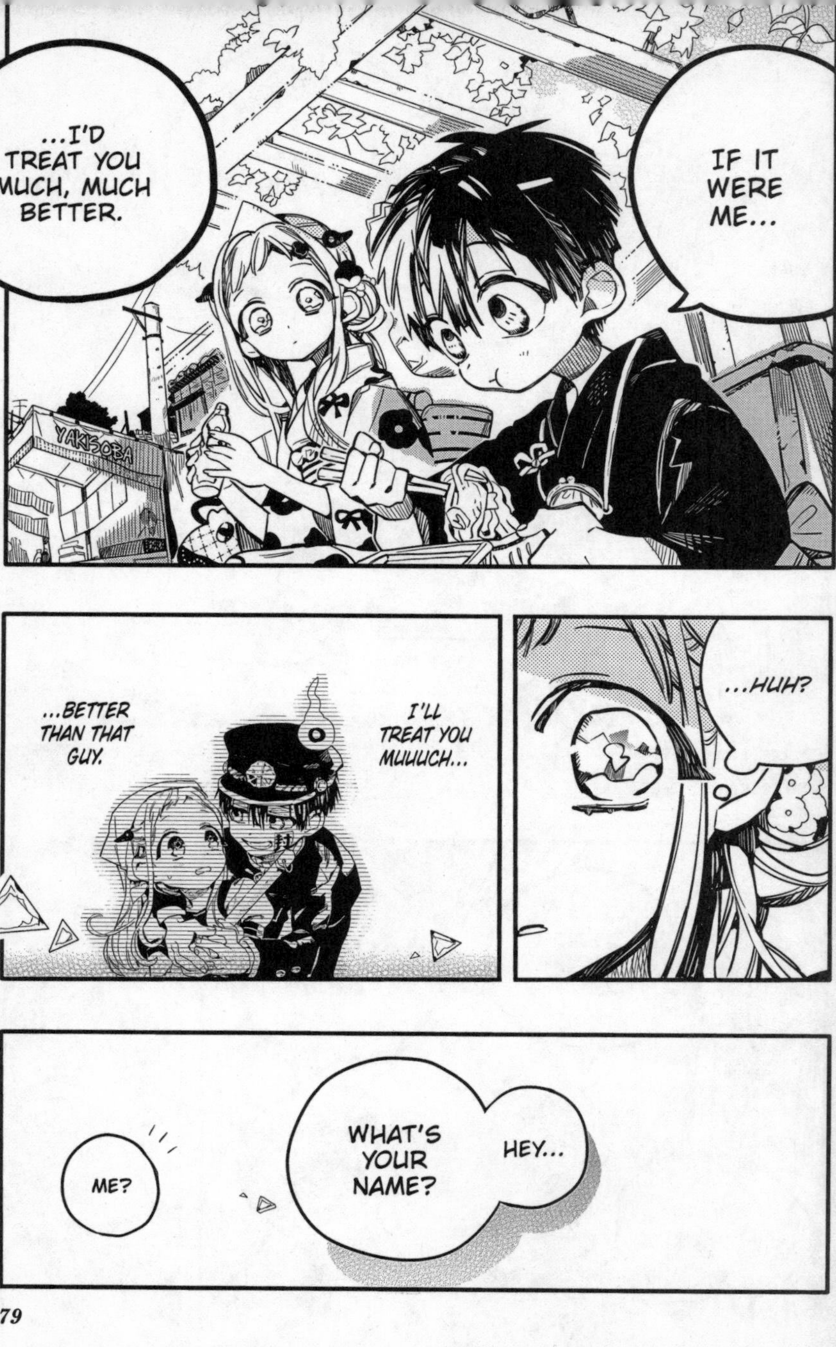
IF IT WERE ME...
...I'D TREAT YOU MUCH, MUCH BETTER.
YAKISOBA
...HUH?
I'LL TREAT YOU MUUUCH...
...BETTER THAN THAT GUY.
HEY...
WHAT'S YOUR NAME?
ME?

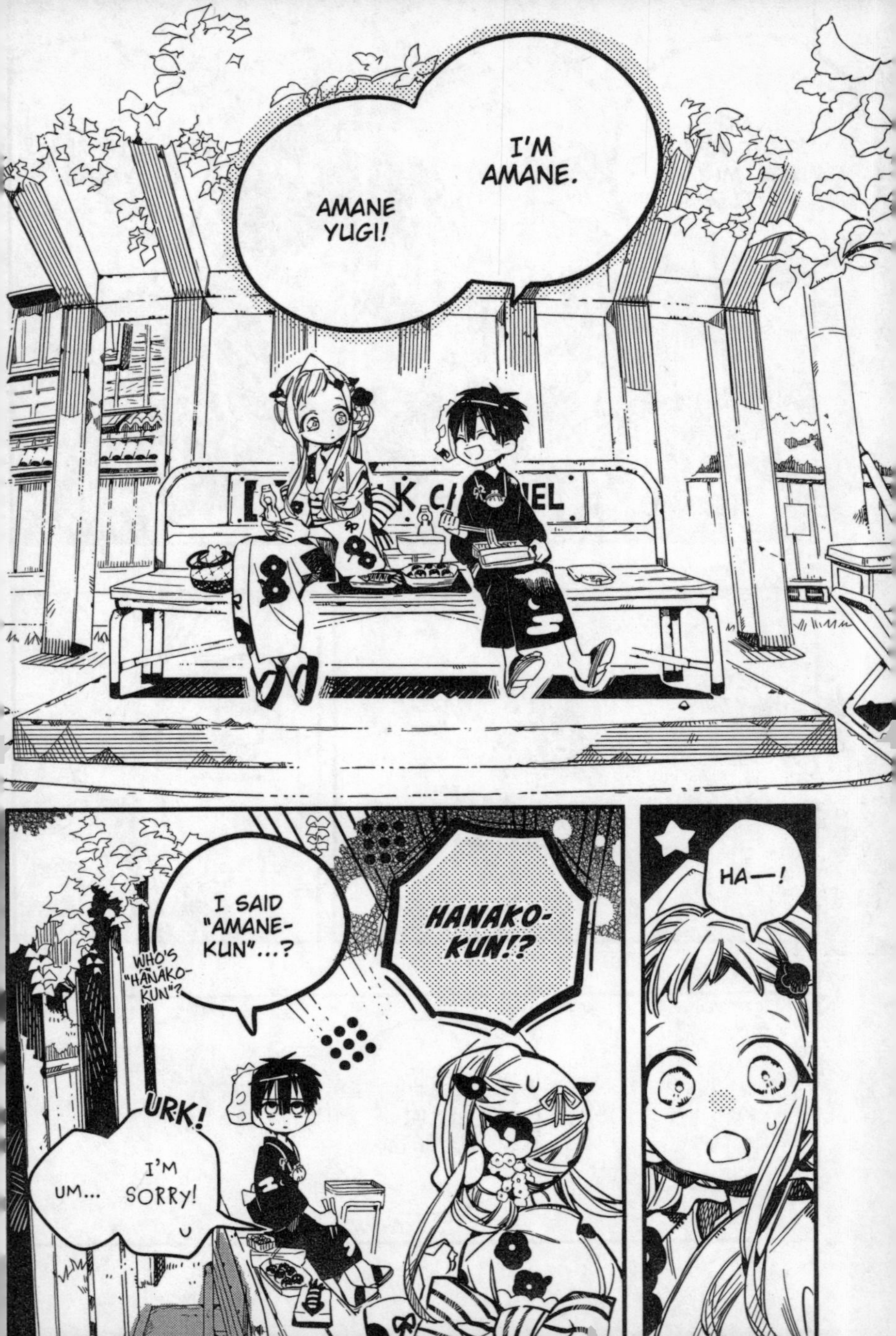
I'M AMANE.
AMANE YUGI!
HA—!
HANAKO-KUN!?
I SAID "AMANE-KUN"...?
WHO'S "HANAKO-KUN"?
URK!
UM... I'M SORRY!

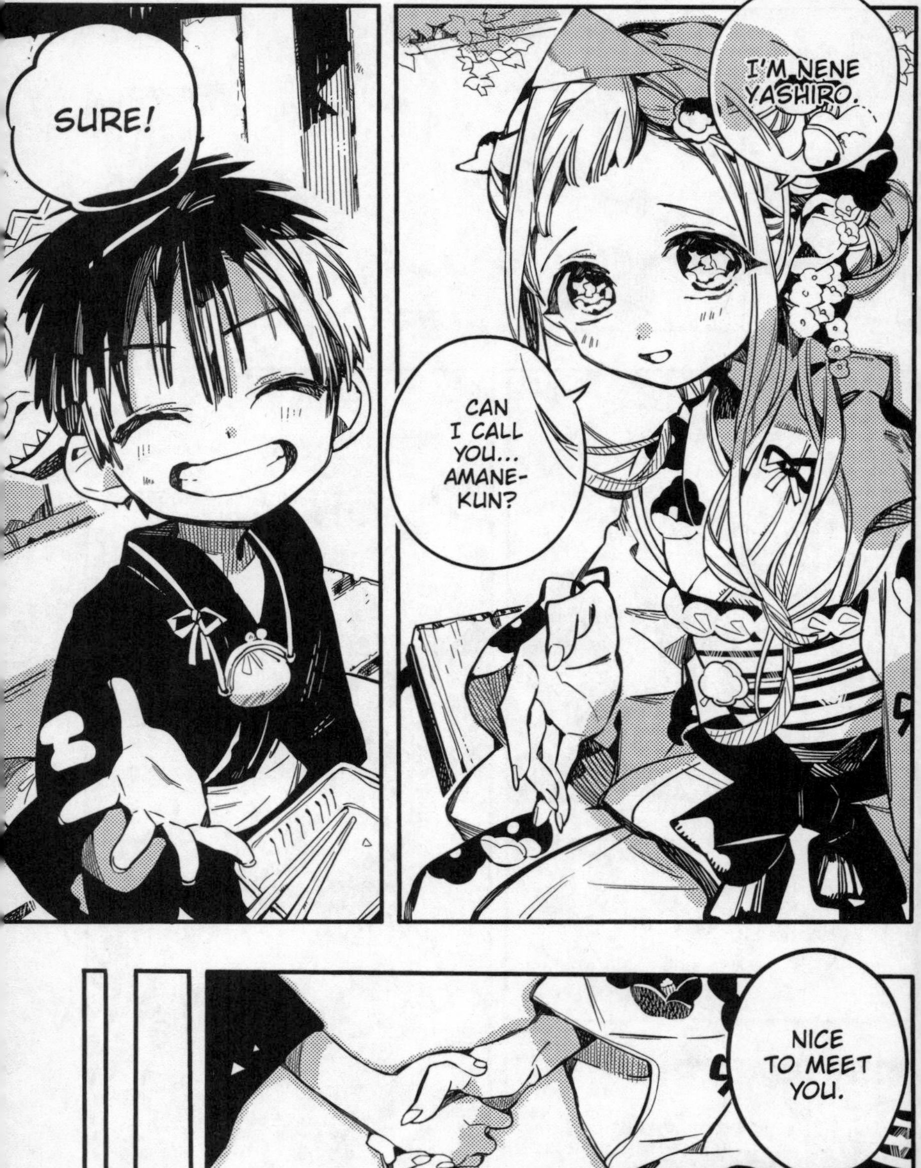
I'M NENE YASHIRO.
CAN I CALL YOU... AMANE-KUN?
SURE!
NICE TO MEET YOU.

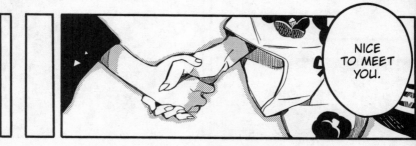

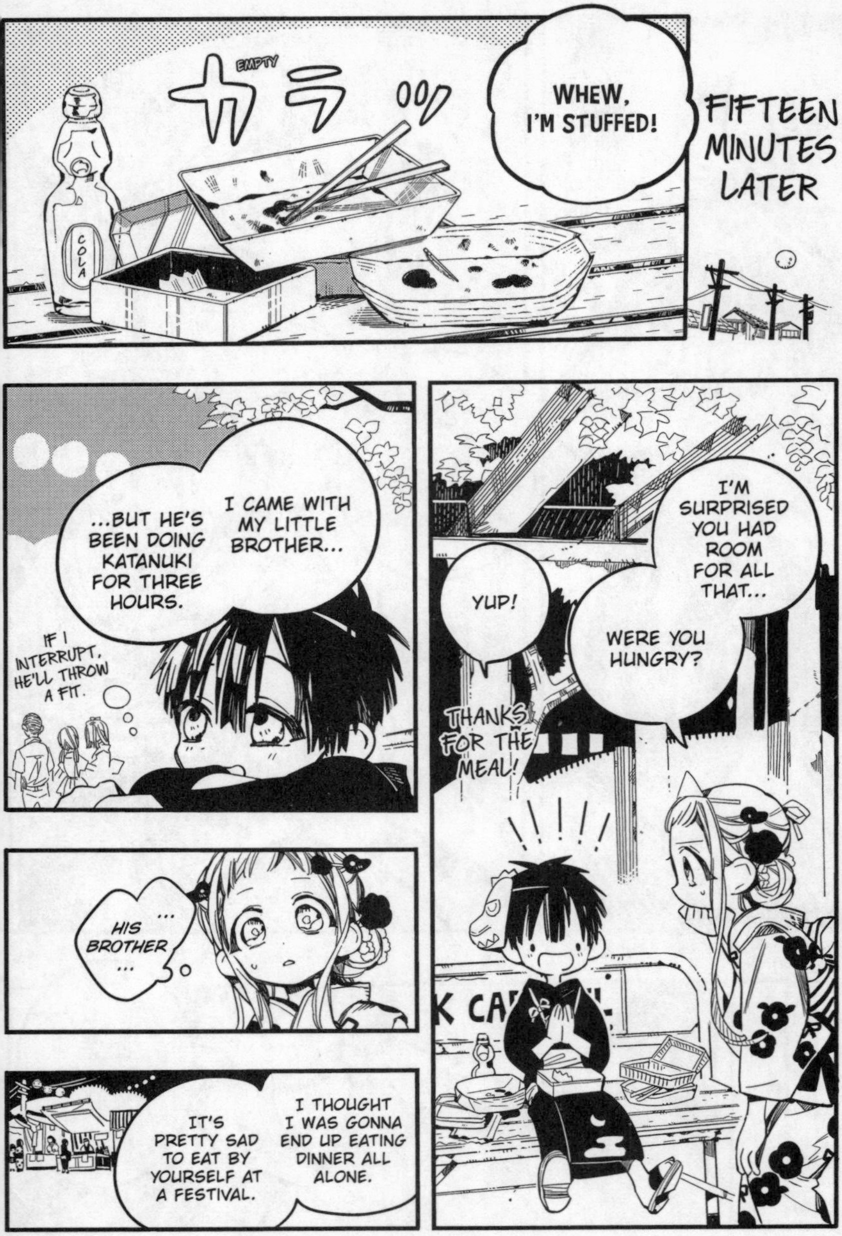

FIFTEEN MINUTES LATER
WHEW, I'M STUFFED!
EMPTY
カラ
COLA
THANKS FOR THE MEAL!
I'M SURPRISED YOU HAD ROOM FOR ALL THAT...
WERE YOU HUNGRY?
YUP!
I CAME WITH MY LITTLE BROTHER...
...BUT HE'S BEEN DOING KATANUKI FOR THREE HOURS.
IF I INTERRUPT, HE'LL THROW A FIT.
...HIS BROTHER...
I THOUGHT I WAS GONNA END UP EATING DINNER ALL ALONE.
IT'S PRETTY SAD TO EAT BY YOURSELF AT A FESTIVAL.

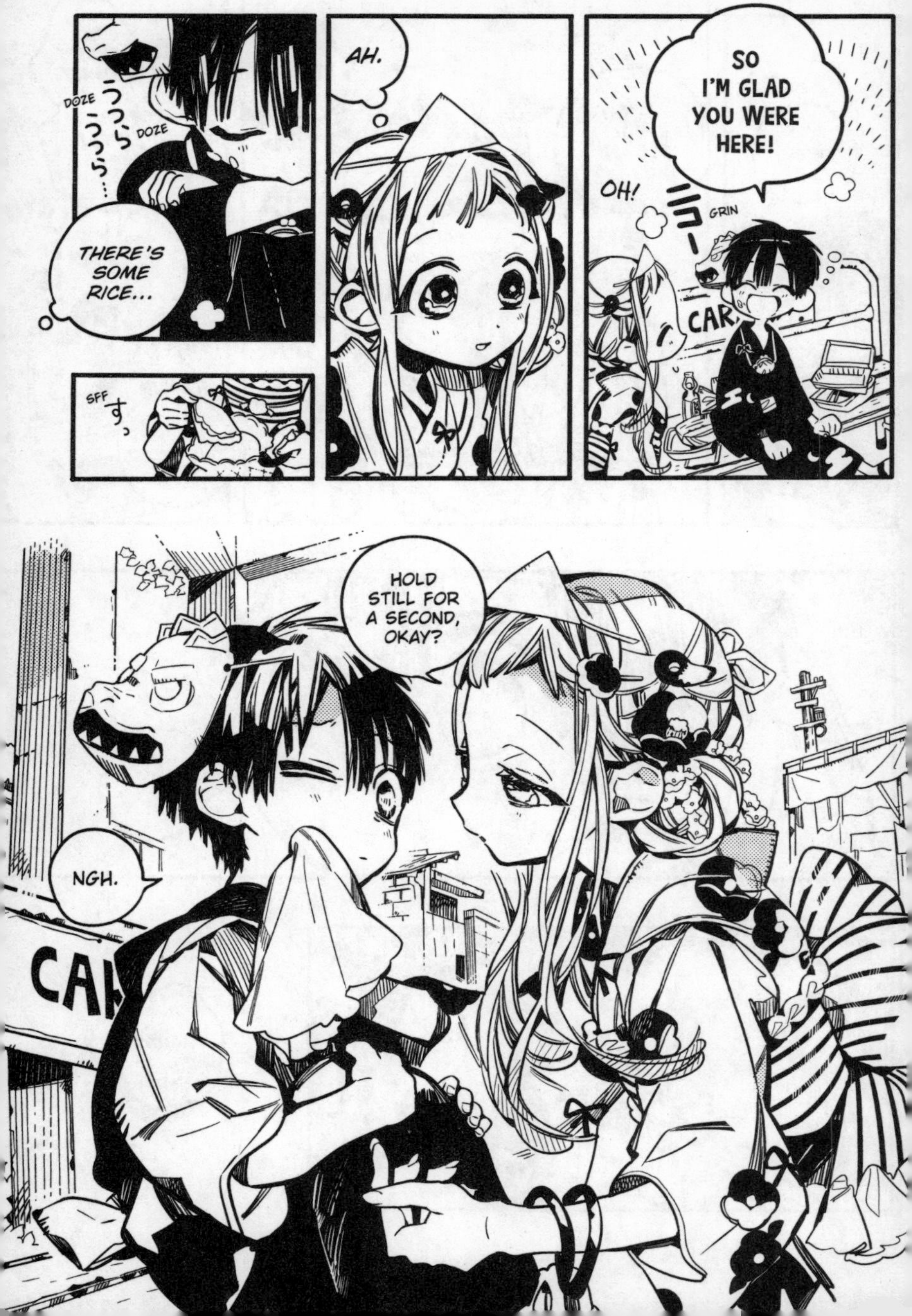
SO I'M GLAD YOU WERE HERE!
OH!
ニコー
GRIN
CAR
AH.
うつら うつら…
DOZE
DOZE
THERE'S SOME RICE...
す
SFF
HOLD STILL FOR A SECOND, OKAY?
NGH.
CAK

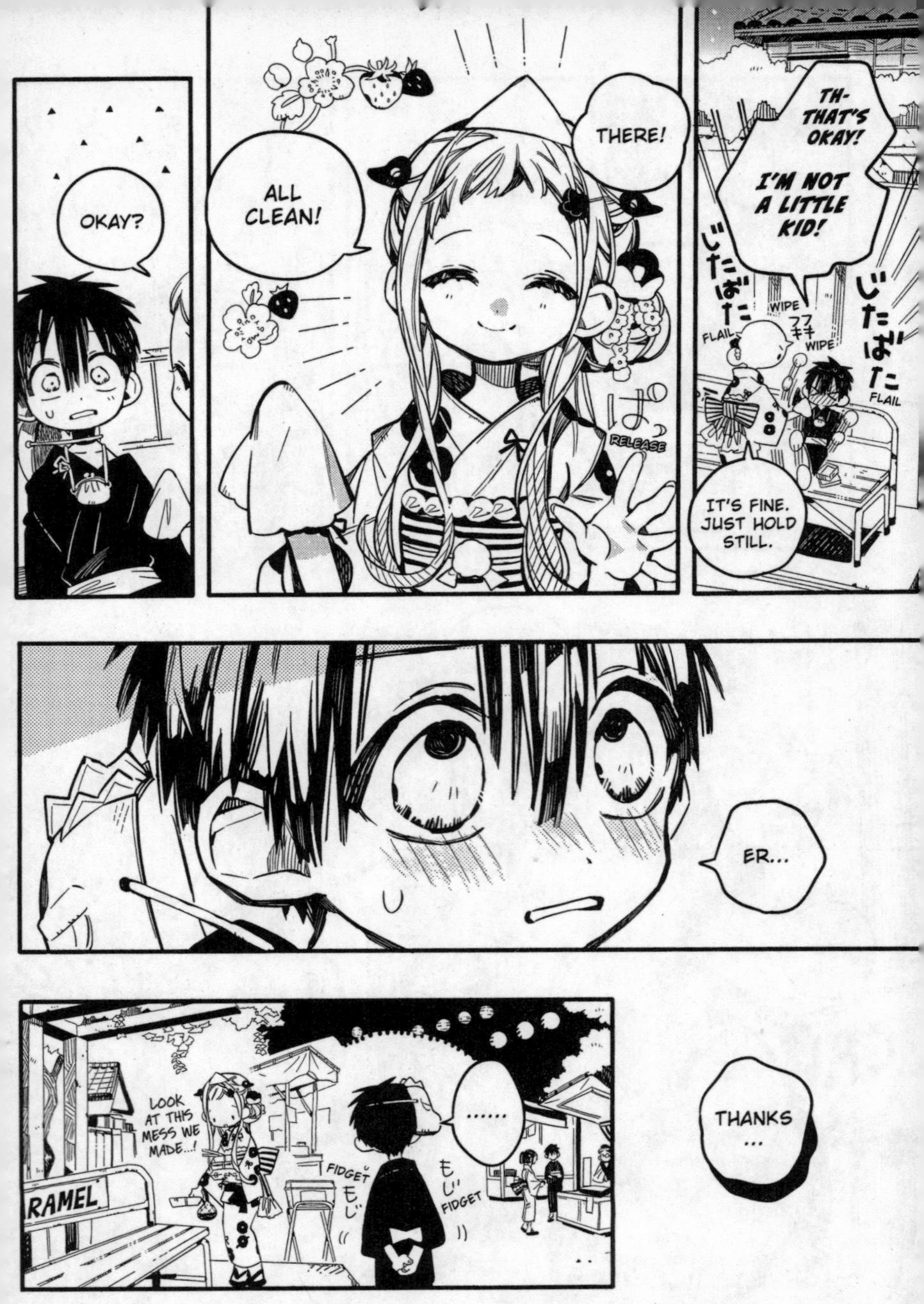
TH-THAT'S OKAY! I'M NOT A LITTLE KID!
じたばた
FLAIL
じたばた
FLAIL
WIPE
フキフキ
WIPE
IT'S FINE. JUST HOLD STILL.
THERE!
ALL CLEAN!
ぱっ
RELEASE
OKAY?
ER...
THANKS...
......
LOOK AT THIS MESS WE MADE...!
もじもじ
FIDGET
FIDGET
RAMEL

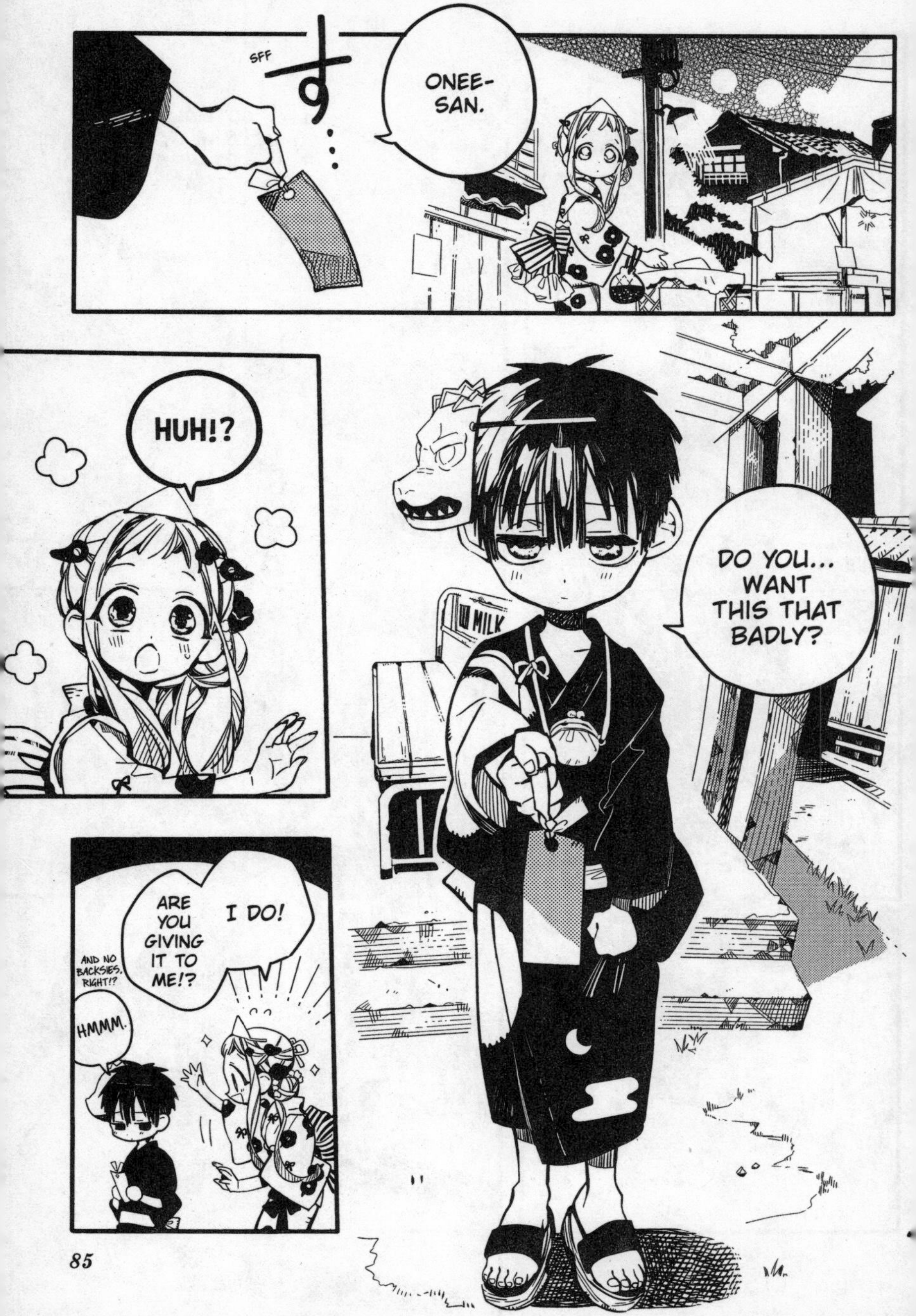
ONEE-SAN.
SFF
す
DO YOU... WANT THIS THAT BADLY?
HUH!?
I DO!
ARE YOU GIVING IT TO ME!?
AND NO BACKSIES, RIGHT!?
HMMM.
MILK

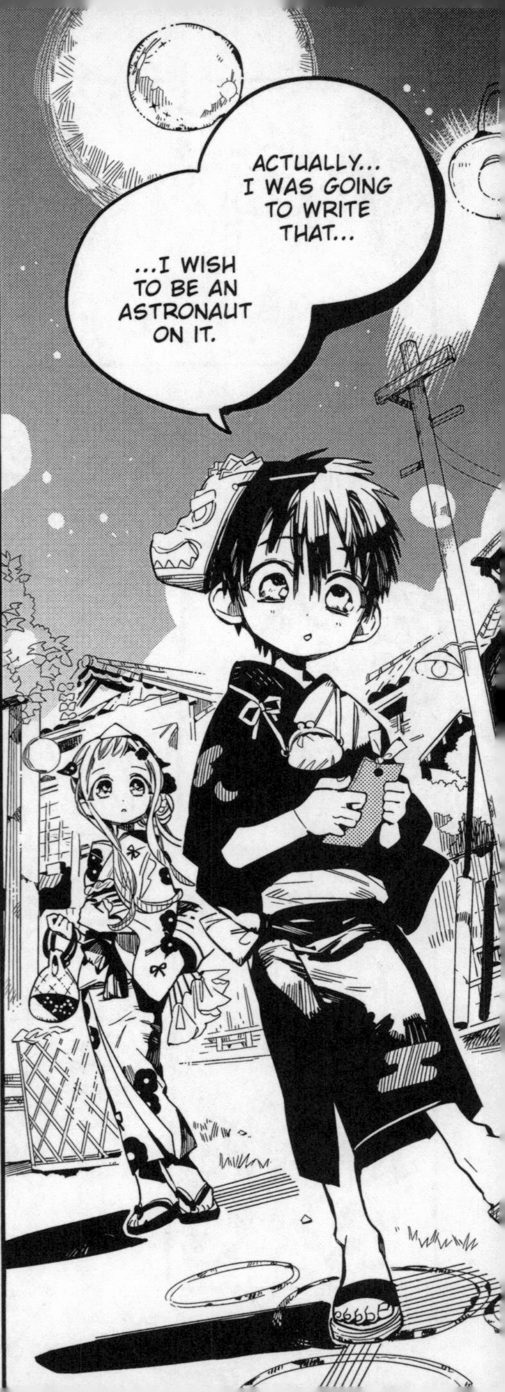
ACTUALLY... I WAS GOING TO WRITE THAT...
...I WISH TO BE AN ASTRONAUT ON IT.

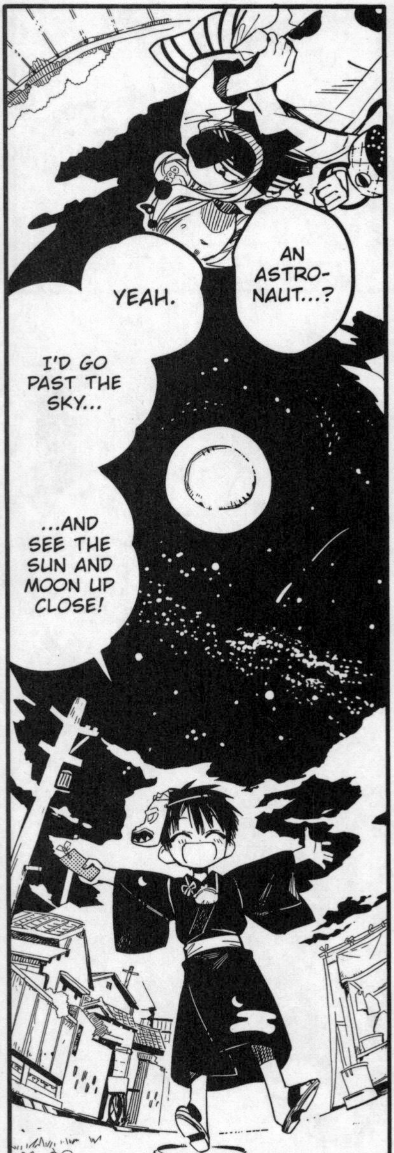
AN ASTRO-NAUT...?
YEAH.
I'D GO PAST THE SKY...
...AND SEE THE SUN AND MOON UP CLOSE!

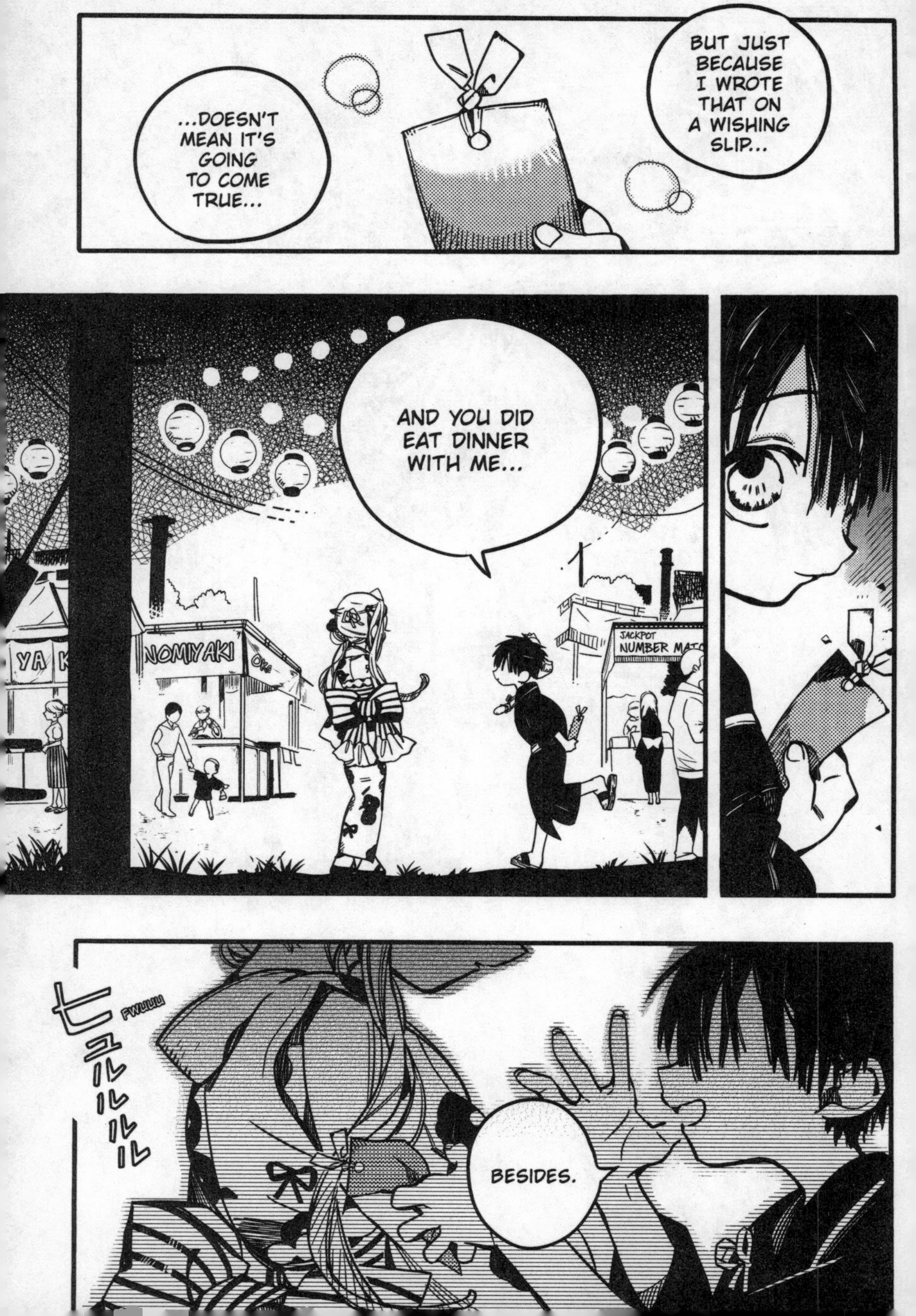
BUT JUST BECAUSE I WROTE THAT ON A WISHING SLIP...
...DOESN'T MEAN IT'S GOING TO COME TRUE...
AND YOU DID EAT DINNER WITH ME...
JACKPOT
NOMIYAKI
ヒュルルルル
FWUUU
BESIDES.

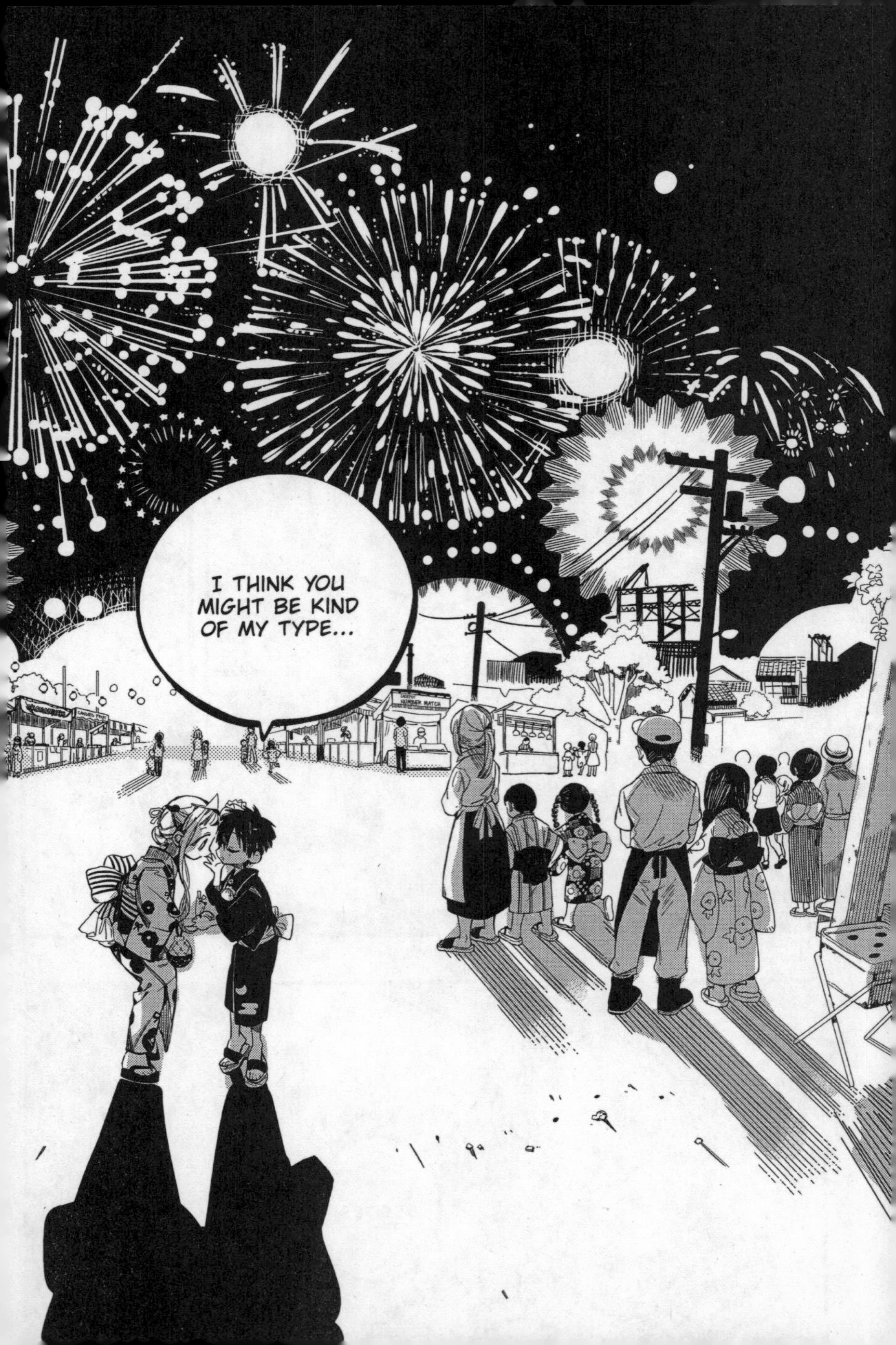
I THINK YOU MIGHT BE KIND OF MY TYPE...
NUMBER MATCH
CANDIED FRUIT

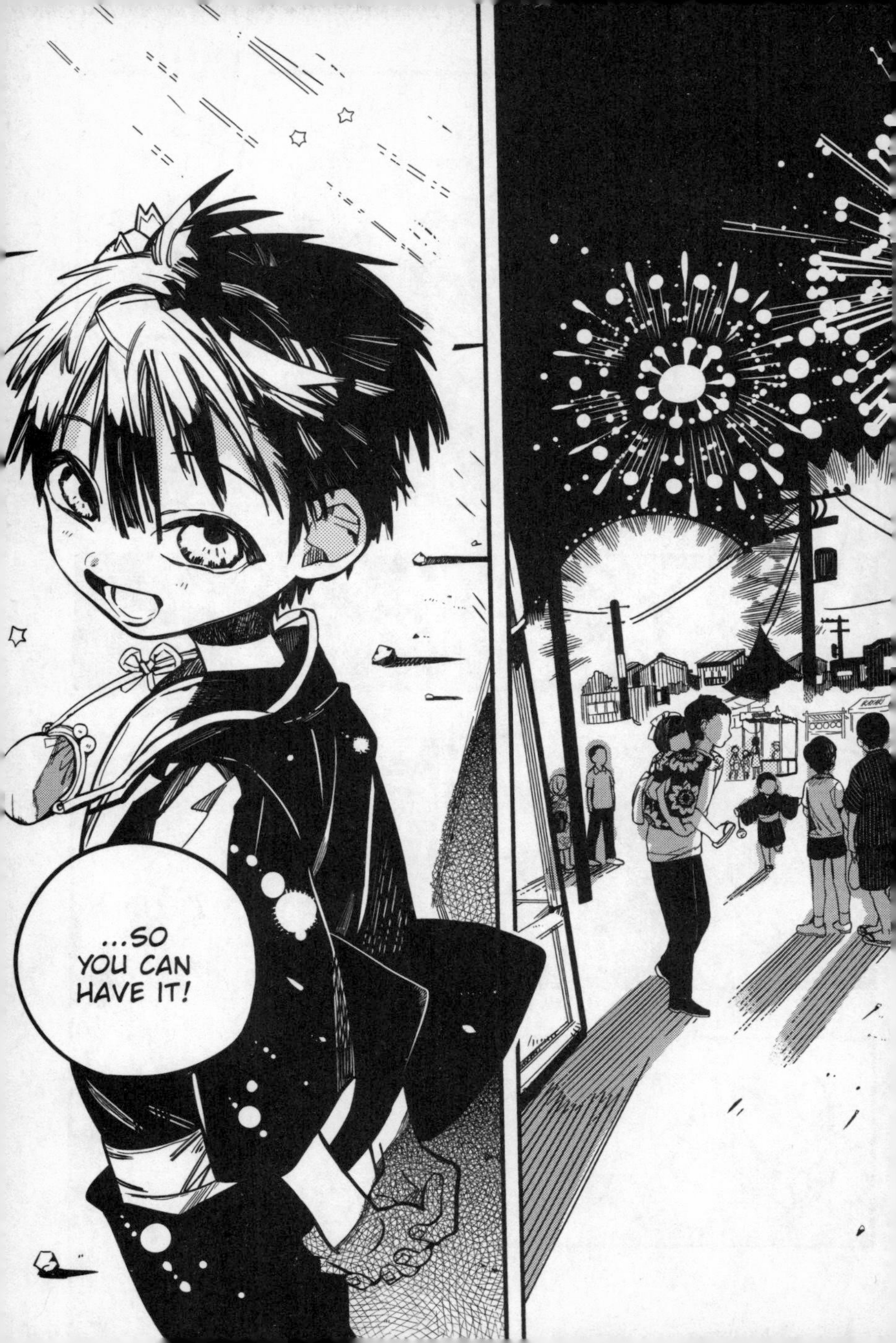
...SO YOU CAN HAVE IT!

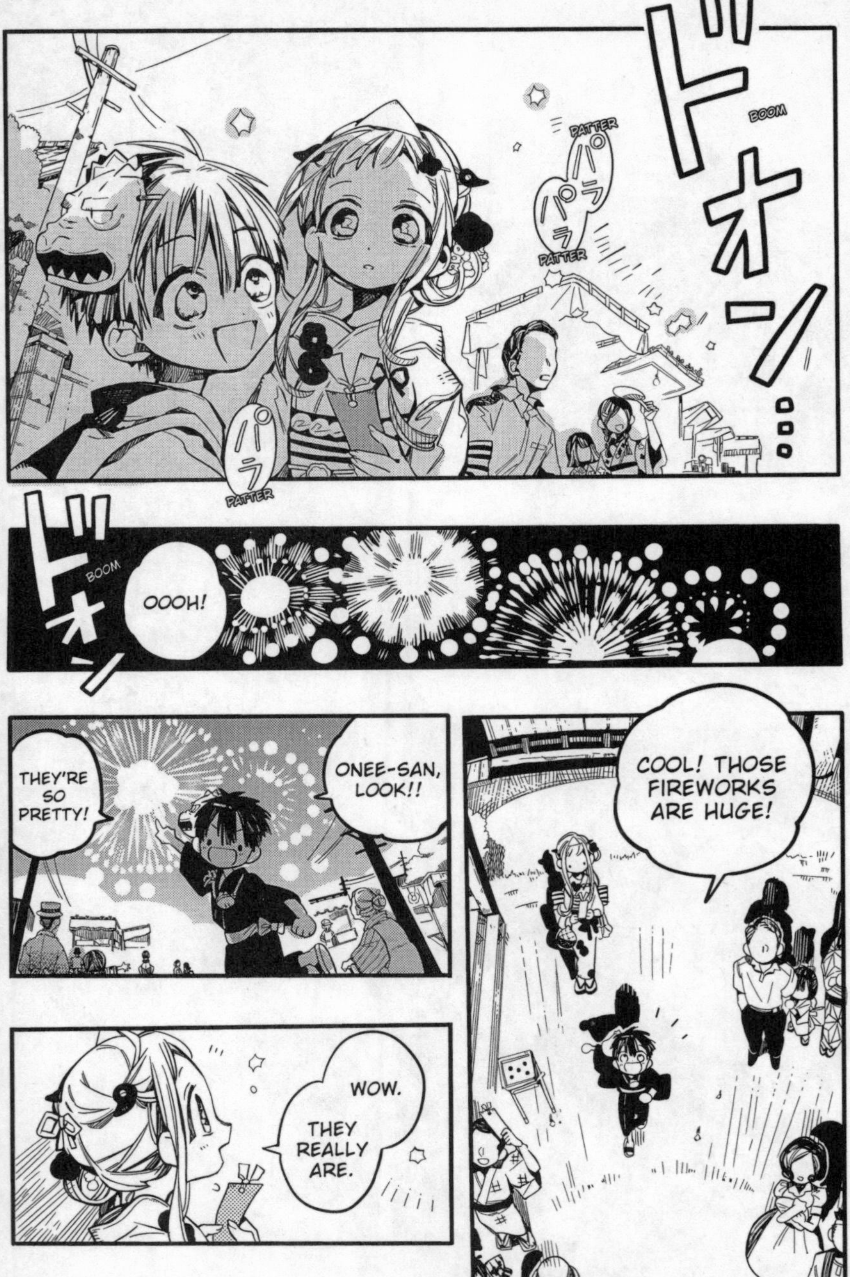
ドオーン…
BOOM
パラパラ
PATTER
PATTER
パラ
PATTER
ドオン
BOOM
OOOH!
COOL! THOSE FIREWORKS ARE HUGE!
ONEE-SAN, LOOK!!
THEY'RE SO PRETTY!
WOW.
THEY REALLY ARE.

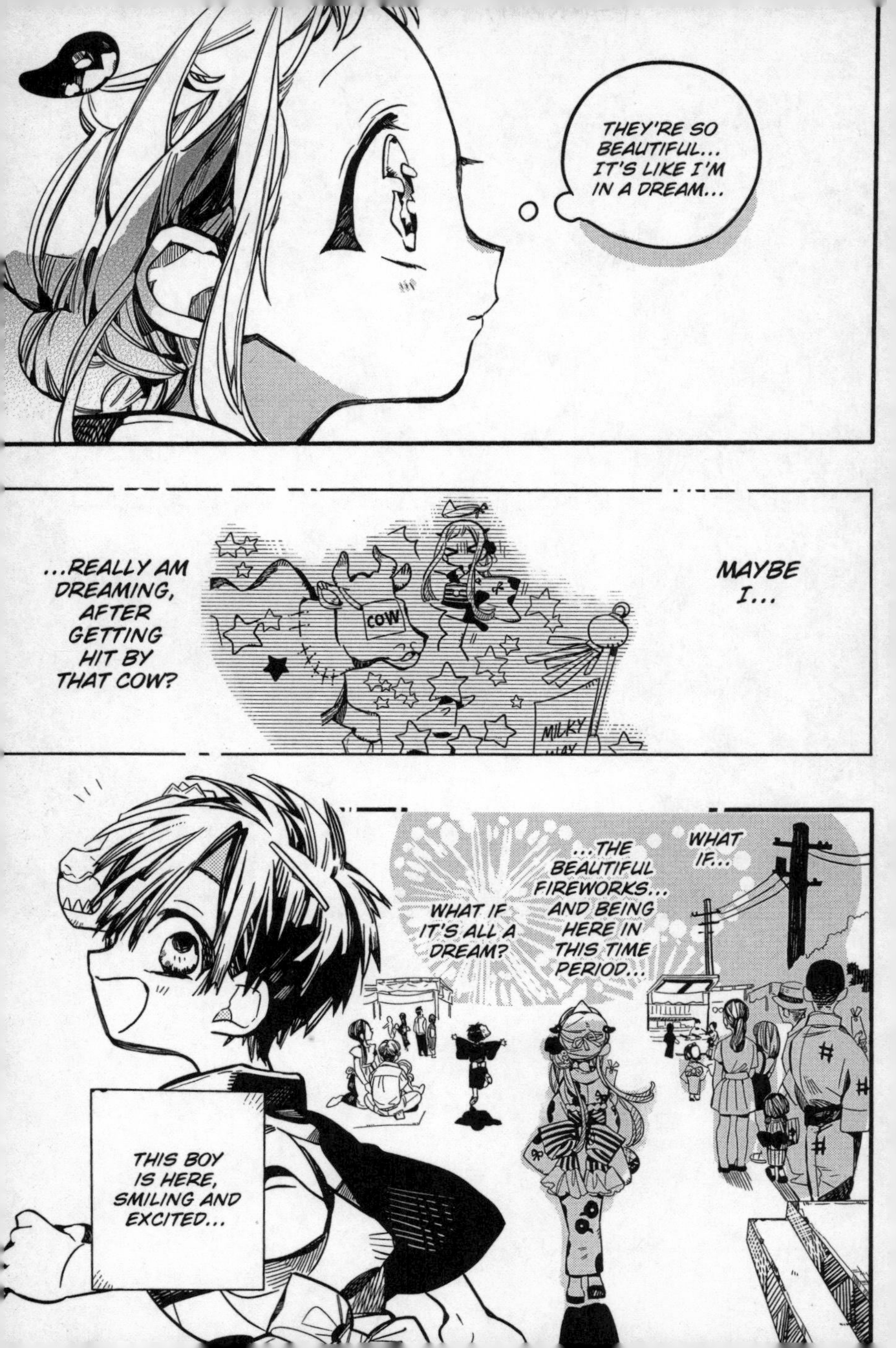
THEY'RE SO BEAUTIFUL... IT'S LIKE I'M IN A DREAM...
MAYBE I...
...REALLY AM DREAMING, AFTER GETTING HIT BY THAT COW?
COW
MILKY
WHAT IF...
...THE BEAUTIFUL FIREWORKS... AND BEING HERE IN THIS TIME PERIOD...
WHAT IF IT'S ALL A DREAM?
THIS BOY IS HERE, SMILING AND EXCITED...

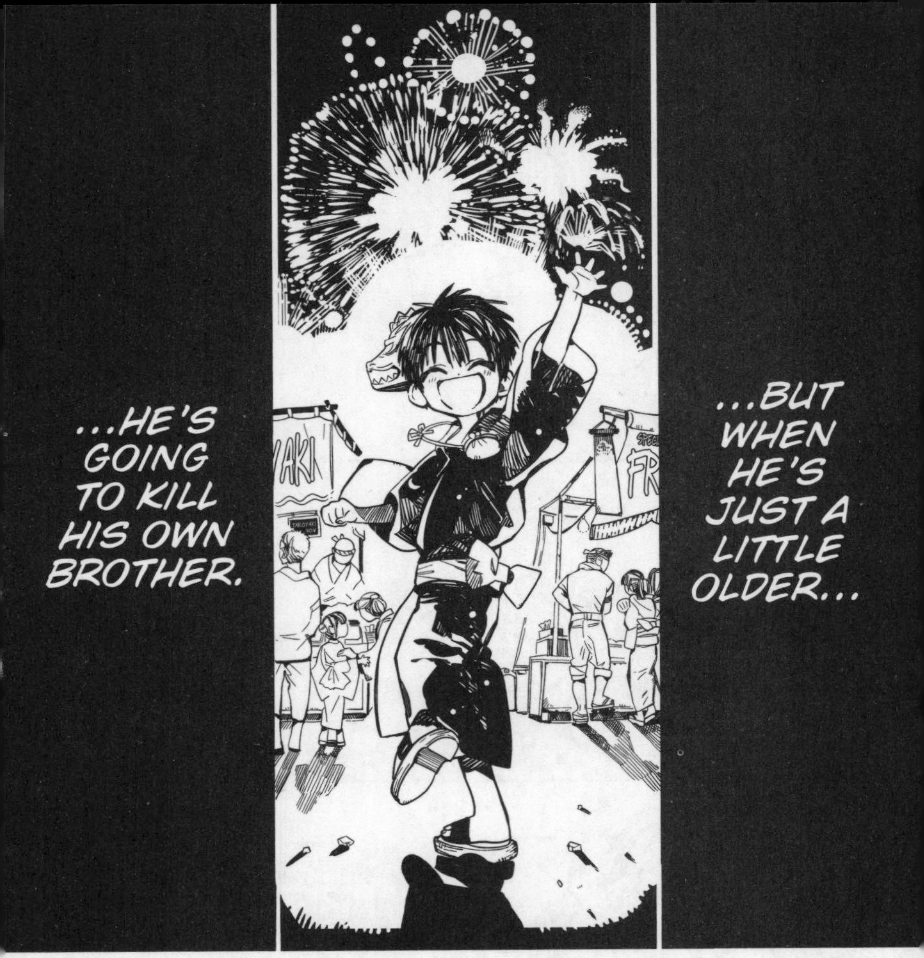
...BUT WHEN HE'S JUST A LITTLE OLDER...
...HE'S GOING TO KILL HIS OWN BROTHER.

IF ONLY THAT WERE ALL THE DREAM.

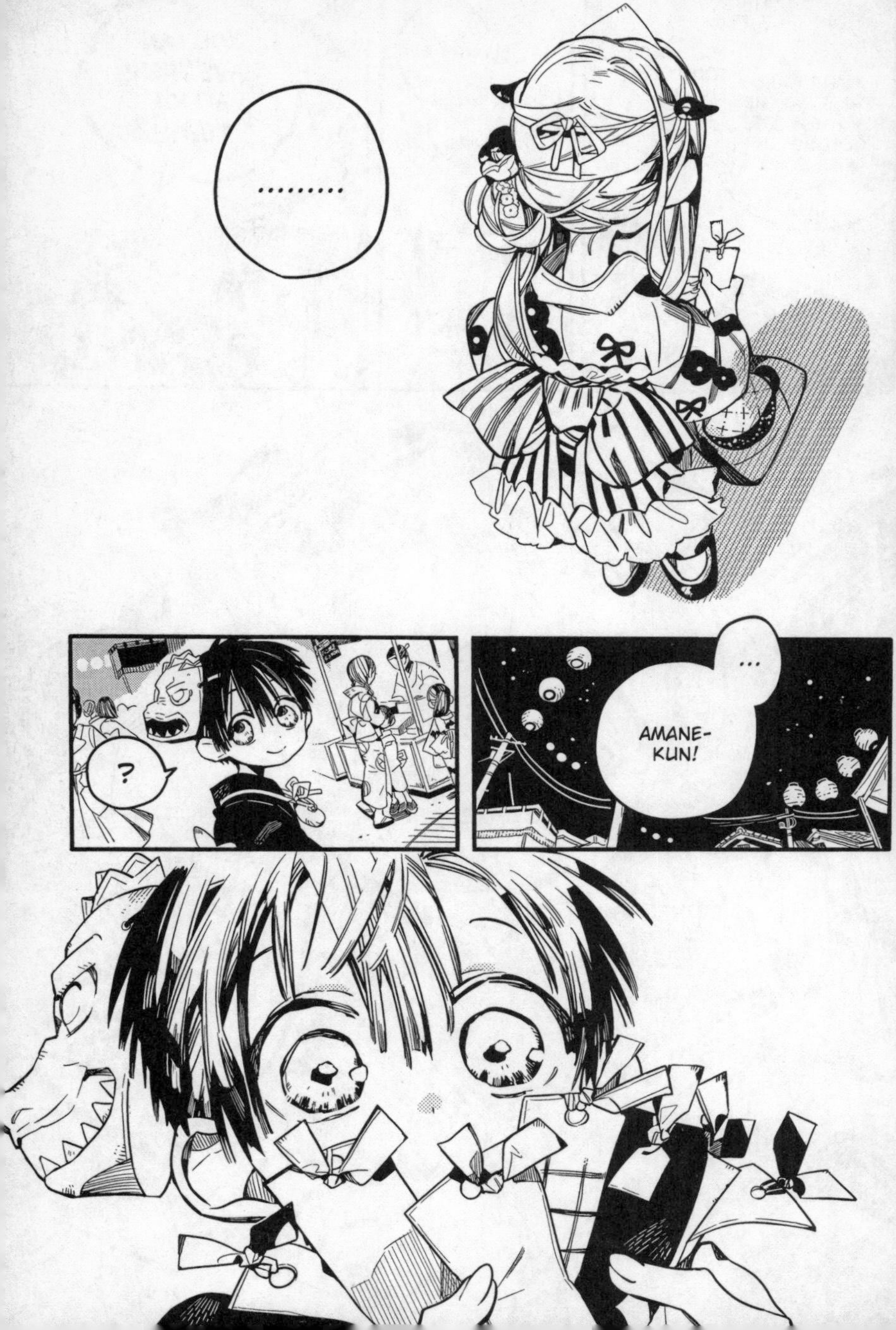

....
...
AMANE-KUN!
?

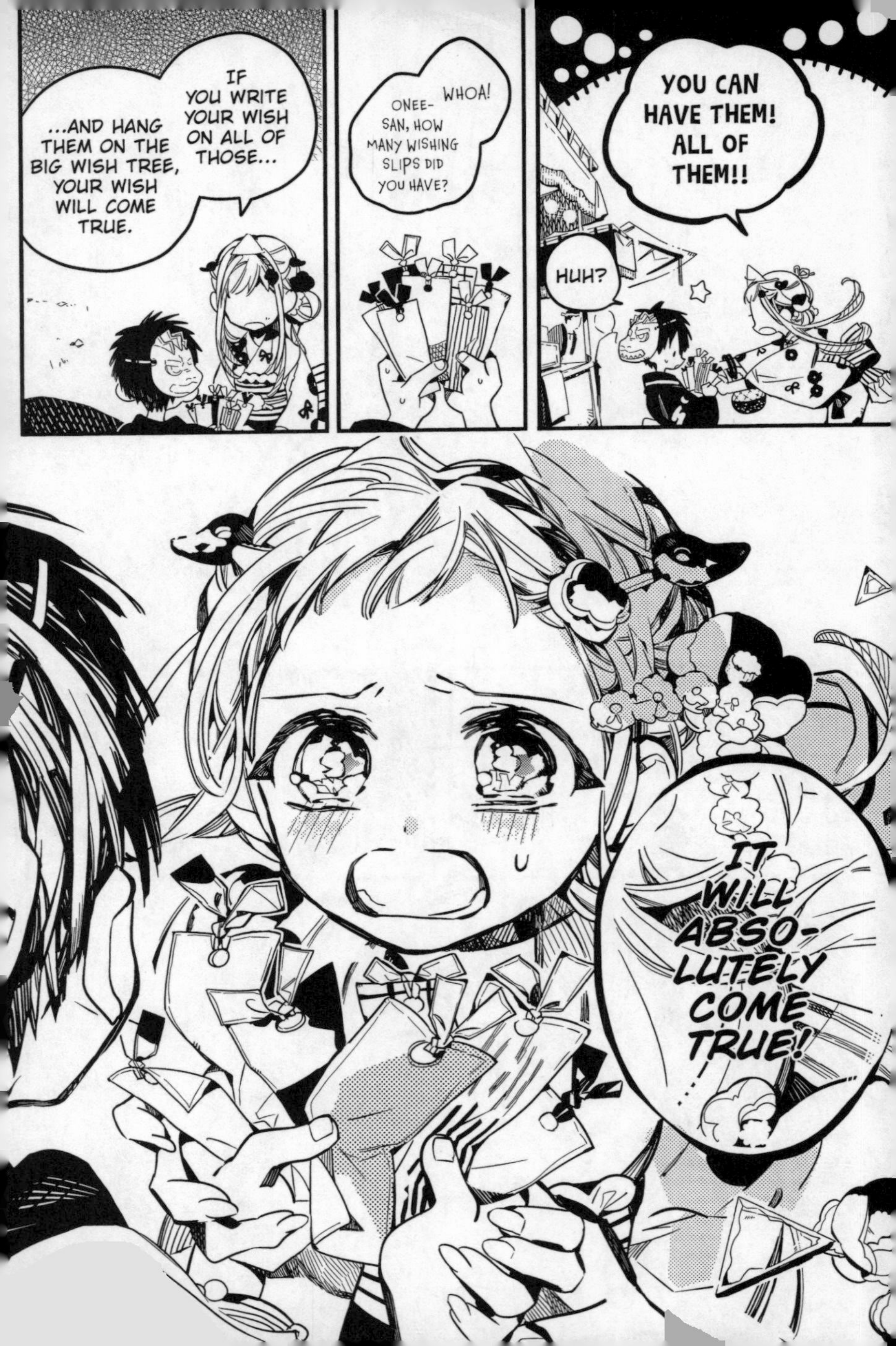

YOU CAN HAVE THEM! ALL OF THEM!!
HUH?
WHOA!
ONEE-SAN, HOW MANY WISHING SLIPS DID YOU HAVE?
IF YOU WRITE YOUR WISH ON ALL OF THOSE...
...AND HANG THEM ON THE BIG WISH TREE, YOUR WISH WILL COME TRUE.
IT WILL ABSO-LUTELY COME TRUE!

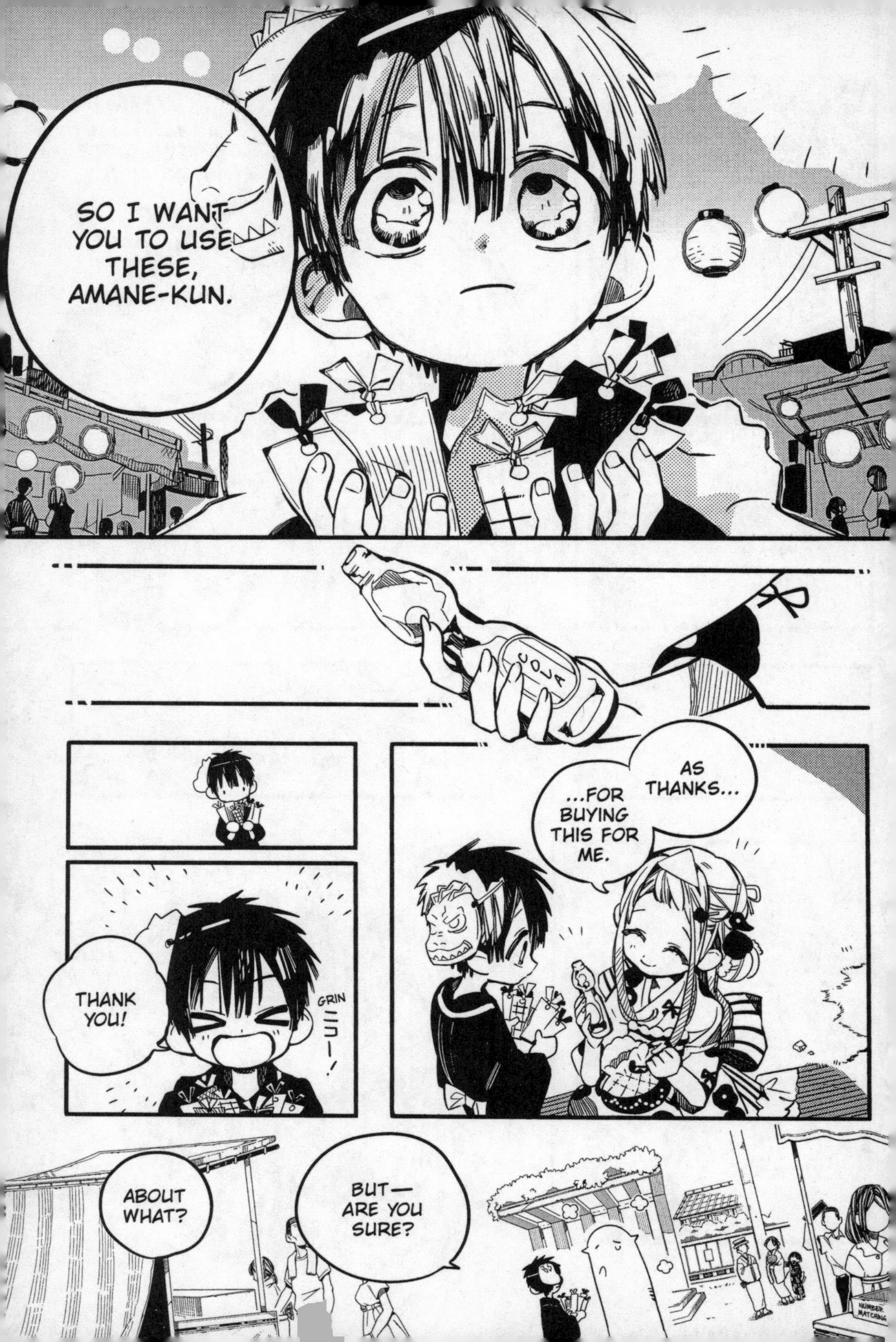

SO I WANT YOU TO USE THESE, AMANE-KUN.
AS THANKS...
...FOR BUYING THIS FOR ME.
THANK YOU!
GRIN
BUT— ARE YOU SURE?
ABOUT WHAT?
NUMBER MATCHING

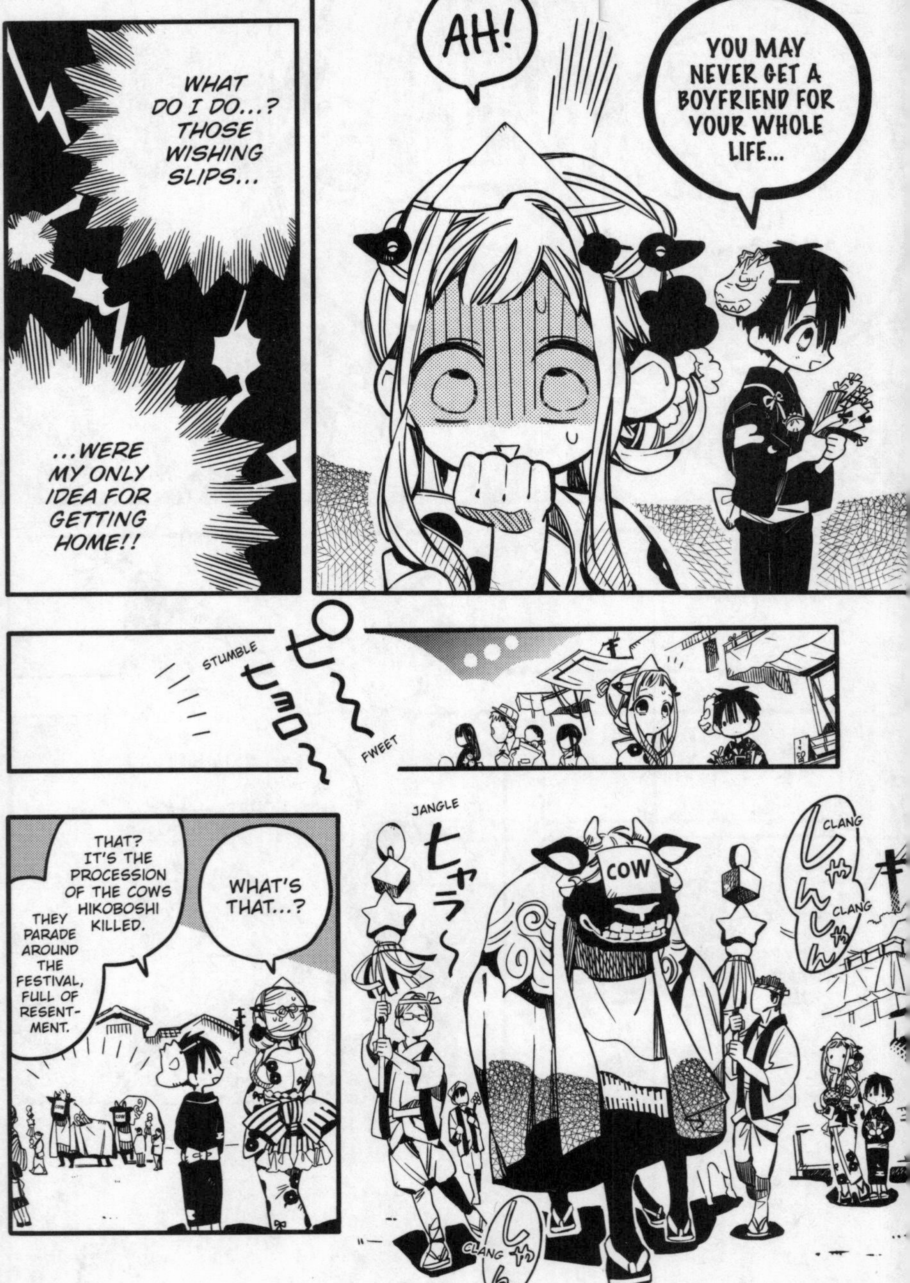
AH!
YOU MAY NEVER GET A BOYFRIEND FOR YOUR WHOLE LIFE...
WHAT DO I DO...? THOSE WISHING SLIPS...
...WERE MY ONLY IDEA FOR GETTING HOME!!
ピ〜
ヒョロ〜
FWEET
STUMBLE
JANGLE
ヒャラ〜
しゃん
CLANG
しゃん
CLANG
COW
しゃん
CLANG
WHAT'S THAT...?
THAT? IT'S THE PROCESSION OF THE COWS HIKOBOSHI KILLED.
THEY PARADE AROUND THE FESTIVAL, FULL OF RESENT-MENT.

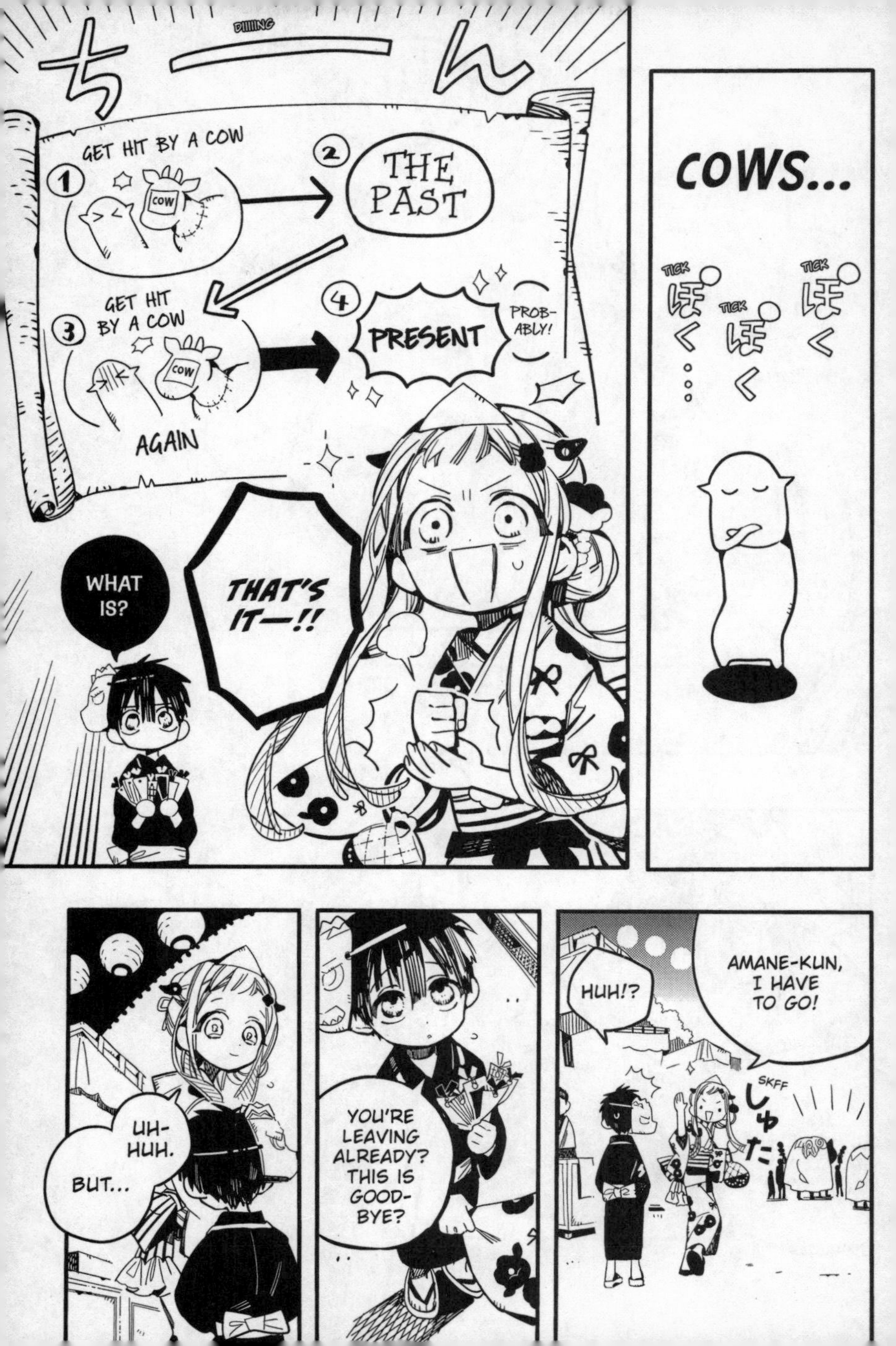
COWS...
TICK
TICK
TICK
ちーん
DIIIING
GET HIT BY A COW
1
COW
2
THE PAST
3
GET HIT BY A COW
COW
AGAIN
4
PRESENT
PROB-ABLY!
THAT'S IT—!!
WHAT IS?
AMANE-KUN, I HAVE TO GO!
HUH!?
SKFF
YOU'RE LEAVING ALREADY? THIS IS GOOD-BYE?
UH-HUH.
BUT...

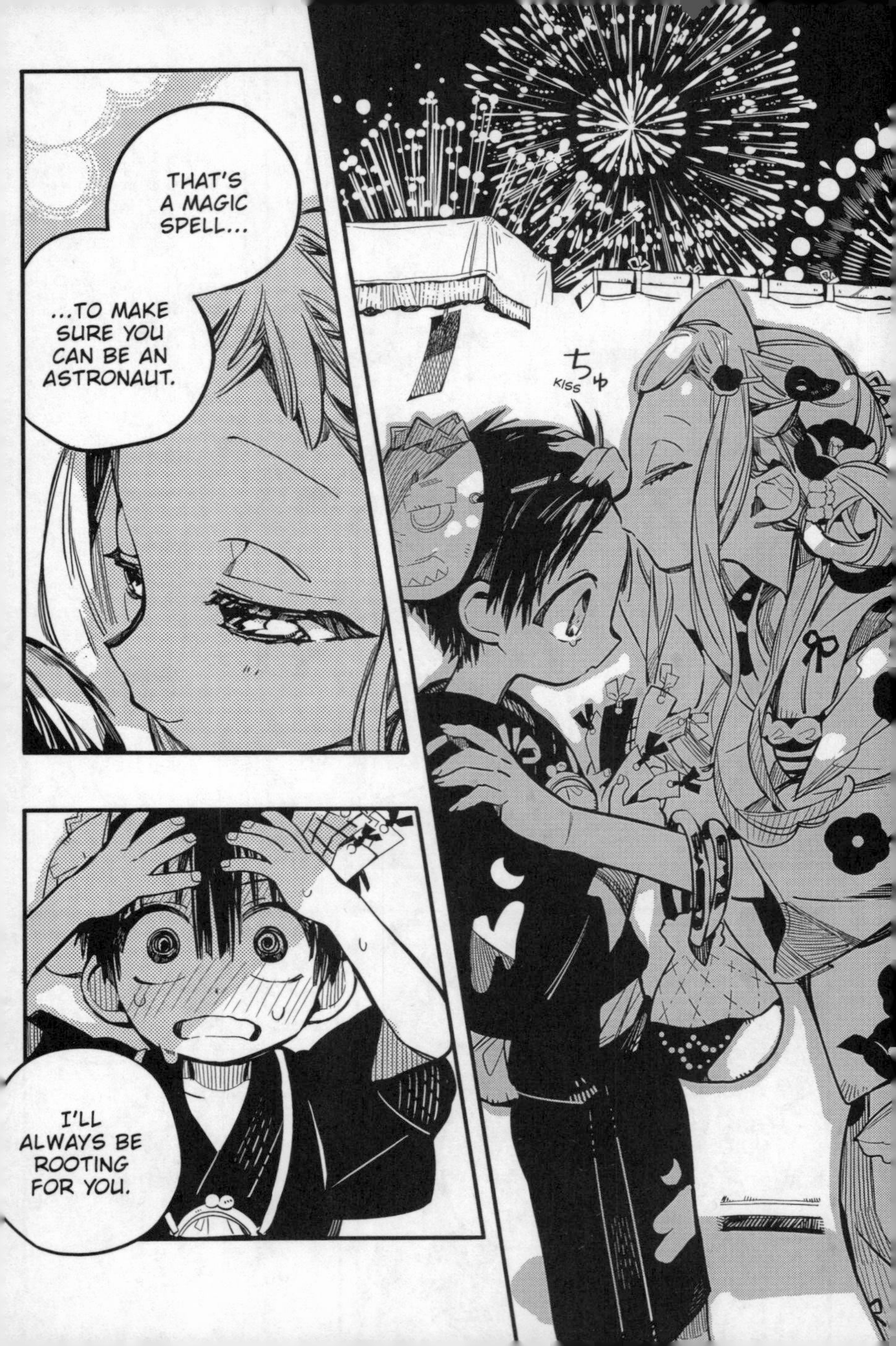
ちゅ KISS
THAT'S A MAGIC SPELL...
...TO MAKE SURE YOU CAN BE AN ASTRONAUT.
I'LL ALWAYS BE ROOTING FOR YOU.

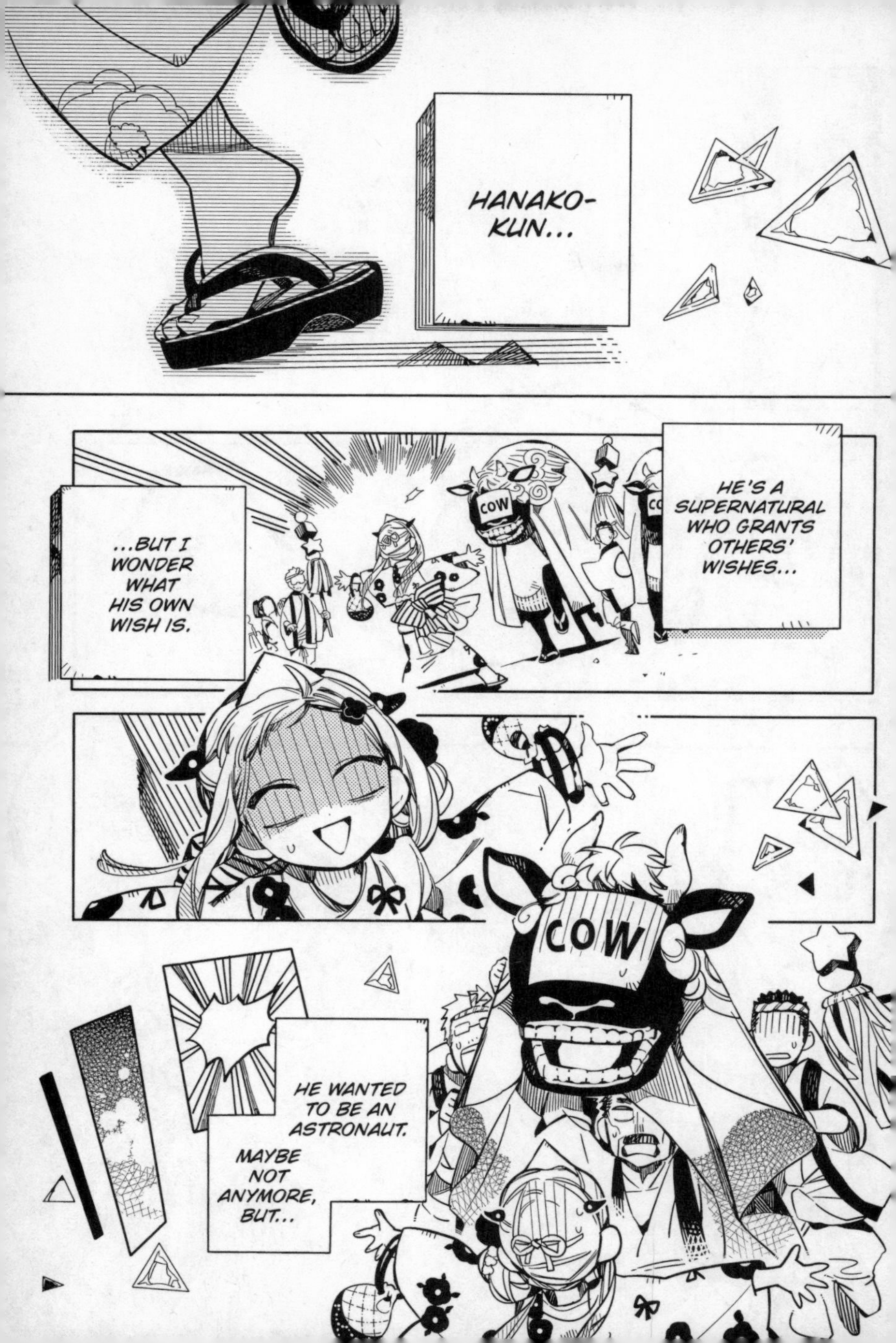

HANAKO-KUN...
HE'S A SUPERNATURAL WHO GRANTS OTHERS' WISHES...
COW
...BUT I WONDER WHAT HIS OWN WISH IS.
COW
HE WANTED TO BE AN ASTRONAUT.
MAYBE NOT ANYMORE, BUT...

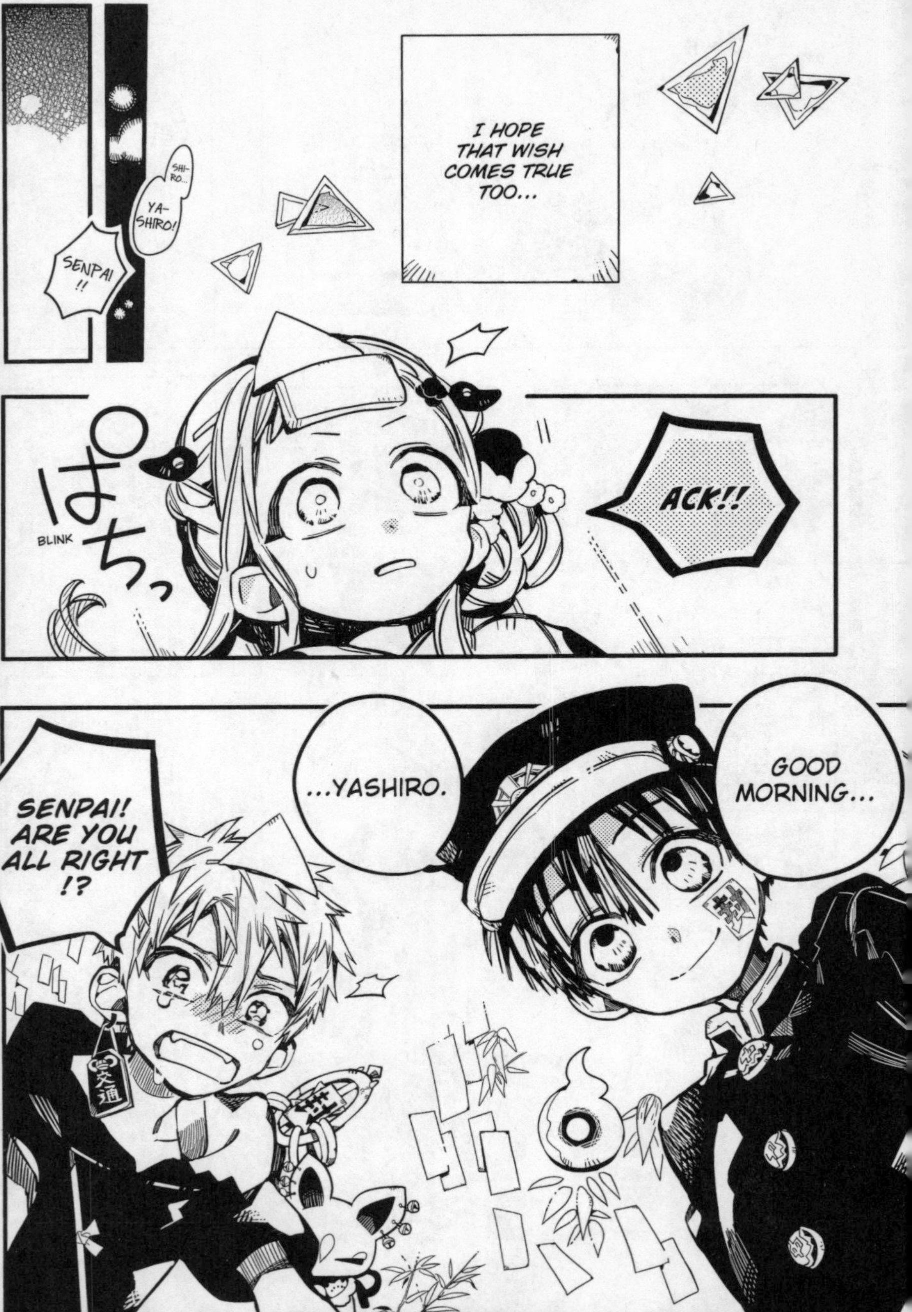
I HOPE THAT WISH COMES TRUE TOO...
SHI-RO...
YA-SHIRO!
SENPAI!!
ACK!!
ぱちっ
BLINK
GOOD MORNING...
...YASHIRO.
SENPAI! ARE YOU ALL RIGHT!?

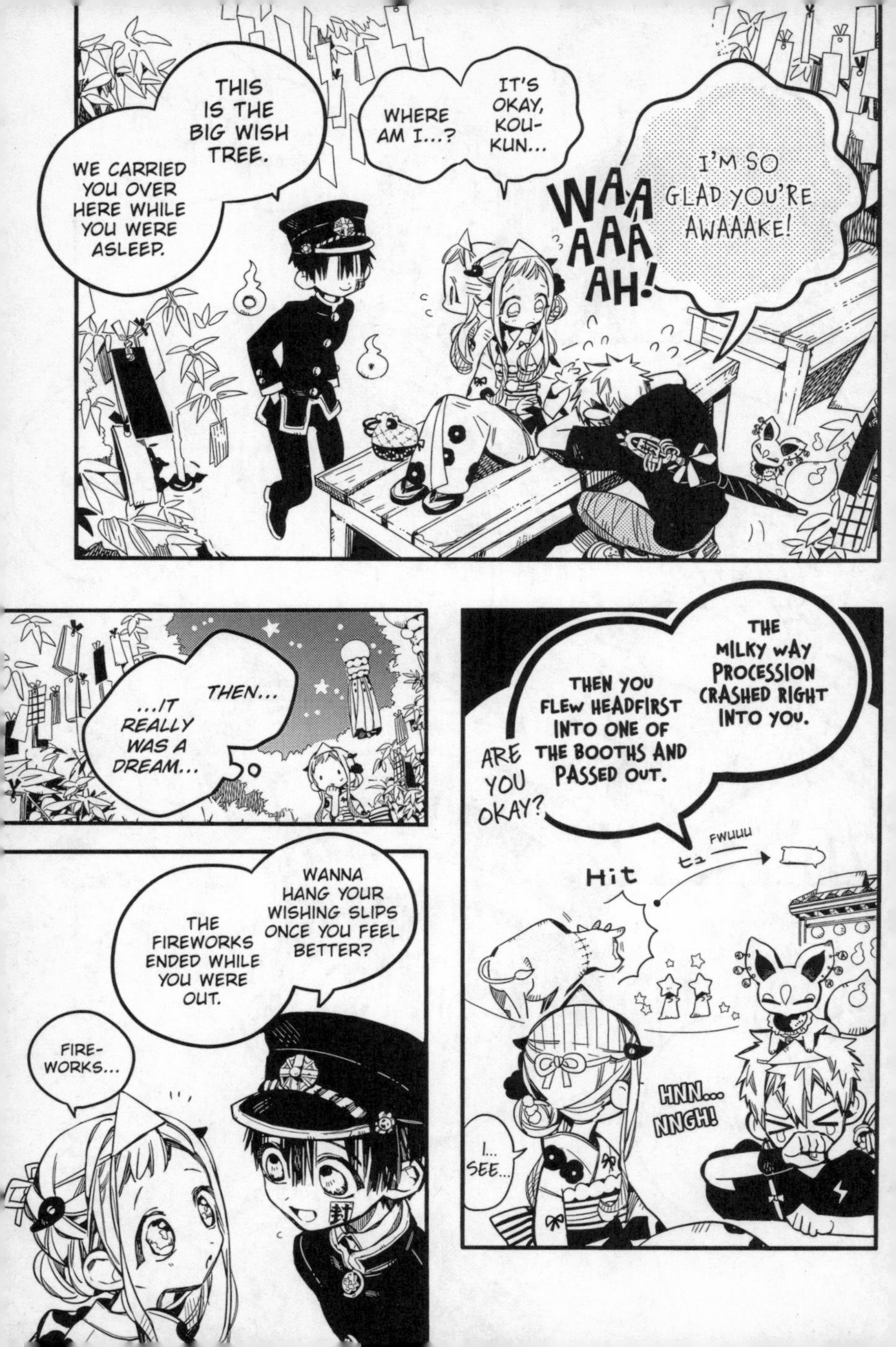
I'M SO GLAD YOU'RE AWAAAKE!
WAAAAAAH!
IT'S OKAY, KOU-KUN...
WHERE AM I...?
THIS IS THE BIG WISH TREE.
WE CARRIED YOU OVER HERE WHILE YOU WERE ASLEEP.
THE MILKY WAY PROCESSION CRASHED RIGHT INTO YOU.
THEN YOU FLEW HEADFIRST INTO ONE OF THE BOOTHS AND PASSED OUT.
ARE YOU OKAY?
ヒュ
FWUUU
Hit
HNN... NNGH!
I... SEE...
THEN...
...IT REALLY WAS A DREAM...
WANNA HANG YOUR WISHING SLIPS ONCE YOU FEEL BETTER?
THE FIREWORKS ENDED WHILE YOU WERE OUT.
FIRE-WORKS...

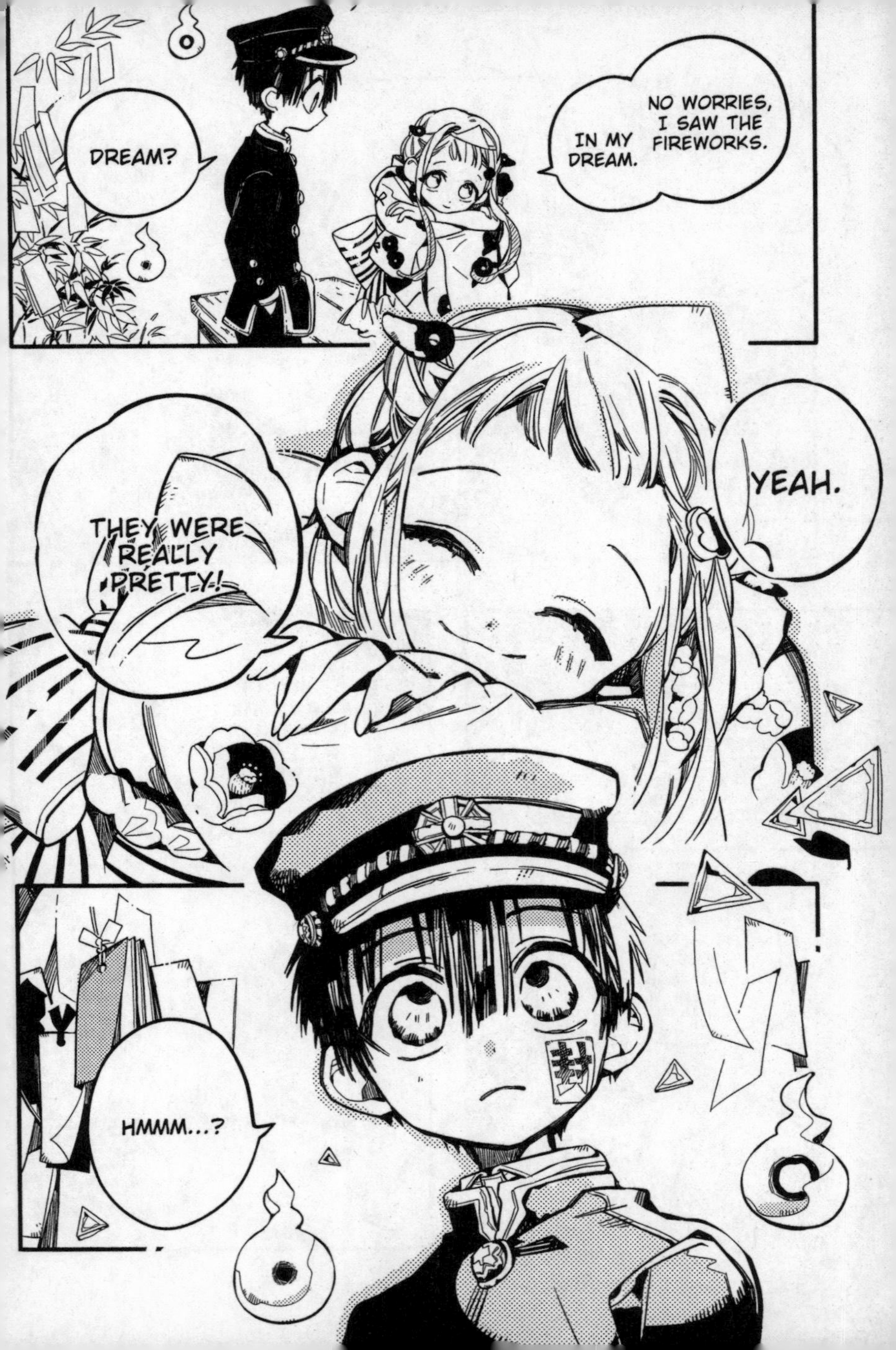
NO WORRIES, I SAW THE FIREWORKS. IN MY DREAM.
DREAM?
YEAH.
THEY WERE REALLY PRETTY!
HMMM...?

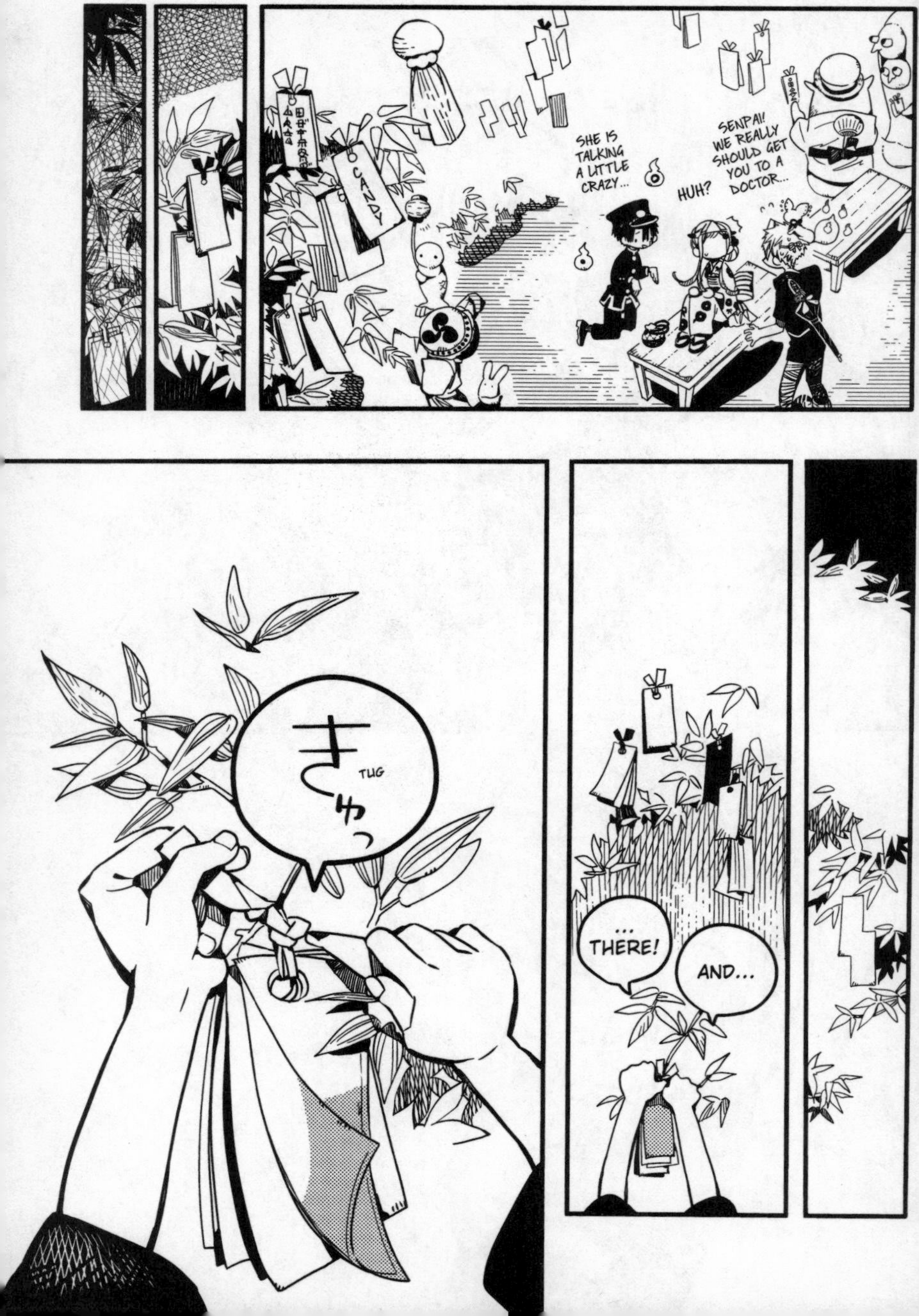
SENPAI! WE REALLY SHOULD GET YOU TO A DOCTOR...
HUH?
SHE IS TALKING A LITTLE CRAZY...
CANDY
...THERE!
AND...
きゅっ
TUG

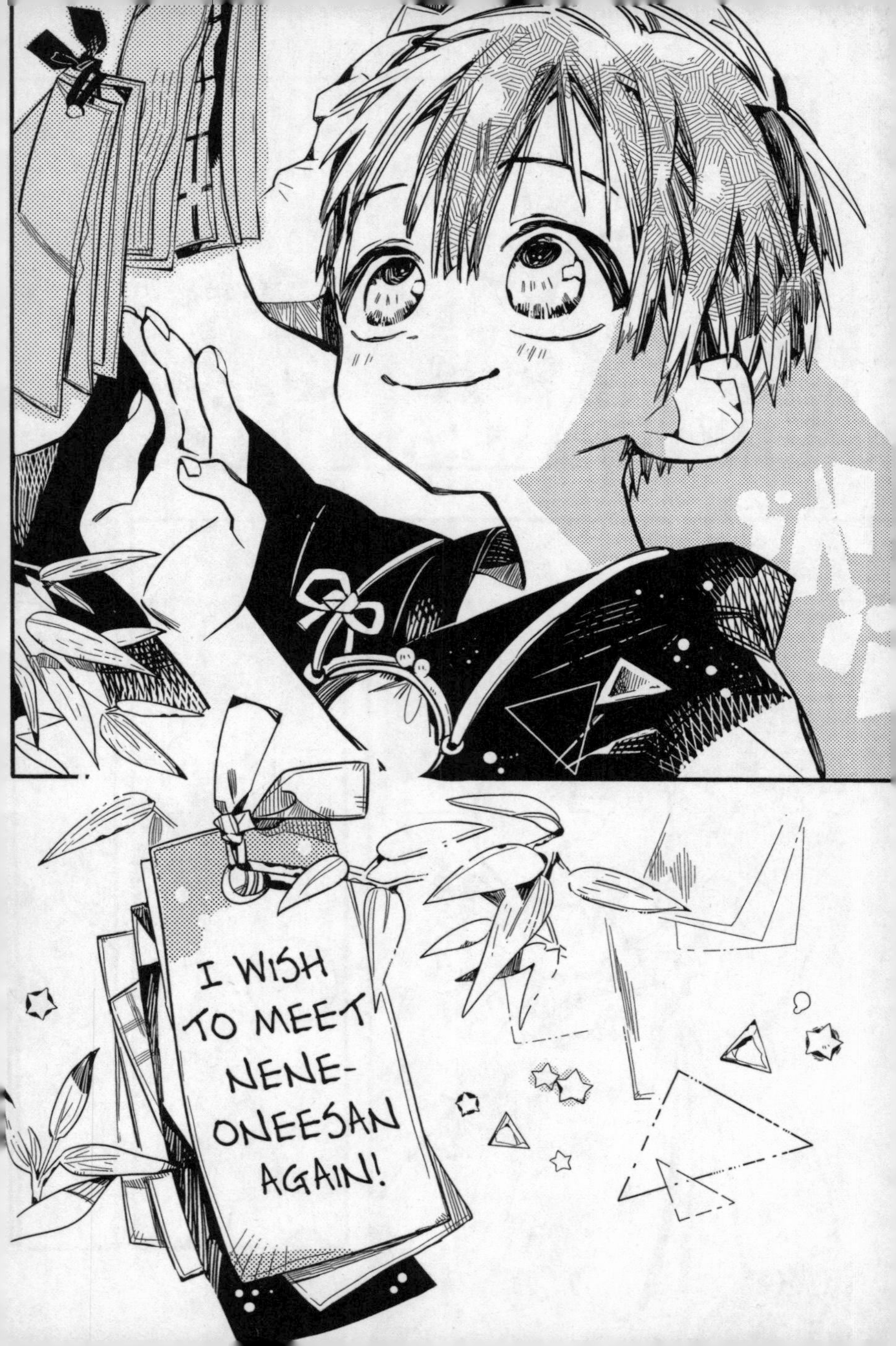
I WISH TO MEET NENE-ONEESAN AGAIN!

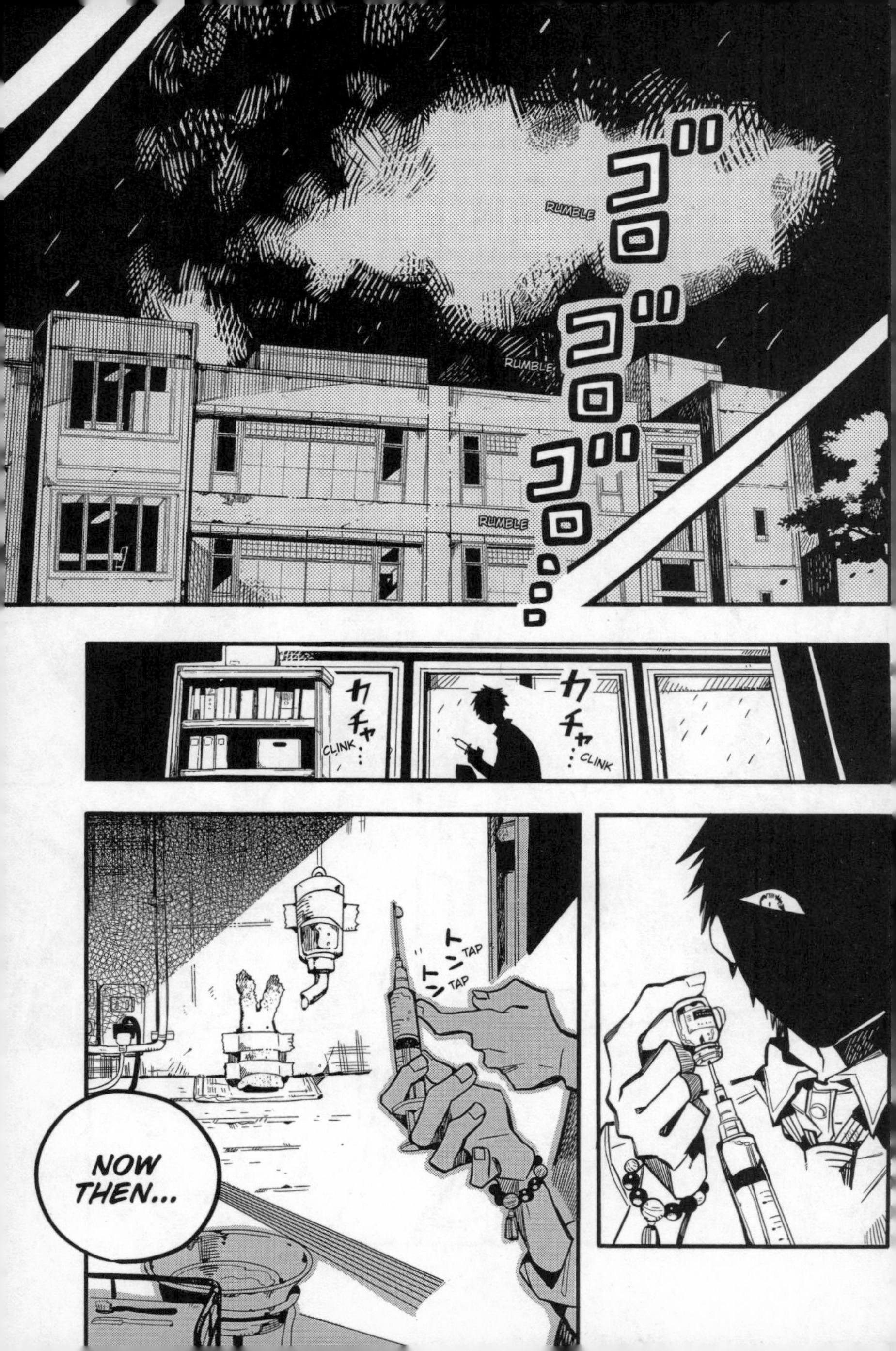
ゴロゴロゴロ...
RUMBLE
RUMBLE
RUMBLE
カチャ...
CLINK
カチャ...
CLINK
トン
TAP
トン
TAP
NOW THEN...

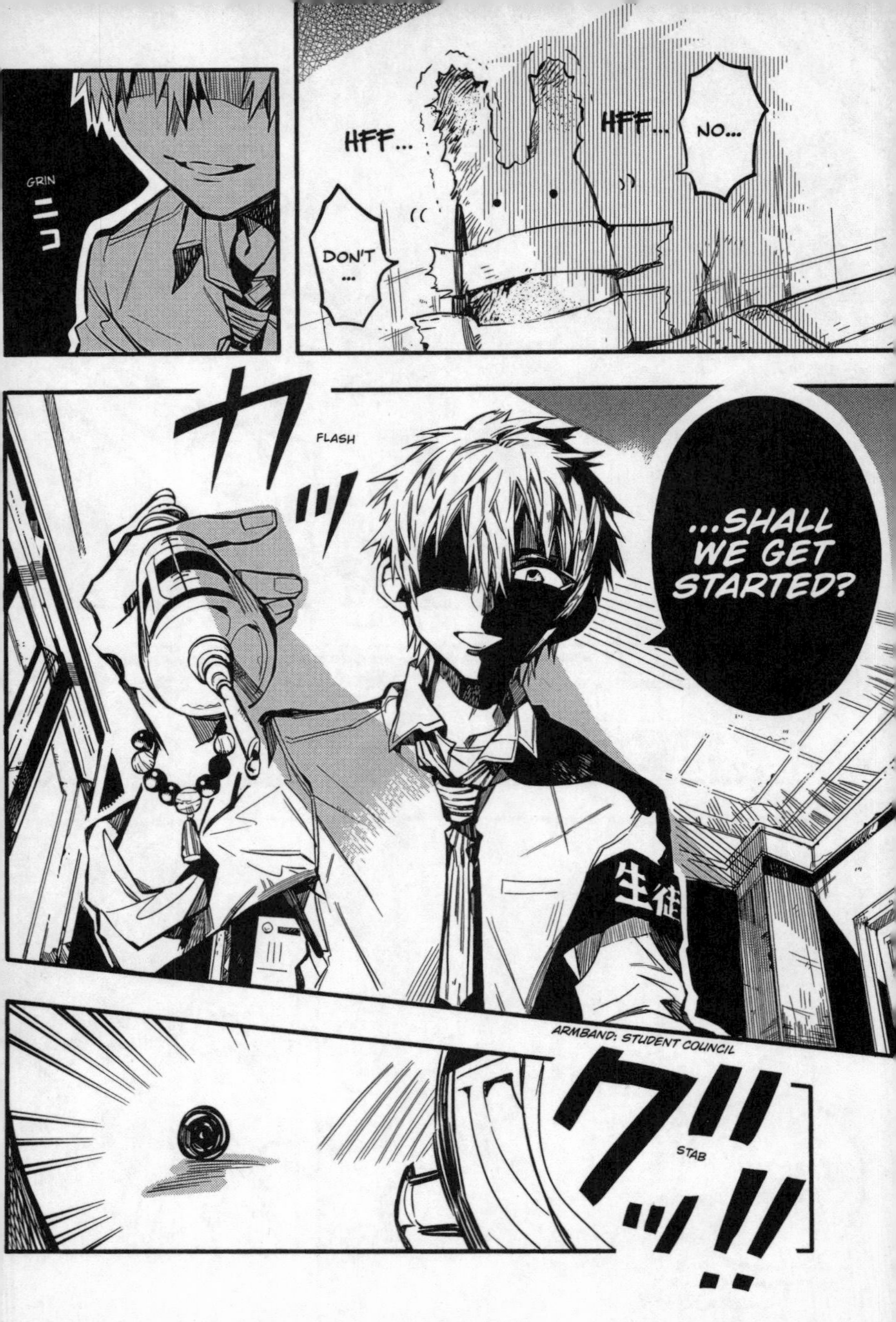
NO...
HFF...
HFF...
DON'T ...
GRIN
ニコ
...SHALL WE GET STARTED?
カッ
FLASH
生徒
ARMBAND: STUDENT COUNCIL
グッ!!
STAB

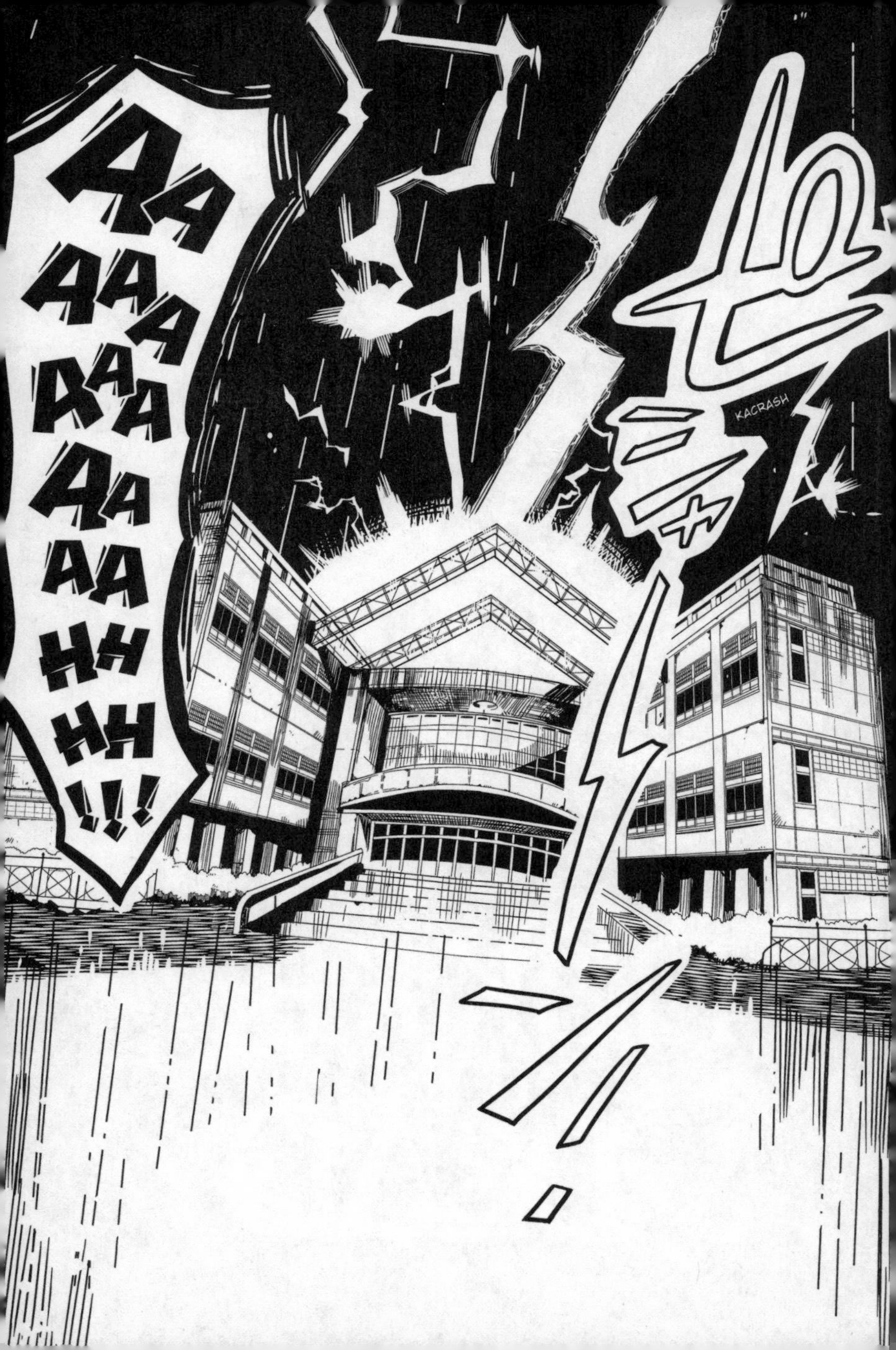
AAAAAAAAAAAAAHHHH!!!
KACRASH

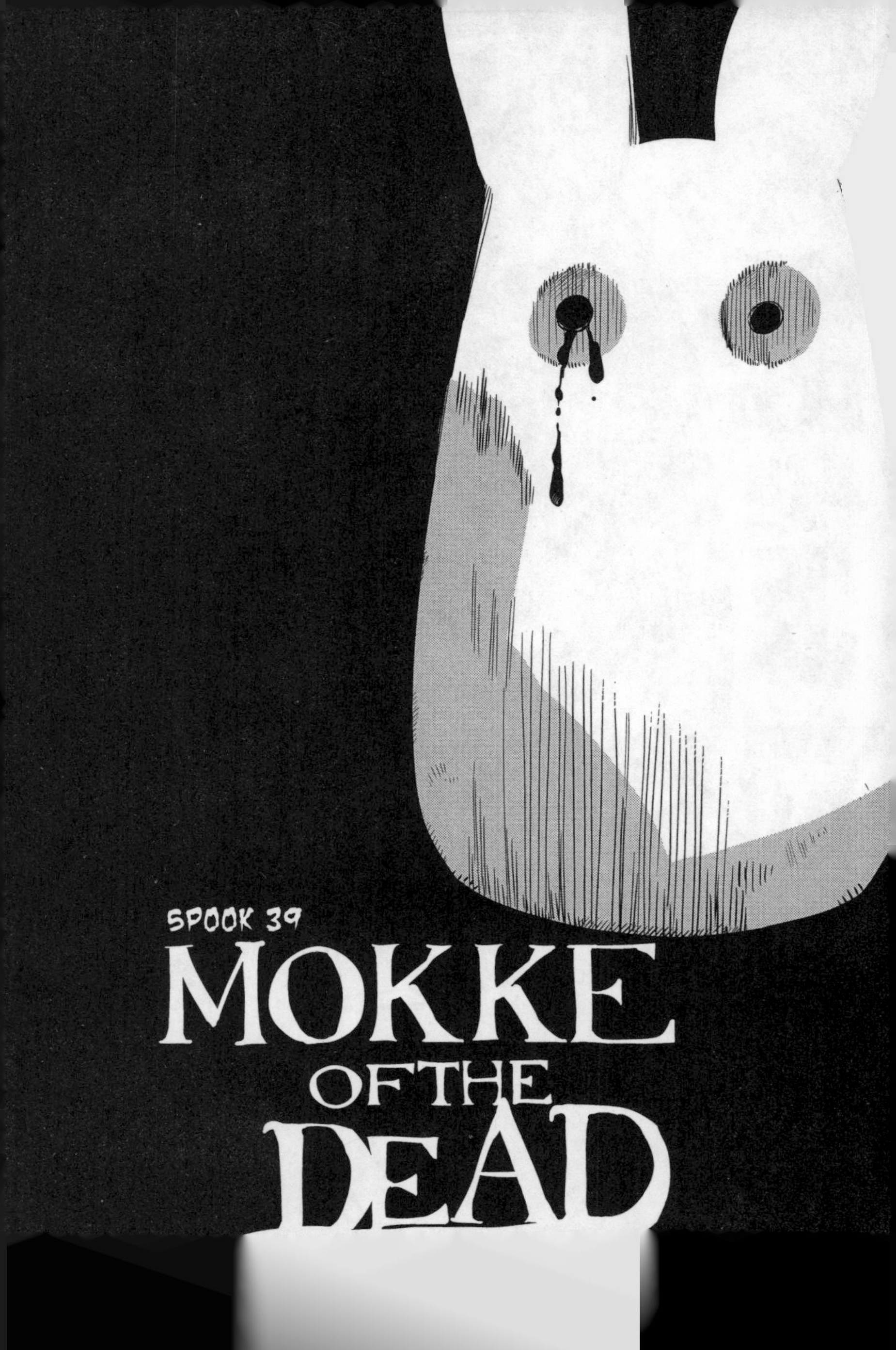
SPOOK 39
MOKKE OF THE DEAD

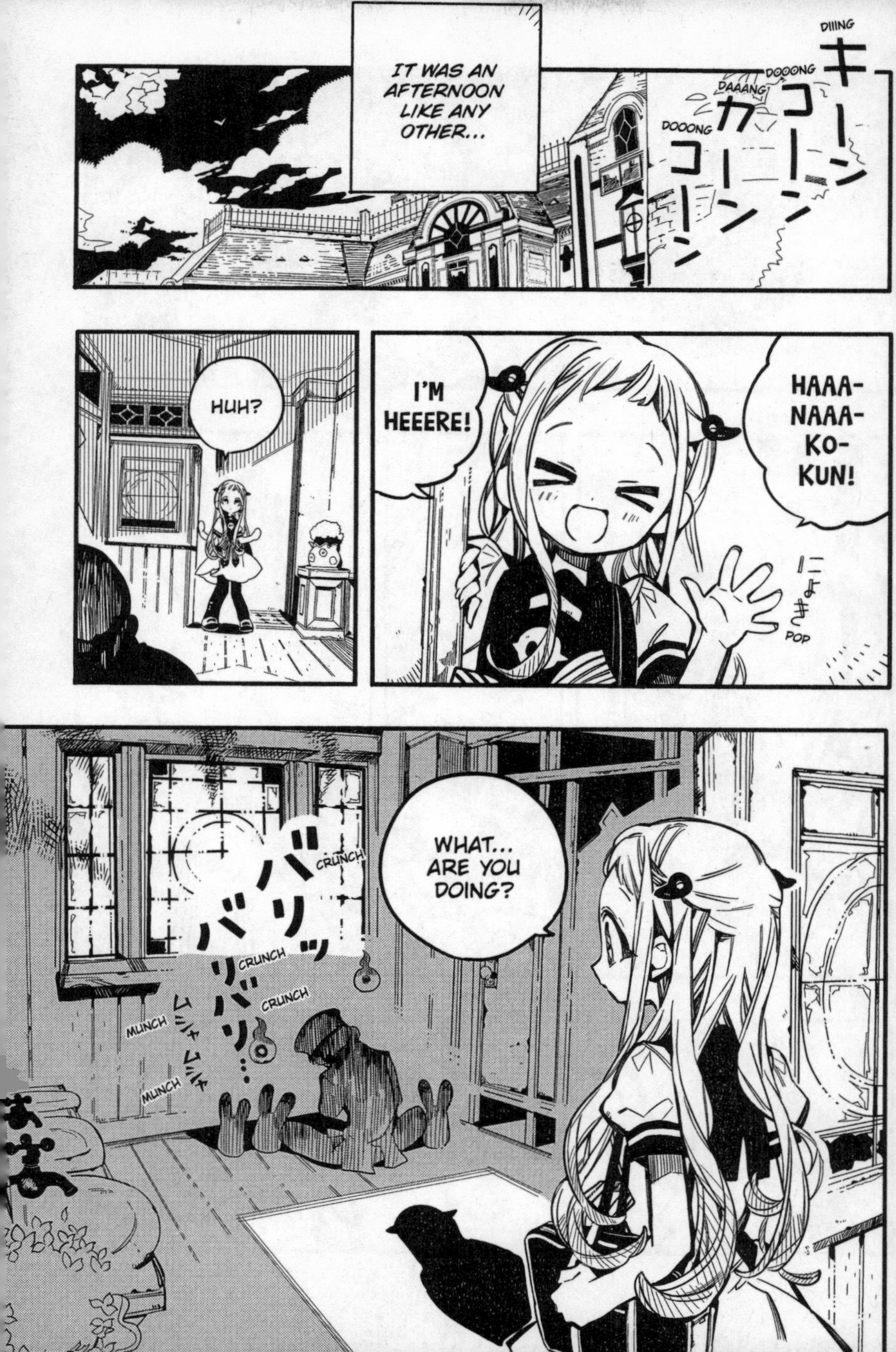

DIIING
DOOONG
DAAANG
DOOONG
IT WAS AN AFTERNOON LIKE ANY OTHER...
HAAA-NAAA-KO-KUN!
I'M HEEERE!
POP
HUH?
WHAT... ARE YOU DOING?
CRUNCH
CRUNCH
CRUNCH
MUNCH
MUNCH

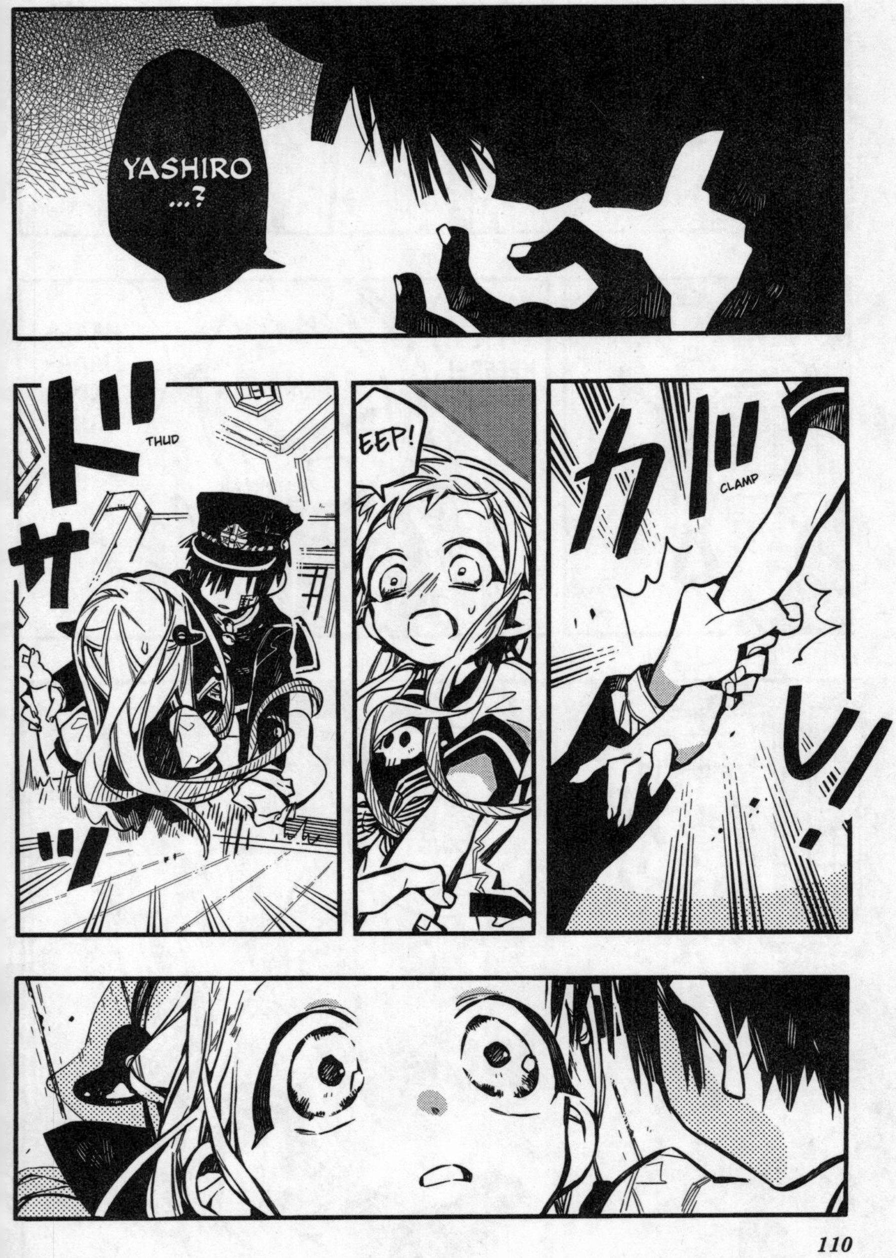
YASHIRO ...?
ガッ
CLAMP
EEP!
ドサッ
THUD

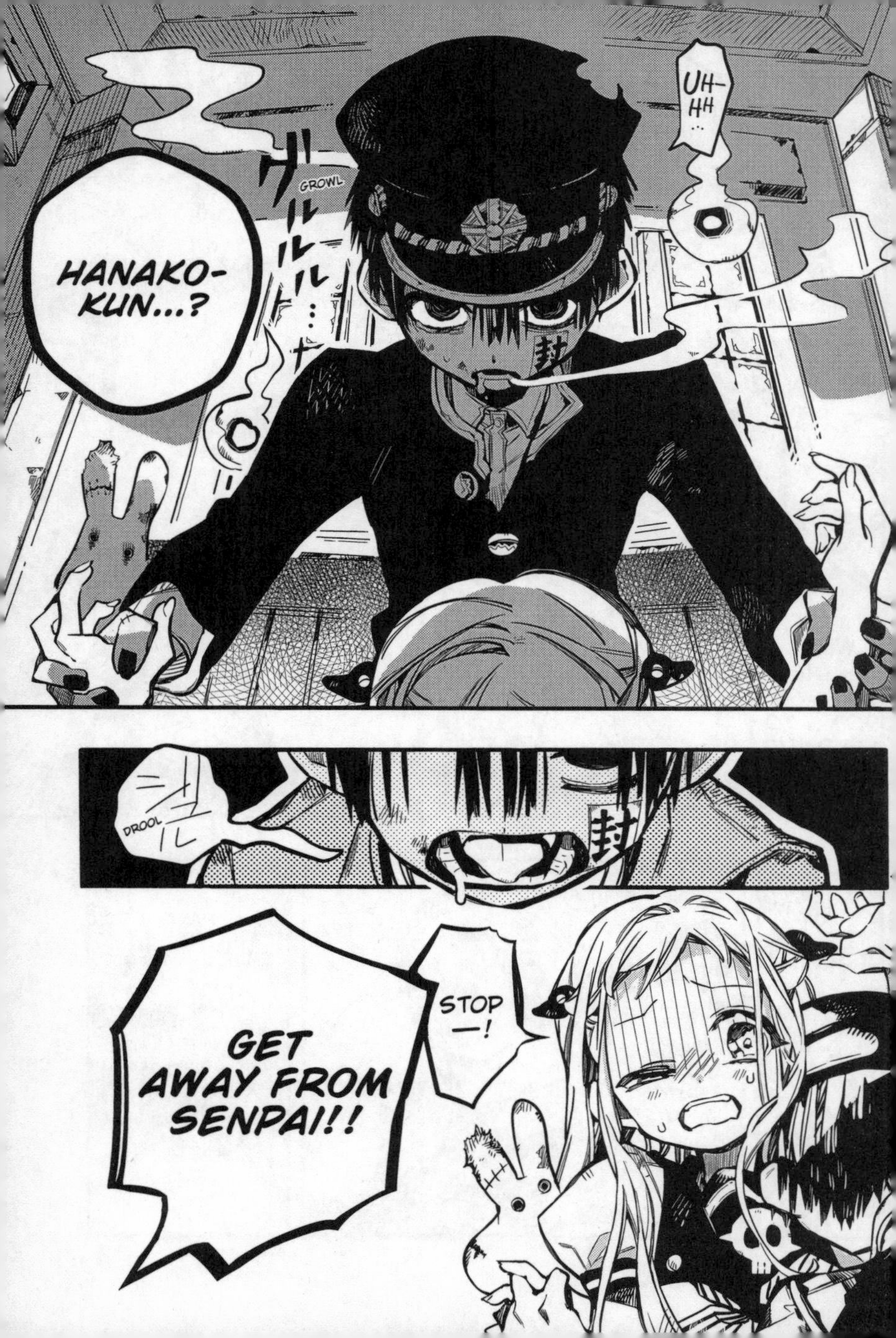
UH-HH...
GROWL
HANAKO-KUN...?
DROOL
STOP—!
GET AWAY FROM SENPAI!!

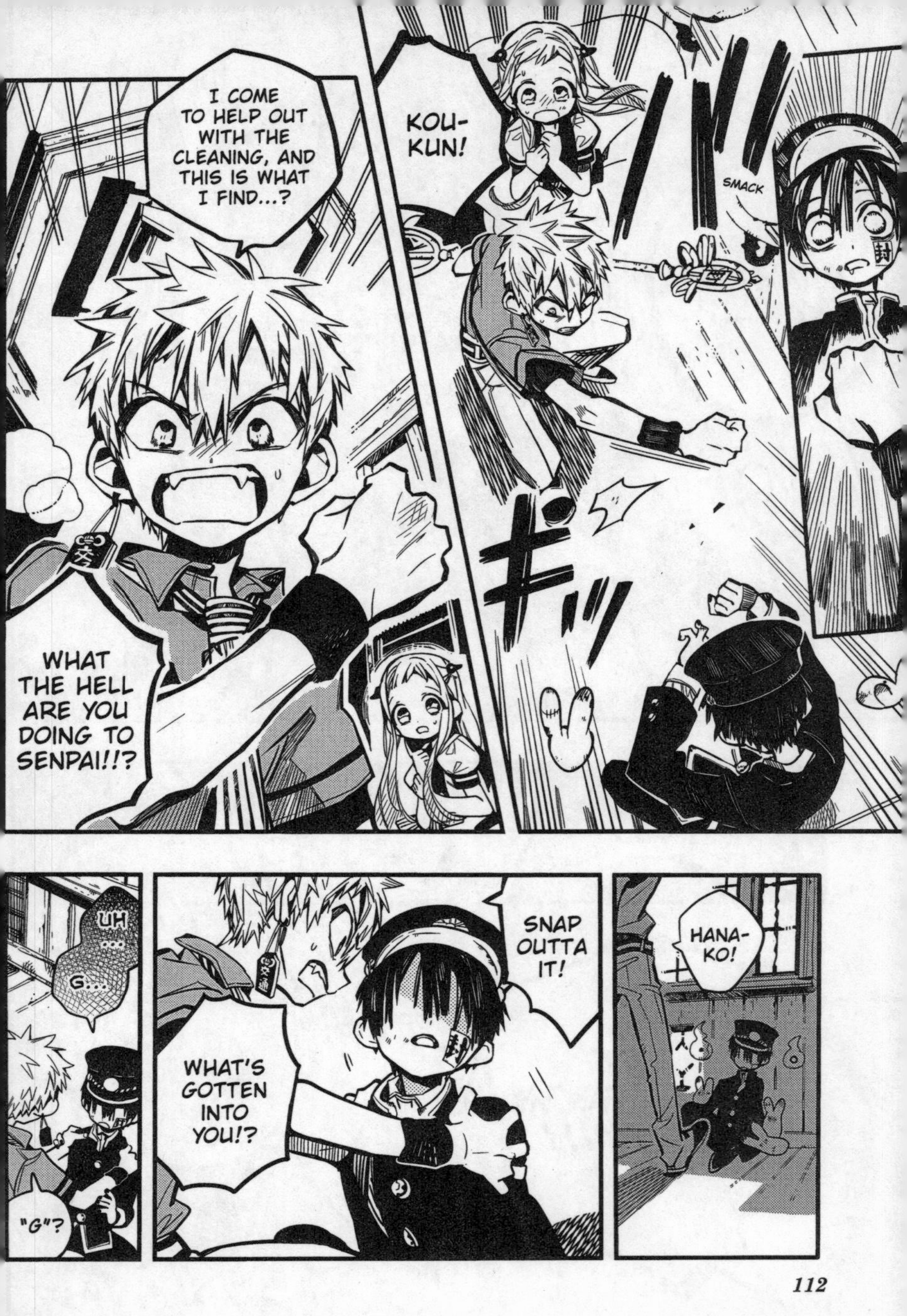
KOU-KUN!
SMACK
ギッ
I COME TO HELP OUT WITH THE CLEANING, AND THIS IS WHAT I FIND...?
WHAT THE HELL ARE YOU DOING TO SENPAI!!?
HANA-KO!
SNAP OUTTA IT!
WHAT'S GOTTEN INTO YOU!?
UH ...
G...
"G"?

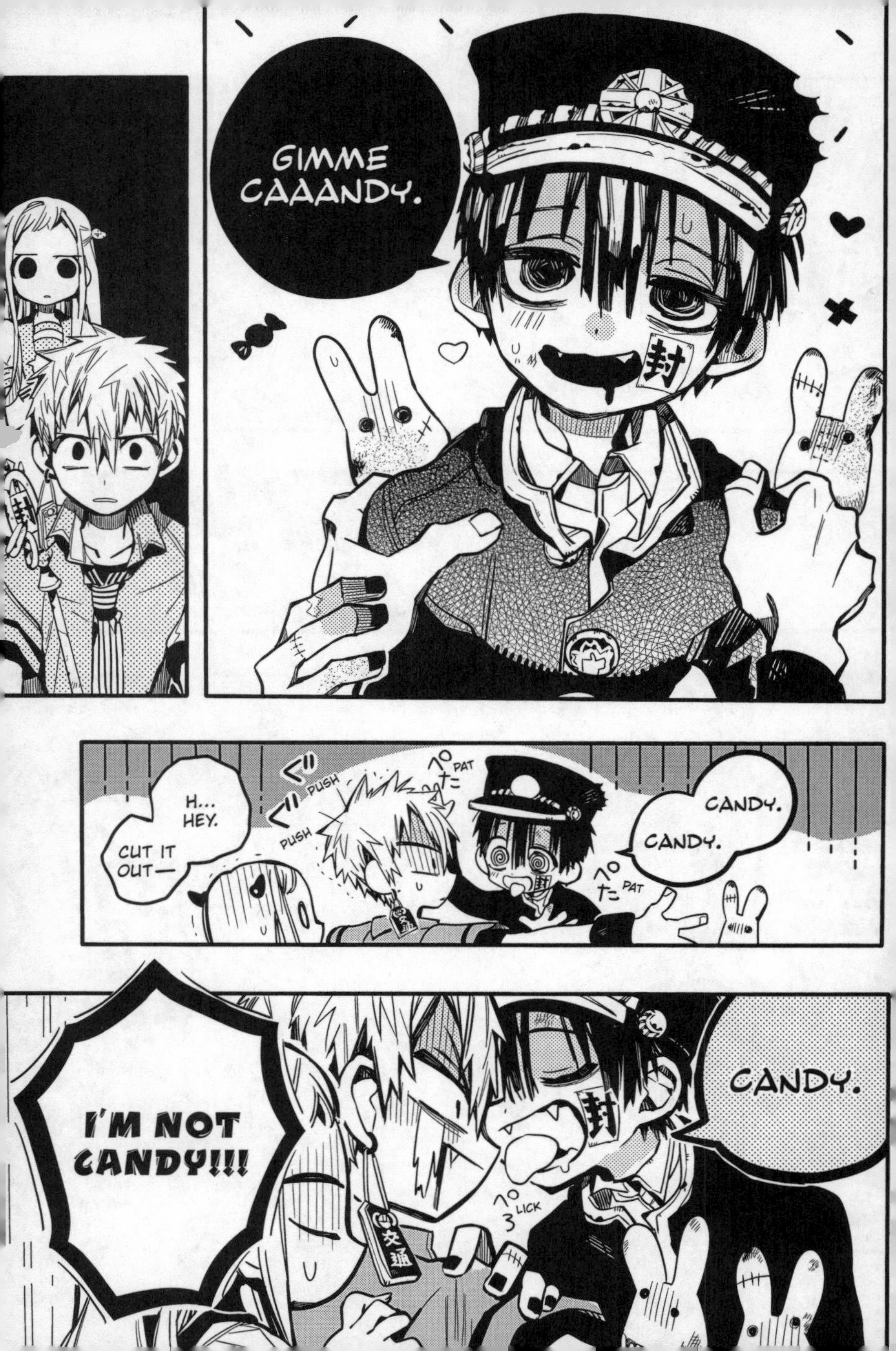

GIMME CAAANDY.
CANDY.
CANDY.
ぺた PAT
ぺた PAT
ぐい PUSH
ぐい PUSH
H... HEY.
CUT IT OUT—
CANDY.
ぺろ LICK
I'M NOT CANDY!!!

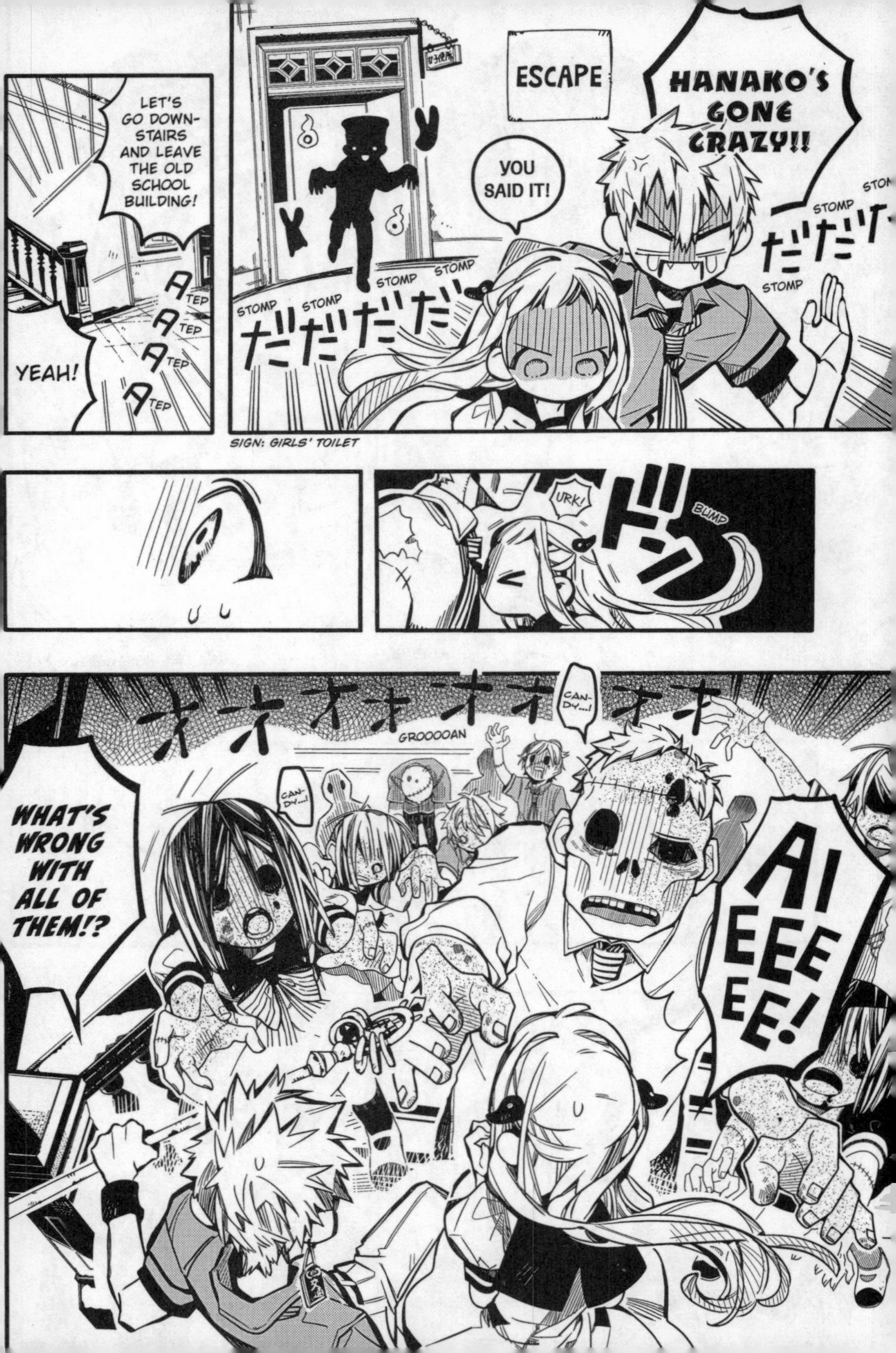
ESCAPE
HANAKO'S GONE CRAZY!!
YOU SAID IT!
STOMP STOMP STOMP STOMP
だだだだ
STOMP STOMP
だだだ
SIGN: GIRLS' TOILET
LET'S GO DOWN-STAIRS AND LEAVE THE OLD SCHOOL BUILDING!
YEAH!
ATEP ATEP ATEP ATEP
URK!
ドン
BUMP
オオオオオオオ
GROOOOAN
CAN-DY...!
CAN-DY...!
AIEEEEEE!
WHAT'S WRONG WITH ALL OF THEM!?

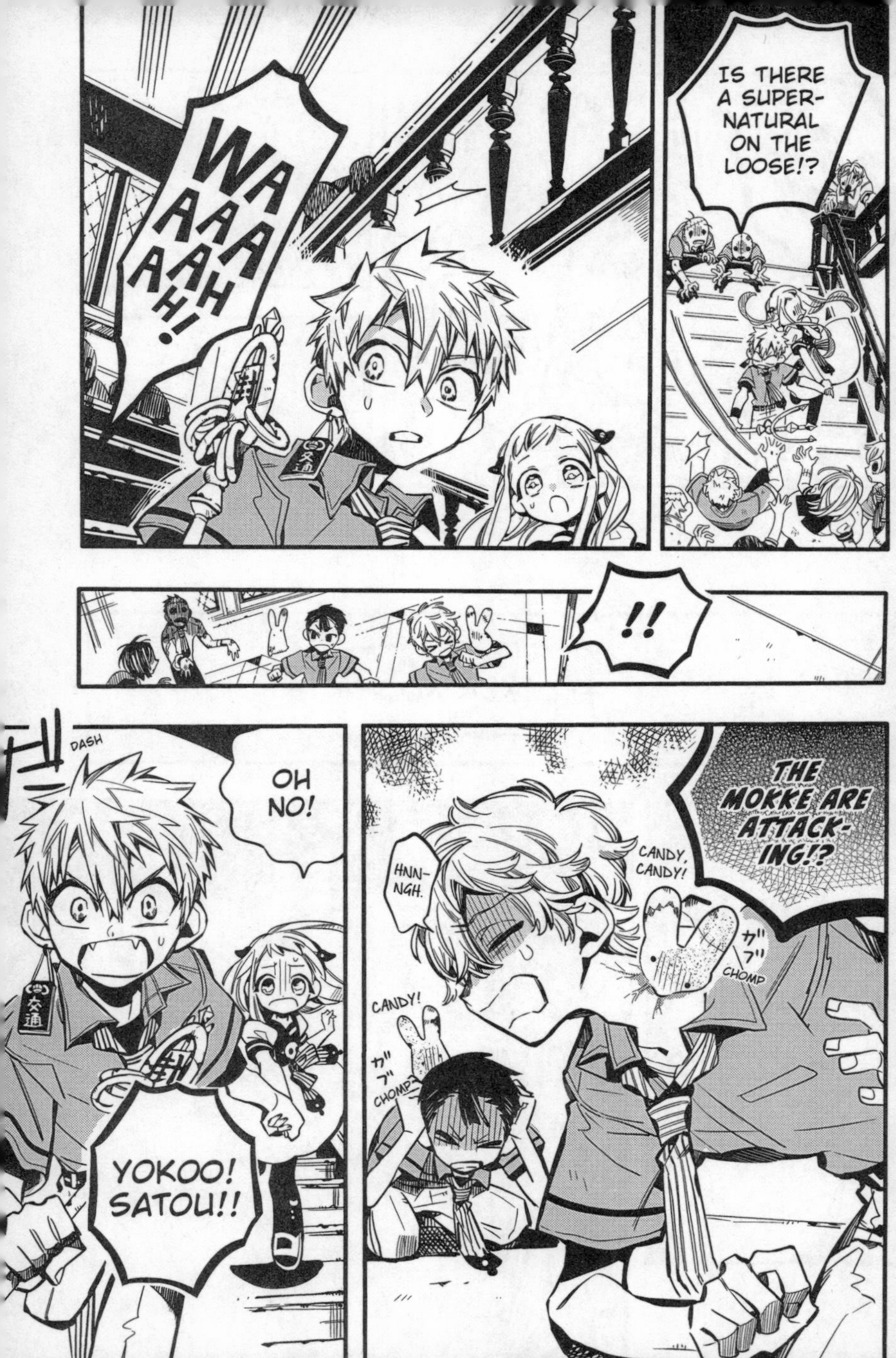
IS THERE A SUPER-NATURAL ON THE LOOSE!?
WAAAAAAAAHAH!
!!
THE MOKKE ARE ATTACK-ING!?
CANDY, CANDY!
HNN-NGH.
ガブ
CHOMP
CANDY!
ガブ
CHOMP
DASH
OH NO!
YOKOO! SATOU!!

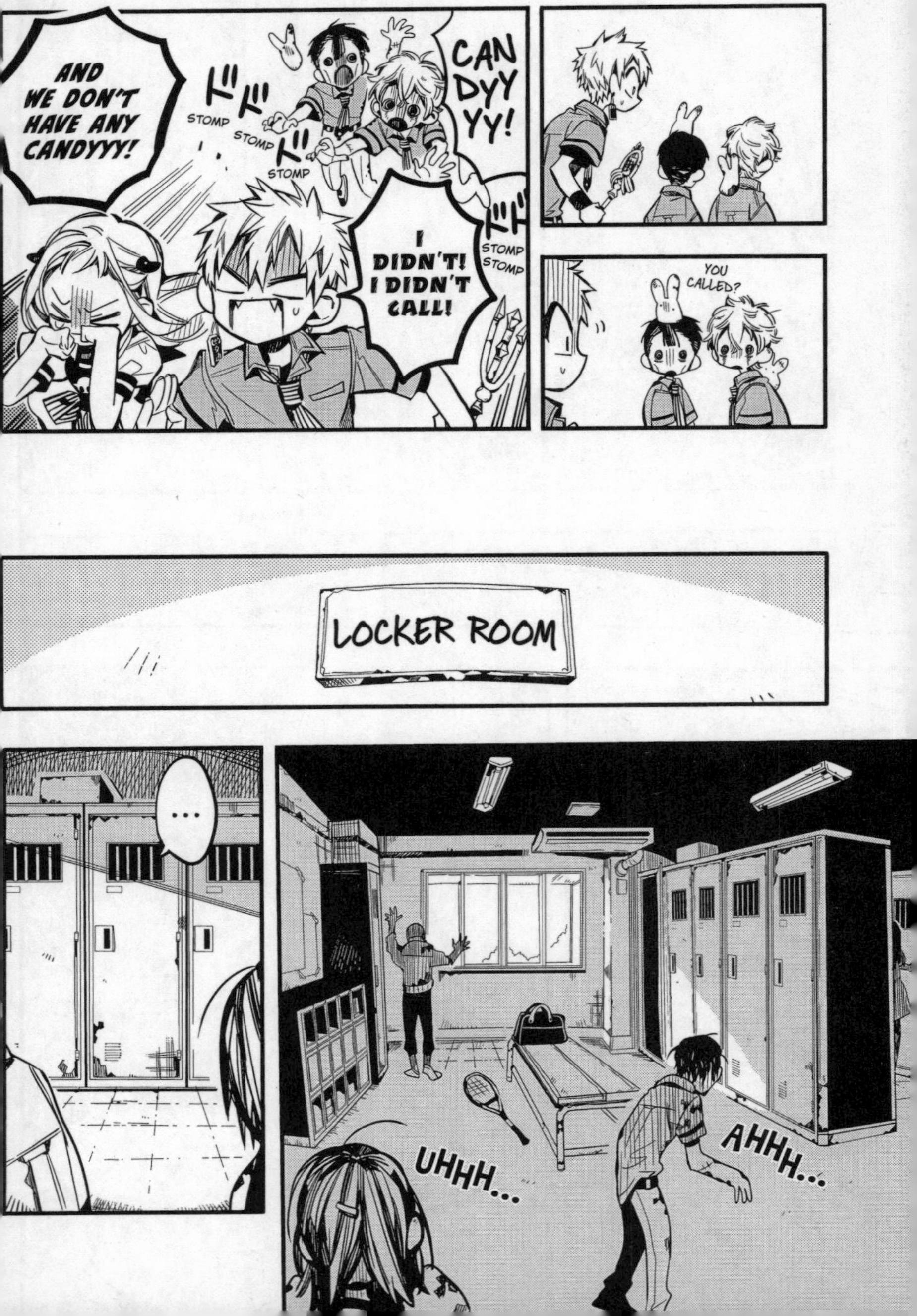
YOU CALLED?
CAN DYY YY!
ドド
STOMP STOMP
I DIDN'T! I DIDN'T CALL!
ドド
STOMP
STOMP
STOMP
AND WE DON'T HAVE ANY CANDYYY!
LOCKER ROOM
AHHH...
UHHH...
...

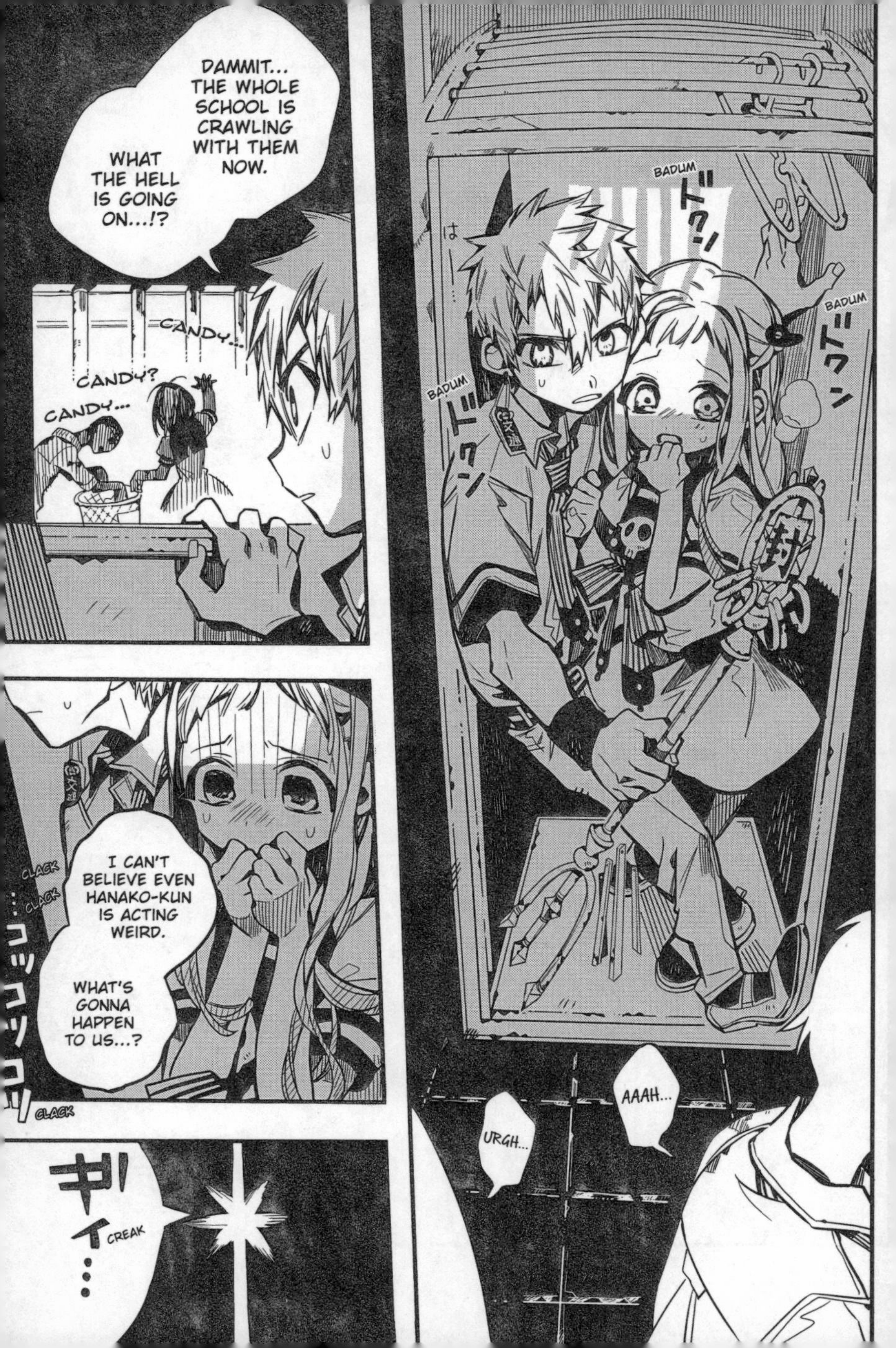

BADUM
ドクン
BADUM
ドクン
BADUM
ドクン
DAMMIT... THE WHOLE SCHOOL IS CRAWLING WITH THEM NOW.
WHAT THE HELL IS GOING ON...!?
CANDY...
CANDY?
CANDY...
I CAN'T BELIEVE EVEN HANAKO-KUN IS ACTING WEIRD.
WHAT'S GONNA HAPPEN TO US...?
CLACK
CLACK
CLACK
AAAH...
URGH...
ギイ…
CREAK

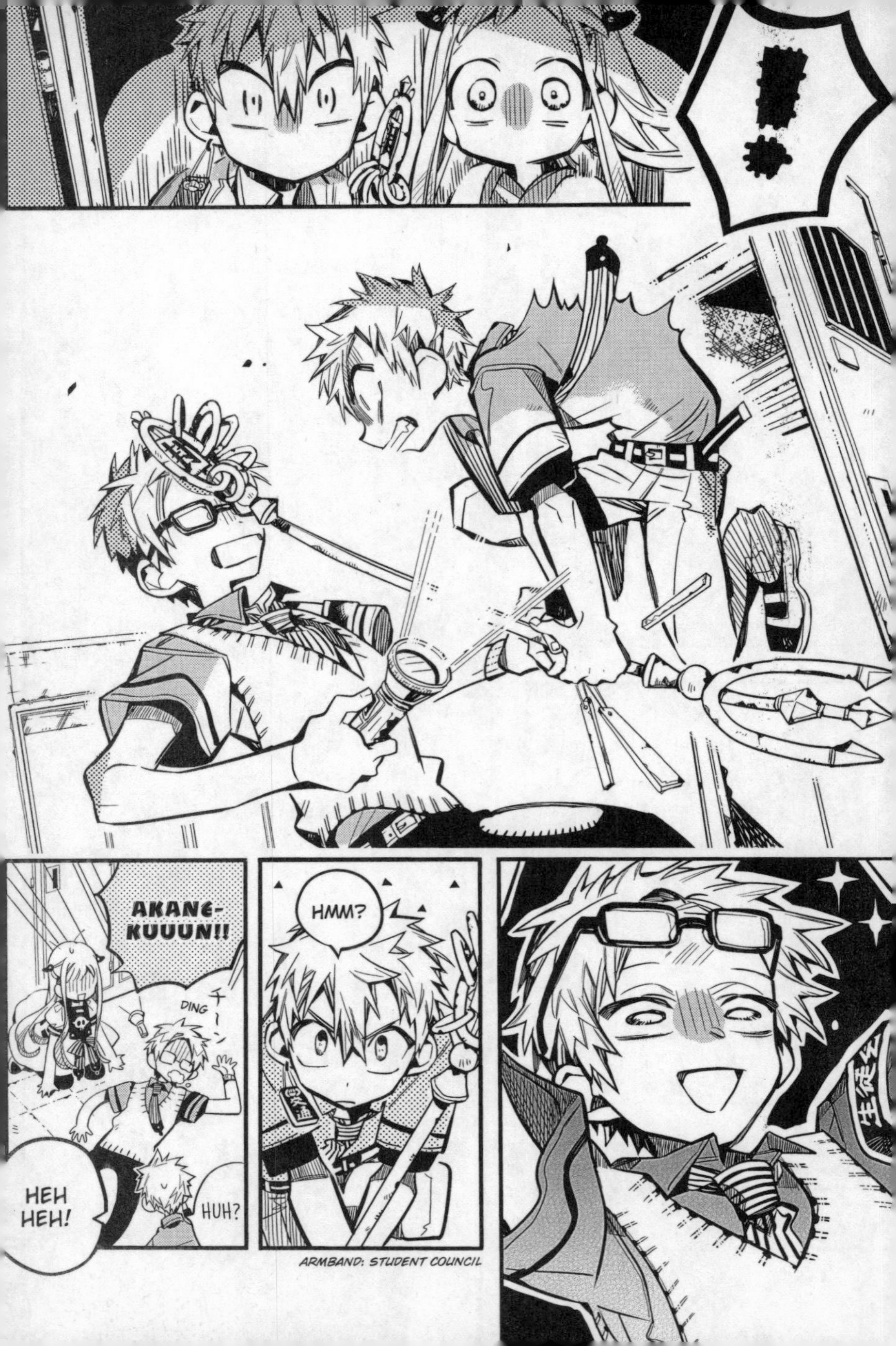
!!
HMM?
ARMBAND: STUDENT COUNCIL
AKANE-KUUUN!!
チーン
DING
HUH?
HEH HEH!

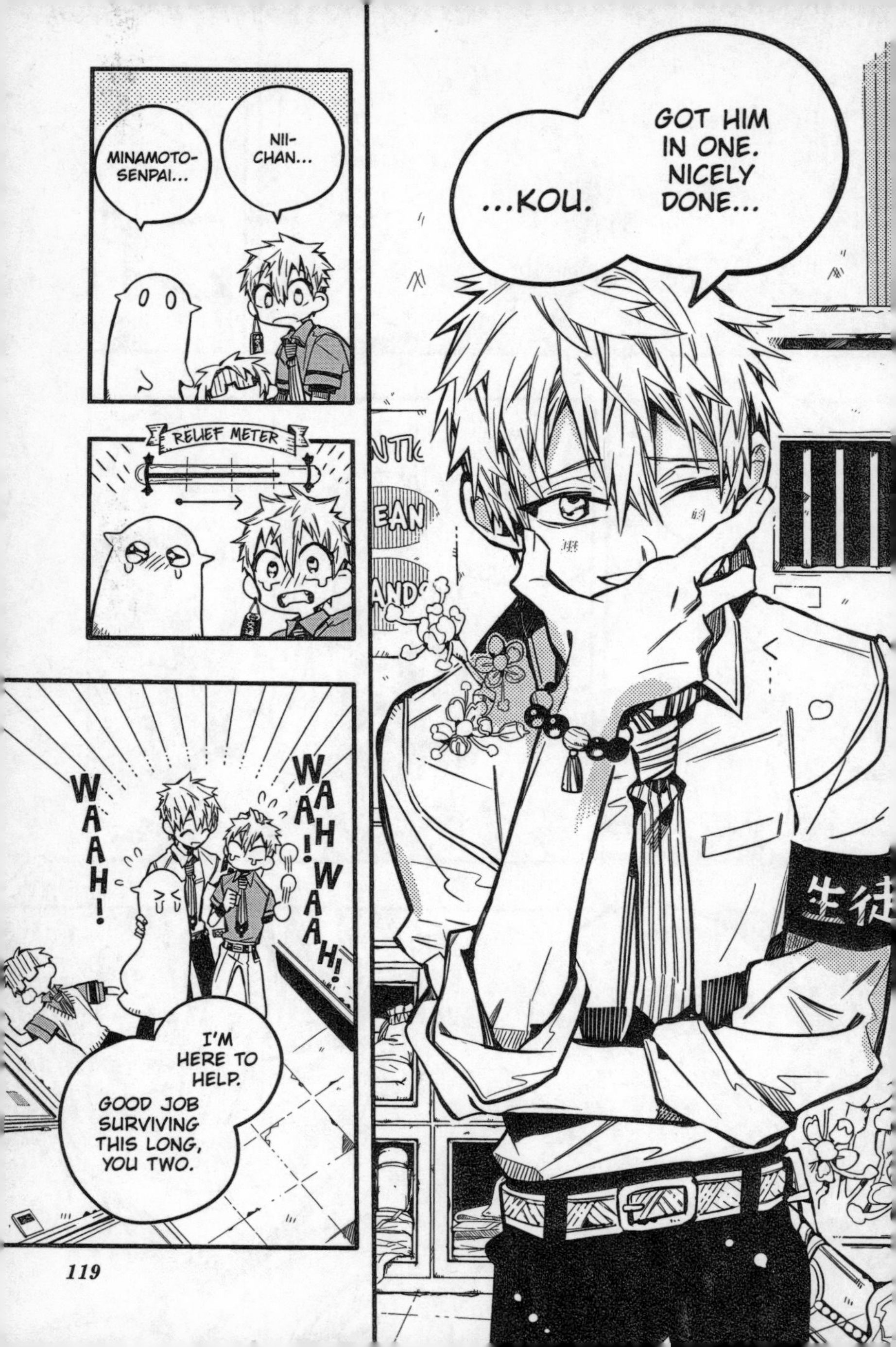
GOT HIM IN ONE. NICELY DONE... ...KOU.
NII-CHAN...
MINAMOTO-SENPAI...
RELIEF METER
WAH! WAH WAAAH!
WAAH!
I'M HERE TO HELP. GOOD JOB SURVIVING THIS LONG, YOU TWO.

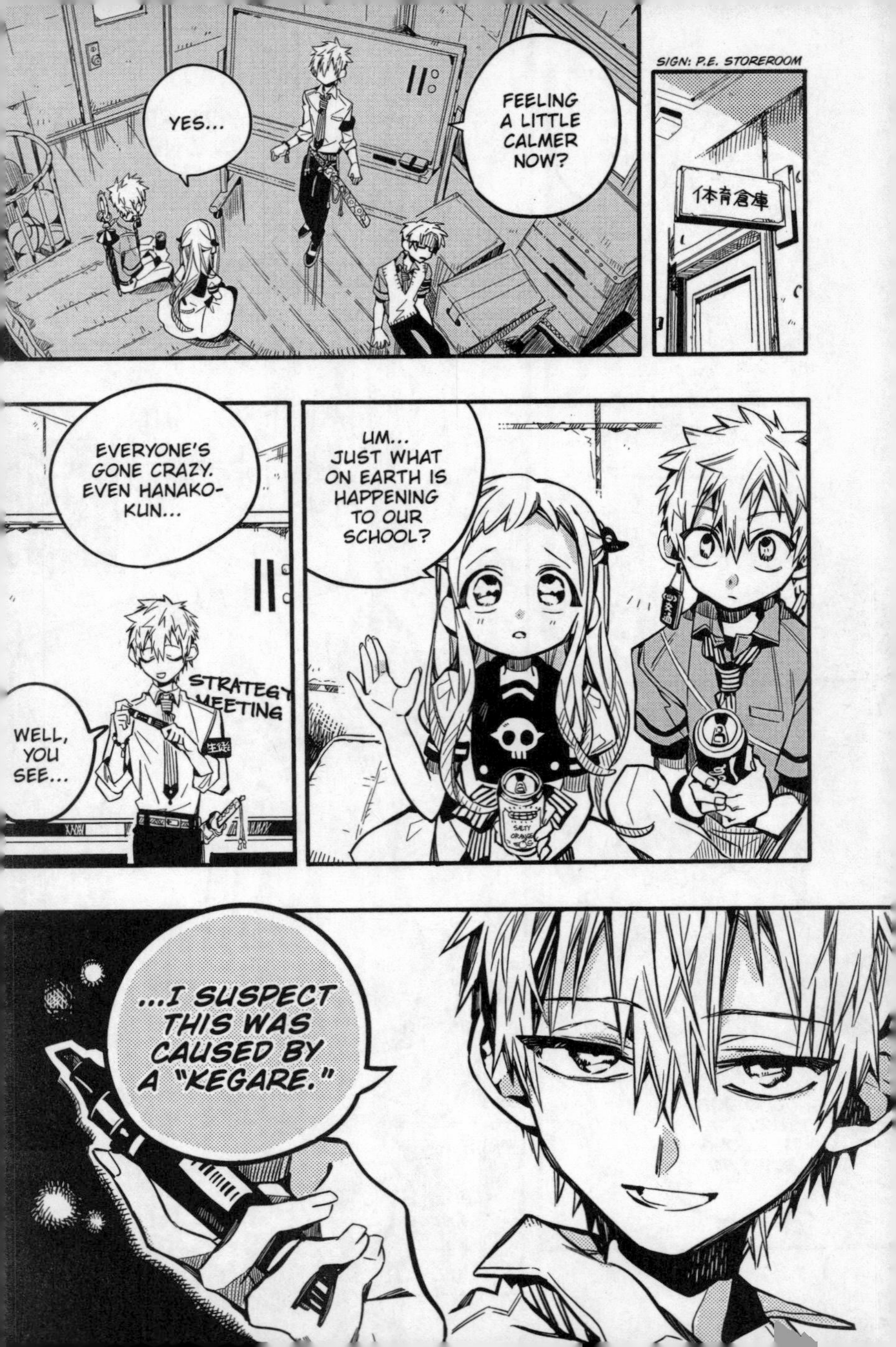
SIGN: P.E. STOREROOM
体育倉庫
FEELING A LITTLE CALMER NOW?
YES...
UM... JUST WHAT ON EARTH IS HAPPENING TO OUR SCHOOL?
EVERYONE'S GONE CRAZY. EVEN HANAKO-KUN...
STRATEGY MEETING
WELL, YOU SEE...
...I SUSPECT THIS WAS CAUSED BY A "KEGARE."

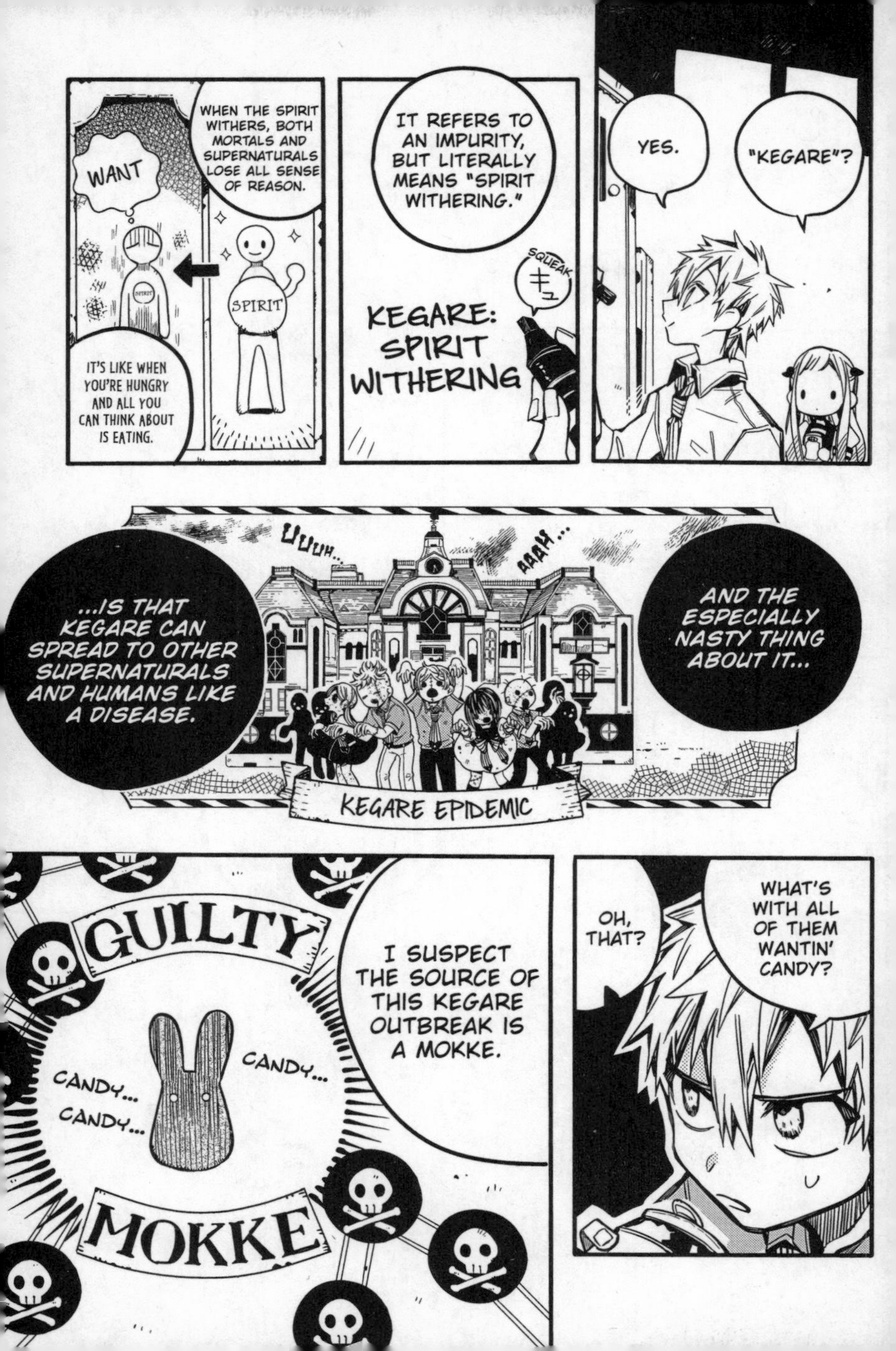
"KEGARE"?
YES.
IT REFERS TO AN IMPURITY, BUT LITERALLY MEANS "SPIRIT WITHERING."
SQUEAK
キュ
KEGARE: SPIRIT WITHERING
WHEN THE SPIRIT WITHERS, BOTH MORTALS AND SUPERNATURALS LOSE ALL SENSE OF REASON.
WANT
SPIRIT
SPIRIT
IT'S LIKE WHEN YOU'RE HUNGRY AND ALL YOU CAN THINK ABOUT IS EATING.
AND THE ESPECIALLY NASTY THING ABOUT IT...
AAAH...
UUUH...
...IS THAT KEGARE CAN SPREAD TO OTHER SUPERNATURALS AND HUMANS LIKE A DISEASE.
KEGARE EPIDEMIC
WHAT'S WITH ALL OF THEM WANTIN' CANDY?
OH, THAT?
I SUSPECT THE SOURCE OF THIS KEGARE OUTBREAK IS A MOKKE.
GUILTY
CANDY...
CANDY...
CANDY...
MOKKE

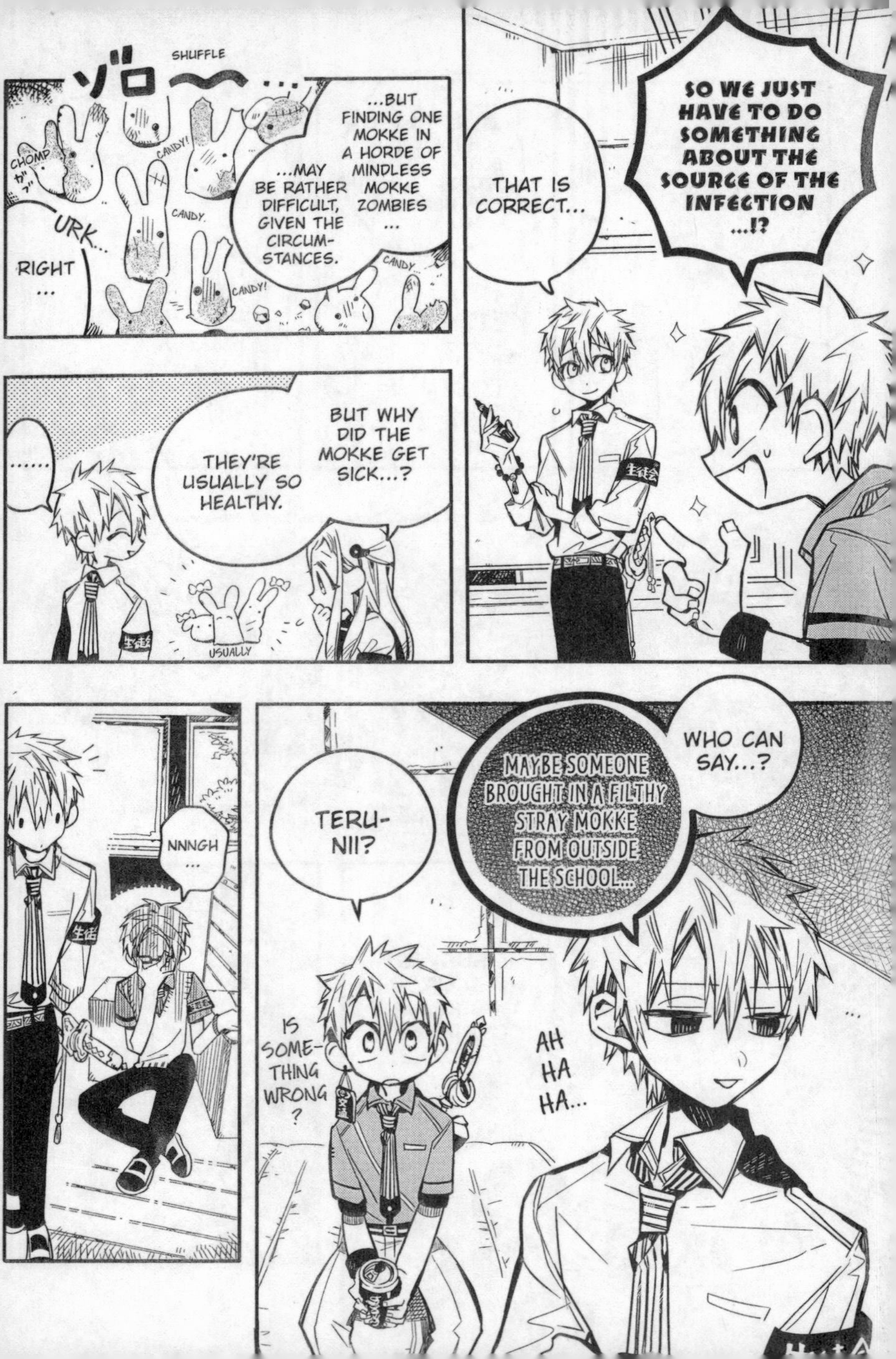

SO WE JUST HAVE TO DO SOMETHING ABOUT THE SOURCE OF THE INFECTION ...!?
THAT IS CORRECT...
ゾロ〜〜...
SHUFFLE
...BUT FINDING ONE MOKKE IN A HORDE OF MINDLESS MOKKE ZOMBIES ...
...MAY BE RATHER DIFFICULT, GIVEN THE CIRCUMSTANCES.
CANDY!
CHOMP
ガブ
CANDY.
URK...
RIGHT ...
CANDY...
CANDY!
BUT WHY DID THE MOKKE GET SICK...?
THEY'RE USUALLY SO HEALTHY.
......
USUALLY
WHO CAN SAY...?
MAYBE SOMEONE BROUGHT IN A FILTHY STRAY MOKKE FROM OUTSIDE THE SCHOOL...
TERU-NII?
...
AH HA HA...
IS SOME-THING WRONG?
NNNGH ...

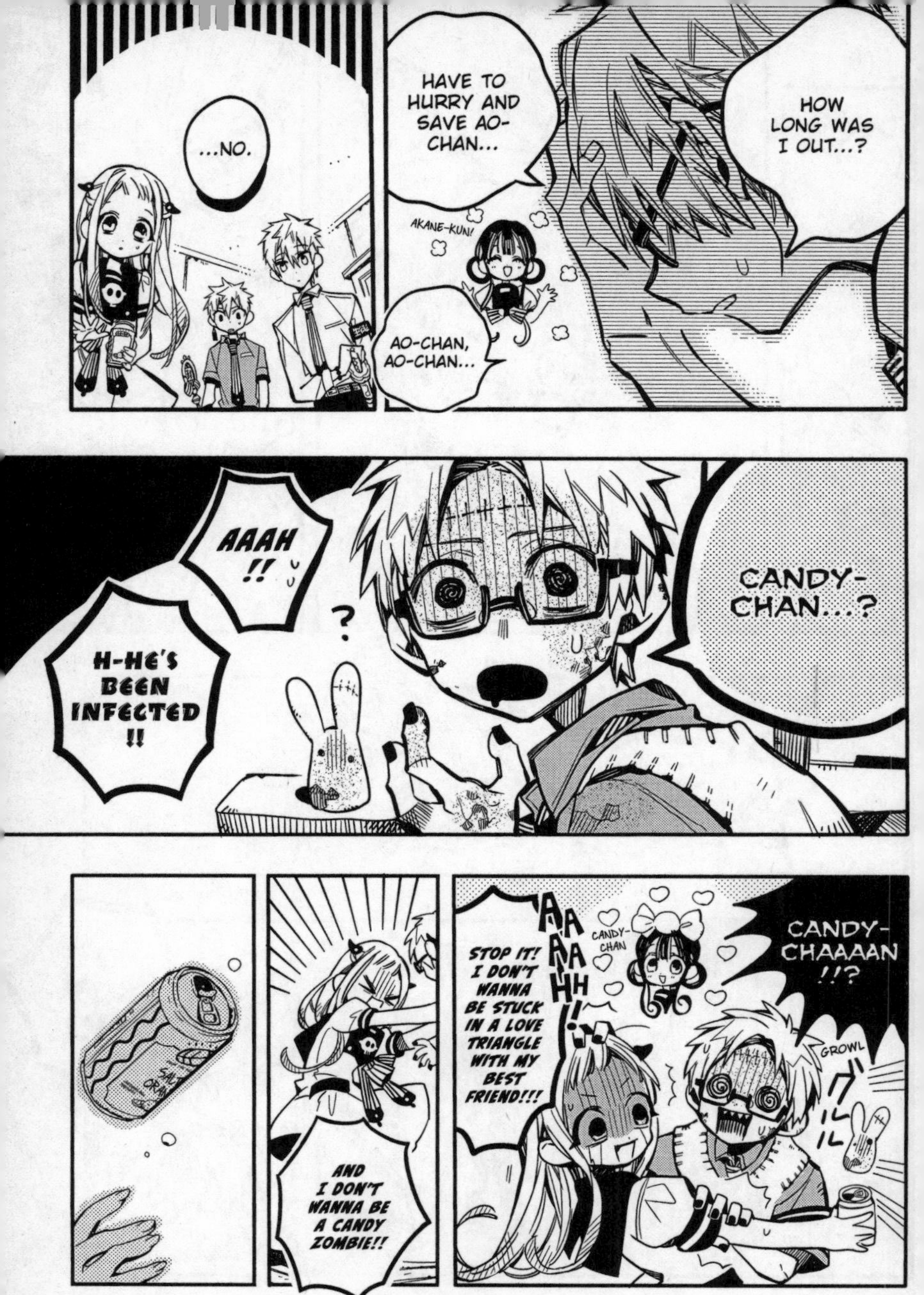
HOW LONG WAS I OUT...?
HAVE TO HURRY AND SAVE AO-CHAN...
AKANE-KUN!
AO-CHAN, AO-CHAN...
...NO.
CANDY-CHAN...?
AAAH!!
H-HE'S BEEN INFECTED!!
CANDY-CHAAAAN!!?
GROWL
AAAHH!
CANDY-CHAN
STOP IT! I DON'T WANNA BE STUCK IN A LOVE TRIANGLE WITH MY BEST FRIEND!!!
AND I DON'T WANNA BE A CANDY ZOMBIE!!

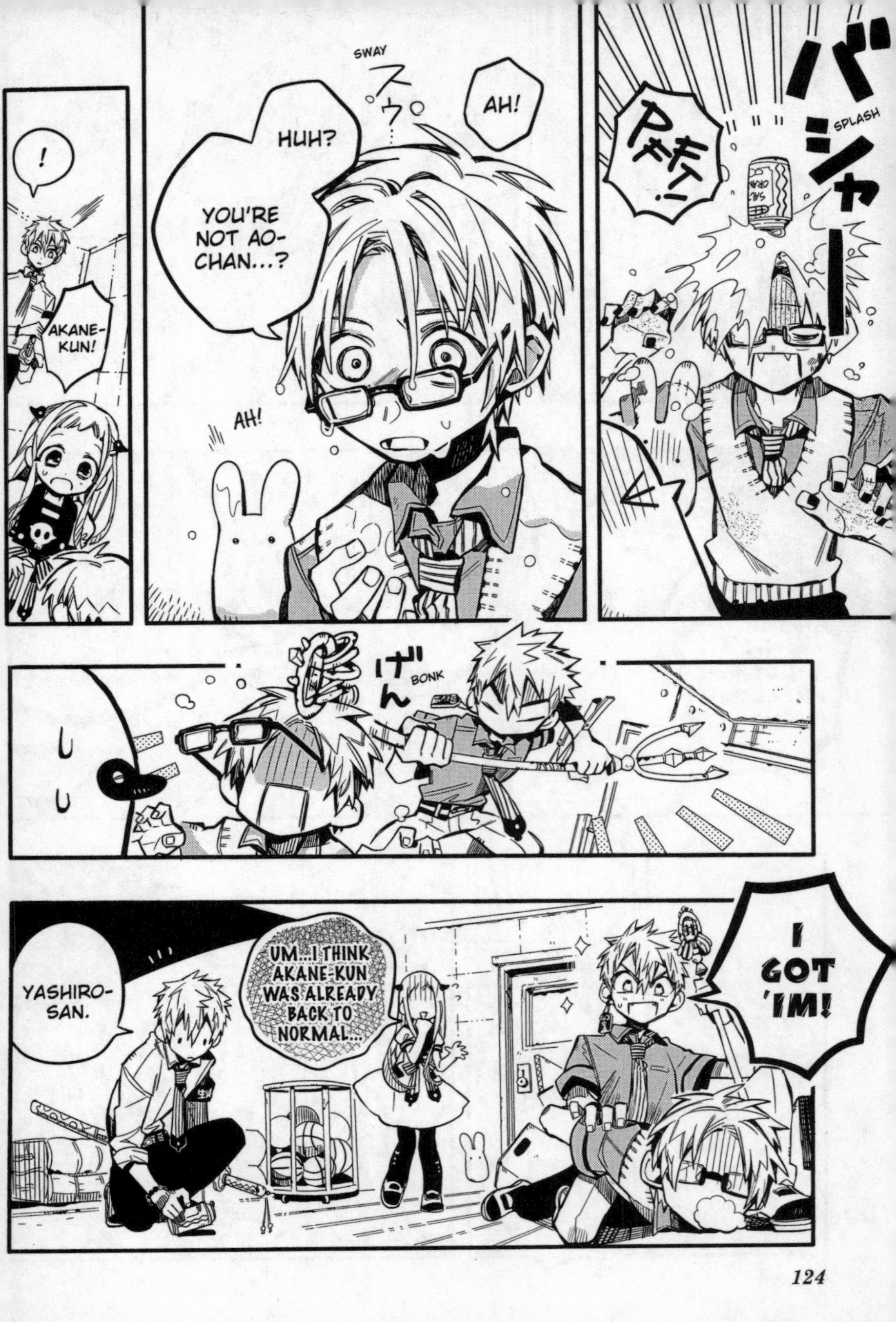

PFFT!!
バシャー
SPLASH
AH!
スゥ
SWAY
HUH?
YOU'RE NOT AO-CHAN...?
AH!
!
AKANE-KUN!
げん
BONK
I GOT 'IM!
UM...I THINK AKANE-KUN WAS ALREADY BACK TO NORMAL...
YASHIRO-SAN.

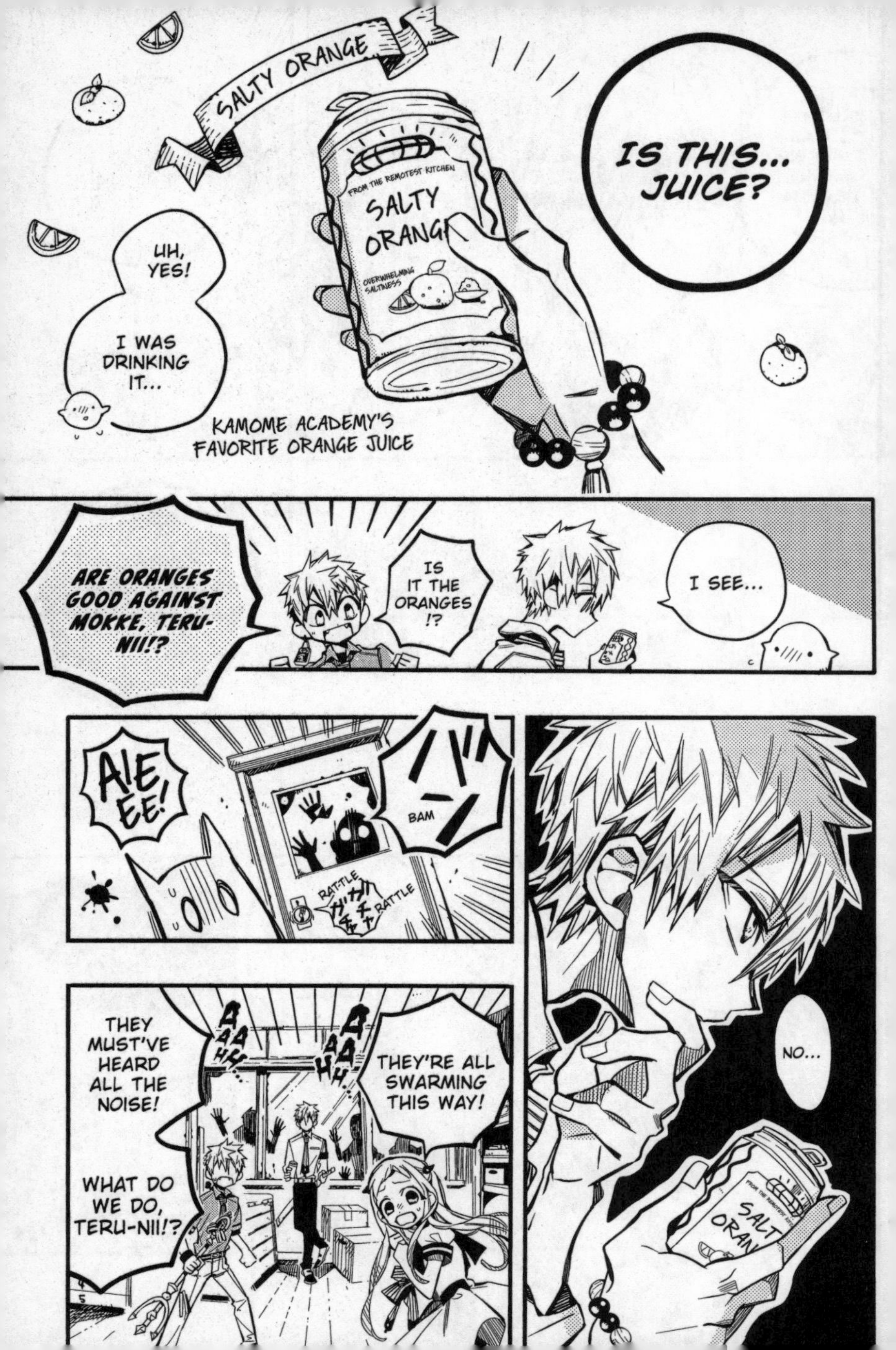
IS THIS... JUICE?
SALTY ORANGE
FROM THE REMOTEST KITCHEN
SALTY ORANG
OVERWHELMING SALTINESS
UH, YES! I WAS DRINKING IT...
KAMOME ACADEMY'S FAVORITE ORANGE JUICE
I SEE...
IS IT THE ORANGES!?
ARE ORANGES GOOD AGAINST MOKKE, TERU-NII!?
NO...
SALT ORAN
BAM
RATTLE RATTLE
AIEEE!
THEY'RE ALL SWARMING THIS WAY!
AAAHH
AAAHH
THEY MUST'VE HEARD ALL THE NOISE!
WHAT DO WE DO, TERU-NII!?

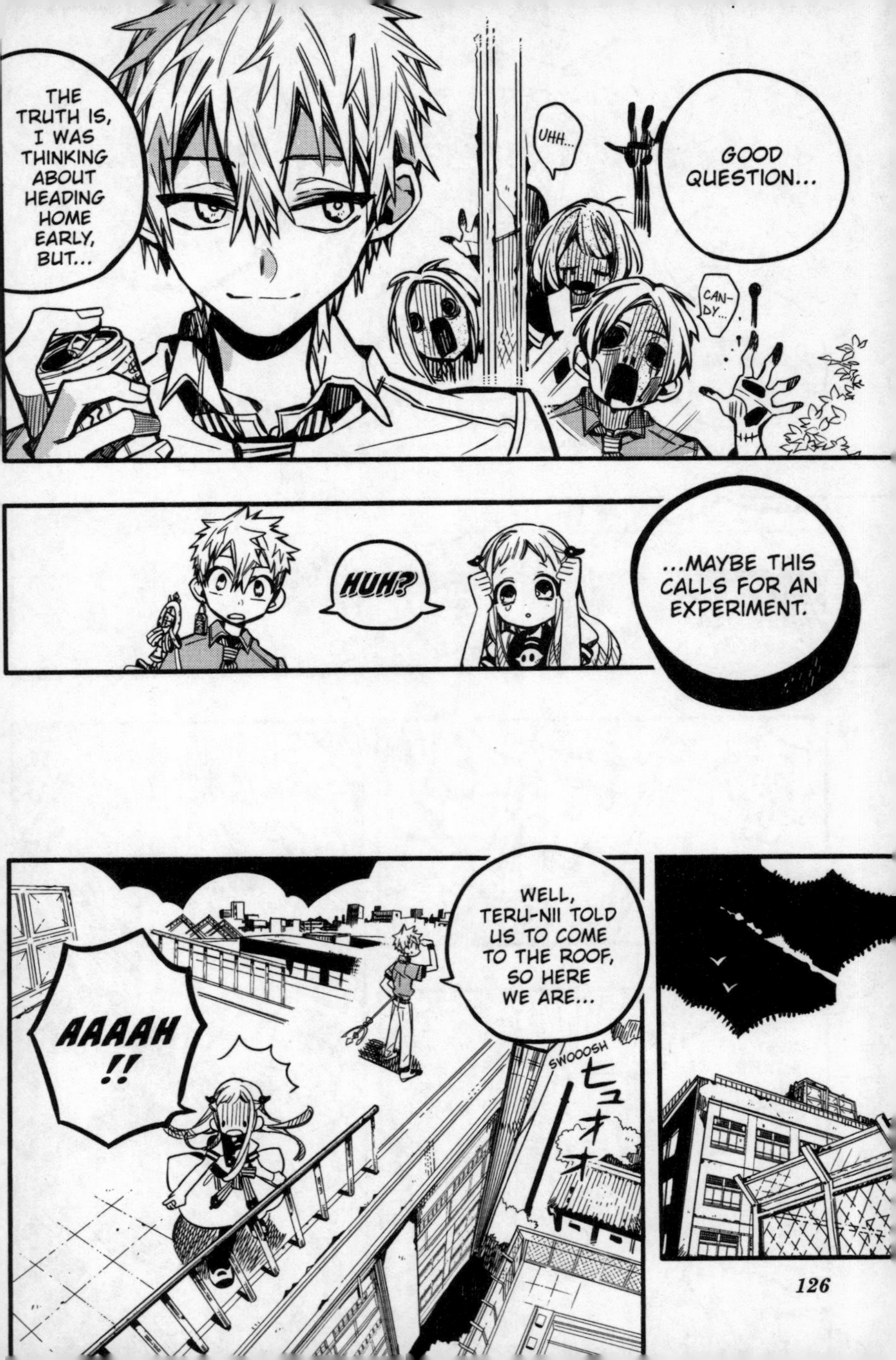
GOOD QUESTION...
UHH...
CAN-DY...
THE TRUTH IS, I WAS THINKING ABOUT HEADING HOME EARLY, BUT...
...MAYBE THIS CALLS FOR AN EXPERIMENT.
HUH?
WELL, TERU-NII TOLD US TO COME TO THE ROOF, SO HERE WE ARE...
SWOOOSH
ヒュオオ
AAAAH!!

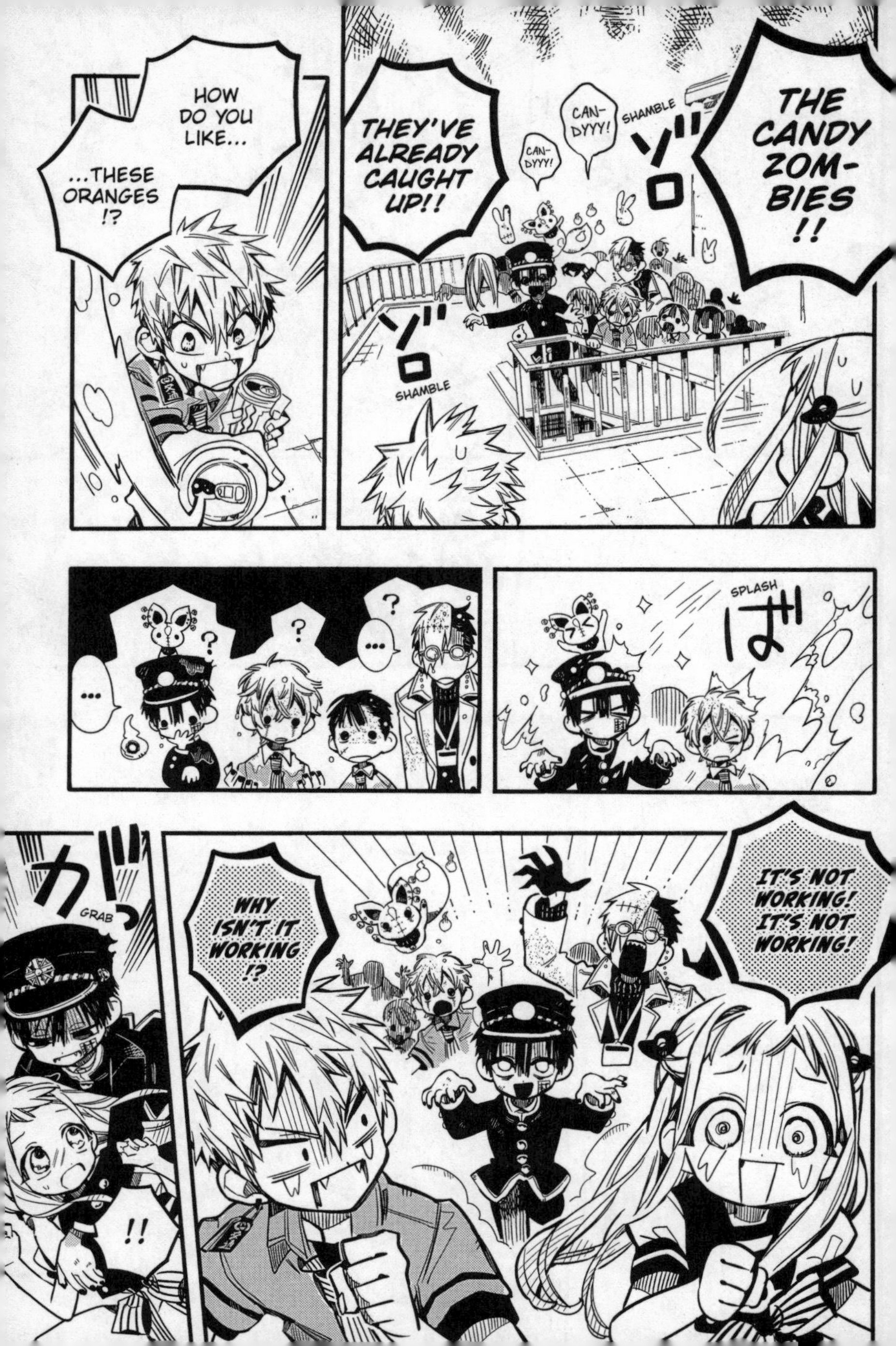
THE CANDY ZOM-BIES!!
SHAMBLE
ゾロ
CAN-DYYY!
CAN-DYYY!
THEY'VE ALREADY CAUGHT UP!!
ゾロ
SHAMBLE
HOW DO YOU LIKE...
...THESE ORANGES!?
SPLASH
ば
?
...
?
?
...
IT'S NOT WORKING! IT'S NOT WORKING!
WHY ISN'T IT WORKING!?
ガッ
GRAB
!!

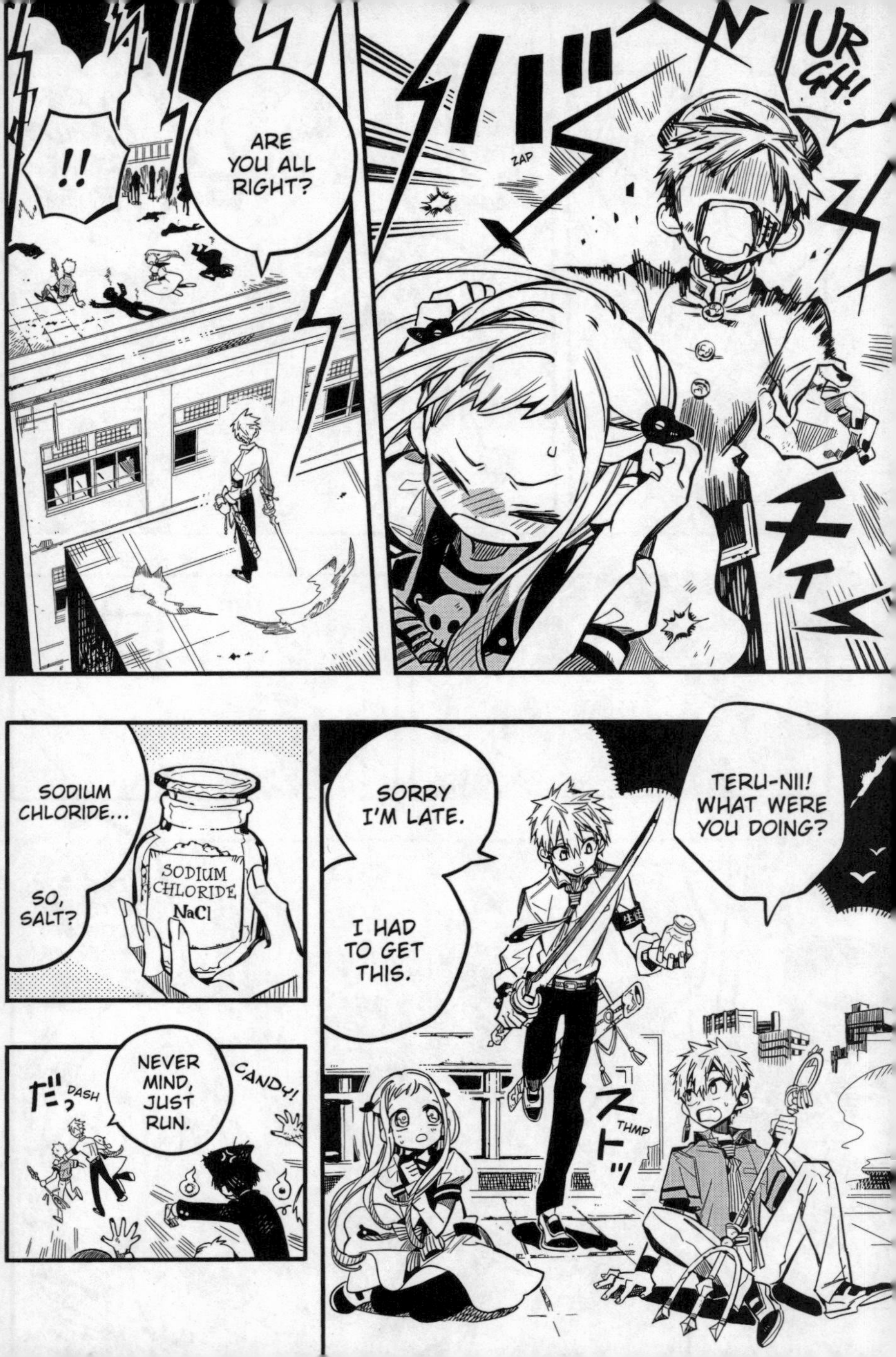
URGH!
ZAP
ARE YOU ALL RIGHT?
!!
TERU-NII! WHAT WERE YOU DOING?
SORRY I'M LATE.
I HAD TO GET THIS.
THMP
SODIUM CHLORIDE...
SODIUM CHLORIDE NaCl
SO, SALT?
CANDY!
NEVER MIND, JUST RUN.
DASH

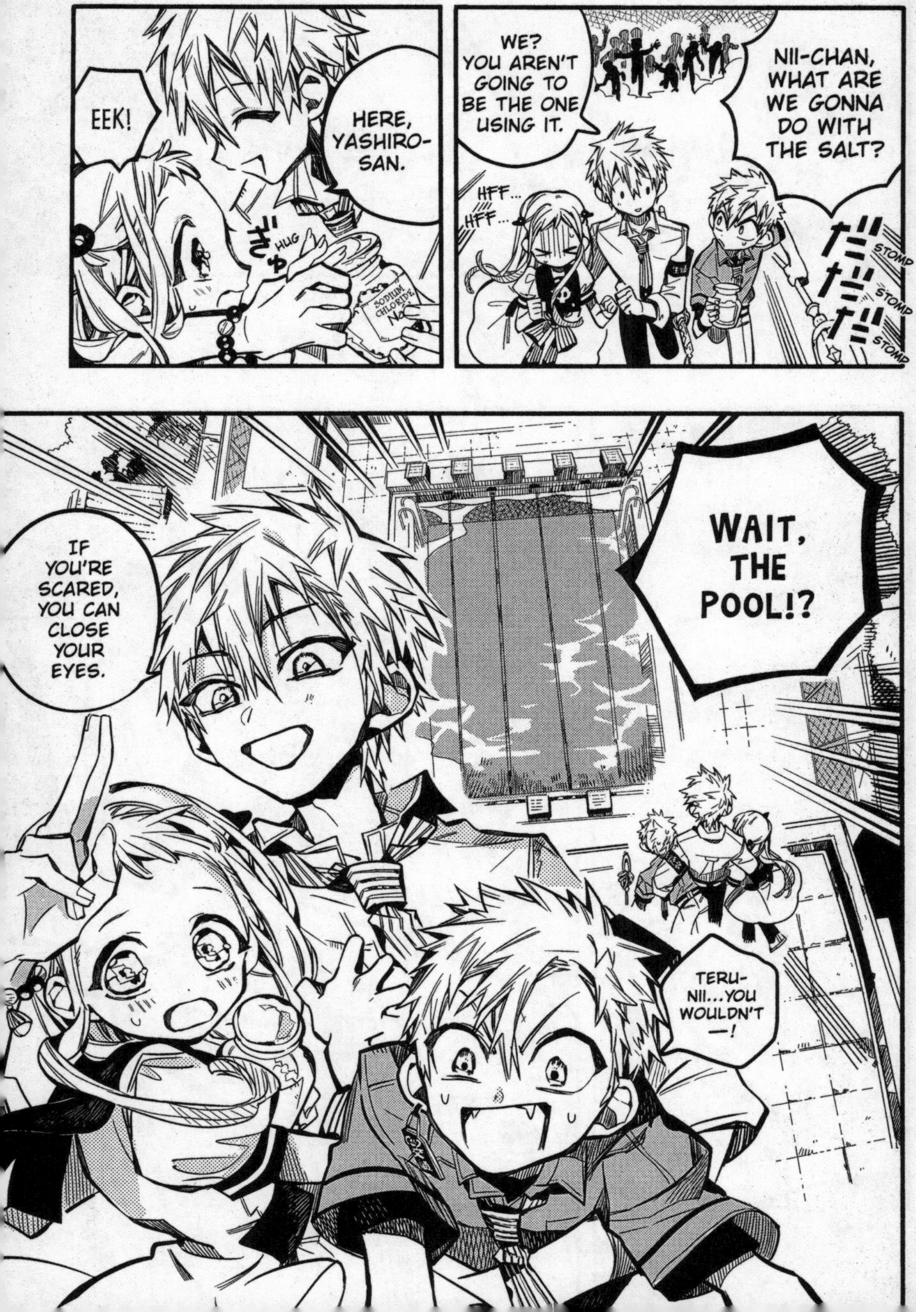
NII-CHAN, WHAT ARE WE GONNA DO WITH THE SALT?
WE? YOU AREN'T GOING TO BE THE ONE USING IT.
HFF... HFF...
だだだ
STOMP STOMP STOMP
HERE, YASHIRO-SAN.
EEK!
ぎゅ
HUG
SODIUM CHLORIDE Na
WAIT, THE POOL!?
IF YOU'RE SCARED, YOU CAN CLOSE YOUR EYES.
TERU-NII...YOU WOULDN'T—!

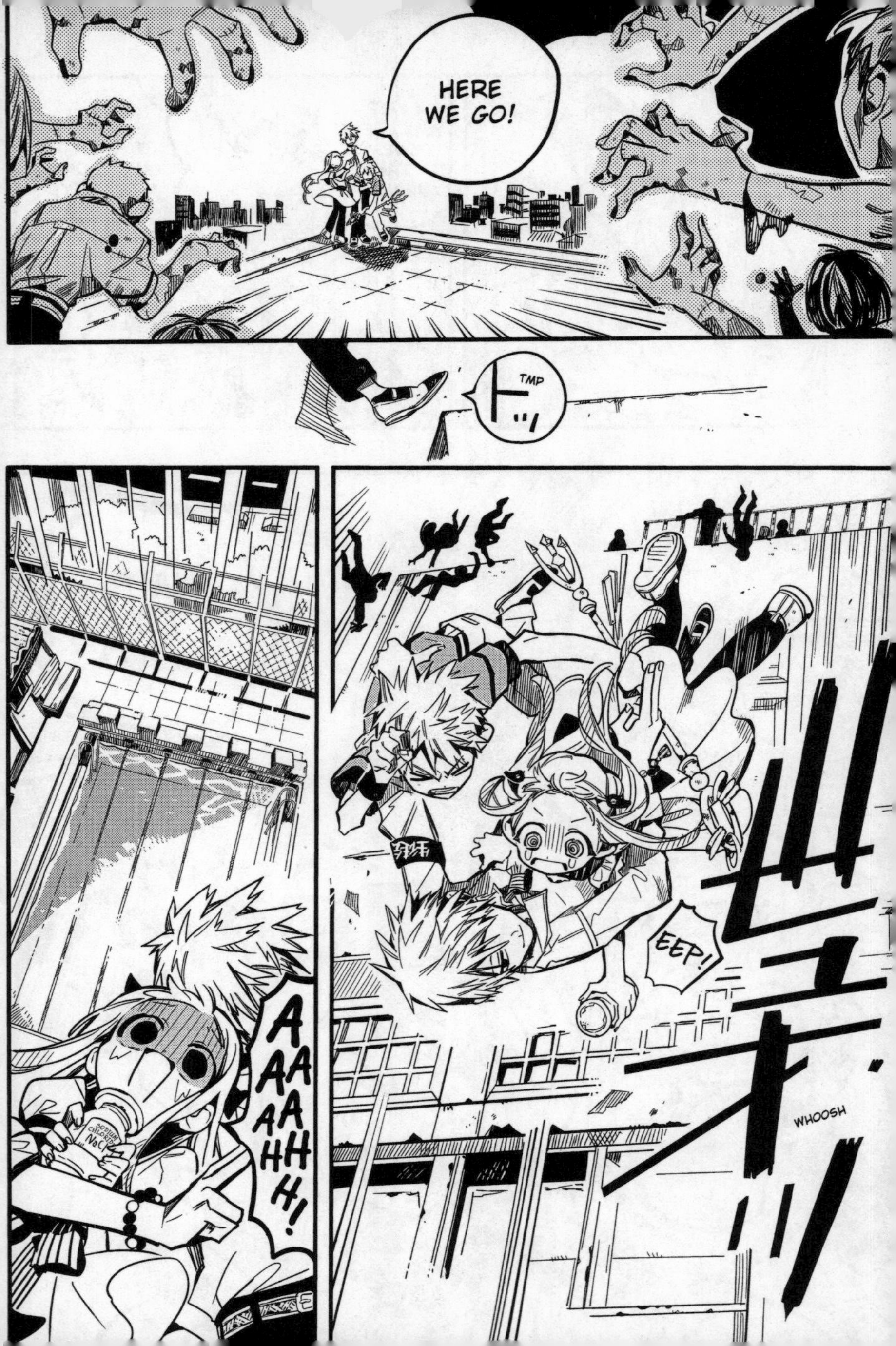
HERE WE GO!
TMP
トッ
EEP!
WHOOSH
AAAAAHHH!
SODIUM CHLORIDE NaCl

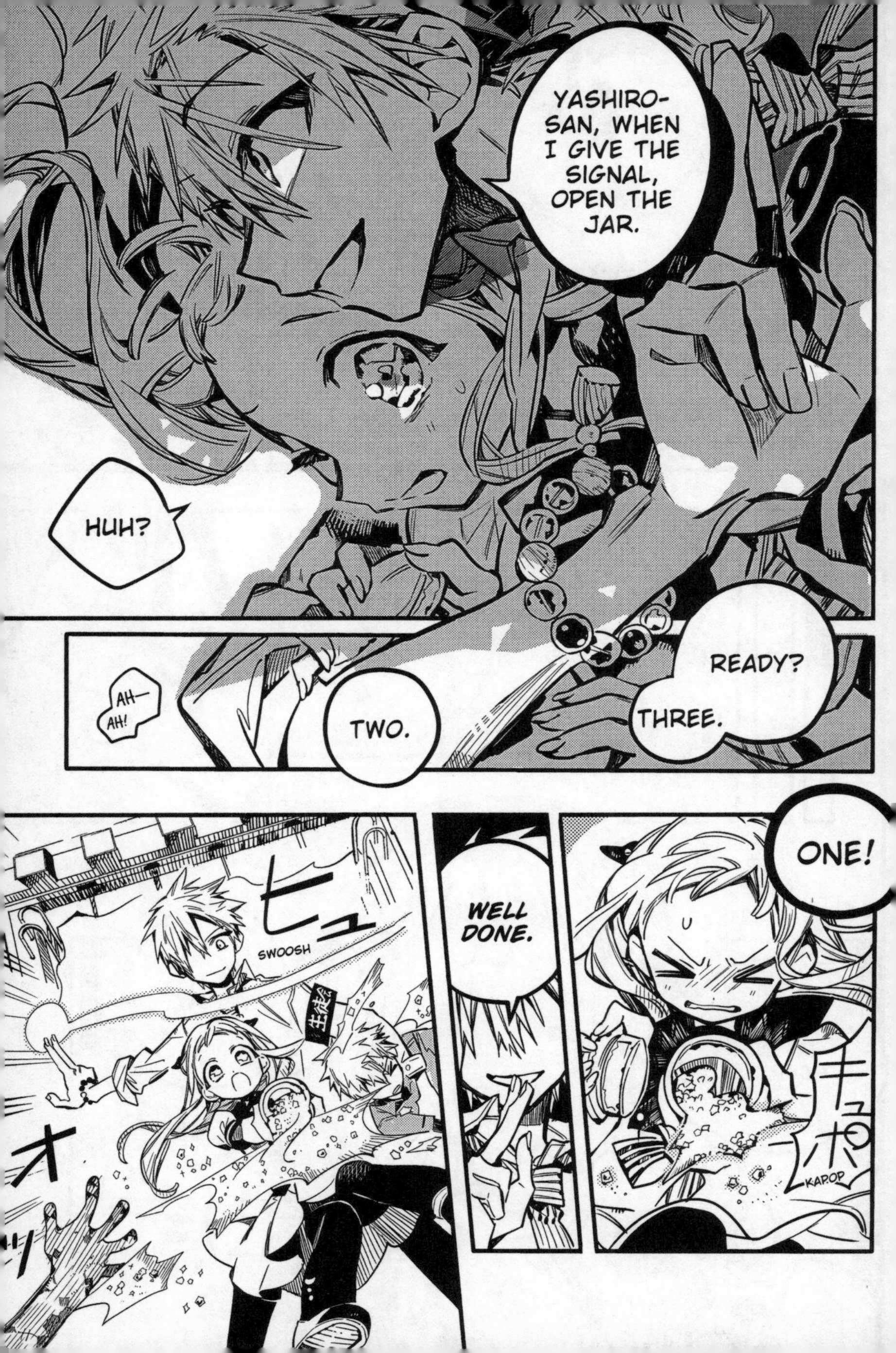
YASHIRO-SAN, WHEN I GIVE THE SIGNAL, OPEN THE JAR.
HUH?
READY?
THREE.
TWO.
AH— AH!
ONE!
キュポ
KAPOP
WELL DONE.
ヒュ
SWOOSH

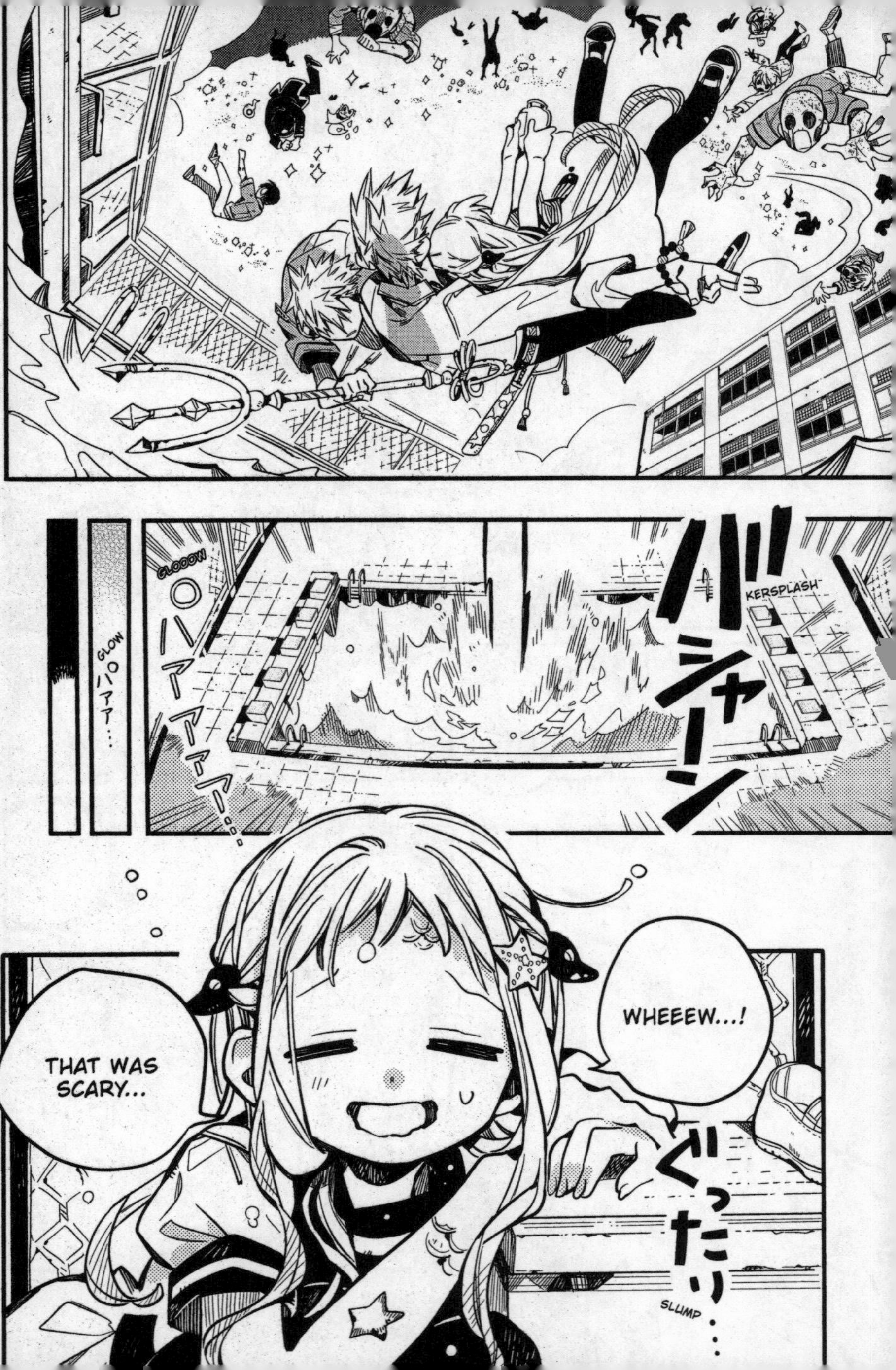
バシャーン
KERSPLASH
ハァァァー…
GLOOOW
ハァア…
GLOW
WHEEEW…!
ぐったり…
SLUMP
THAT WAS SCARY…

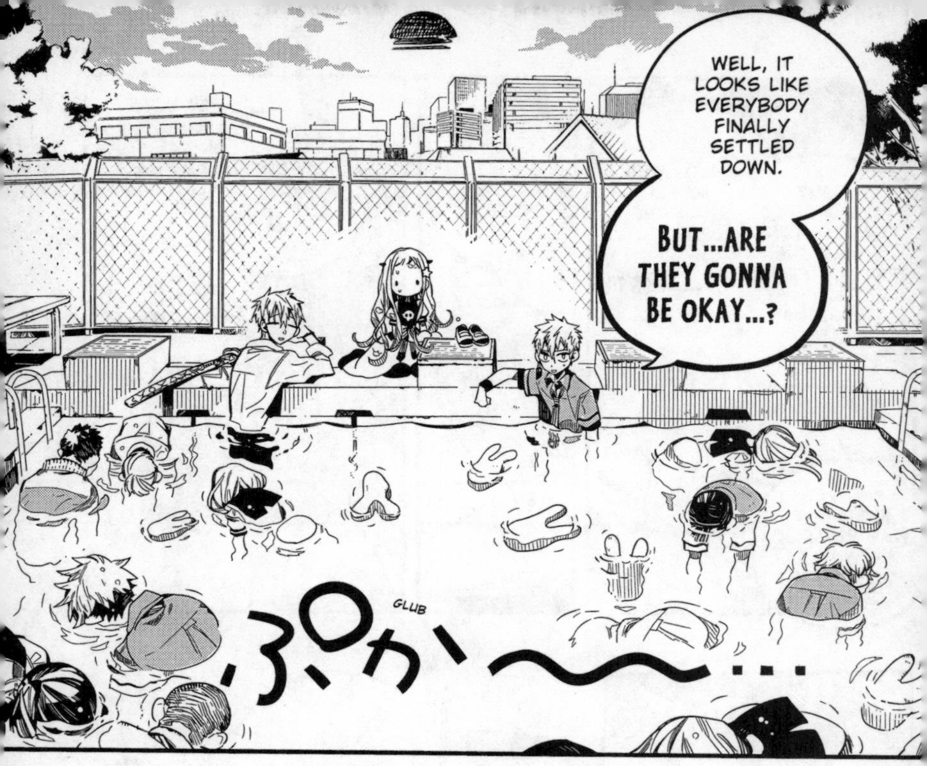
WELL, IT LOOKS LIKE EVERYBODY FINALLY SETTLED DOWN.
BUT...ARE THEY GONNA BE OKAY...?
ぷか〜〜…
GLUB

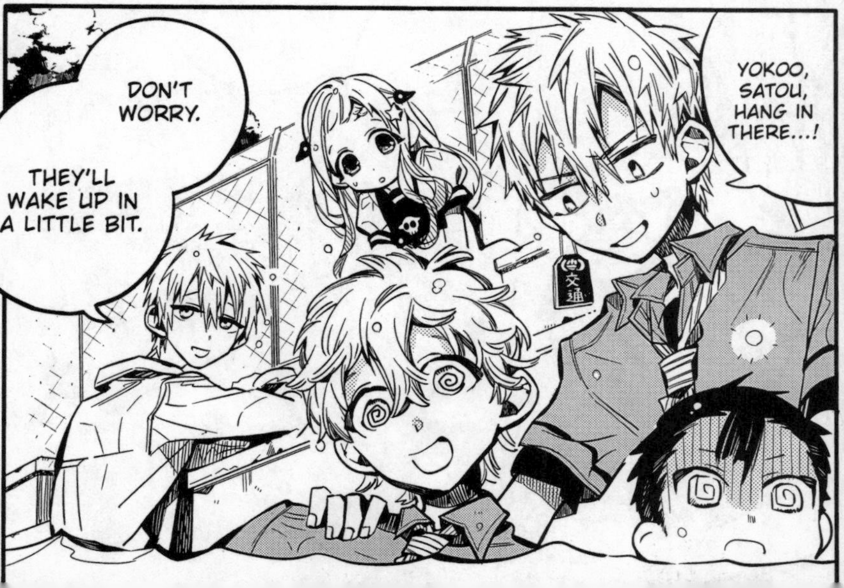
YOKOO, SATOU, HANG IN THERE...!
DON'T WORRY.
THEY'LL WAKE UP IN A LITTLE BIT.

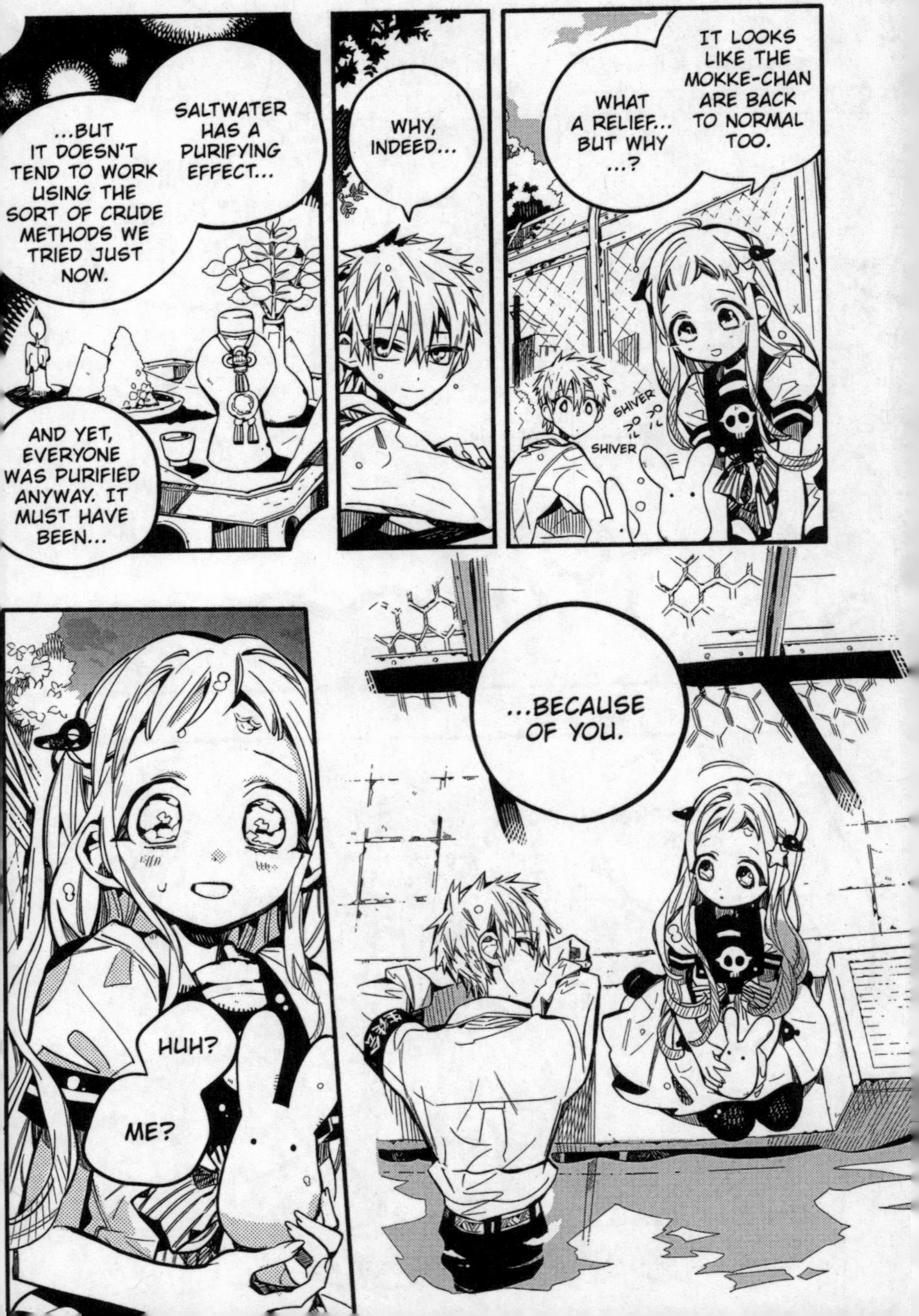
IT LOOKS LIKE THE MOKKE-CHAN ARE BACK TO NORMAL TOO.
WHAT A RELIEF... BUT WHY ...?
SHIVER
SHIVER
WHY, INDEED...
SALTWATER HAS A PURIFYING EFFECT...
...BUT IT DOESN'T TEND TO WORK USING THE SORT OF CRUDE METHODS WE TRIED JUST NOW.
AND YET, EVERYONE WAS PURIFIED ANYWAY. IT MUST HAVE BEEN...
...BECAUSE OF YOU.
HUH?
ME?

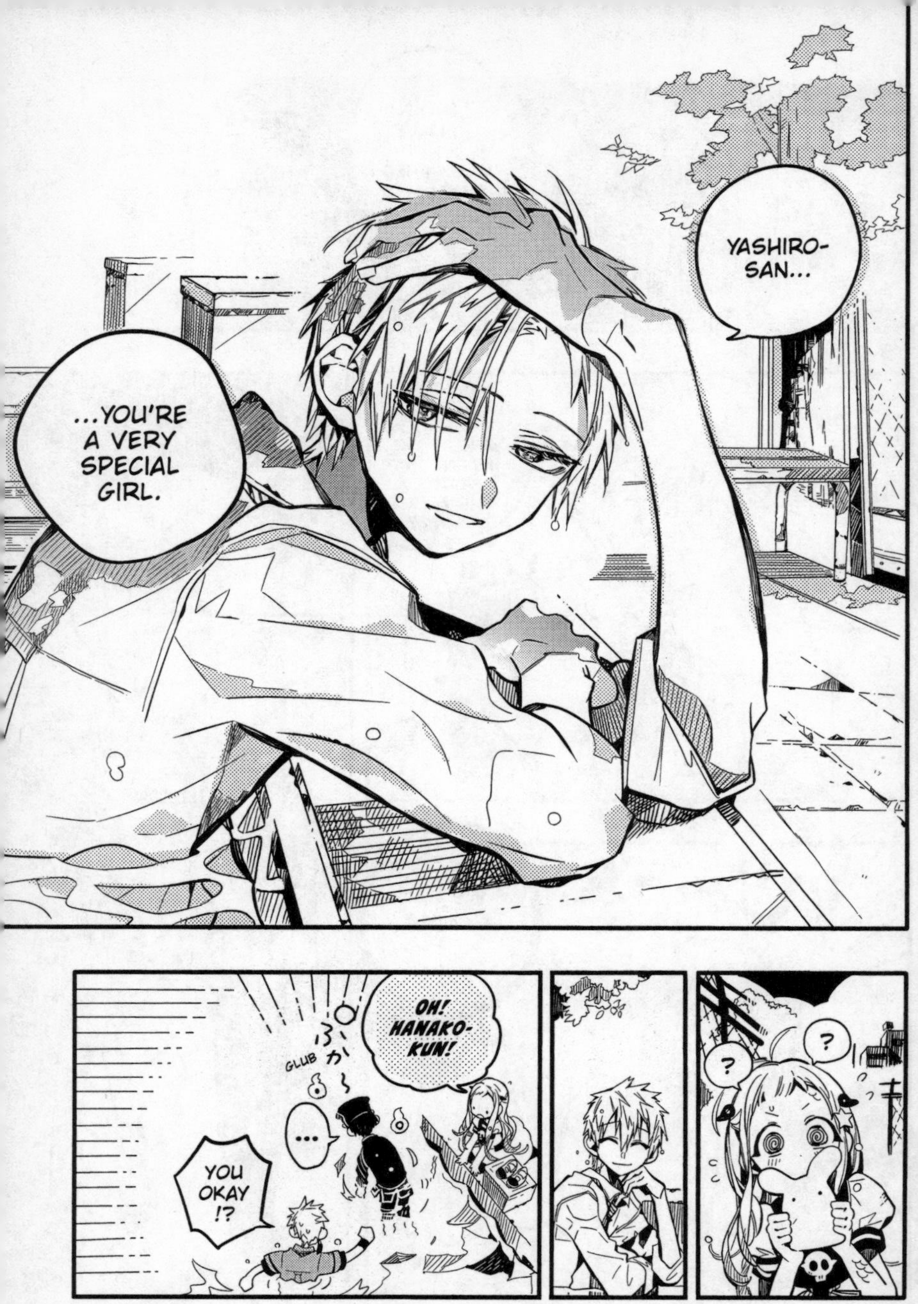
YASHIRO-SAN...
...YOU'RE A VERY SPECIAL GIRL.
?
?
OH! HANAKO-KUN!
GLUB
...
YOU OKAY !?

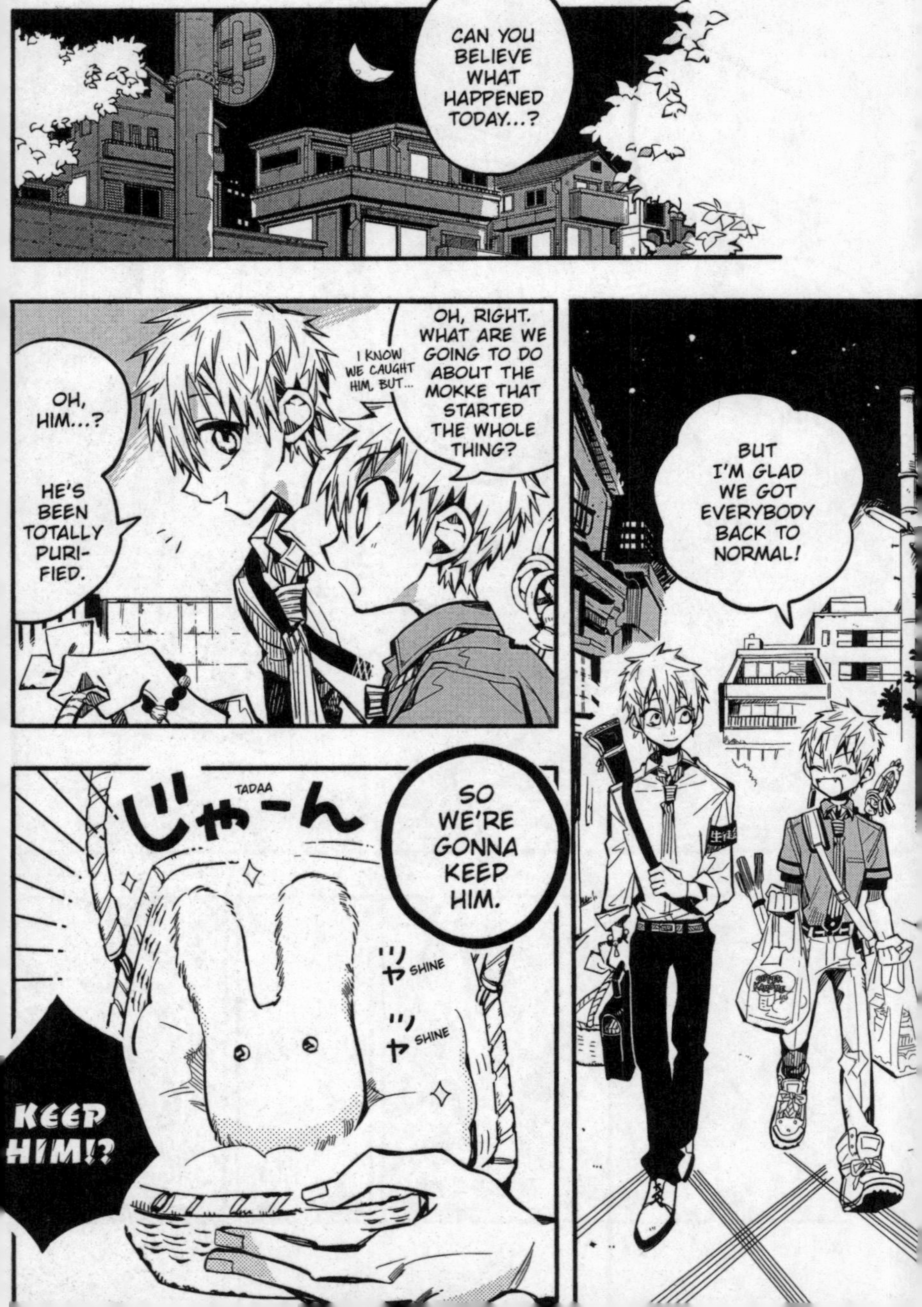
CAN YOU BELIEVE WHAT HAPPENED TODAY...?
BUT I'M GLAD WE GOT EVERYBODY BACK TO NORMAL!
OH, RIGHT. WHAT ARE WE GOING TO DO ABOUT THE MOKKE THAT STARTED THE WHOLE THING?
I KNOW WE CAUGHT HIM, BUT...
OH, HIM...?
HE'S BEEN TOTALLY PURIFIED.
SO WE'RE GONNA KEEP HIM.
じゃーん TADAA
ツヤ SHINE
ツヤ SHINE
KEEP HIM!?

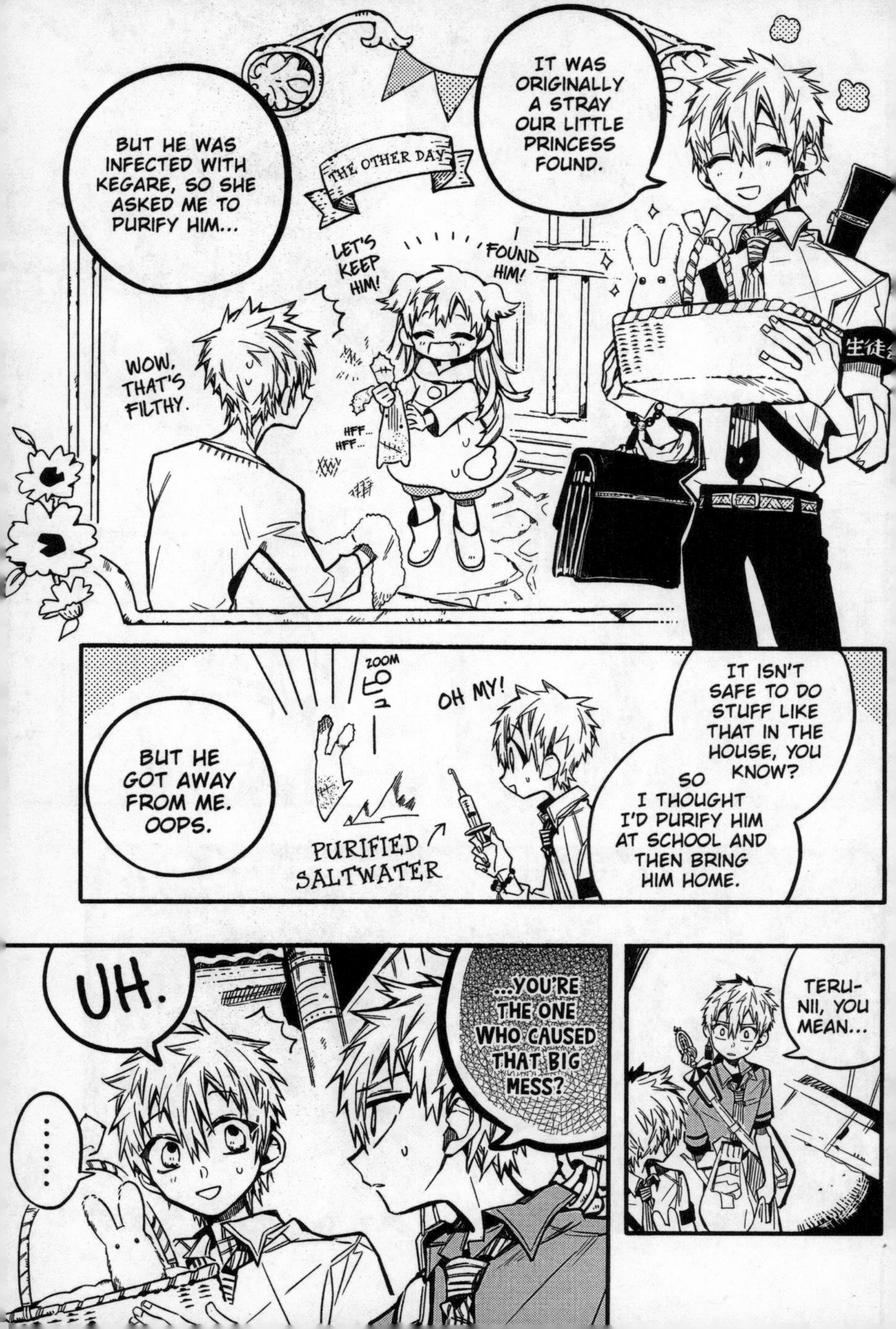
IT WAS ORIGINALLY A STRAY OUR LITTLE PRINCESS FOUND.
THE OTHER DAY
BUT HE WAS INFECTED WITH KEGARE, SO SHE ASKED ME TO PURIFY HIM...
I FOUND HIM!
LET'S KEEP HIM!
HFF... HFF...
WOW, THAT'S FILTHY.
IT ISN'T SAFE TO DO STUFF LIKE THAT IN THE HOUSE, YOU KNOW?
SO I THOUGHT I'D PURIFY HIM AT SCHOOL AND THEN BRING HIM HOME.
OH MY!
ZOOM
PURIFIED SALTWATER
BUT HE GOT AWAY FROM ME. OOPS.
TERU-NII, YOU MEAN...
...YOU'RE THE ONE WHO CAUSED THAT BIG MESS?
UH.
......

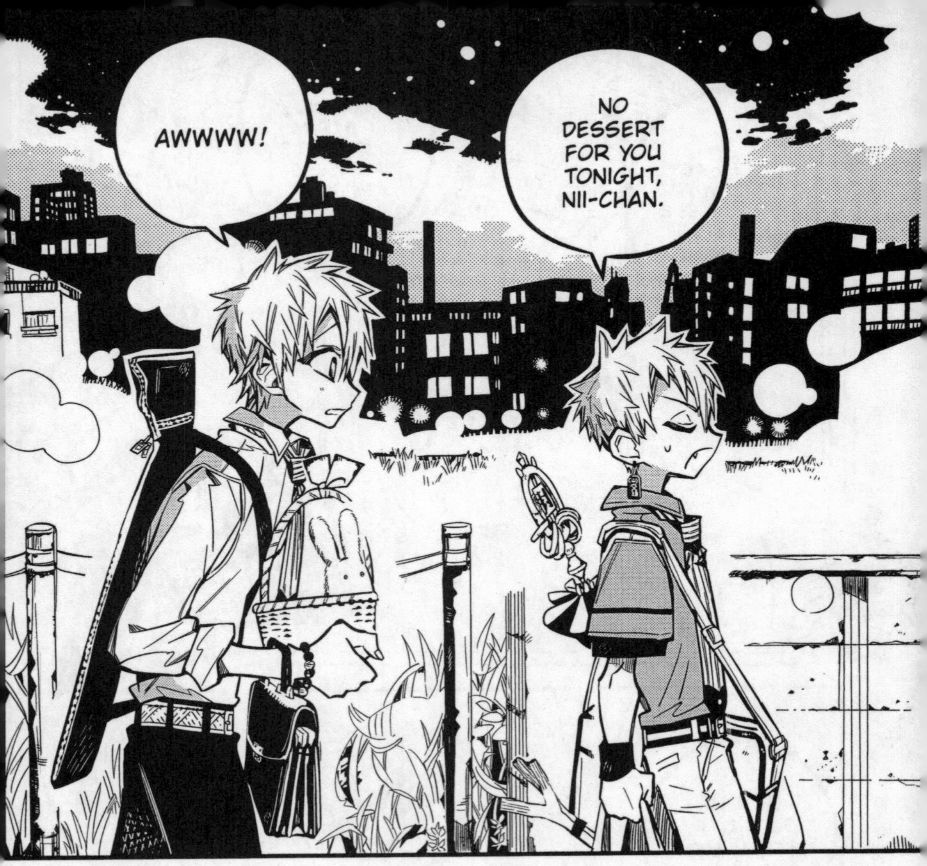
NO DESSERT FOR YOU TONIGHT, NII-CHAN.
AWWWW!

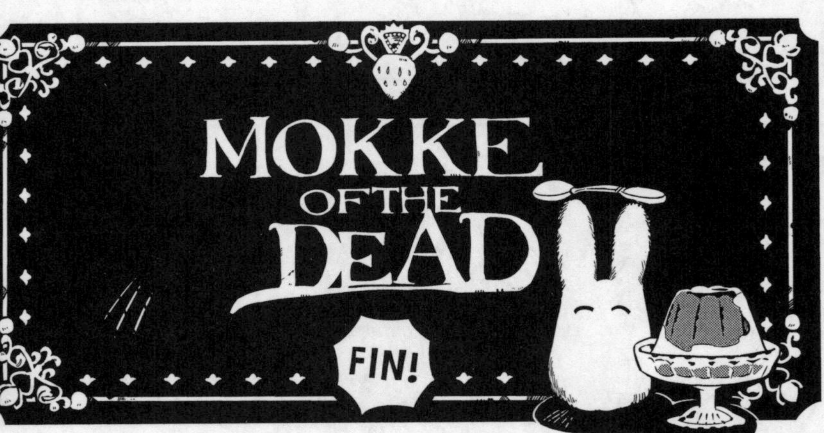
MOKKE OF THE DEAD
FIN!

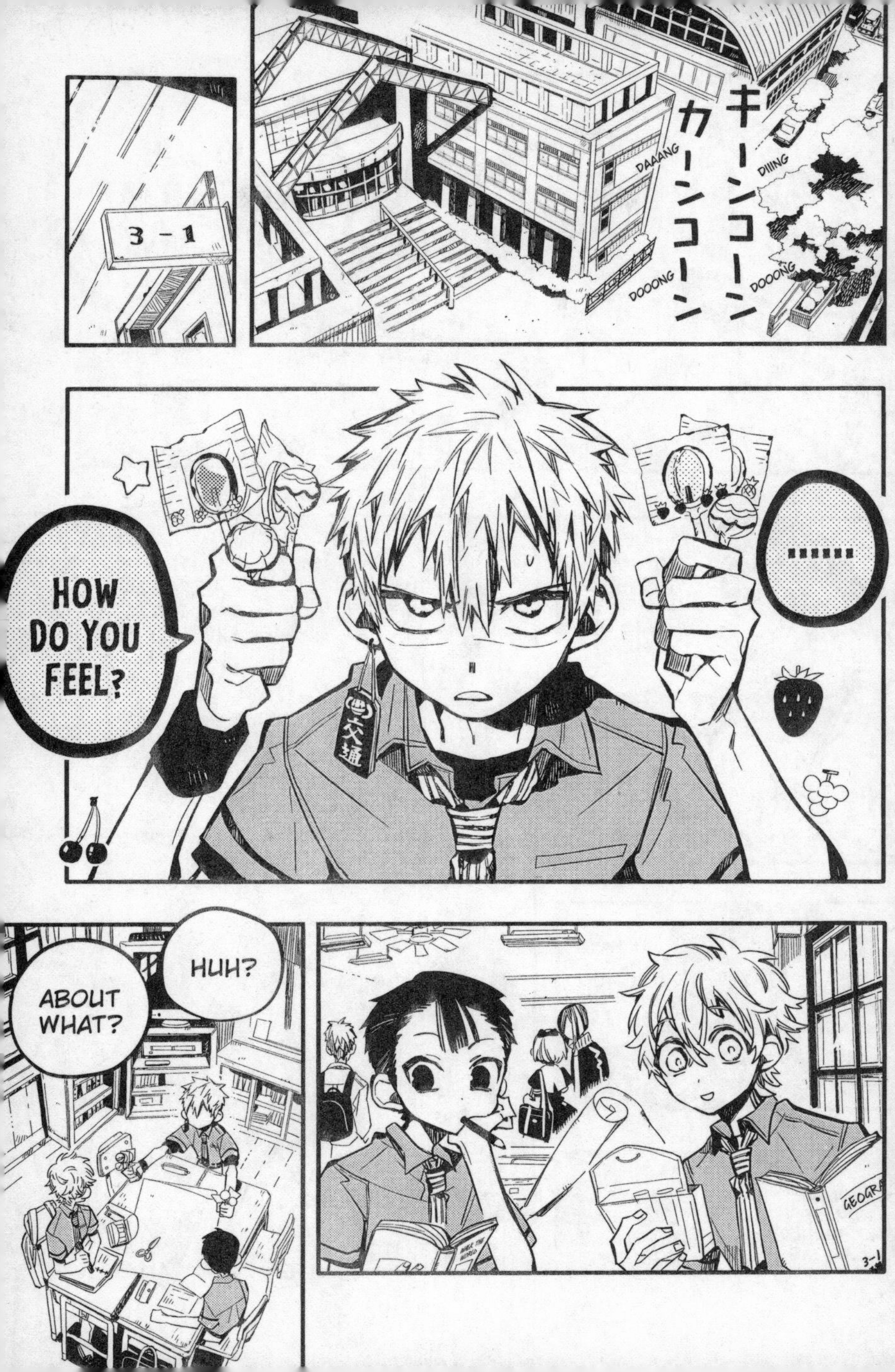
キーンコーン
DIIING
DOOONG
カーンコーン
DAAANG
DOOONG
3-1
......
HOW DO YOU FEEL?
3-1
HUH?
ABOUT WHAT?

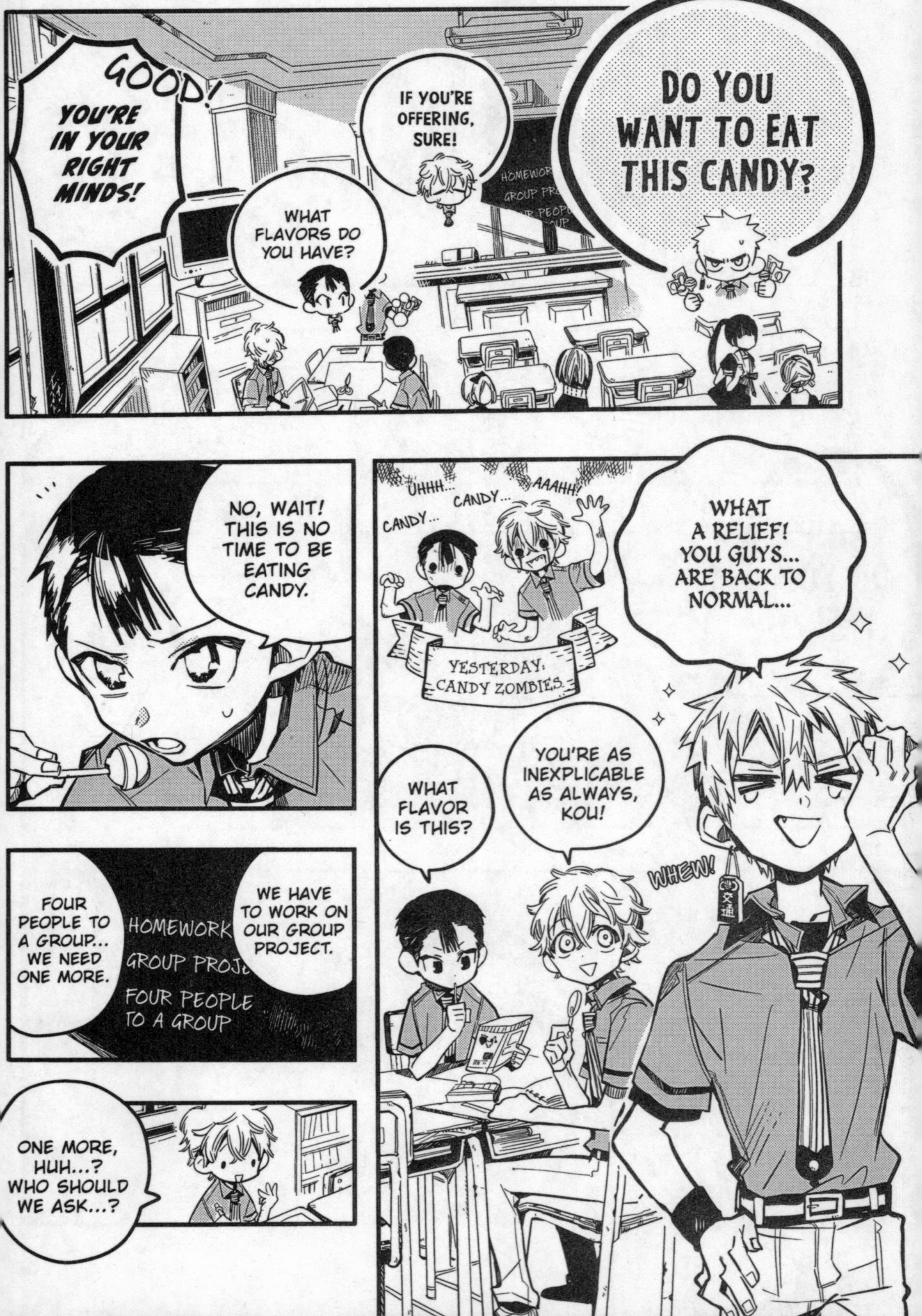
DO YOU WANT TO EAT THIS CANDY?
IF YOU'RE OFFERING, SURE!
WHAT FLAVORS DO YOU HAVE?
GOOD! YOU'RE IN YOUR RIGHT MINDS!
WHAT A RELIEF! YOU GUYS... ARE BACK TO NORMAL...
AAAHH!
CANDY...
UHHH...
CANDY...
YESTERDAY: CANDY ZOMBIES
YOU'RE AS INEXPLICABLE AS ALWAYS, KOU!
WHAT FLAVOR IS THIS?
WHEW!
NO, WAIT! THIS IS NO TIME TO BE EATING CANDY.
WE HAVE TO WORK ON OUR GROUP PROJECT.
HOMEWORK
GROUP PROJ
FOUR PEOPLE TO A GROUP
FOUR PEOPLE TO A GROUP... WE NEED ONE MORE.
ONE MORE, HUH...? WHO SHOULD WE ASK...?

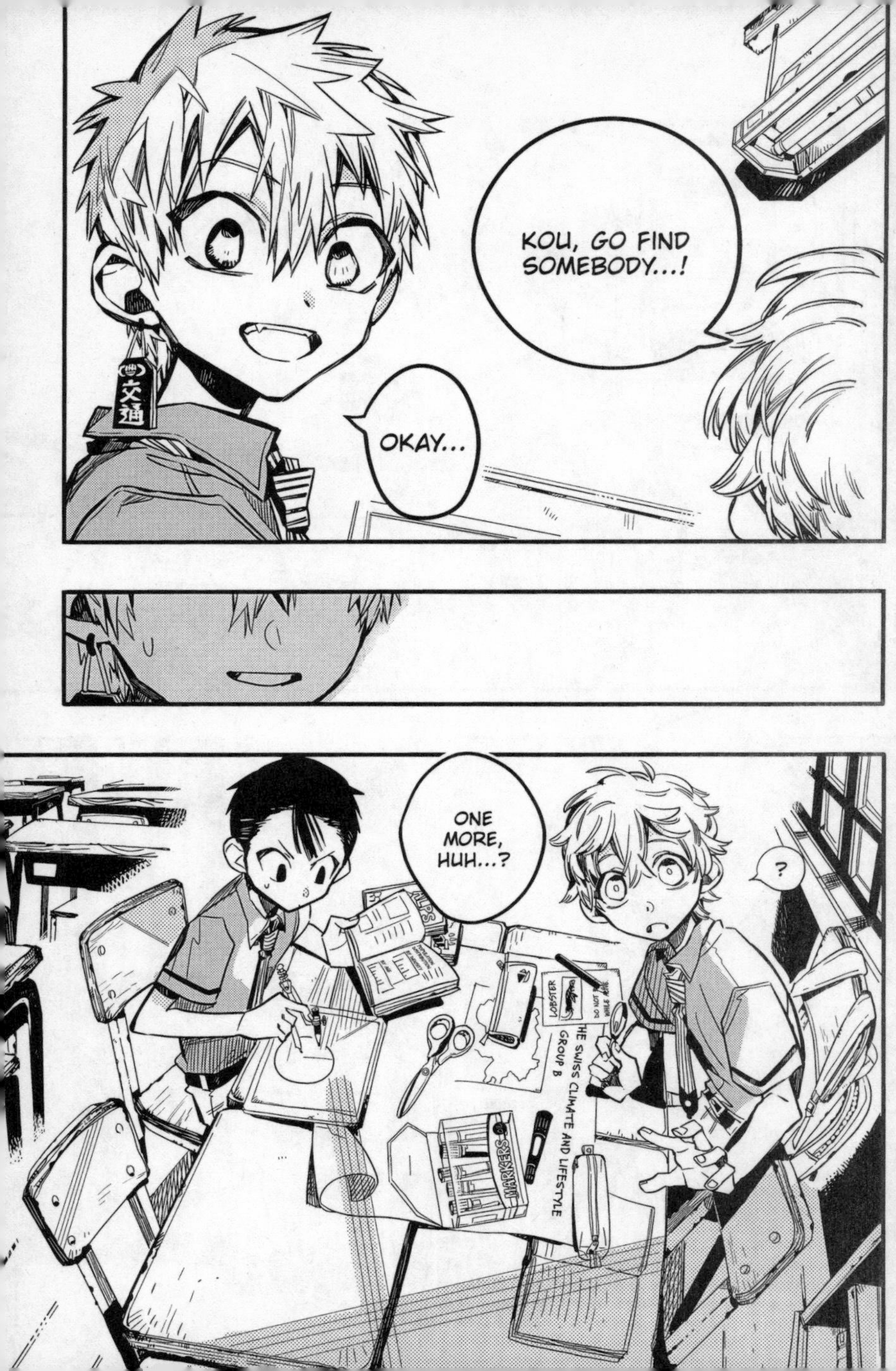
KOU, GO FIND SOMEBODY...!
OKAY...
?
ONE MORE, HUH...?
LOBSTER
THE SWISS CLIMATE AND LIFESTYLE GROUP B
MARKERS

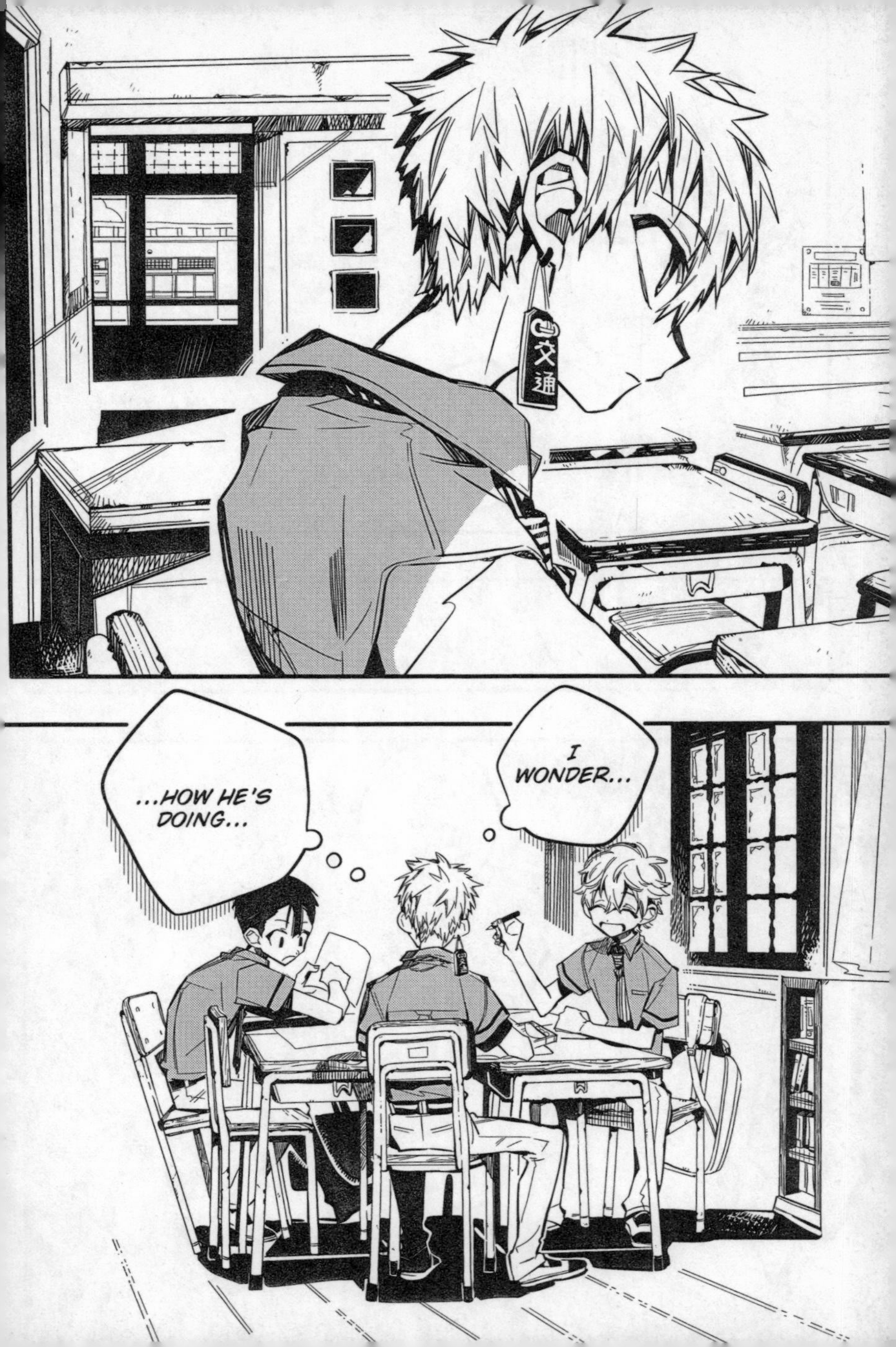
交通
I WONDER...
...HOW HE'S DOING...

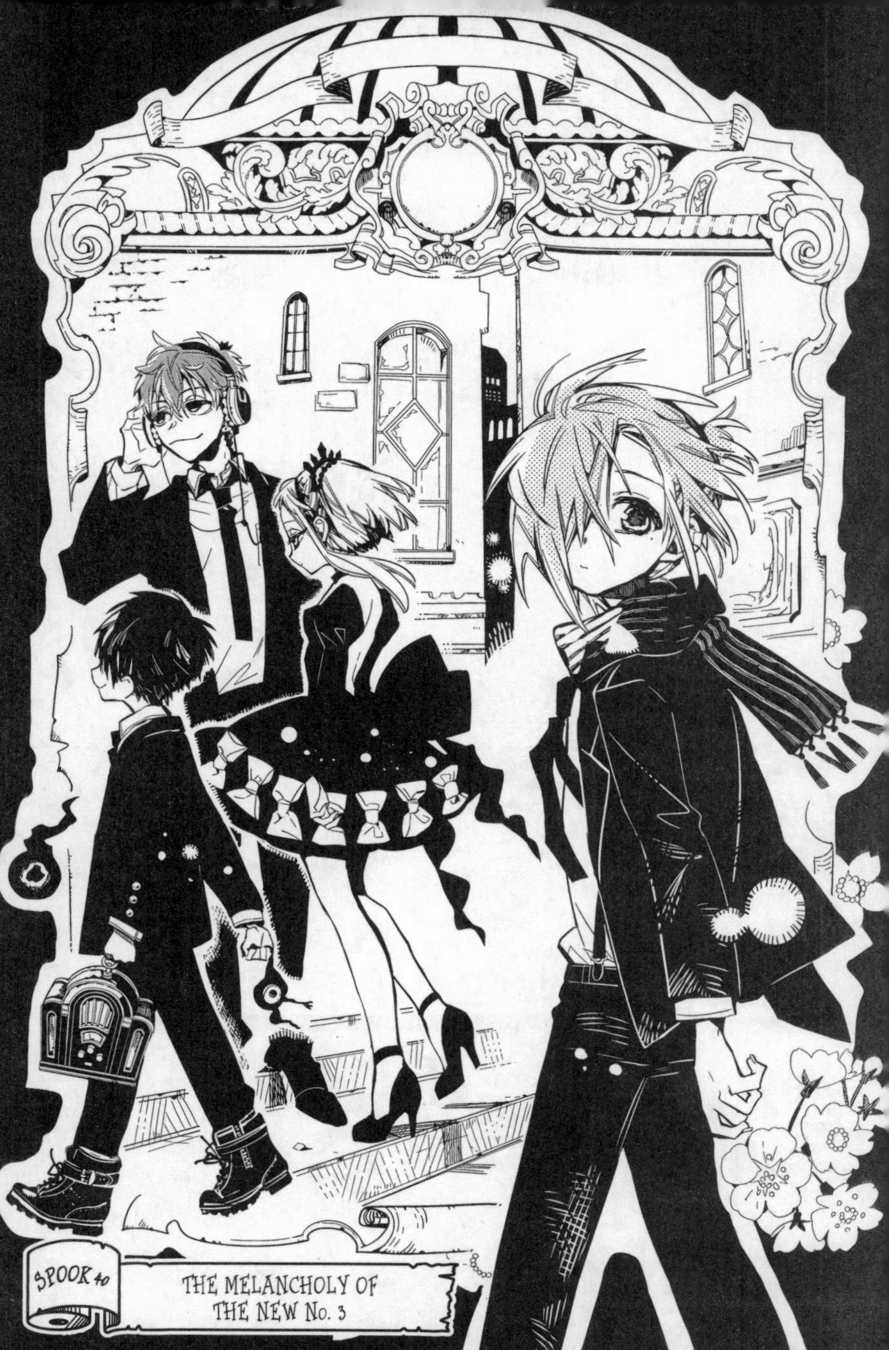
SPOOK 40
THE MELANCHOLY OF
THE NEW No. 3

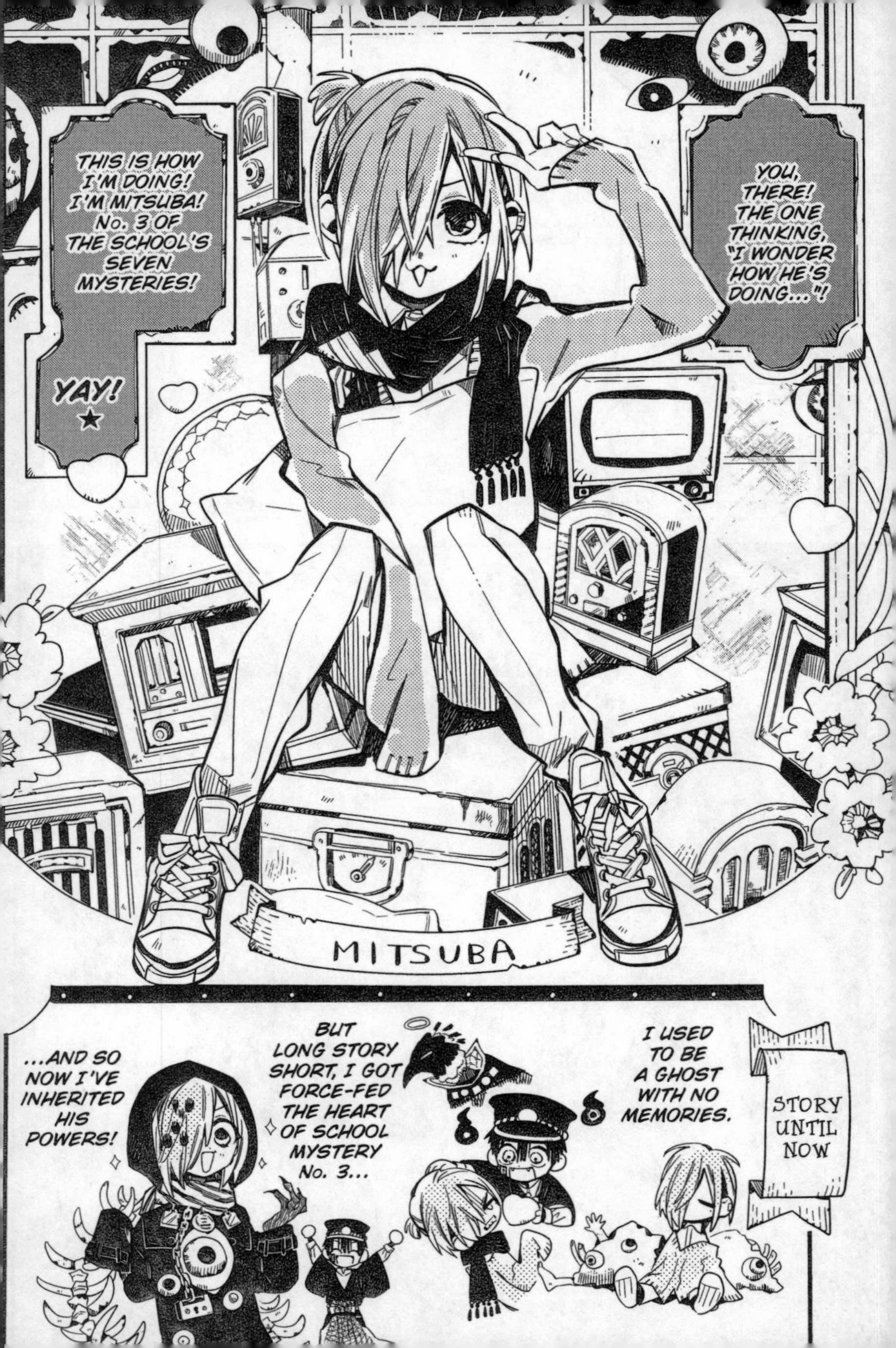
YOU, THERE! THE ONE THINKING, "I WONDER HOW HE'S DOING..."!
THIS IS HOW I'M DOING! I'M MITSUBA! No. 3 OF THE SCHOOL'S SEVEN MYSTERIES!
YAY! ★
MITSUBA
STORY UNTIL NOW
I USED TO BE A GHOST WITH NO MEMORIES.
BUT LONG STORY SHORT, I GOT FORCE-FED THE HEART OF SCHOOL MYSTERY No. 3...
...AND SO NOW I'VE INHERITED HIS POWERS!

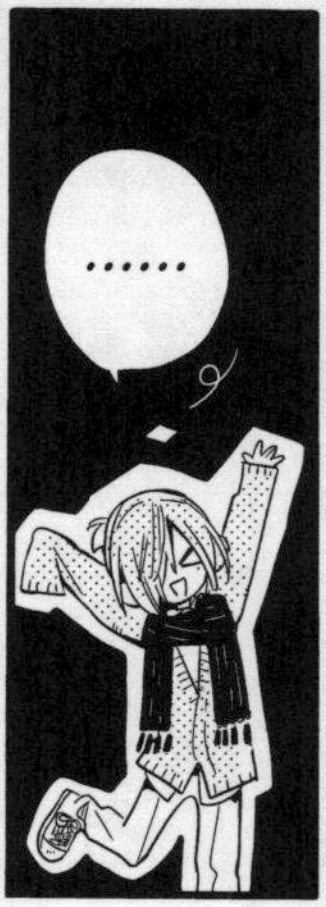
......

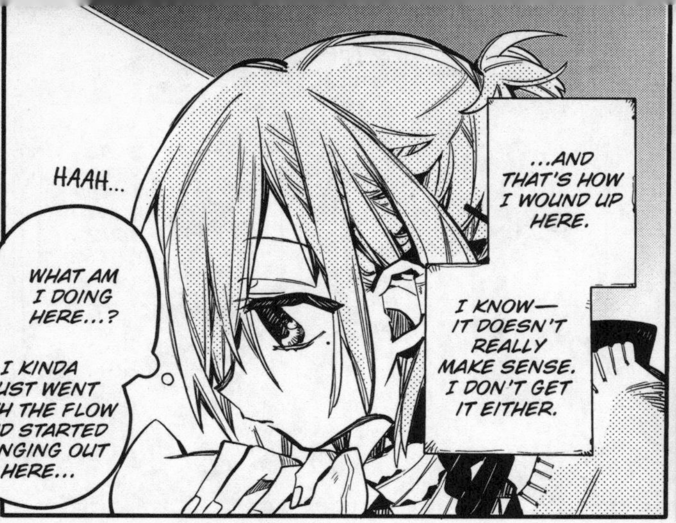
...AND THAT'S HOW I WOUND UP HERE.
HAAH...
I KNOW— IT DOESN'T REALLY MAKE SENSE. I DON'T GET IT EITHER.
WHAT AM I DOING HERE...?
I KINDA JUST WENT WITH THE FLOW AND STARTED HANGING OUT HERE...

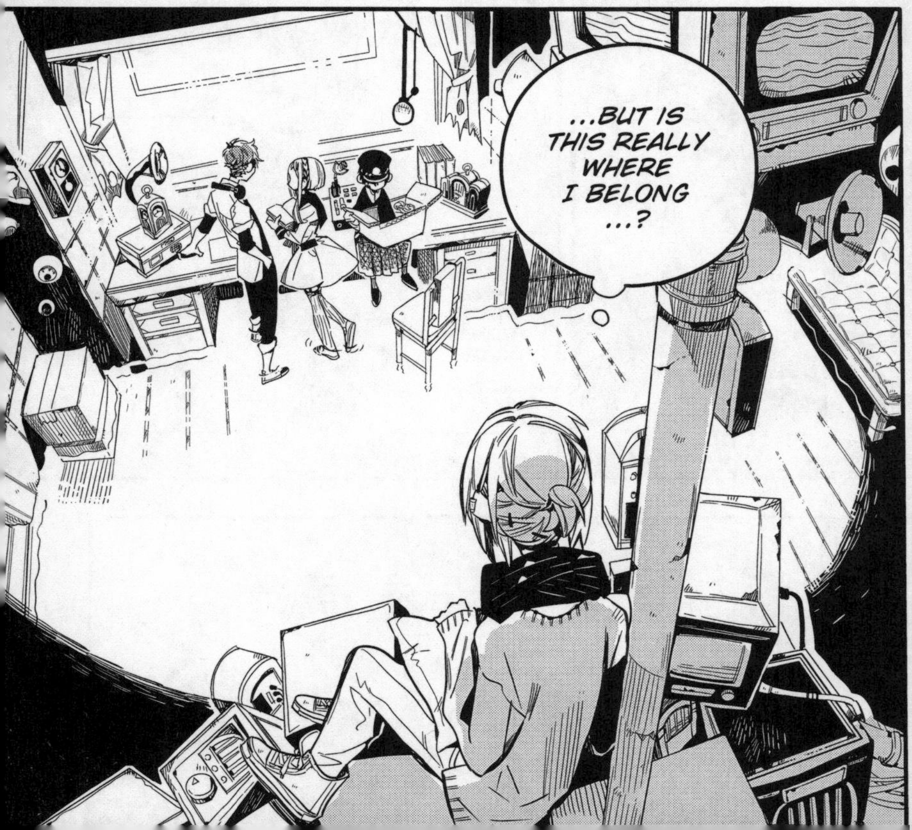
...BUT IS THIS REALLY WHERE I BELONG ...?

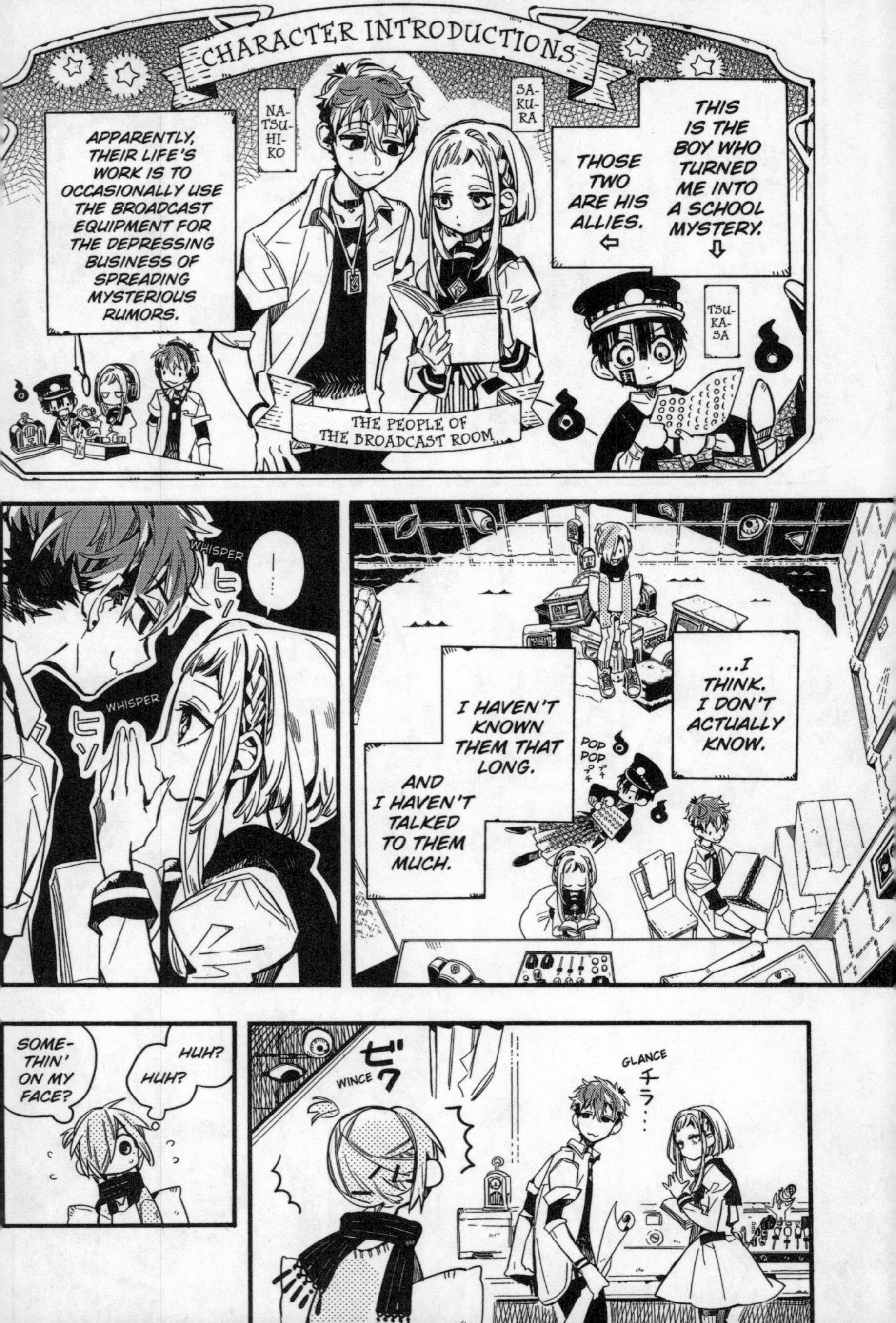
CHARACTER INTRODUCTIONS
THIS IS THE BOY WHO TURNED ME INTO A SCHOOL MYSTERY. ⇩
THOSE TWO ARE HIS ALLIES. ⇦
SA-KU-RA
NA-TSU-HI-KO
APPARENTLY, THEIR LIFE'S WORK IS TO OCCASIONALLY USE THE BROADCAST EQUIPMENT FOR THE DEPRESSING BUSINESS OF SPREADING MYSTERIOUS RUMORS.
TSU-KA-SA
THE PEOPLE OF THE BROADCAST ROOM
...I THINK. I DON'T ACTUALLY KNOW.
I HAVEN'T KNOWN THEM THAT LONG.
POP POP
AND I HAVEN'T TALKED TO THEM MUCH.
WHISPER
!...
WHISPER
GLANCE
WINCE
HUH? HUH?
SOMETHIN' ON MY FACE?

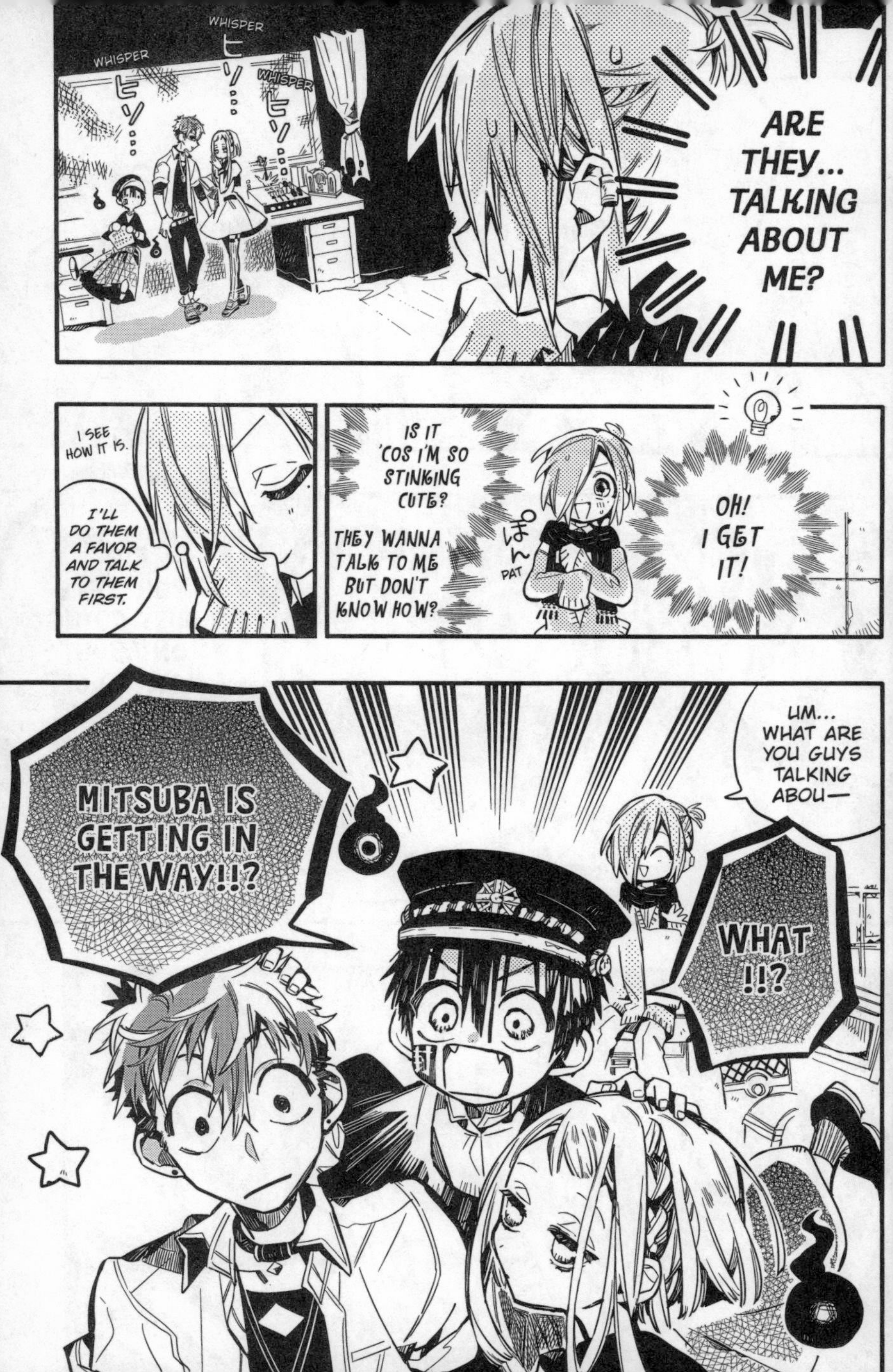
WHISPER
ヒソ...
WHISPER
ヒソ...
WHISPER
ヒソ...
ARE THEY... TALKING ABOUT ME?
OH! I GET IT!
ぽん
PAT
IS IT 'COS I'M SO STINKING CUTE?
THEY WANNA TALK TO ME BUT DON'T KNOW HOW?
I SEE HOW IT IS.
I'LL DO THEM A FAVOR AND TALK TO THEM FIRST.
UM... WHAT ARE YOU GUYS TALKING ABOU—
WHAT!!?
MITSUBA IS GETTING IN THE WAY!!?

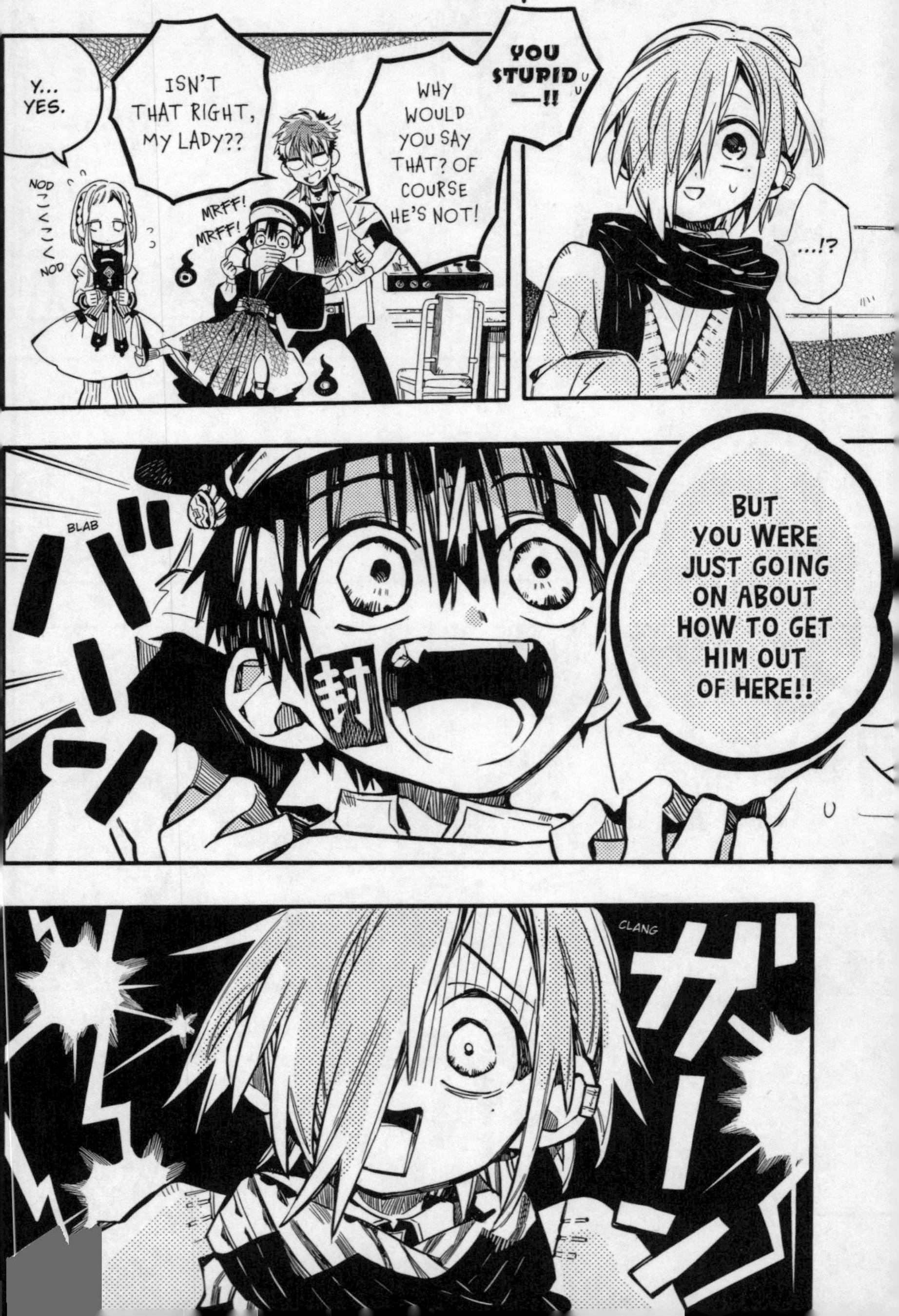
...!?
YOU STUPID—!!
WHY WOULD YOU SAY THAT? OF COURSE HE'S NOT!
MRFF! MRFF!
ISN'T THAT RIGHT, MY LADY??
NOD NOD
Y... YES.
BUT YOU WERE JUST GOING ON ABOUT HOW TO GET HIM OUT OF HERE!!
BLAB
CLANG

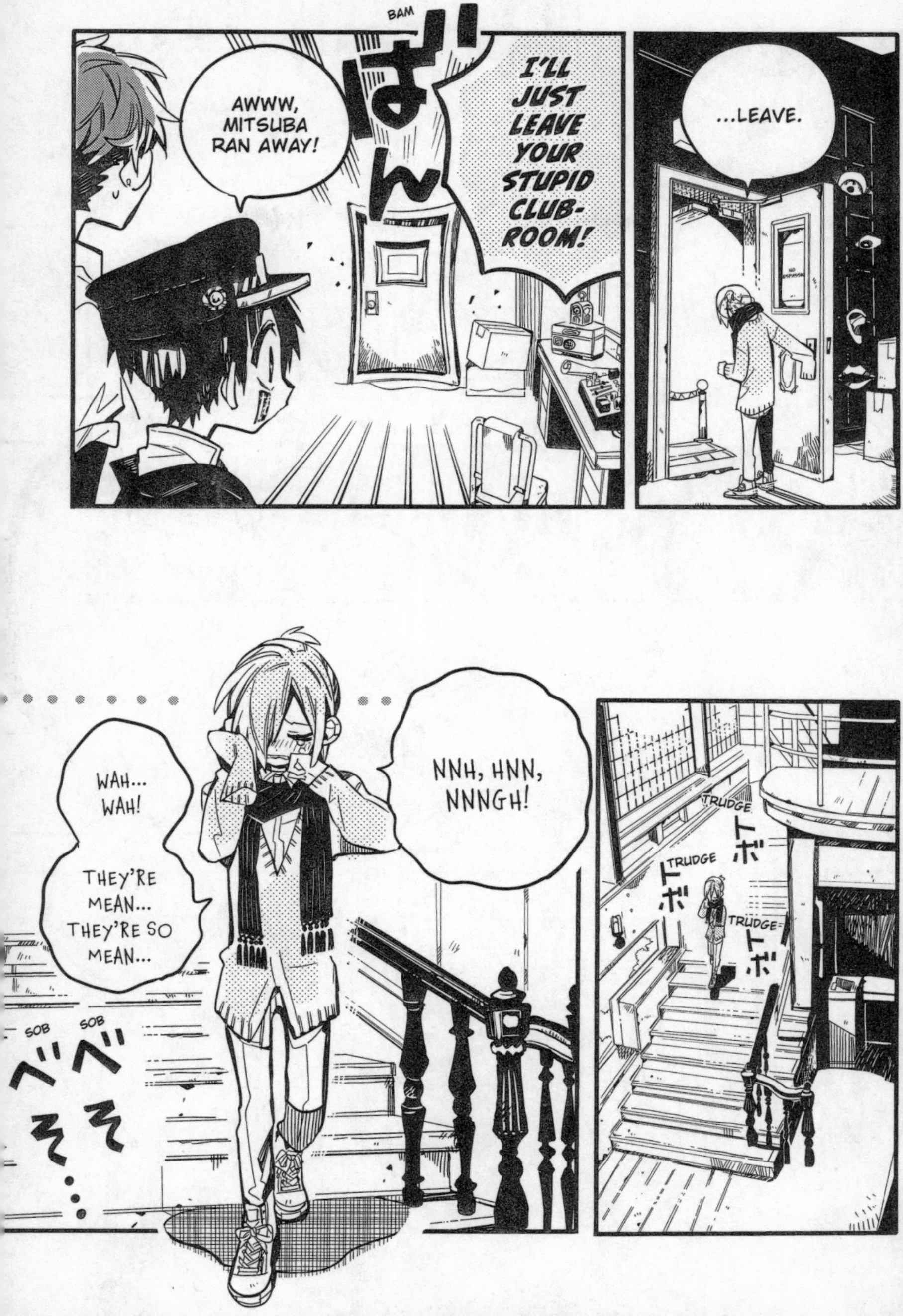

...LEAVE.
BAM
ばん
I'LL JUST LEAVE YOUR STUPID CLUB-ROOM!
AWWW, MITSUBA RAN AWAY!
TRUDGE
トボ
TRUDGE
トボ
TRUDGE
トボ
NNH, HNN, NNNGH!
WAH... WAH!
THEY'RE MEAN... THEY'RE SO MEAN...
SOB SOB
べべそそ...

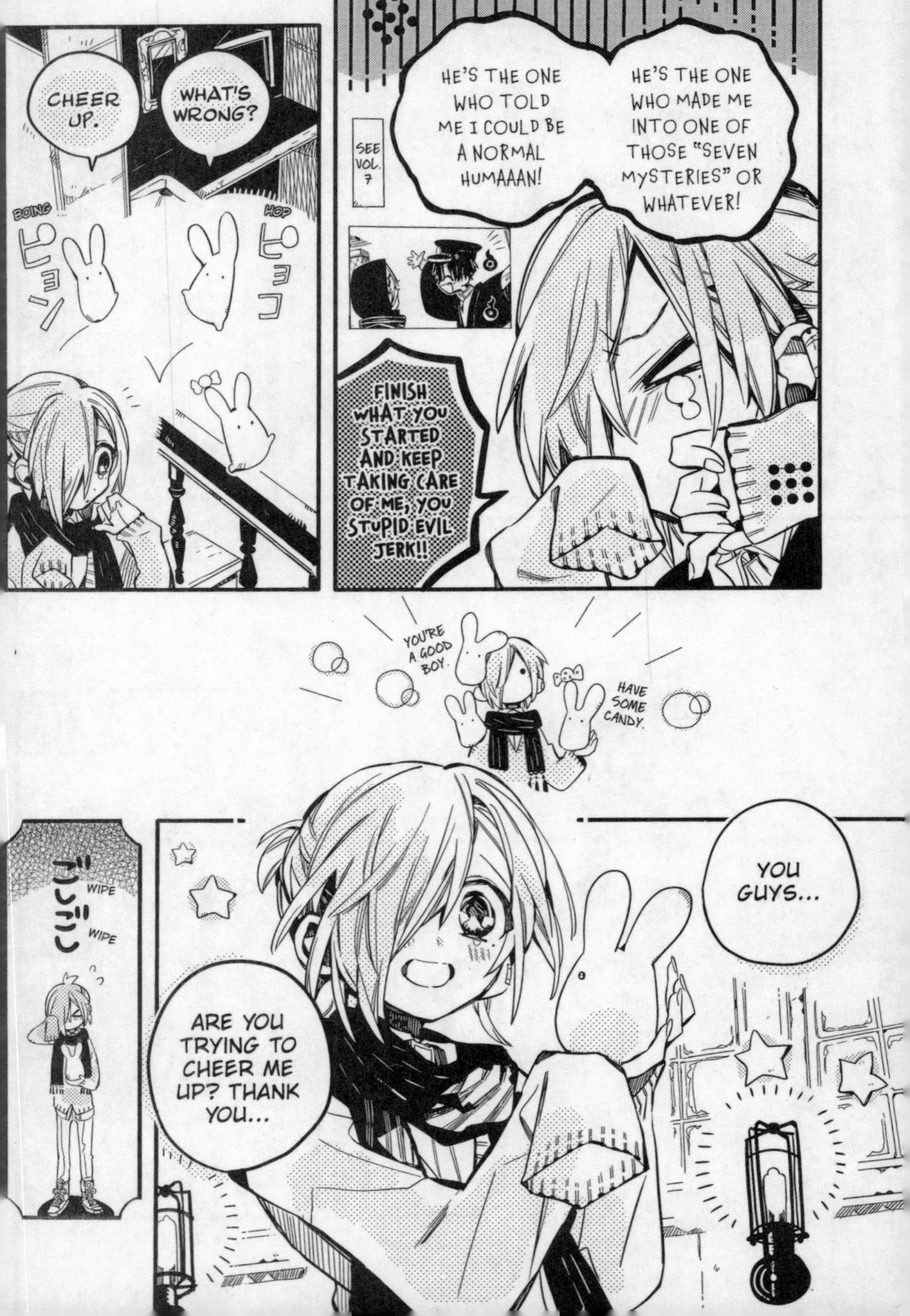

HE'S THE ONE WHO MADE ME INTO ONE OF THOSE "SEVEN MYSTERIES" OR WHATEVER!
HE'S THE ONE WHO TOLD ME I COULD BE A NORMAL HUMAAAN!
SEE VOL. 7
FINISH WHAT YOU STARTED AND KEEP TAKING CARE OF ME, YOU STUPID EVIL JERK!!
WHAT'S WRONG?
CHEER UP.
HOP
BOING
HAVE SOME CANDY.
YOU'RE A GOOD BOY.
YOU GUYS...
ARE YOU TRYING TO CHEER ME UP? THANK YOU...
WIPE
WIPE

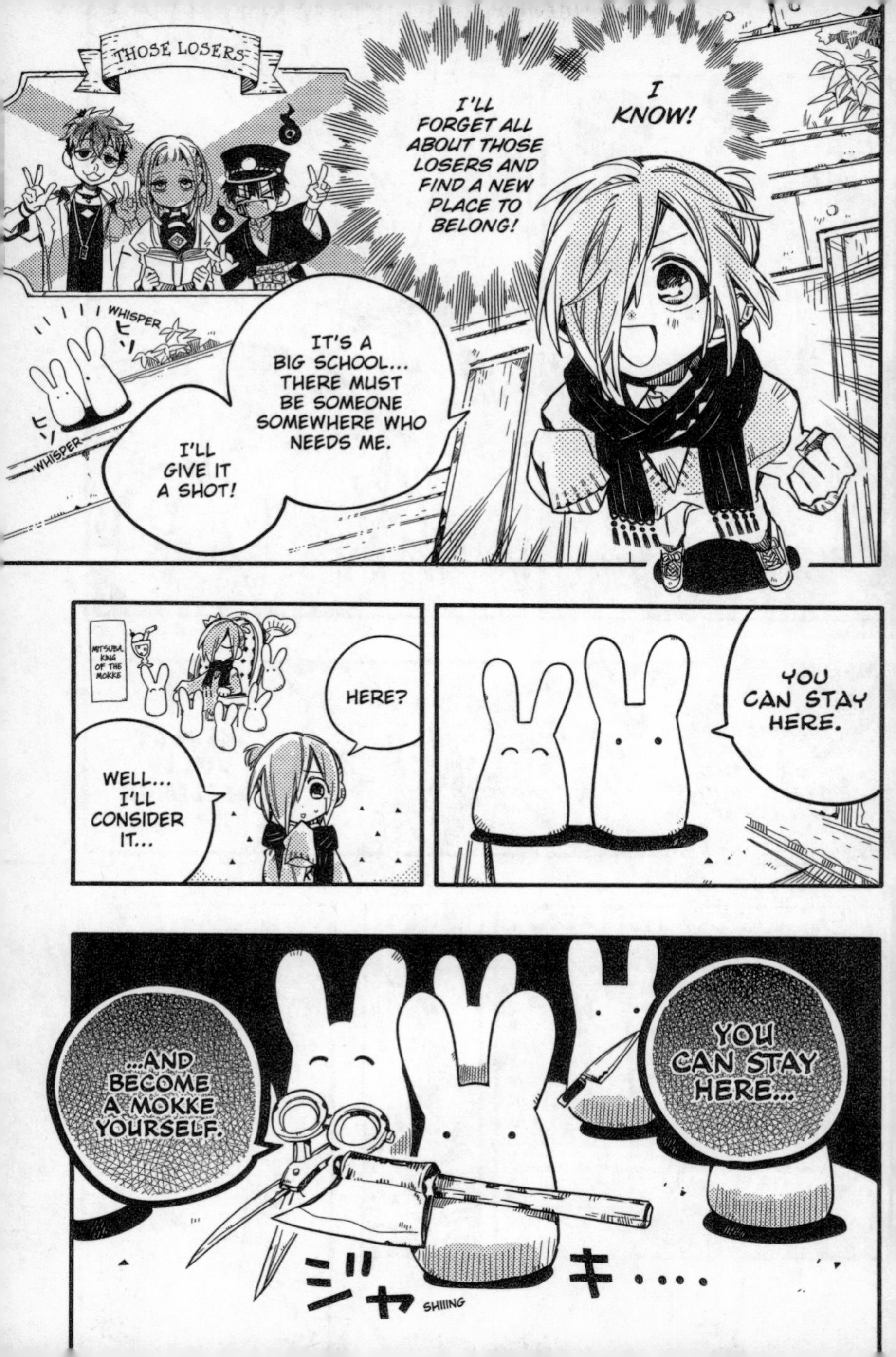
I KNOW!
I'LL FORGET ALL ABOUT THOSE LOSERS AND FIND A NEW PLACE TO BELONG!
THOSE LOSERS
ヒソ WHISPER
ヒソ WHISPER
IT'S A BIG SCHOOL... THERE MUST BE SOMEONE SOMEWHERE WHO NEEDS ME.
I'LL GIVE IT A SHOT!
YOU CAN STAY HERE.
HERE?
MITSUBA, KING OF THE MOKKE
WELL... I'LL CONSIDER IT...
YOU CAN STAY HERE...
...AND BECOME A MOKKE YOURSELF.
ジャキ.... SHIIING

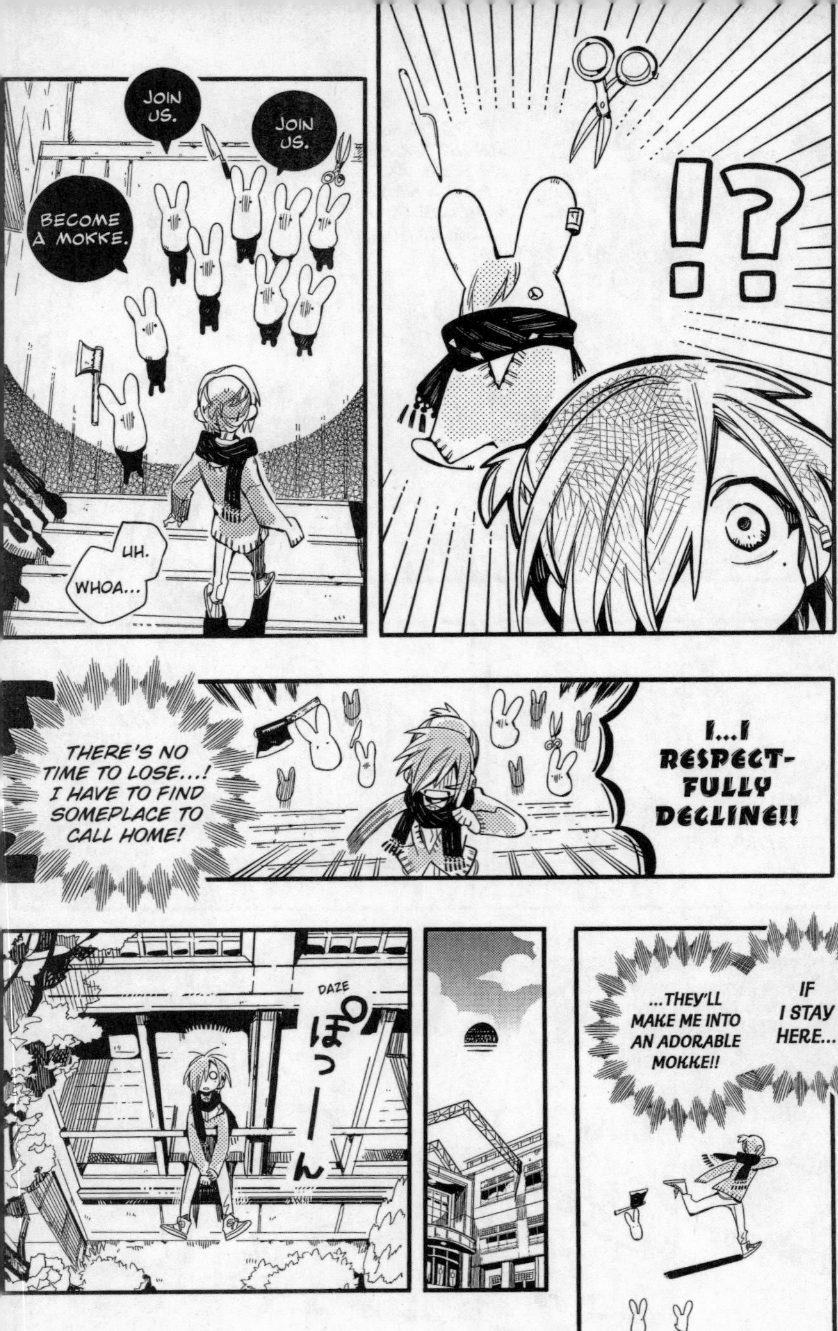
!?
JOIN US.
JOIN US.
BECOME A MOKKE.
UH.
WHOA...
I...I RESPECT-FULLY DECLINE!!
THERE'S NO TIME TO LOSE...! I HAVE TO FIND SOMEPLACE TO CALL HOME!
IF I STAY HERE...
...THEY'LL MAKE ME INTO AN ADORABLE MOKKE!!
ぽっーん
DAZE

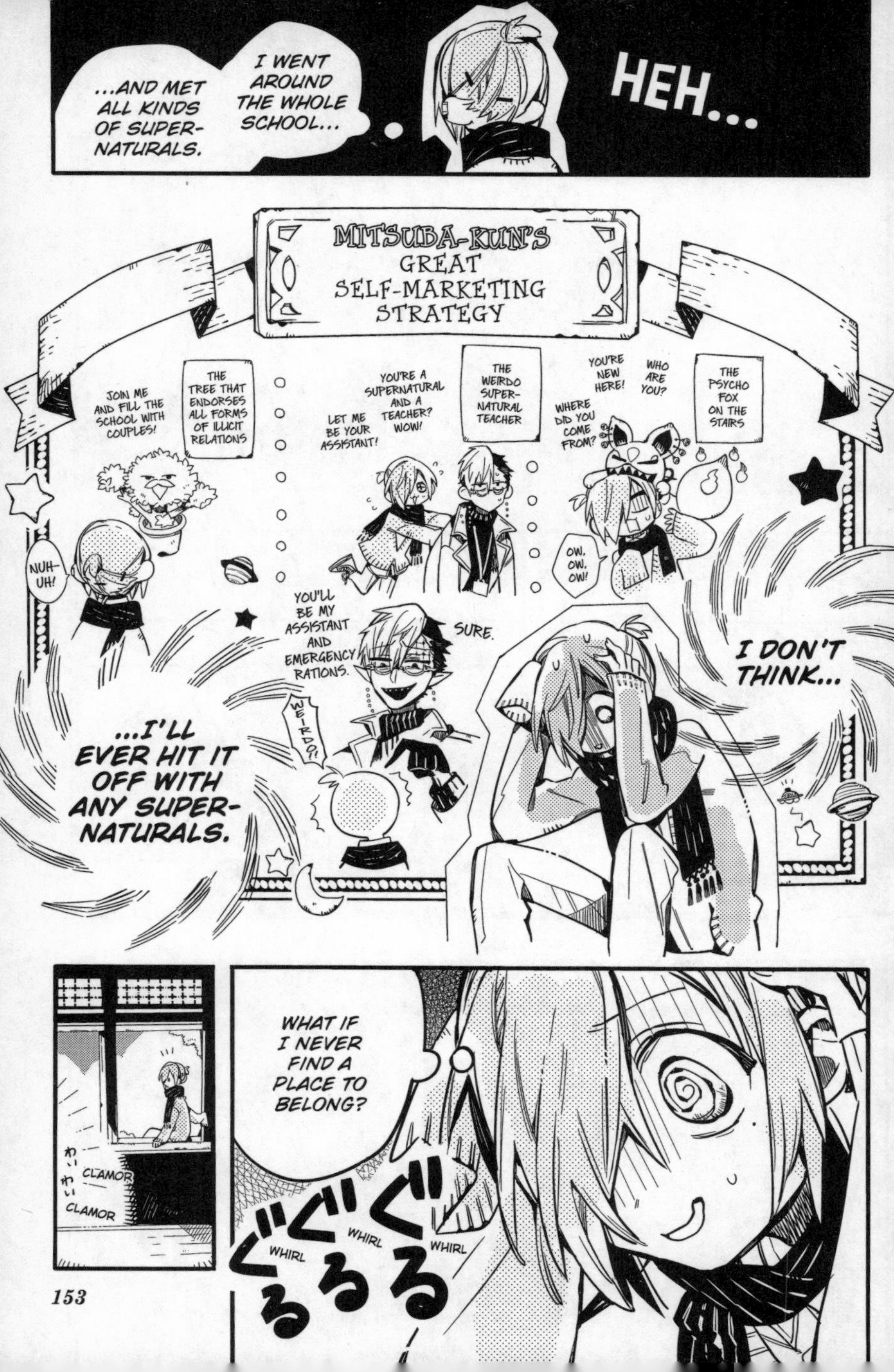
HEH...
I WENT AROUND THE WHOLE SCHOOL...
...AND MET ALL KINDS OF SUPER-NATURALS.
MITSUBA-KUN'S GREAT SELF-MARKETING STRATEGY
THE PSYCHO FOX ON THE STAIRS
WHO ARE YOU?
YOU'RE NEW HERE!
WHERE DID YOU COME FROM?
OW, OW, OW!
THE WEIRDO SUPER-NATURAL TEACHER
YOU'RE A SUPERNATURAL AND A TEACHER? WOW!
LET ME BE YOUR ASSISTANT!
THE TREE THAT ENDORSES ALL FORMS OF ILLICIT RELATIONS
JOIN ME AND FILL THE SCHOOL WITH COUPLES!
NUH-UH!
I DON'T THINK...
SURE.
YOU'LL BE MY ASSISTANT AND EMERGENCY RATIONS.
WEIRDO?!
...I'LL EVER HIT IT OFF WITH ANY SUPER-NATURALS.
WHAT IF I NEVER FIND A PLACE TO BELONG?
ぐるぐるぐる ぐるるる
WHIRL
WHIRL
WHIRL
わいわい
CLAMOR
CLAMOR

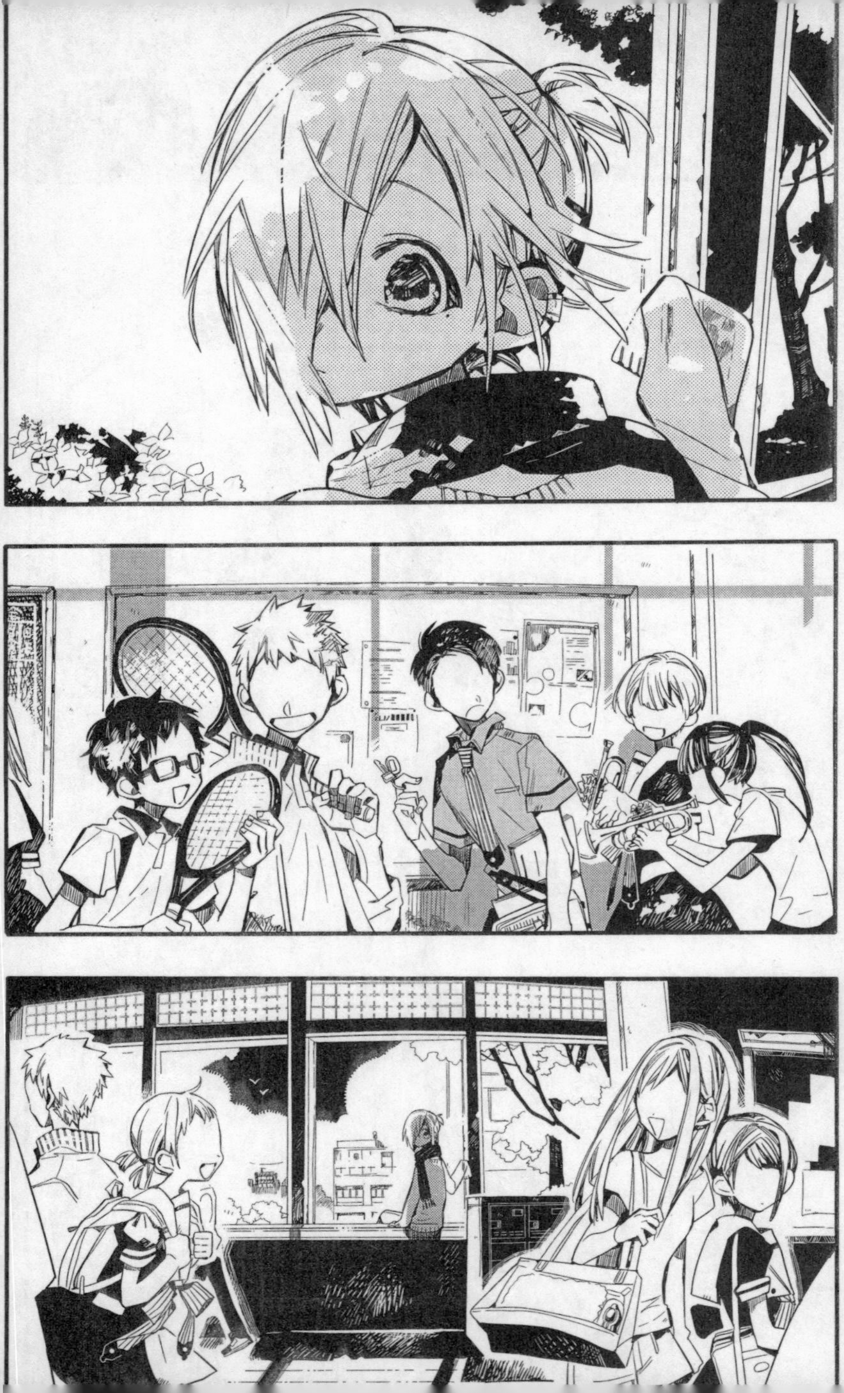

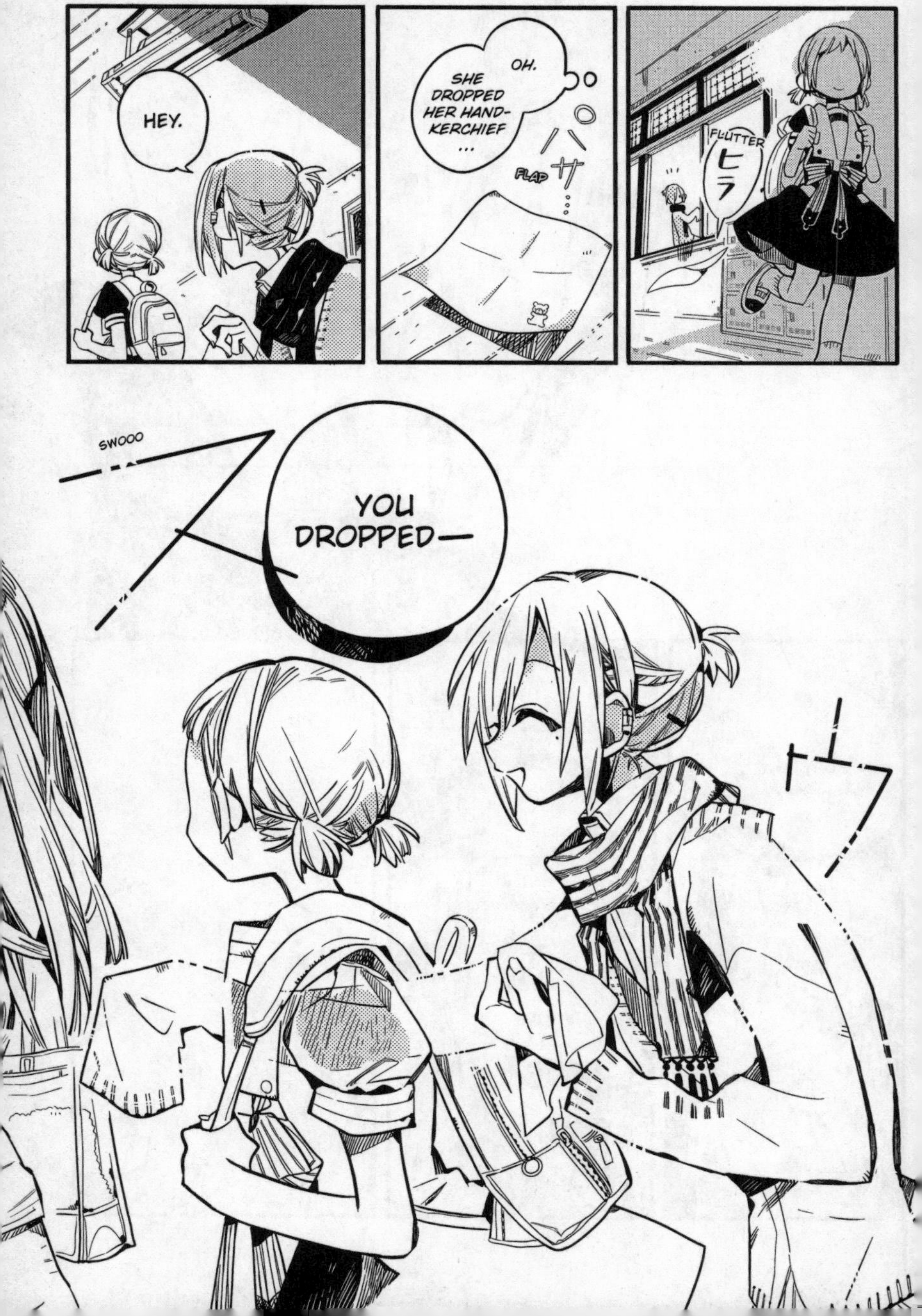
FLUTTER
ヒラ
OH.
SHE DROPPED HER HANDKERCHIEF...
ハサ
FLAP
HEY.
SWOOO
YOU DROPPED—

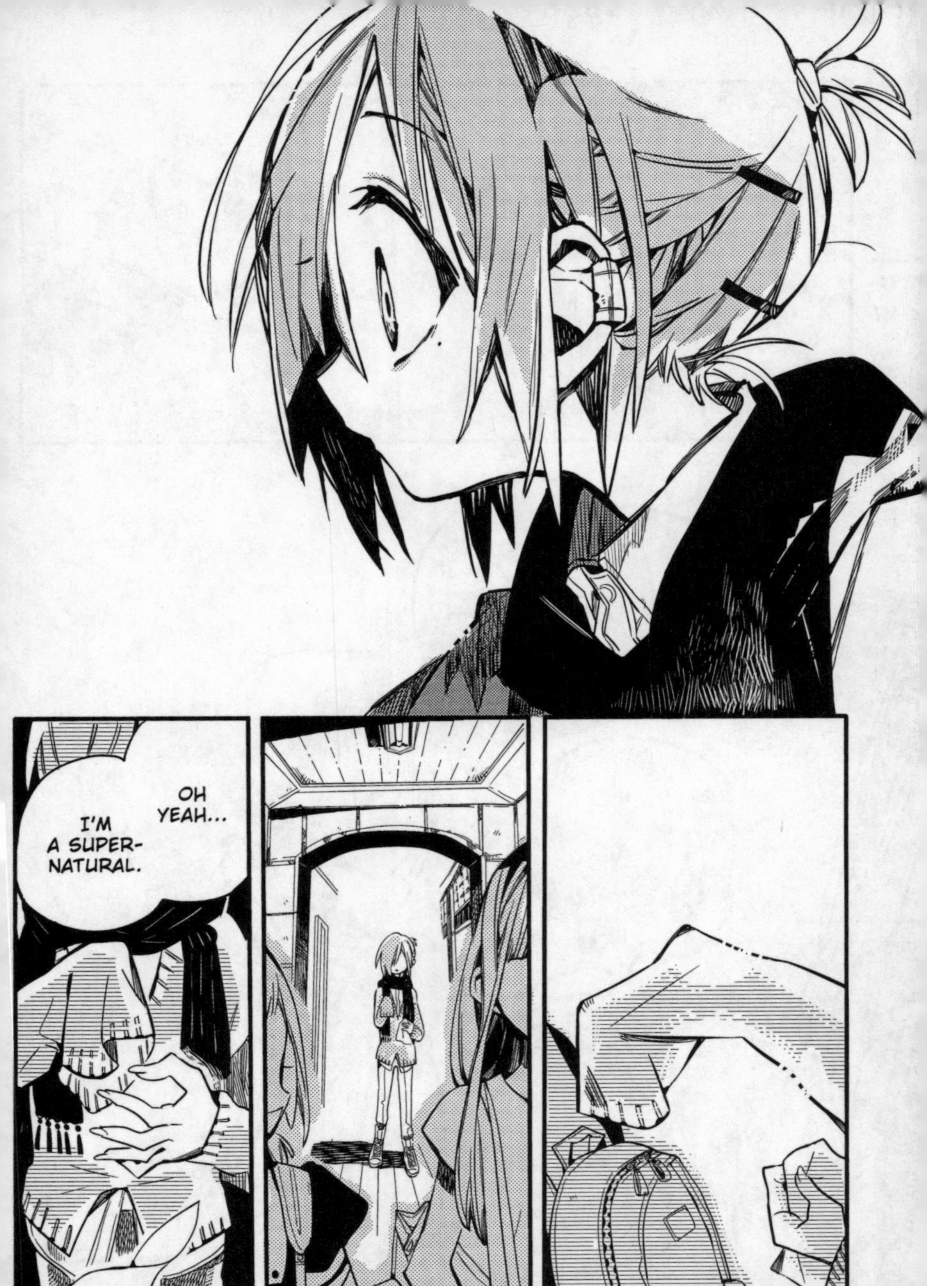
OH YEAH...
I'M A SUPER-NATURAL.

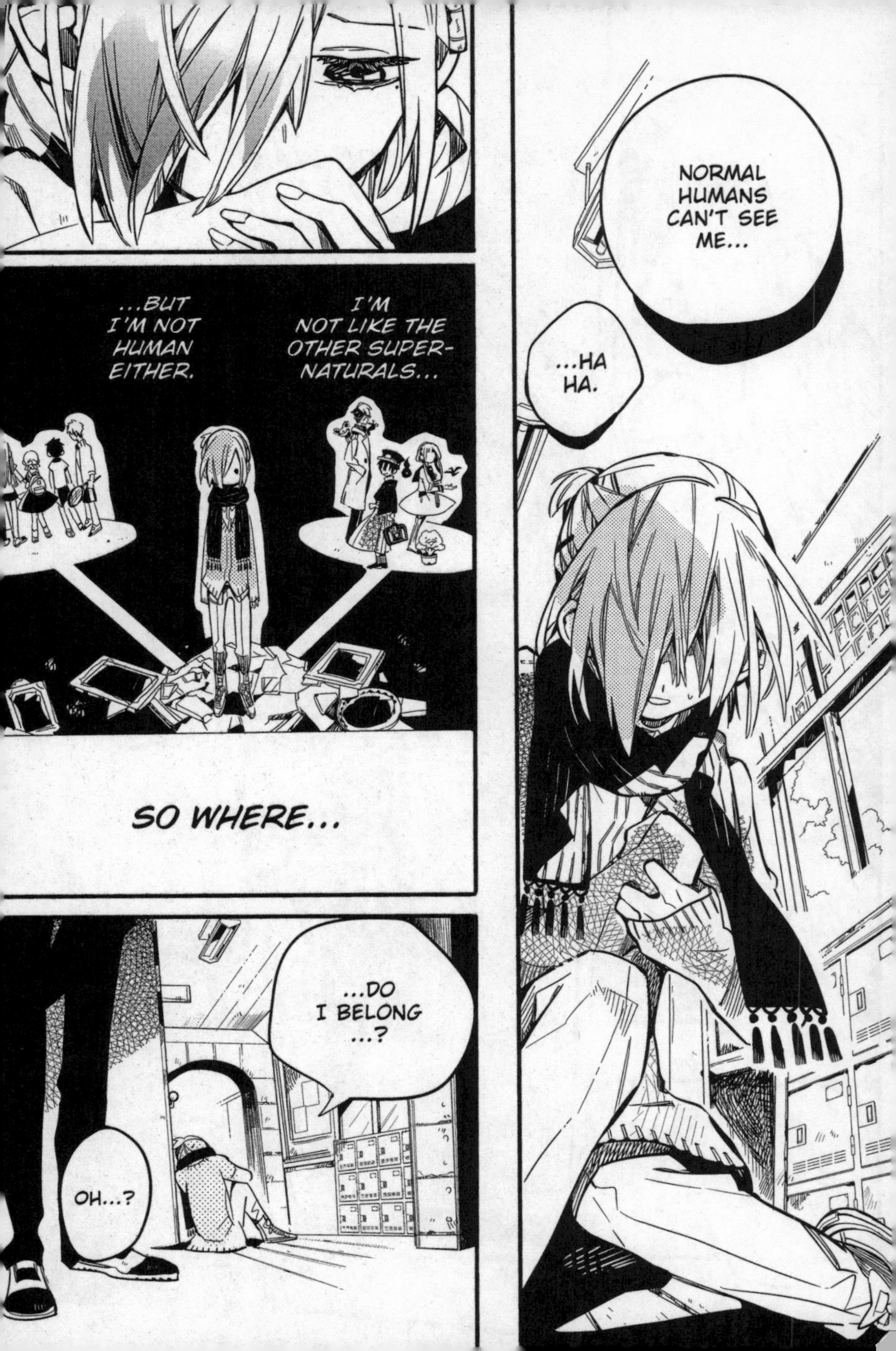
NORMAL HUMANS CAN'T SEE ME...
...HA HA.
I'M NOT LIKE THE OTHER SUPER-NATURALS...
...BUT I'M NOT HUMAN EITHER.
SO WHERE...
...DO I BELONG ...?
OH...?

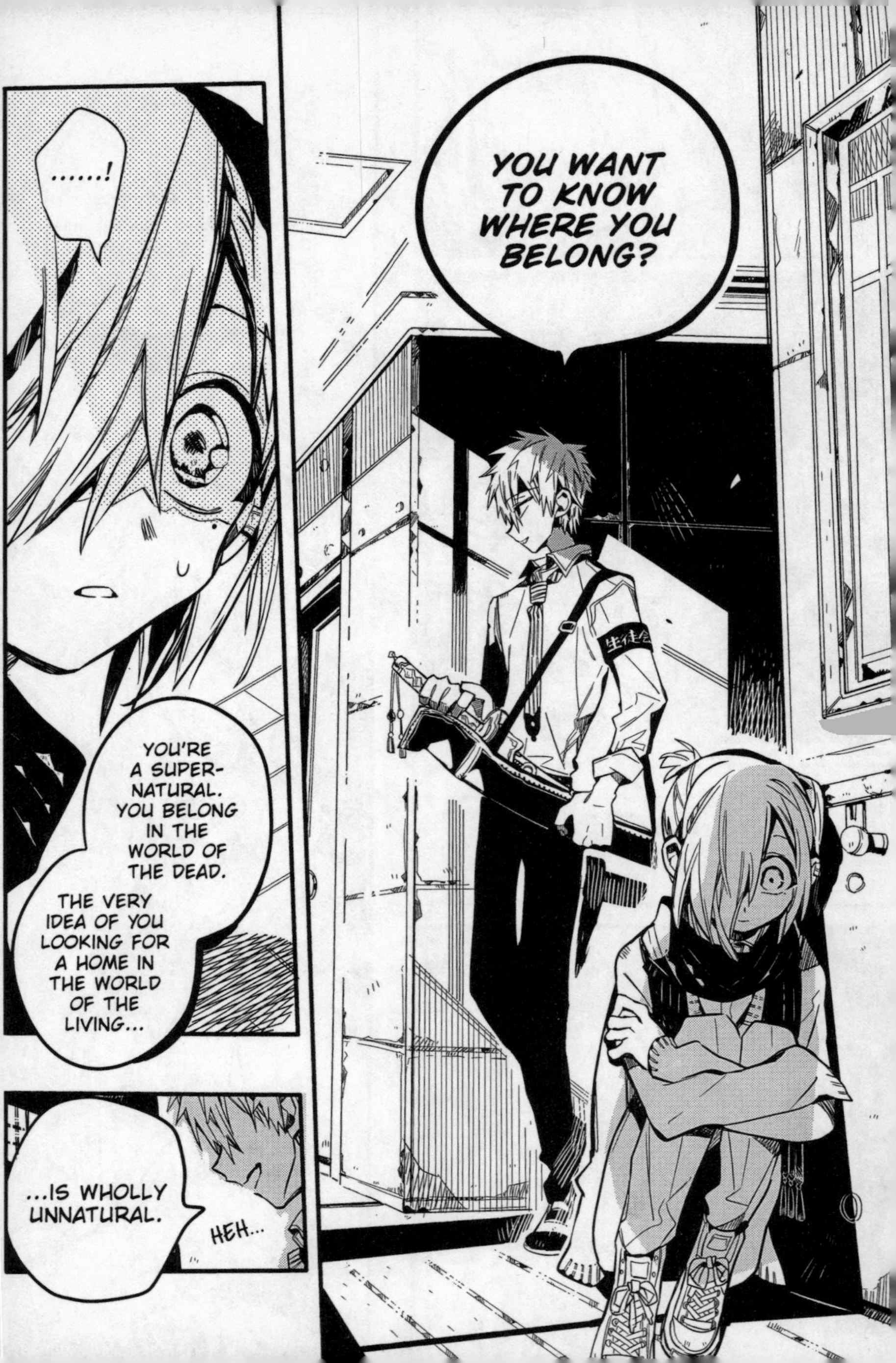
YOU WANT TO KNOW WHERE YOU BELONG?
生徒会
......!
YOU'RE A SUPER-NATURAL. YOU BELONG IN THE WORLD OF THE DEAD.
THE VERY IDEA OF YOU LOOKING FOR A HOME IN THE WORLD OF THE LIVING...
...IS WHOLLY UNNATURAL.
HEH...

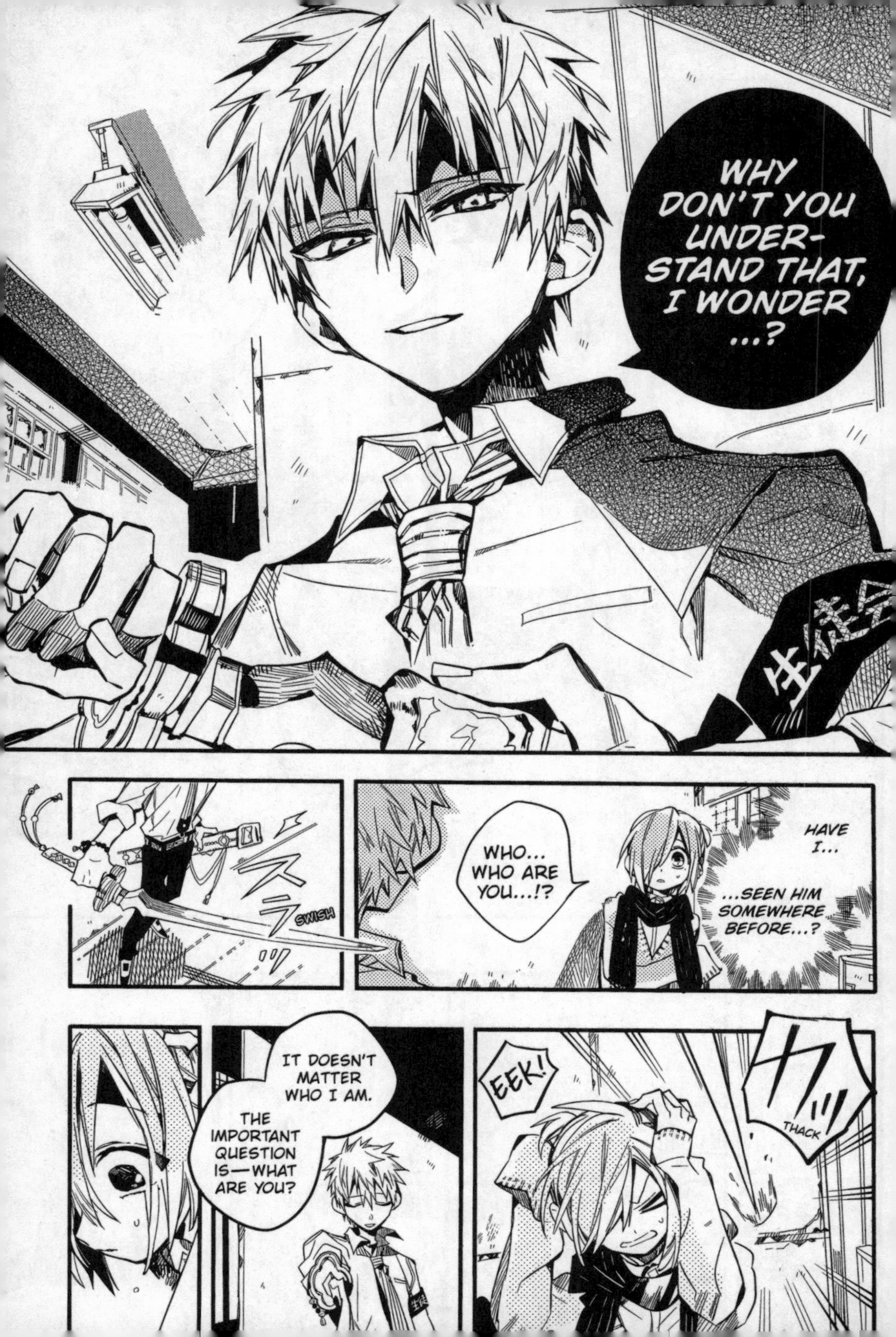
WHY DON'T YOU UNDER- STAND THAT, I WONDER ...?
WHO... WHO ARE YOU...!?
HAVE I...
...SEEN HIM SOMEWHERE BEFORE...?
SWISH
THACK
EEK!
IT DOESN'T MATTER WHO I AM.
THE IMPORTANT QUESTION IS—WHAT ARE YOU?

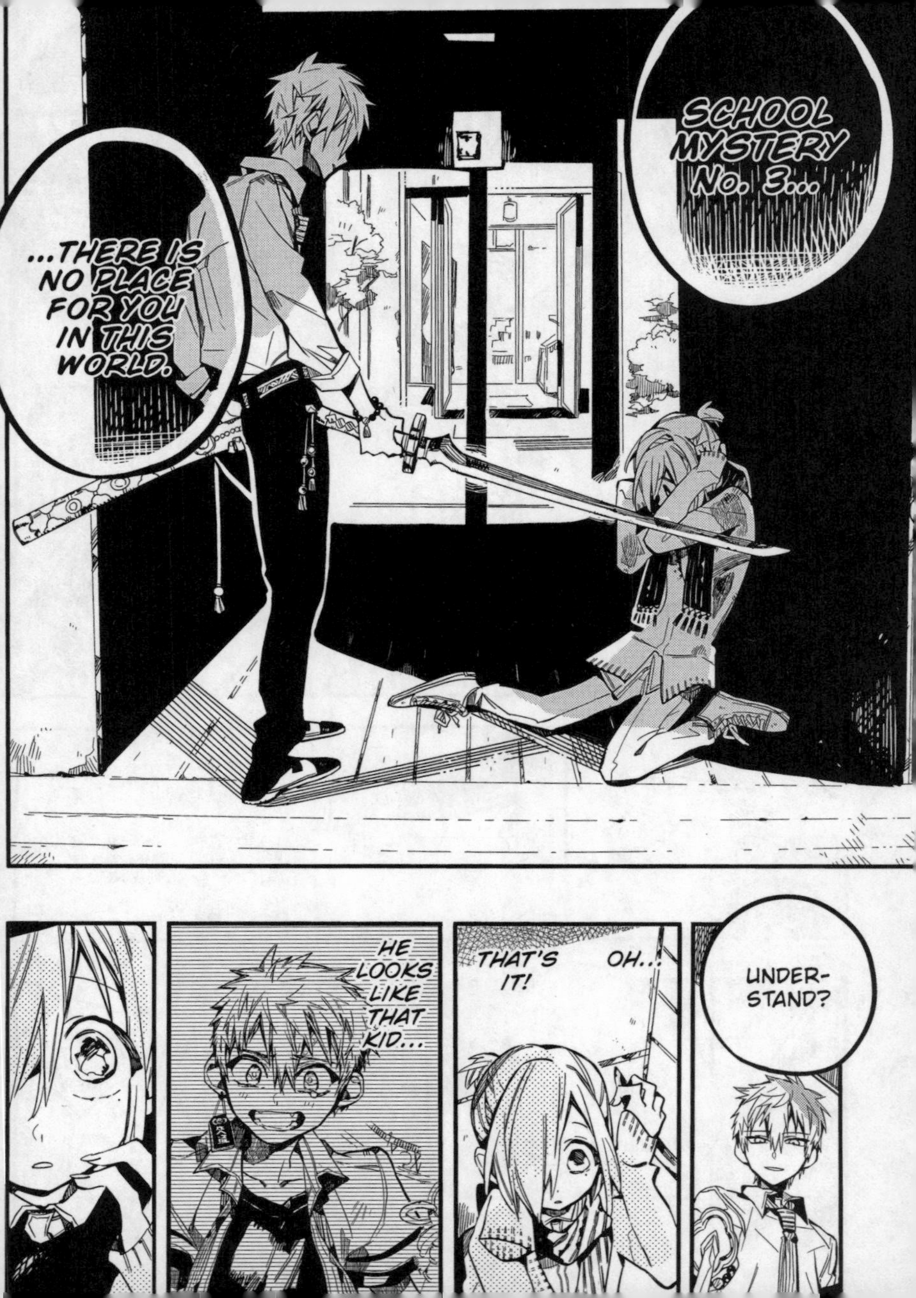
SCHOOL MYSTERY No. 3...
...THERE IS NO PLACE FOR YOU IN THIS WORLD.
UNDER-STAND?
OH...
THAT'S IT!
HE LOOKS LIKE THAT KID...

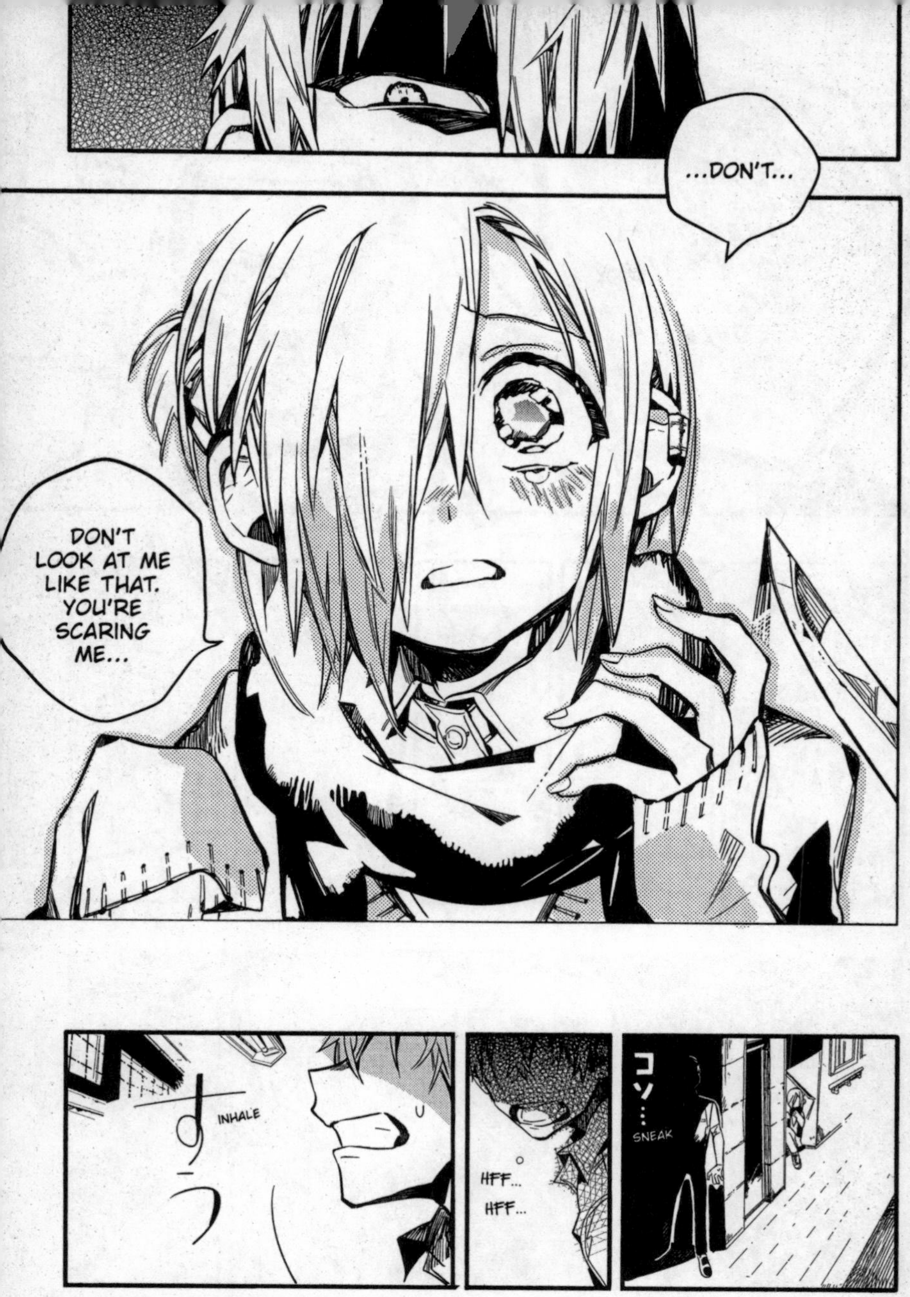
...DON'T...
DON'T LOOK AT ME LIKE THAT. YOU'RE SCARING ME...
コソ…
SNEAK
HFF...
HFF...
INHALE

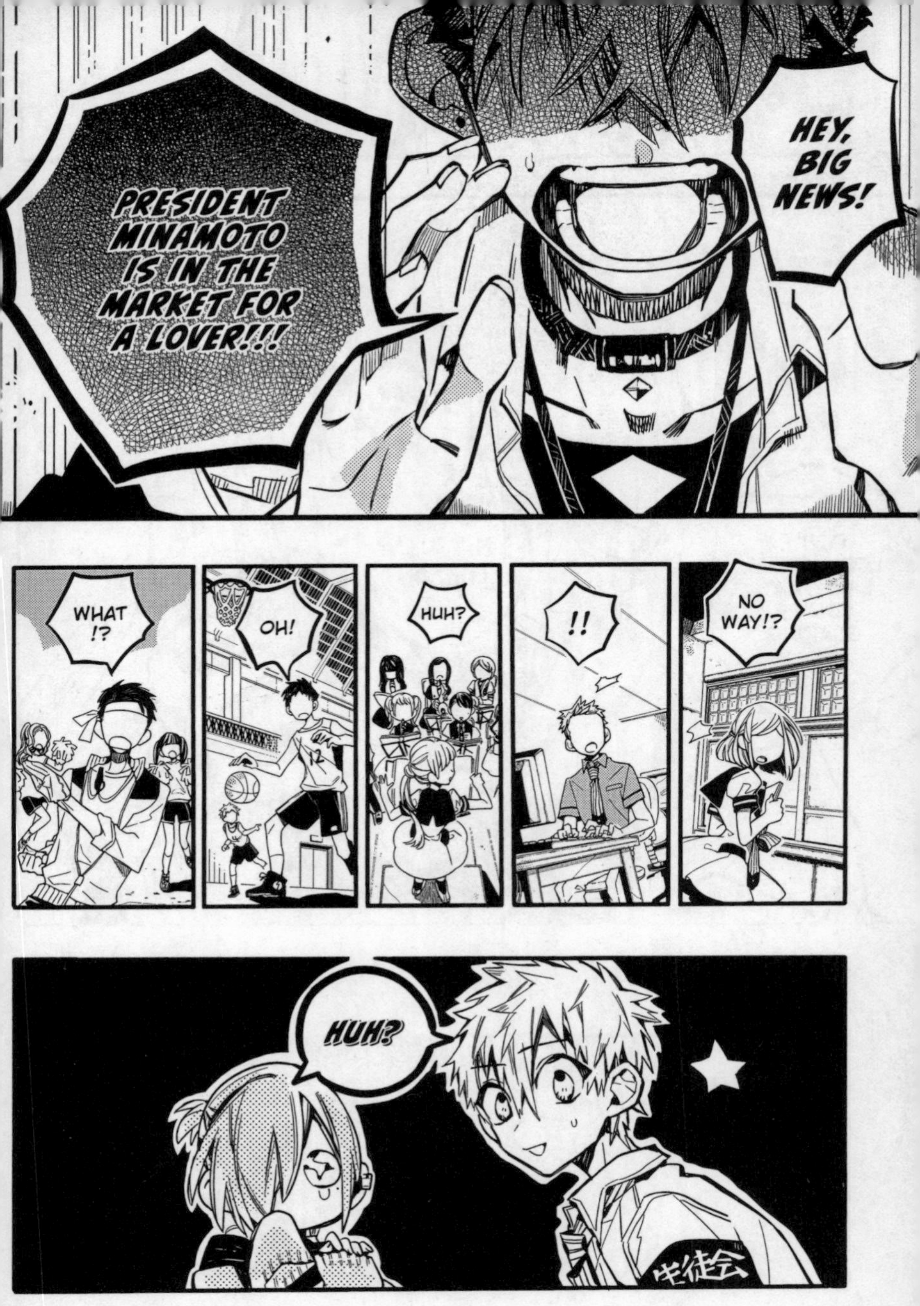
HEY, BIG NEWS!
PRESIDENT MINAMOTO IS IN THE MARKET FOR A LOVER!!!
NO WAY!?
!!
HUH?
OH!
WHAT!?
HUH?

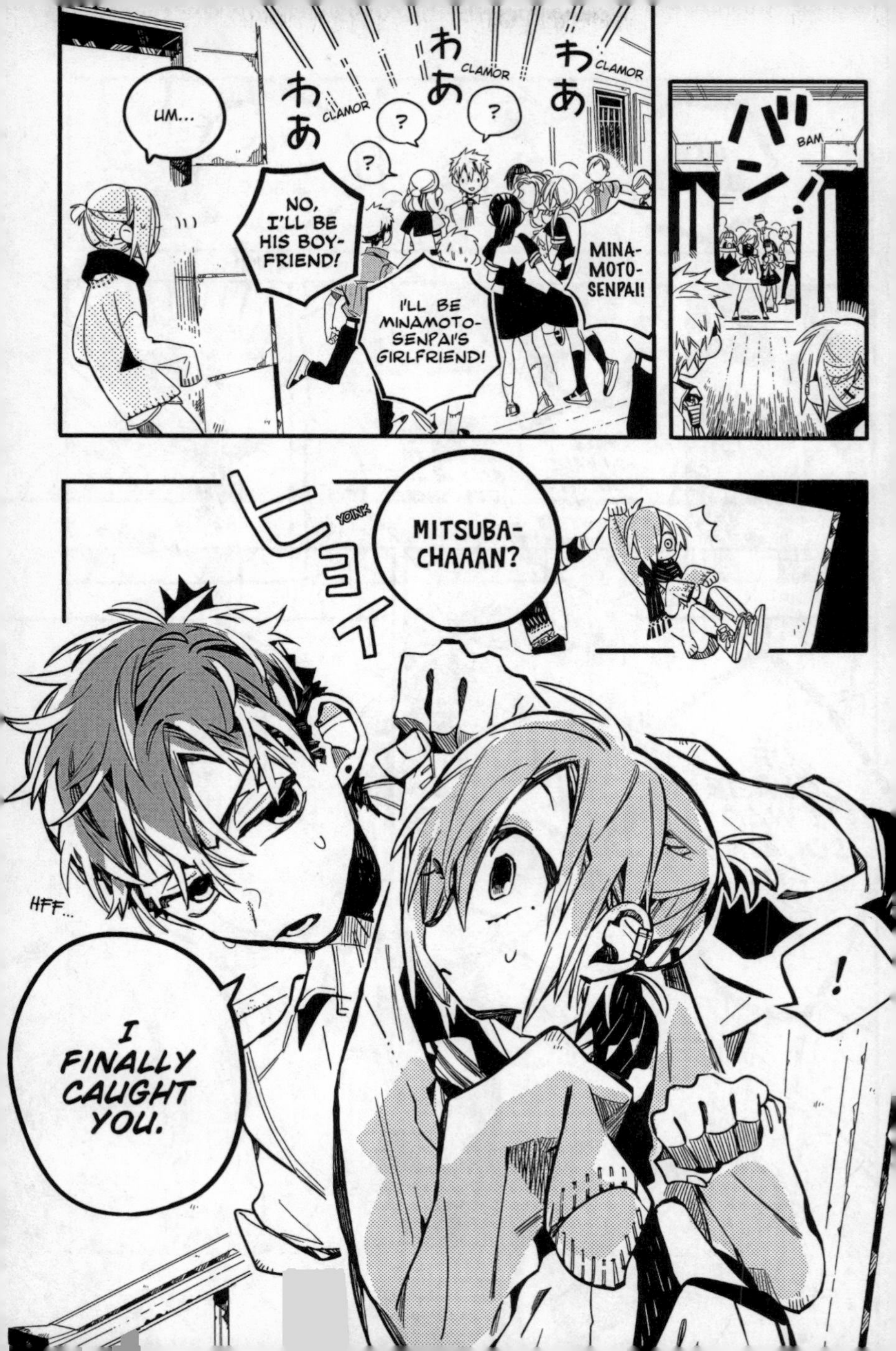
バン!
BAM
わあ
CLAMOR
わあ
CLAMOR
わあ
CLAMOR
?
?
?
MINAMOTO-SENPAI!
I'LL BE MINAMOTO-SENPAI'S GIRLFRIEND!
NO, I'LL BE HIS BOYFRIEND!
UM...
MITSUBA-CHAAAN?
ヒョイ
YOINK
!
HFF...
I FINALLY CAUGHT YOU.

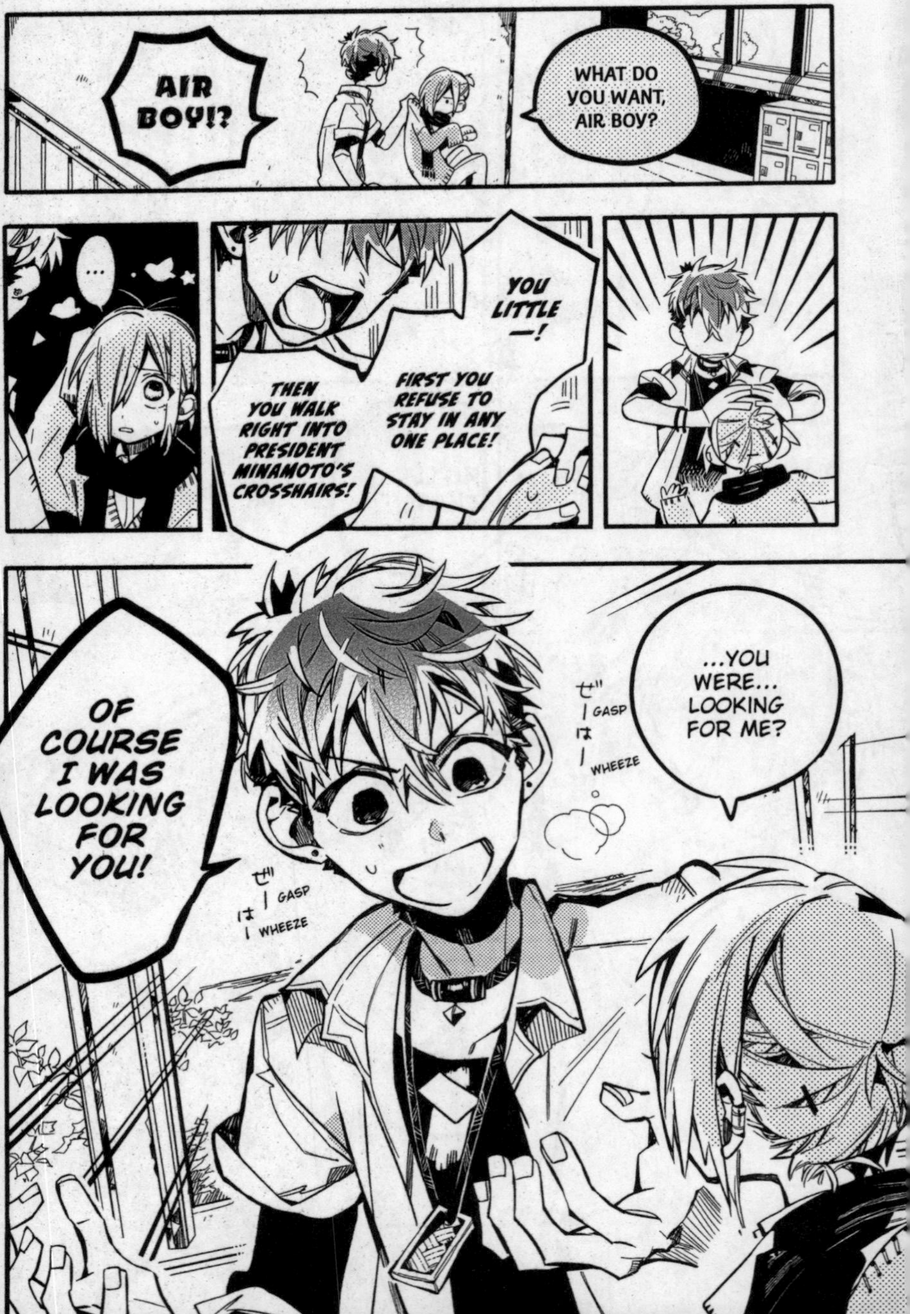
WHAT DO YOU WANT, AIR BOY?
AIR BOY!?
YOU LITTLE —!
FIRST YOU REFUSE TO STAY IN ANY ONE PLACE!
THEN YOU WALK RIGHT INTO PRESIDENT MINAMOTO'S CROSSHAIRS!
...
...YOU WERE... LOOKING FOR ME?
ゼ GASP
は WHEEZE
OF COURSE I WAS LOOKING FOR YOU!
ゼ GASP
は WHEEZE

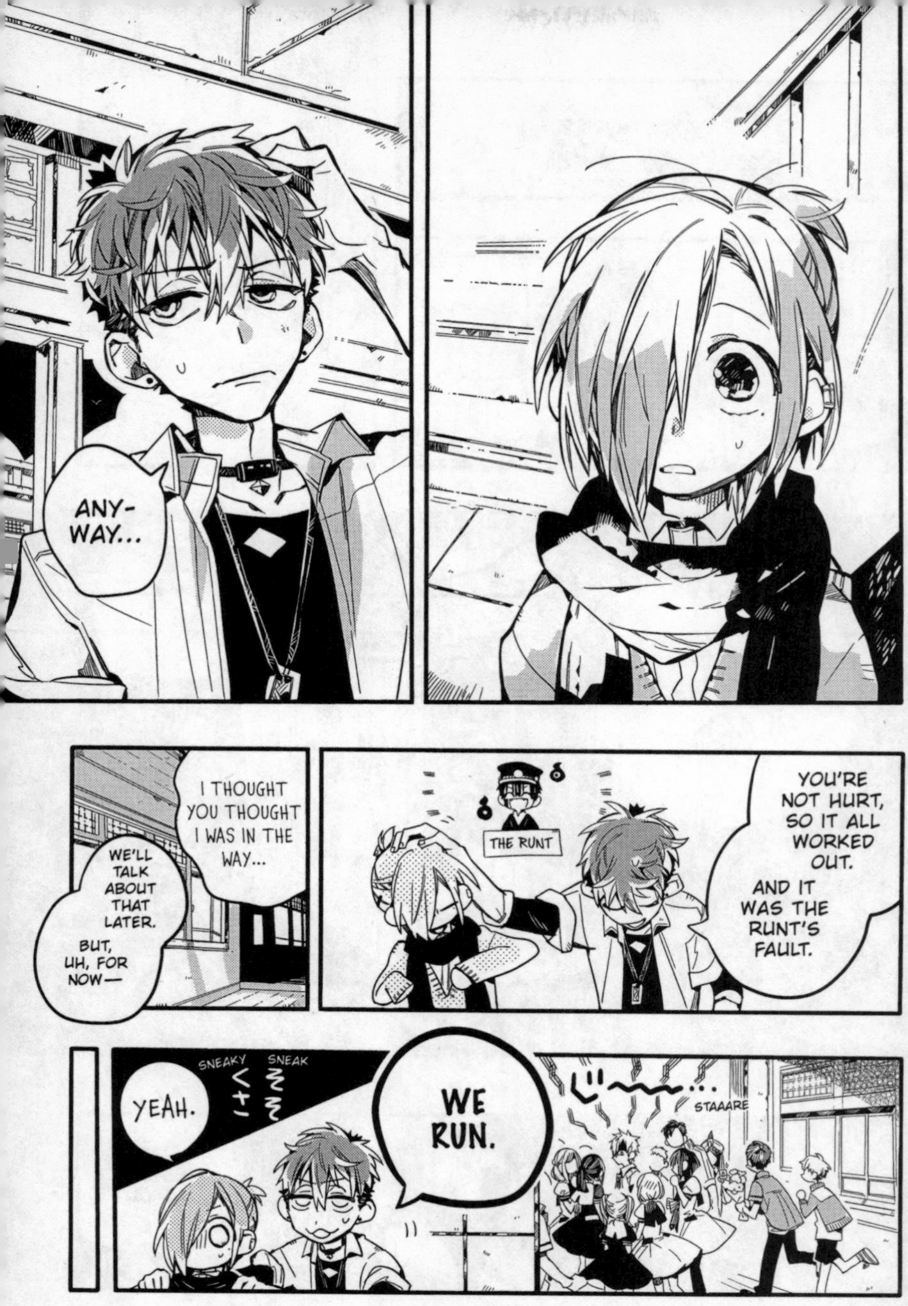
ANY-WAY...
THE RUNT
YOU'RE NOT HURT, SO IT ALL WORKED OUT.
AND IT WAS THE RUNT'S FAULT.
I THOUGHT YOU THOUGHT I WAS IN THE WAY...
WE'LL TALK ABOUT THAT LATER.
BUT, UH, FOR NOW—
STAAARE
WE RUN.
SNEAK
SNEAKY
YEAH.

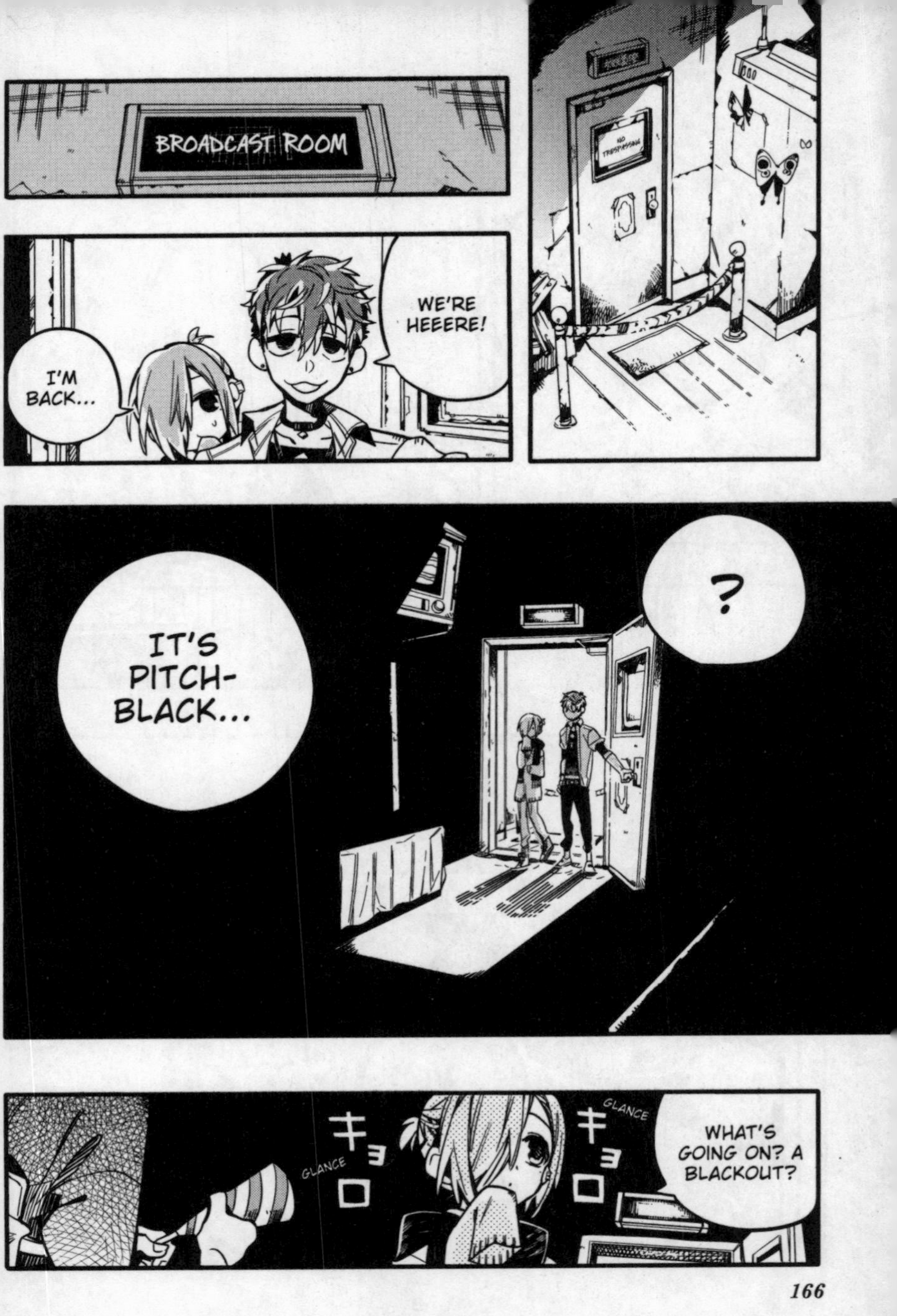
NO TRESPASSING
BROADCAST ROOM
WE'RE HEEERE!
I'M BACK...
?
IT'S PITCH-BLACK...
WHAT'S GOING ON? A BLACKOUT?
GLANCE
キョロ
GLANCE
キョロ

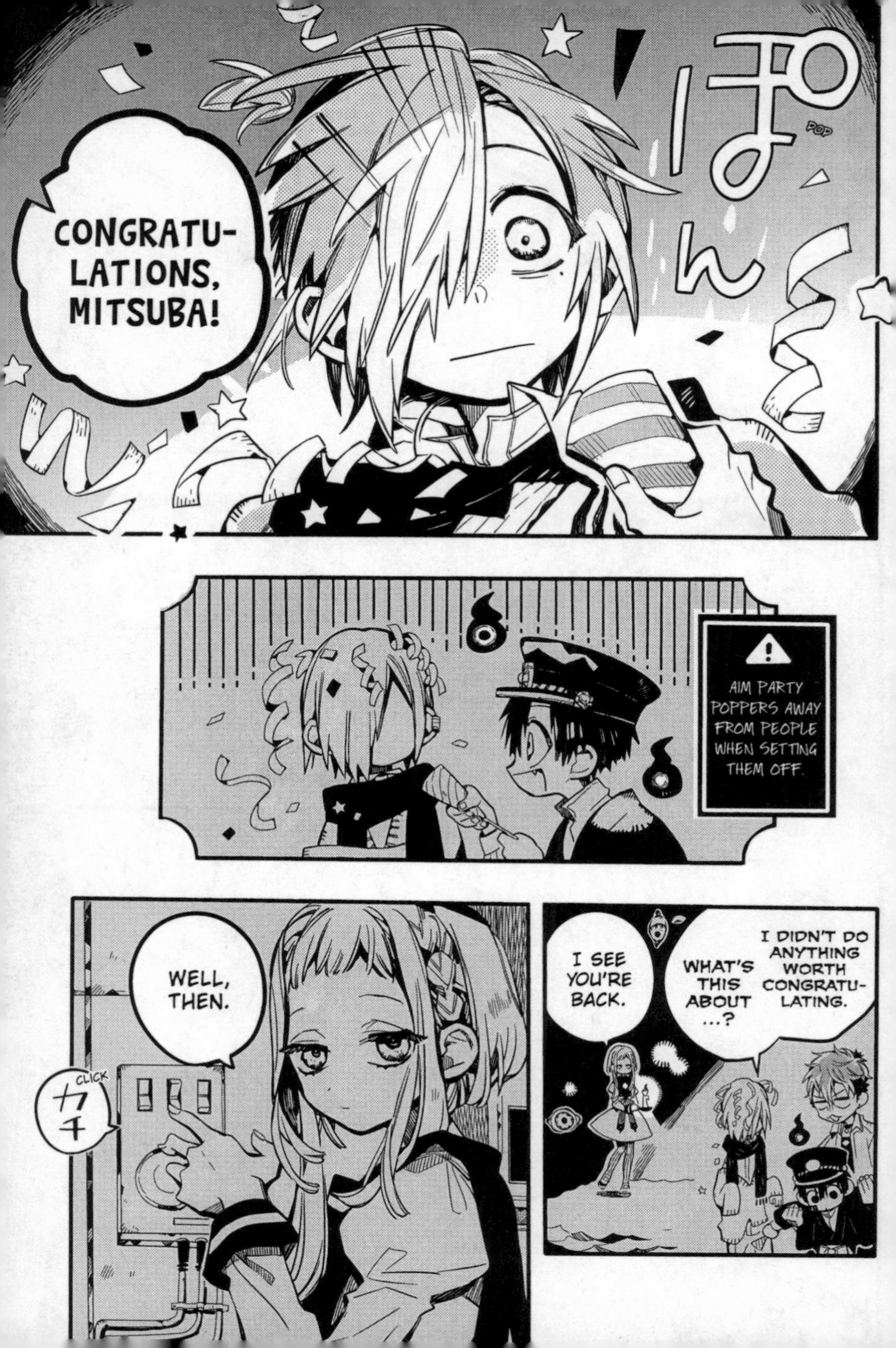
ぽん
POP
CONGRATU-LATIONS, MITSUBA!
AIM PARTY POPPERS AWAY FROM PEOPLE WHEN SETTING THEM OFF.
I DIDN'T DO ANYTHING WORTH CONGRATU-LATING.
WHAT'S THIS ABOUT ...?
I SEE YOU'RE BACK.
WELL, THEN.
カチ
CLICK

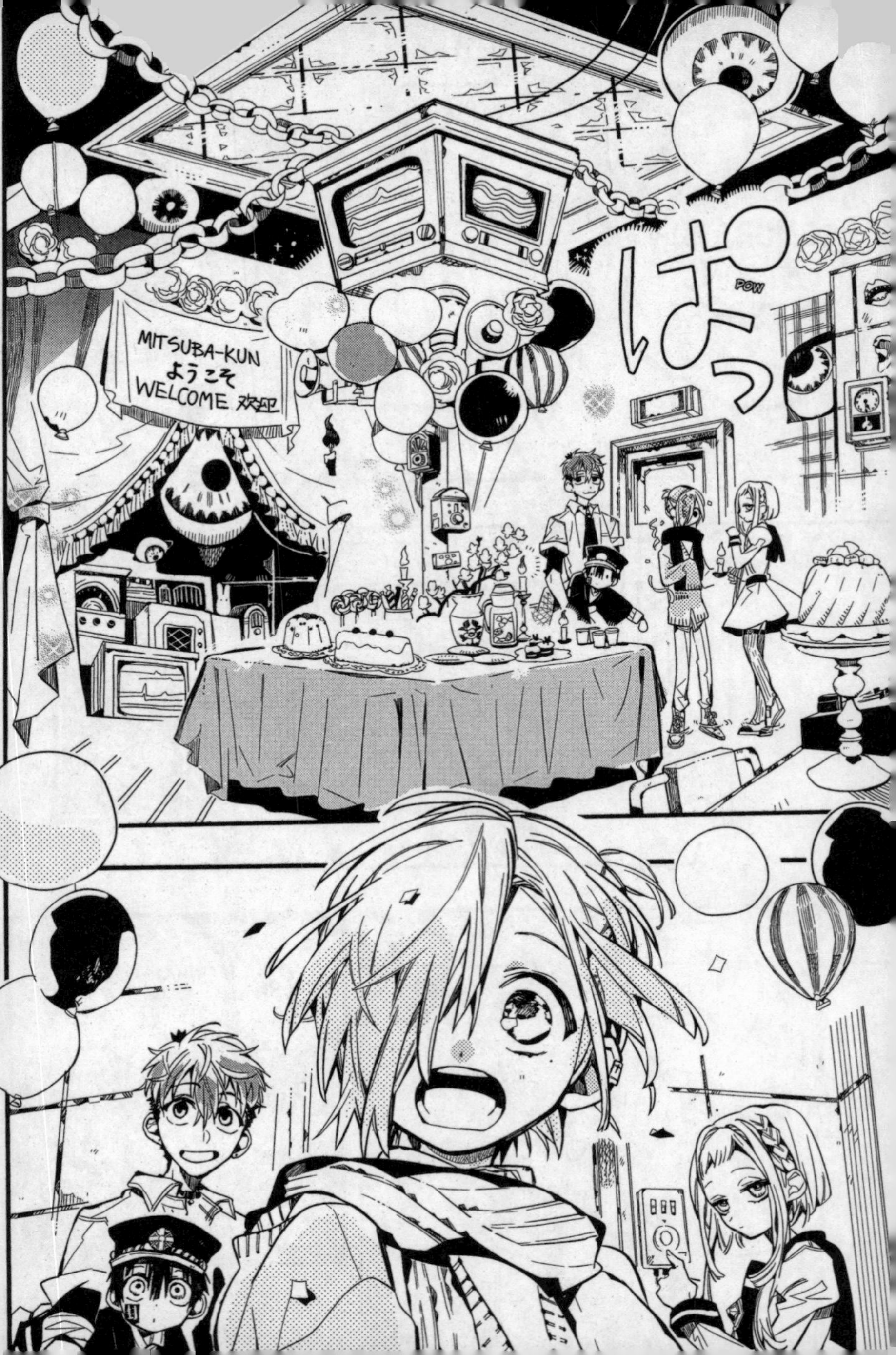
ぱっ
POW
MITSUBA-KUN
ようこそ
WELCOME 欢迎

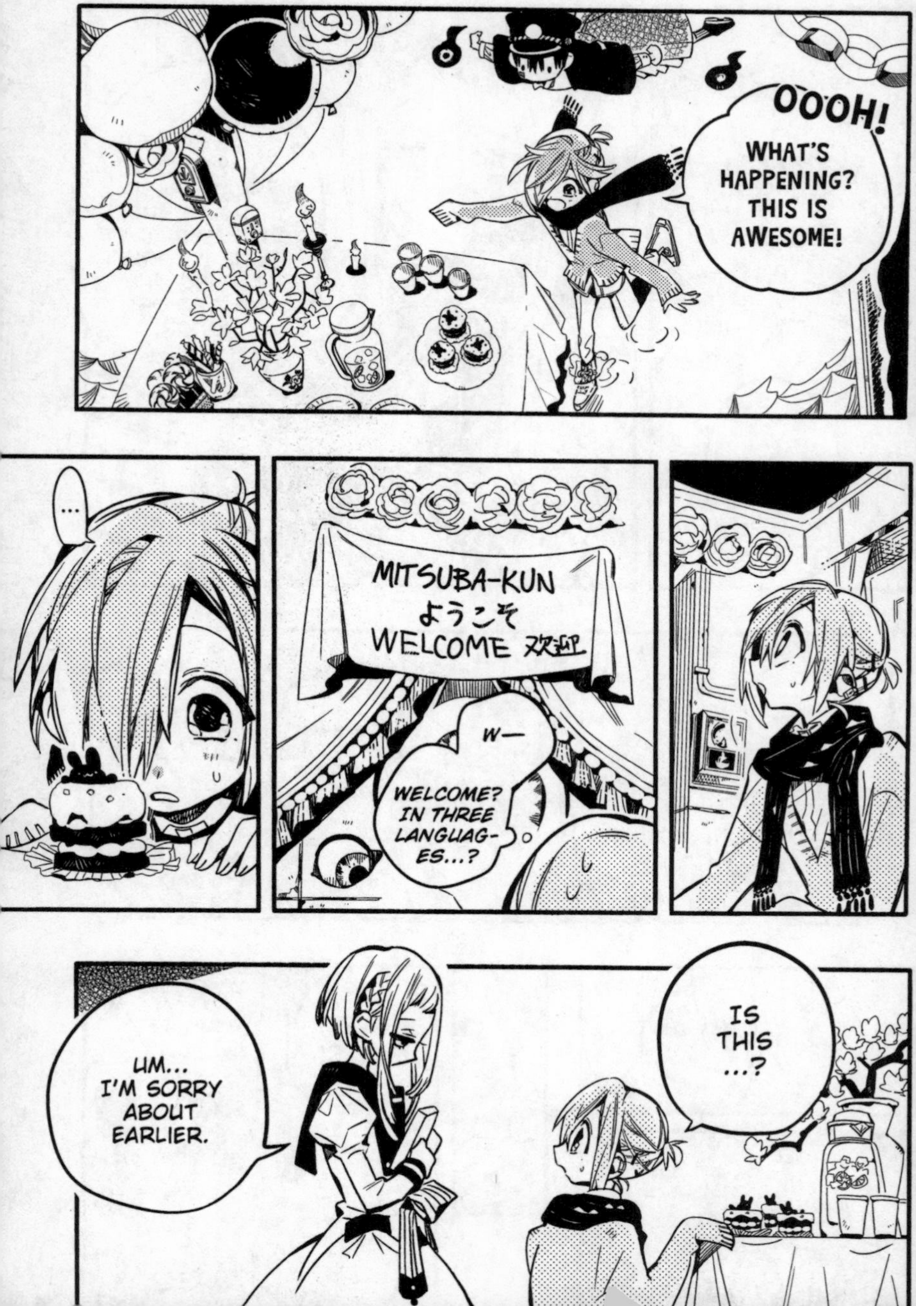
OOOH!
WHAT'S HAPPENING? THIS IS AWESOME!
MITSUBA-KUN ようこそ WELCOME 欢迎
W—
WELCOME? IN THREE LANGUAG-ES...?
...
IS THIS ...?
UM... I'M SORRY ABOUT EARLIER.

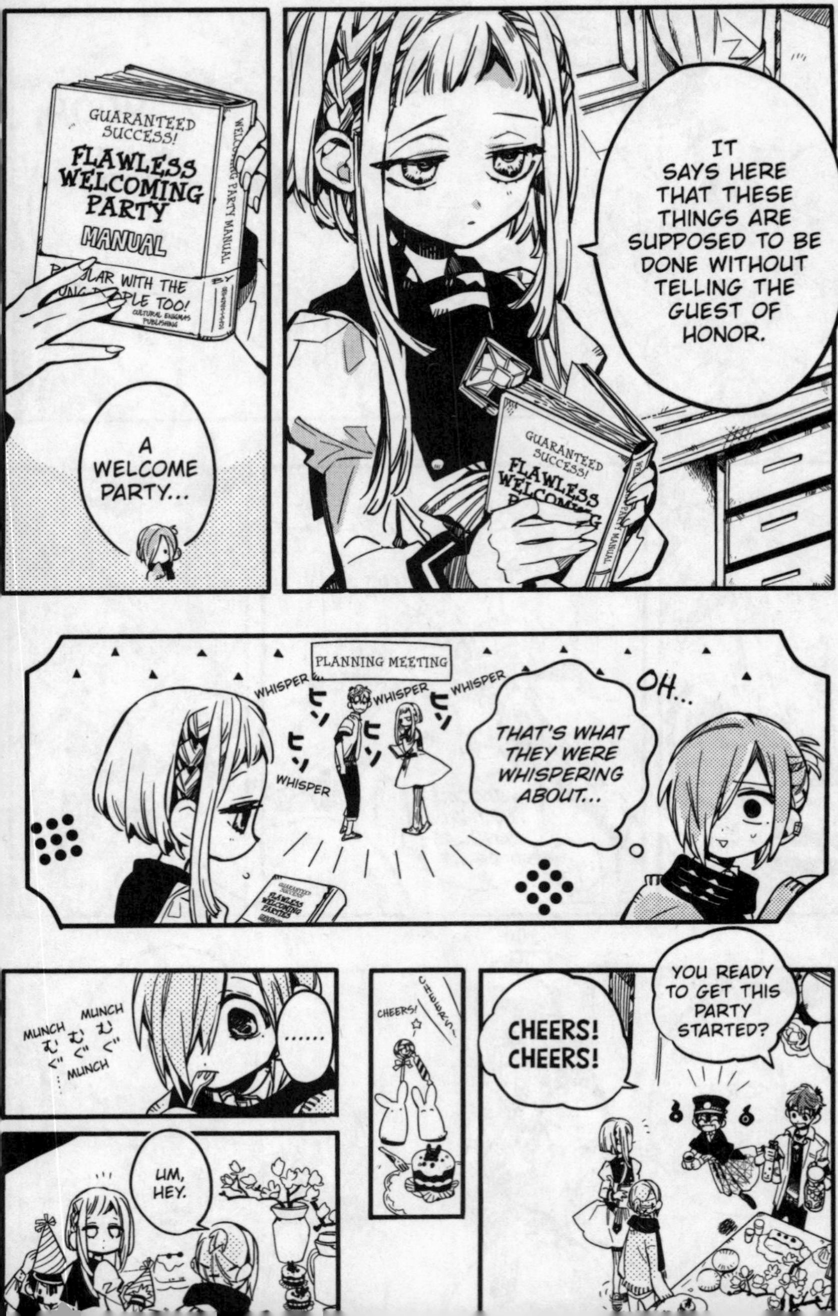
IT SAYS HERE THAT THESE THINGS ARE SUPPOSED TO BE DONE WITHOUT TELLING THE GUEST OF HONOR.
GUARANTEED SUCCESS! FLAWLESS WELCOMING
GUARANTEED SUCCESS!
FLAWLESS WELCOMING PARTY
MANUAL
WELCOMING PARTY MANUAL
CULTURAL ENIGMAS PUBLISHING
A WELCOME PARTY...
OH...
THAT'S WHAT THEY WERE WHISPERING ABOUT...
PLANNING MEETING
WHISPER
WHISPER
WHISPER
WHISPER
FLAWLESS WELCOMING PARTIES
YOU READY TO GET THIS PARTY STARTED?
CHEERS! CHEERS!
CHEERS!
MUNCH MUNCH MUNCH MUNCH
......
UM, HEY.

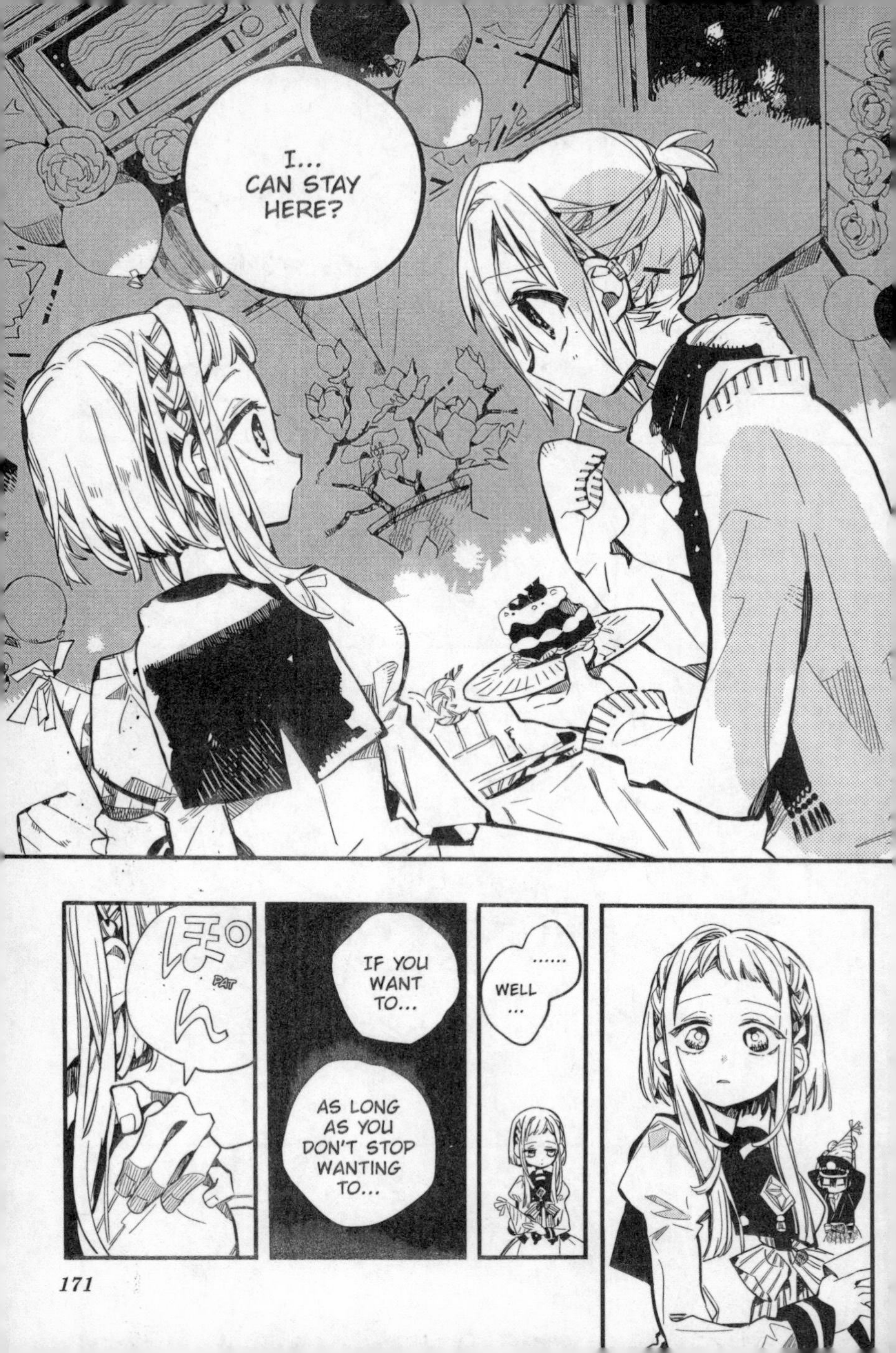
I... CAN STAY HERE?
...... WELL ...
IF YOU WANT TO...
AS LONG AS YOU DON'T STOP WANTING TO...
ぽん
PAT

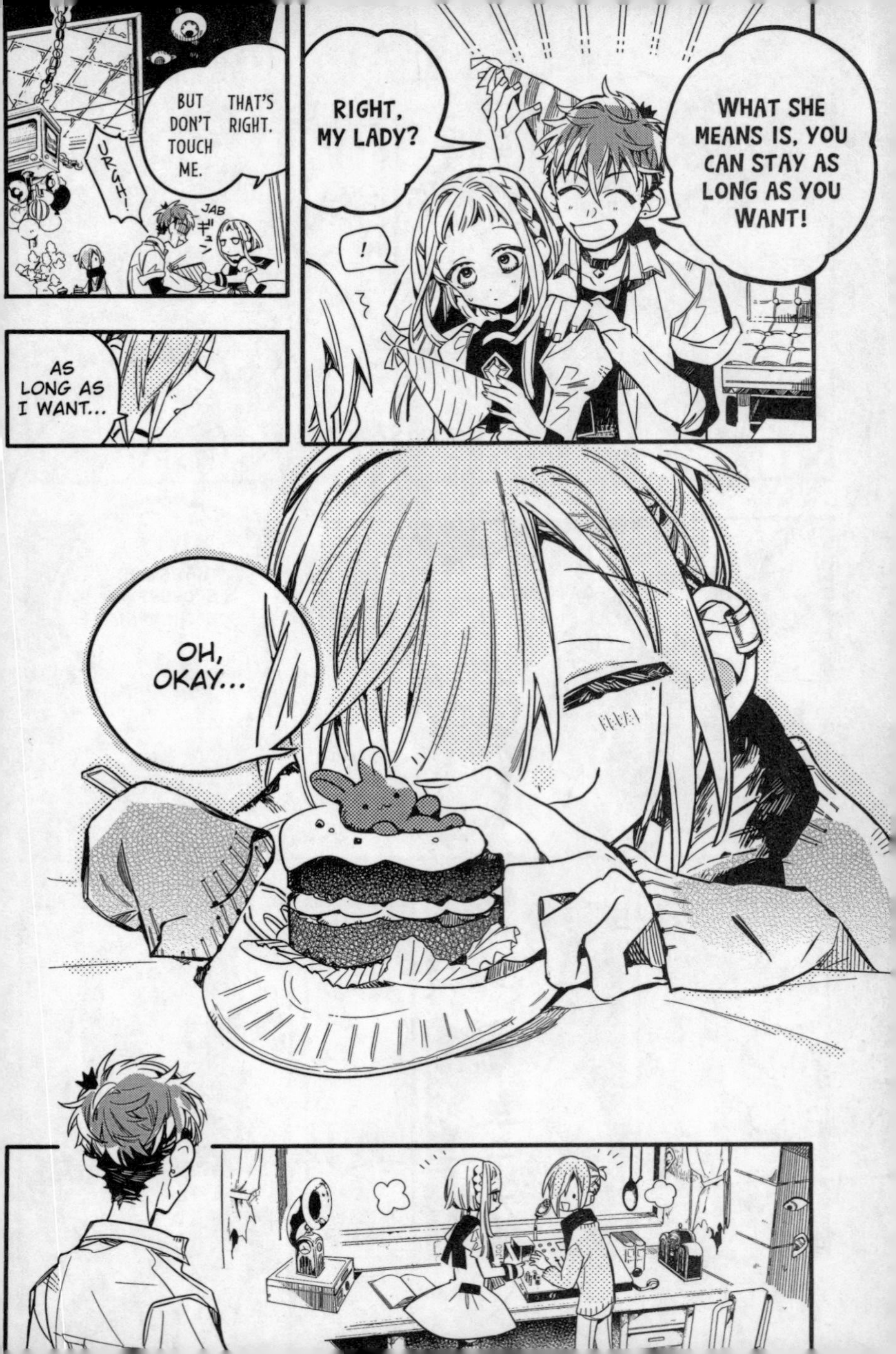

WHAT SHE MEANS IS, YOU CAN STAY AS LONG AS YOU WANT!
RIGHT, MY LADY?
!
THAT'S RIGHT.
BUT DON'T TOUCH ME.
URGH!
JAB
AS LONG AS I WANT...
OH, OKAY...

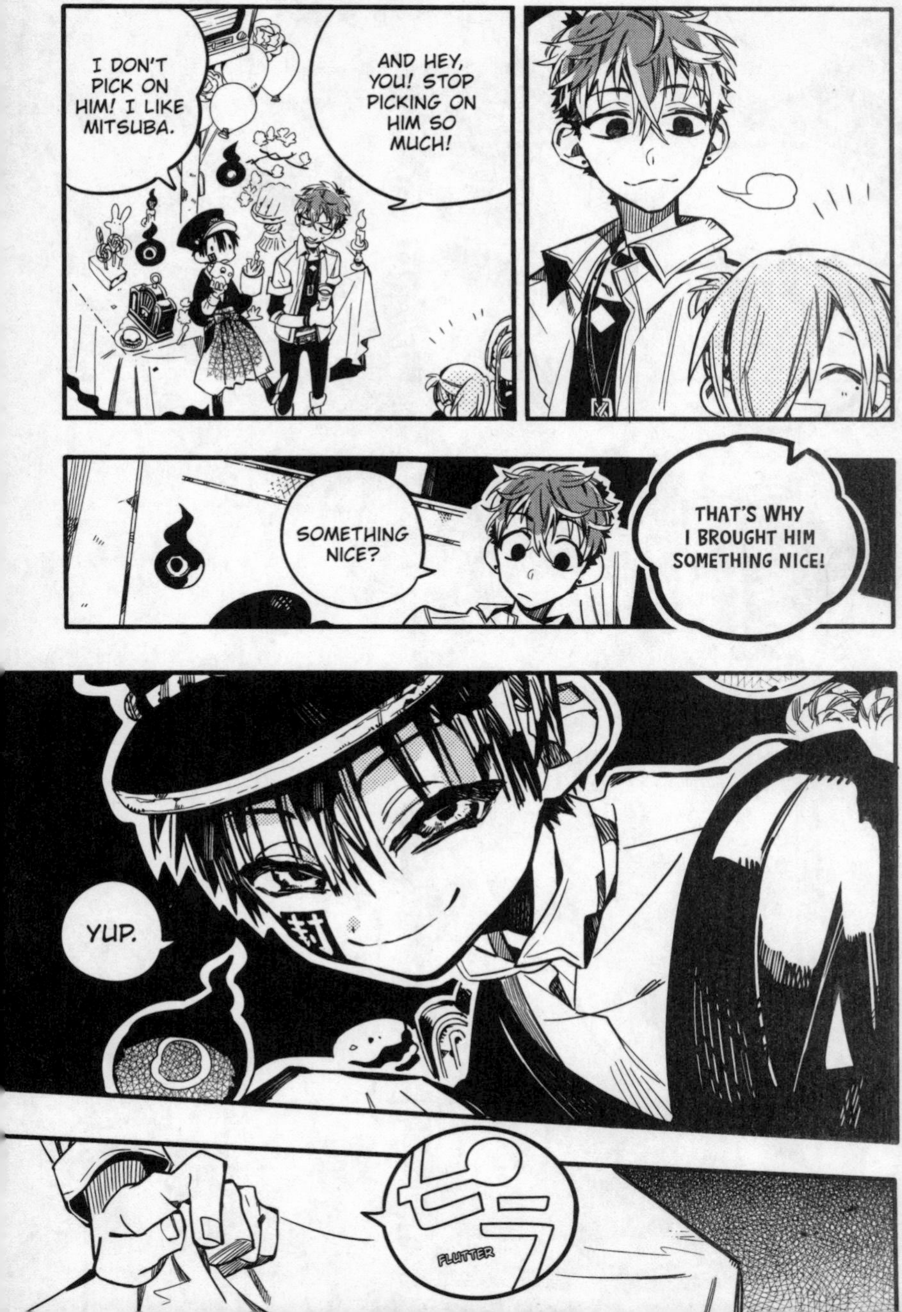
AND HEY, YOU! STOP PICKING ON HIM SO MUCH!
I DON'T PICK ON HIM! I LIKE MITSUBA.
THAT'S WHY I BROUGHT HIM SOMETHING NICE!
SOMETHING NICE?
YUP.
ヒラ
FLUTTER

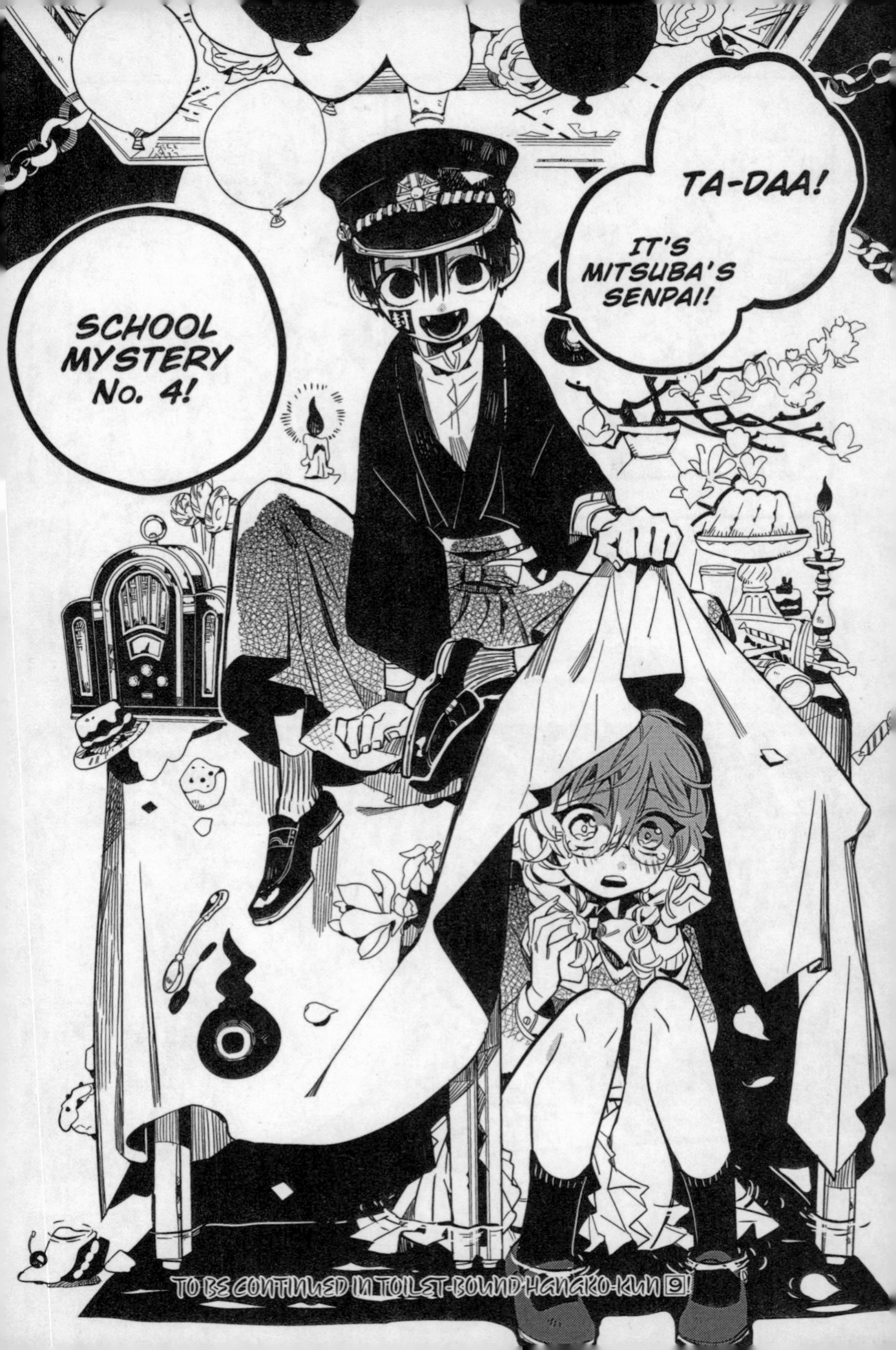
TA-DAA!
IT'S MITSUBA'S SENPAI!
SCHOOL MYSTERY No. 4!
TO BE CONTINUED IN TOILET-BOUND HANAKO-KUN 9!

TRANSLATION NOTES

Common Honorifics

no honorific: Indicates familiarity or closeness; if used without permission or reason, addressing someone in this manner would constitute an insult.

-san: The Japanese equivalent of Mr./Mrs./Miss. If a situation calls for politeness, this is the fail-safe honorific.

-sama: Conveys great respect; may also indicate that the social status of the speaker is lower than that of the addressee.

-kun: Used most often when referring to boys, this indicates affection or familiarity. Occasionally used by older men among their peers, but it may also be used by anyone referring to a person of lower standing.

-chan: An affectionate honorific indicating familiarity used mostly in reference to girls; also used in reference to cute persons or animals of either gender.

-senpai: A suffix used to address upperclassmen or more experienced coworkers.

-sensei: A respectful term for teachers, artists, or high-level professionals.

-onee-san: A way to address young women whom the speaker thinks of as an older-sister type.

Page 34

Tanabata is a holiday on July 7 that celebrates the annual reunion of Orihime and Hikoboshi, two deities whose love so distracted them from their duties that the Milky Way was put between them to keep them apart for the rest of the year. It is customary to make wishes on this holiday by writing them on slips of paper called *tanzaku* and tying them to the bamboo branches used to decorate for the holiday.

Page 36

A *yukata* is a type of casual summer kimono and a very popular item to wear at summer festivals.

Page 42

A "triangle crown" or *tenkan* (literally "heavenly crown") is a white, triangular cloth headband that corpses were traditionally dressed in. More ornate versions were originally worn by figures in Buddhist mythology and during the anointing of an emperor, but the cloth version mimicking the same shape became a way for the dead to claim

similarly high status and avoid giving offense to King Enma, who judges the dead. While *tenkan* are no longer commonly used at funerals, Japanese ghosts are often still depicted as wearing them and white clothes as a useful shorthand for "something only a dead person would wear."

Page 47

Mochi is a chewy traditional Japanese sweet made from rice pounded into a paste.

Page 48

Amazake is a traditional Japanese drink made from fermented rice. It has very low alcohol content and thus is popular with people of all ages. It is not uncommon to see it at folk festivals, traditional teahouses, or shrines.

Page 57

Water yo-yos are part of a traditional Japanese carnival game. The goal is to fish them out of a pool of water by using a hook at the end of a paper string to drag the yo-yo out by its elastic finger loop. Since the paper quickly tears apart once wet, the challenge is to scoop them out by only submerging the hook and without making too many waves.

Page 71

Castella is a kind of Japanese sponge cake that is cut into rectangular slices, originating from the Portuguese *Pão d'Castela* (bread from Castile) that was brought to Japan in the 1500s.

Page 77

Ikayaki is grilled squid, a popular festival food.

Page 82

Literally meaning "shape removal," *katanuki* is a festival activity where a pushpin or other pointy object is used to cut a shape out of a candy wafer. Sometimes prizes are given for doing a good job. The wafer has an outline on it as a guide, and the more complicated shapes yield better rewards.

Page 96

Hikoboshi was a cowherd, and because his love for Orihime consumed his every waking moment, his cattle went about unattended. With no one to care for them, they starved, fell ill, and, in this version, apparently died.

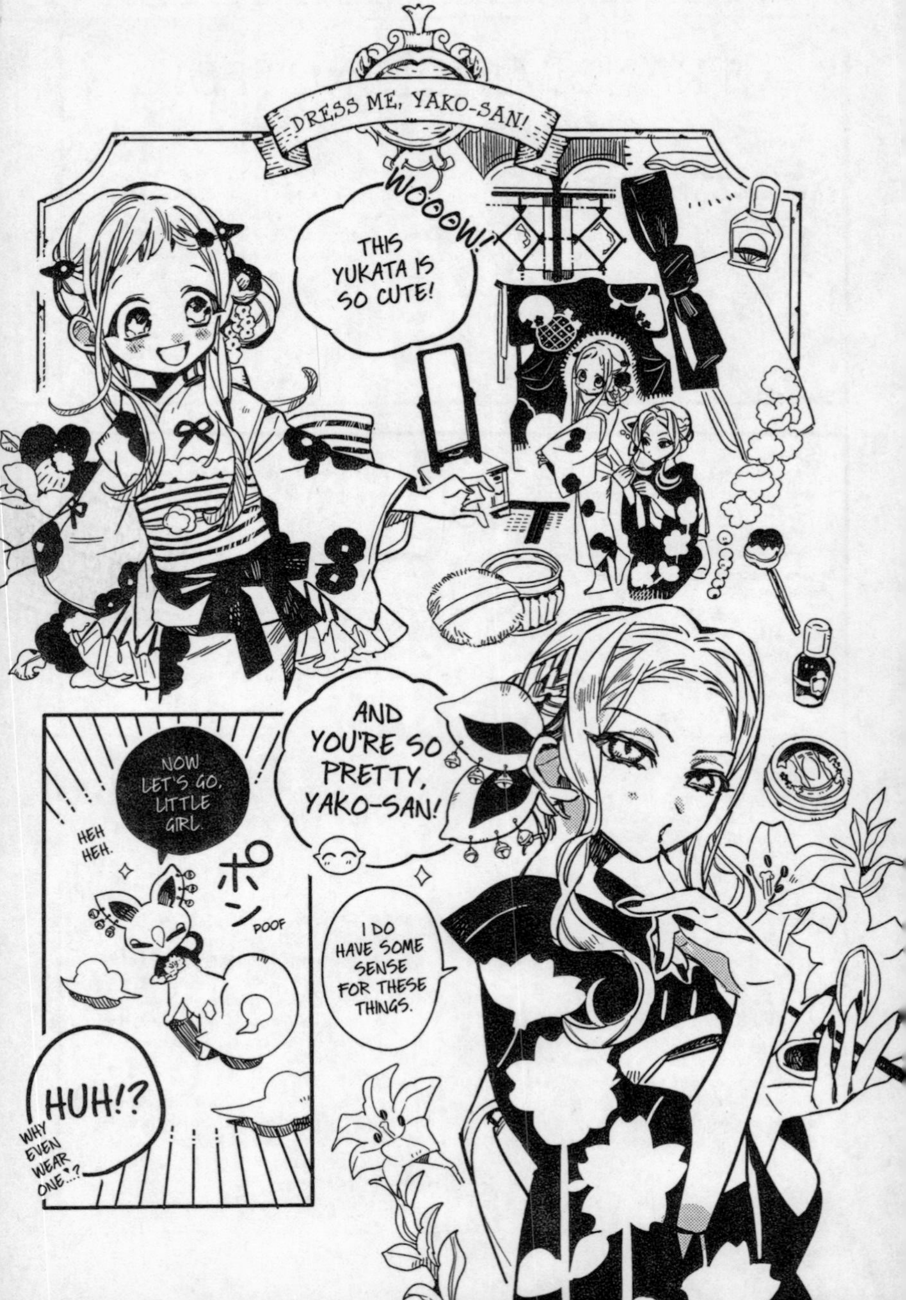
DRESS ME, YAKO-SAN!
WOOOOW!
THIS YUKATA IS SO CUTE!
AND YOU'RE SO PRETTY, YAKO-SAN!
I DO HAVE SOME SENSE FOR THESE THINGS.
NOW LET'S GO, LITTLE GIRL.
HEH HEH.
ポン
POOF
HUH!?
WHY EVEN WEAR ONE...?

DELETED SCENE FROM CHAPTER 39

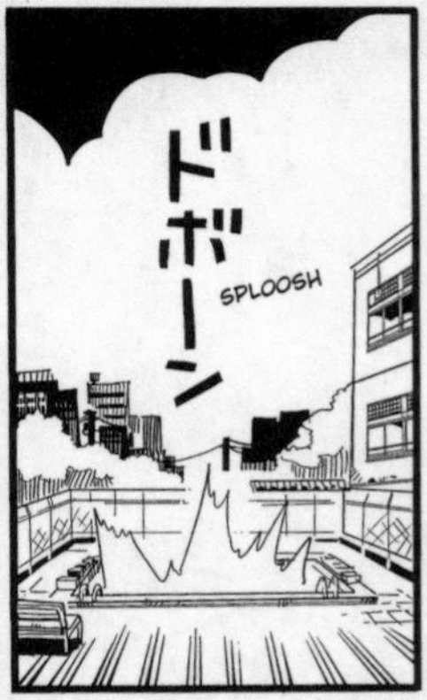
ドボーン
SPLOOSH

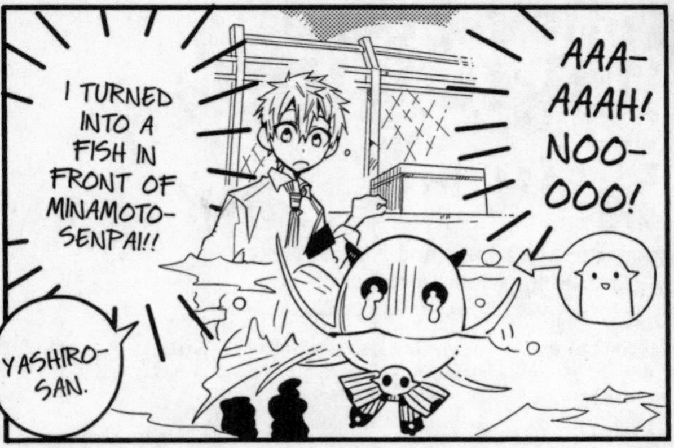
AAA-AAAH! NOO-OOO!
I TURNED INTO A FISH IN FRONT OF MINAMOTO-SENPAI!!
YASHIRO-SAN.

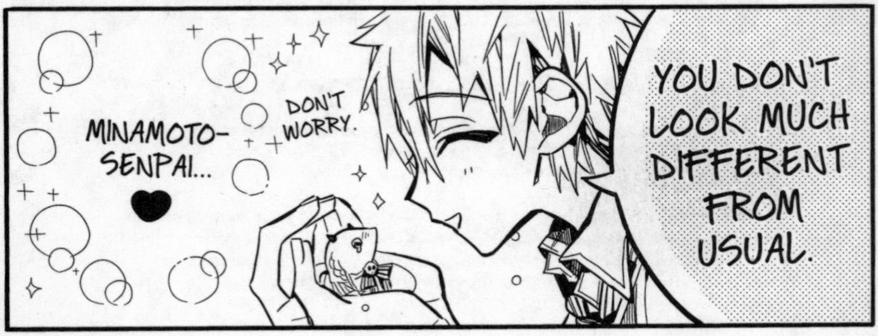
YOU DON'T LOOK MUCH DIFFERENT FROM USUAL.
DON'T WORRY.
MINAMOTO-SENPAI...

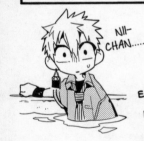

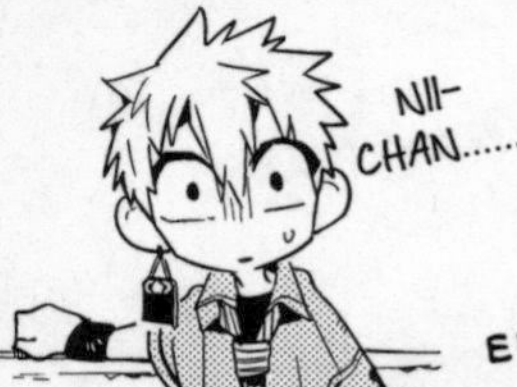
NII-CHAN......

SPECIAL THANKS ♡

EKE-CHAN OMAYU-TAN YUUJI-CHAN

RUI-CHAN REYU-CHAN ANNE-CHAN

MY EDITOR IMANITY

COVER DESIGN NAKAMURA-SAMA

AND YOU

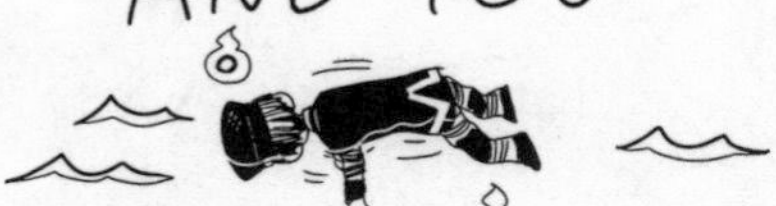

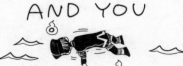

Toilet-bound Hanako-Kun 8

AidaIro

Translation: Alethea Nibley and Athena Nibley
Lettering: Nicole Dochych

JIBAKU SHONEN HANAKO-KUN Volume 8 ©2018 AidaIro / SQUARE ENIX CO., LTD.
First published in Japan in 2018 by SQUARE ENIX CO., LTD. English translation rights arranged with SQUARE ENIX CO., LTD. and Yen Press, LLC through Tuttle-Mori Agency, Inc.

English translation © 2018 by SQUARE ENIX CO., LTD.

Yen Press
150 West 30th Street, 19th Floor
New York, NY 10001

Visit us at yenpress.com • facebook.com/yenpress • twitter.com/yenpress • yenpress.tumblr.com • instagram.com/yenpress

First Yen Press Print Edition: March 2021
Originally published as an ebook in October 2018 by Yen Press.

Yen Press is an imprint of Yen Press, LLC.
The Yen Press name and logo are trademarks of Yen Press, LLC.

The publisher is not responsible for websites (or their content) that are not owned by the publisher.

Library of Congress Control Number: 2019953610

ISBN: 978-1-9753-1140-7 (paperback)

10 9 8 7 6 5 4 3 2 1

BVG

Printed in the United States of America